ARRESTING LANGUAGE

D1489683

MERIDIAN

Crossing Aesthetics

Werner Hamacher

Editor

*Stanford
University
Press*

*Stanford
California
2001*

ARRESTING LANGUAGE

From Leibniz to Benjamin

Peter Fenves

Stanford University Press
Stanford, California

© 2001 by the Board of Trustees of the
Leland Stanford Junior University

Printed in the United States of America

Library of Congress Cataloging-in-Publication Data

Fenves, Peter D. (Peter David)
    Arresting language : from Leibniz to Benjamin / Peter Fenves.
        p.   cm. — (Meridian)
    Includes bibliographical references (p.) and index.
    ISBN 0-8047-3959-5 (alk. paper) —
ISBN 0-8047-3960-9 (pbk. : alk. paper)
    1. Language and languages—Philosophy.   2. Poetry.
I. Title.   II. Meridian (Stanford, Calif)
P107 .F46   2002
401—dc21   2001041087

Original Printing 2001

Last figure below indicates year of this printing:
10 09 08 07 06 05 04 03 02 01

Typeset by James P. Brommer
in 10.9/13 Garamond and Lithos display

0012935464

For Susannah

Contents

Note on Translations and Abbreviations

All translations in this volume, unless otherwise cited, are my own. For the sake of convenience, I have provided references to English translations except when the original texts are very short or when readily available translations include the pagination of the original in the margins.

Walter Benjamin

AP   *Arcades Project*
C   *Correspondence of Walter Benjamin*
GB   *Gesammelte Briefe*
GS   *Gesammelte Schriften*
O   *Origin of German Tragic Drama*
W   *Selected Writings*

Georg Cantor

GA   *Gesammelte Abhandlungen*

Hermann Cohen

LRE *Logik der reinen Erkenntnis*

Johann Peter Hebel

H   *Sämtliche Schriften*

Friedrich Hölderlin

SW   *Sämtliche Werke*

Edmund Husserl

HGW   *Husserliana: Gesammelte Werke*
I   *Ideas Pertaining to a Pure Phenomenology and to a Phenomenological Philosophy*
PRS   "Philosophy as Rigorous Science"

Luce Irigaray

CM   *La Croyance même*
EDS   *Ethique de le différence sexuelle*
ESD   *An Ethics of Sexual Difference*
SG   *Sex and Genealogies*

Immanuel Kant

A, B   *Kritik der reinen Vernunft* ("A" for 1781 ed.; "B" for 1787 ed.)
Ak   *Gesammelte Schriften*

Heinrich von Kleist

BA   *Berliner Abendblätter*
SWB   *Sämtliche Werke und Briefe*

Gottfried von Leibniz

A   *Sämtliche Schriften und Briefe*
FS   *Flores sparsi in tumulum Papissae*
G   *Die philosophischen Schriften*
L   *Philosophical Papers and Letters*
LH   *Die Leibniz-Handschriften der Königlichen Öffentlichen Bibliothek zu Hannover*
T   *Theodicy: Essays on the Goodness of God, the Freedom of Man, and the Origin of Evil*

Moses Mendelssohn

J	*Jerusalem; or, On Religious Power and Judaism*
JubA	*Gesammelte Schriften: Jubiläumsausgabe*

Bertrand Russell

PM	*The Principles of Mathematics*

Friedrich Schelling

HKA	*Historisch-kritisch Ausgabe*

Friedrich Schiller

NA	*Schillers Werke: Nationalausgabe*

ARRESTING LANGUAGE

Introduction: "From an Awkward Perspective"

Hölderlin makes a simple yet startling statement in the final paragraph of his "Remarks on *Antigone*," the last of his critical writings: "Sophocles is right" (SW, 5: 272).[1] Instead of concluding his last "Remarks" by asserting in grandiloquent terms the moral grandeur or intellectual greatness of the Greek tragedian, Hölderlin evaluates him in the most prosaic manner possible—as though Sophocles had successfully solved a routine arithmetical problem. Sophocles is right, however, only because he discovers a perspective other than that of "right" in both senses of the word: a perspective that not only tends to go wrong but also detaches itself from vantage points sanctioned by the order of law (*das Recht*). At the end of the tragedy, Creon, as the supreme representative of the legal order against which Antigone rebels, "is almost abused by his servants. Sophocles is right [*hat Recht*]. . . . The infinite, like the spirit of states and of the world, cannot be grasped other than from an awkward perspective [*aus linkischen Gesichtspunkt*]" (SW, 5: 272). A literal translation of the last phrase would be: "from a left-ish point of view"—that is, a perspective that cannot get its bearings, achieve a stable stance, and set itself on the right course. The rightness of Sophocles lies in the "leftishness" of his perspective. This insight into Sophocles' tragedy can be applied to literature in general: for poets to be right, they must discover perspectives that tend to go wrong. This insight is valid for criticism as well. In order to be right a critic must discover a perspective that goes awry. An unmistakable criterion of error—for critics as well as poets—consists in "having" the right perspective, which is to say, securing a point of view that never goes wrong. The essays in this volume are dedicated to this, Hölderlin's last critical insight.

A *linkisch* perspective is neither "sinister," which is a matter of individual morality, nor "gauche," which is a matter of social mores, although all three terms reflect an ancient privilege of the right hand over the left. Instead of being a matter of morals or mores, a *linkisch* or awkward perspective is concerned with only two "things": "the infinite and the spirit of states." In order to grasp both morals and mores it is not necessary to seek out an awkward perspective; the right one will suffice—whatever it may be. The state, by contrast, cannot be grasped from the right perspective as long as it represents and embodies the order of law (*das Recht*); any grasp of "the right" must be done from the left. And the infinite cannot be grasped from the right perspective for an even more compelling reason: there is *no* perspective on the infinite, other than that of an infinite being, who, however, cannot be ascribed any perspective at all. Since every perspective is correlated with a particular horizon, every one is finite. The "right" perspective from which to grasp the infinite cannot be, moreover, the nonperspective of an infinite being, for the infinite, according to Hölderlin, cannot be grasped as *a being* in the first place: it is not one thing among others, much less the highest from whose vantage point all things are revealed as they truly are. Grasping the infinite is therefore a particularly precarious operation—or balancing act. No infinite thing exists; yet there is a perspective from which to grasp the infinite nevertheless: a perspective in which the balancing act of grasping the nonthing called "the infinite" takes false steps, falters, and founders. The existence of the infinite lies in the awkward perspective from which it is—unsuccessfully—grasped. This paradox does not leave the finite untouched: the definition of finite things *as* finite, definition as such, depends on an awkward perspective that can be rectified only for certain limited times, limited spaces, and limited aims. This is particularly true of the legal order, the "essence" of which is self-rectification. At the borders of the legal order there is always at least one awkward perspective from which it can be grasped, seized, and thereby altered. The essays in this volume follow the direction of Hölderlin's reflections on awkwardness and are therefore principally concerned with the nature of the infinite and the "spirit" of the legal order.

Arresting Language

If Hölderlin seems to treat the author of *Antigone* as though he had scored well on a mathematics quiz ("Sophocles is right"), it is because Sophocles indeed solves a calculus problem. The opening paragraphs of "Remarks on *Antigone*," like those of "Remarks on *Oedipus*," propose and delineate a "lawful calculus" (SW, 5: 195) on the basis of which poetry "among us" can be "elevated to the *mechanē* of the ancients" (SW, 5: 195).[2] Only by means of the new calculus can the incalculable—"the living meaning" (SW, 5: 195)—be determined as such. To insure that the incalculable does not escape calculation after all, the calculus Hölderlin proposes, like the one Leibniz coinvented, must be infinitesimal: its range is "the infinite and continuously determined relation" (SW, 5: 195). The incalculable cannot be determined within the continuum of appearances, not even by the method of exhaustion, for it appears only as the appearance of appearance—and therefore as an irreversible and irrevocable interruption of everything that has hitherto appeared: "*what in poetic meter is called caesura, the pure word, the counterrhythmic interruption [das reine Wort, die gegenrhythmische Unterbrechung]* becomes necessary in order to encounter the rupturing alteration of representations at its summa in such a manner that forthwith no longer the change of representation but representation itself appears [*nicht mehr der Wechsel der Vorstellung, sondern die Vorstellung selber erscheint*]" (SW, 5: 196).

The caesura, as "pure word," does not simply mark an interruption; it carries the interruption out. Such is the decisive character of this word: although it cannot be experienced within a continuum of representations, it structures this continuum by interrupting it and dividing it into unequal parts. Language not only arrests the succession of representations, moreover; language is arrested in turn. This double-sided arrest would be altogether paradoxical if the language that arrests the succession of representations were the same language that was arrested; but it is not—or not quite: the arresting language is the "pure word," whereas the arrested language is the empirical word, which is to say, the word through which appearances are represented. The "pure word," by contrast, says nothing. For this reason, it is by no means certain that the "pure word" is even *a* word—one word among others. Rather, the "pure word" even interrupts the process of judgment through which words are separated from, and connected to, one another. The arresting of empirically verifiable language by the "pure word" renders all accounts based on language—including the calculation that one "has" a language—unreliable. Only one thing is certain about the "pure word" from Hölderlin's dense delineation of its form and function: the arresting agent is without any legal authority or governing power. Thus Hölderlin writes, "In both plays [of Sophocles] the speeches of Tiresias constitute the caesura" (SW, 5: 197).

"The living meaning," as the incalculable moment for which a "lawful calculus" is invented, can make itself known only in the radical disruption of life and the suspension of its meaning: "He [Tiresias] enters the course of fate as the custodian of the natural power [*Naturmacht*] that, in a tragic manner, removes the human being [*den Menschen*] from his sphere of life, the middle-point of his inner life, into another world and tears him into the eccentric sphere of the dead" (SW, 5: 197). The radical interruption of a continuous succession of representations cannot be accomplished by a civil power. Whatever else "natural power" means in this context, at least this much is clear: Tiresias has no legal warrant for breaking into "the course of fate" and tearing human beings out of their vital context and living continuum. Nor does he have divine sanction either. The figure in whom the arresting of language takes place can be determined and identified as such only from a *linkisch* or awkward perspective. And only insofar as Tiresias is without any legal authority or divine sanction can he "constitute" the "pure word, the counterrhythmic interruption." Otherwise, if he were a representative of some legal or divine order, he would be too entangled *in* representation to allow representation *itself* to appear. The essays in this volume gravitate toward Tiresian figures: those who interrupt the continuum of representations without being in a position to justify this interruption, but nevertheless do so in accordance with a "lawful calculus," not as an arbitrary whim or expression of will.

A figure that fulfills a function similar to that of Tiresias in Hölderlin's account of the Sophoclean tragedies is Don Fernando, the dissembling "hero" of Kleist's story, "The Earthquake in Chile." In one of the last scenes of the story, members of a chaotic mob threaten the life of those whom Don Fernando has taken under his wing. Without the slightest authority, he issues an arrest warrant for the instigator of the attack. In the unauthorized words of this warrant, the course of events comes to a halt and a legal order appears; but this order of law appears only in order to appear—not to rectify itself. The chaotic scene in which Don Fernando issues his unauthorized arrest warrant contrasts with an Edenic one. At the center of Kleist's story of physical, civic, and religious collapse is a remarkable scene of social reconciliation in which the human "spirit" rises up and everyone gathered in the redolent garden seems to belong to "*one* family" (SWB, 2: 152).[3] The appearance of a fake legal order brings to light a paradisal condition that, unlike the appearance of *"one* family," does not appear as such; on the contrary, governed by no number, least of all by "one," the fake legal order appears unconscionable, if not downright sinister, and for this reason, it too collapses. The fourth of the eight chapters in this volume is organized around Don Fernando's unauthorized arrest warrant, and so, too, is the volume as a whole. The aim of the volume could thus be summarized in terms of Hölderlin's last "Remarks" and Kleist's first story: to identify certain moments of arresting language and, more generally, to make such moments recognizable in turn. Only from a *linkisch* or awkward perspective can arresting language be recognized as such—and not made into "speech acts" on the basis of which new rules are instituted and new institutions erected.

The essays in this volume are thus all concerned with a "pure word" in which representation as such can appear. Sometimes, as in the first chapter, the interruption occurs as a swooning: Theodore, the hero of a "little fable" (G, 6: 361; T, 369) that Leibniz invents for the conclusion of his *Theodicy*, succumbs to vertigo as he enters the hall in which the very world of which he is a part—"the real true world" (G, 6: 364; T, 372)—appears as in a "theatrical representation" (G, 6: 363; T, 371). He can be revived only when Athena places a "Divine liquor . . . on his tongue [*sur la langue*]" (G, 6: 364; T, 372): his *langue* is purified; he stops speaking, and the doubly infinite continuum that forms the "palace of fates" (G, 6: 362; T, 370) is interrupted, if only for a moment. Other times, as in the second chapter, the arresting of language is enacted in the text itself: Moses Mendelssohn exclaims "O!" at the prospect of a legal order forcing anyone to say once and for all what he or she believes (JubA, 8: 135; J, 67). For, according to Mendelssohn, the communication of beliefs takes time, especially beliefs about those "things"—the Eternal being, above all—that cannot be represented in terms of the temporal continuum. Time must therefore be made for the potentially infinite slowness of linguistic communication. Such is the function of language on a "holy day." Still other chapters, especially the ones concerned with the writings of Walter Benjamin, analyze the relation between linguistic continuity and discontinuity. According to Benjamin, whose work from beginning to end is stamped by Hölderlin's theory and practice of caesura,[4] Greek tragedy is ordered around arrested language: the "infantilism" of tragic heroes (GS, 1: 289; O, 110). The silence of the tragic hero signals and solidifies the new Athenian legal order, which is founded on free speech rather than on rigid formulas; but at the same time—against "the times"—this silence puts on trial the Olympian gods along with the legal order they guard and guarantee. And the last chapter in the volume concentrates on some of the angelic figures who traverse the work of Benjamin and Luce Irigaray, for these figures have been said—by way of both doctrine and anecdote—to enact and announce the radical interruption of self-sustaining regimens and self-rectifying orders. Once they are no longer divinely sanctioned, as sheer media, if not custodians of "natural power," they, too, function as Tiresian figures of "counterrhythmic interruption."[5]

From Leibniz to Benjamin

A guide for a provisional delimitation of the inquiry into arresting language can be found in the last paragraph of Hölderlin's "Remarks on *Antigone*." Almost in passing, Hölderlin offers an abbreviated response to a question for which he would become famous more than a century after he ceased publishing poems, translations, and critical remarks—"what are poets for [*wozu Dichter*]?" (SW, 2: 123): "[to] present the world on an abbreviated scale [*die Welt im verringerten Maasstab darstellt*]" (SW, 5: 272). The idea of a microcosmos is ancient,[6] whereas the exposition of the poetic task as the abbreviation of the world is relatively young. It corresponds to the invention of the technical term and scientific discipline of "aesthetics" among proponents of Leibnizian metaphysics in the middle of the eighteenth century, especially Alexander Baumgarten. As the science of the sensible, aesthetics is an integral component of systematic philosophy, the basis of which is the principle of reason. Aesthetics shows that even the apparently chaotic material of sensation can be pleasantly subordinated to this principle.[7] By perfectly realizing the veritative potential of the senses, poets create beautiful works of art; the most beautiful poem, in turn, would present in an abbreviated manner the most rationally ordered of possible worlds, namely our own. As the surest form of abbreviation, the presentation of a fully formed individual constitutes the "truest" mode of "aesthetic truth."[8] From its call for a "lawful calculus" in the opening paragraphs of the "Remarks on *Oedipus*" to its exposition of the "perspective" from which the infinite can be grasped in the last paragraph of the "Remarks on *Antigone*," Hölderlin's final poetological reflections appropriate and transform Leibnizian terminology—and never so clearly as when he proposes the development of a "poetic logic [*poëtischer Logik*]" (SW, 5: 265). The present inquiry into arresting language therefore takes

its point of departure from Leibniz's idea of philosophical style and orga-
nizes itself around his presentation of *fatum* as the "sentence"—or "stop-
ping" (*arrest*)—of divine wisdom (G, 6: 254; T, 269).

"The all-destroying Kant" (JubA, 3, 2: 71–72), to cite Mendelssohn's fa-
mous phrase, may have dealt a death blow to philosophical systems like
Baumgarten's *Metaphysica,* yet Kant's *Critiques* did not by any means spell
the end of Leibniz's legacy. Throughout the nineteenth century more and
more of his astoundingly diverse writing was published for the first time,
and already published texts appeared in more reliable editions. And at the
beginning of the twentieth century Leibniz's work enjoyed a remarkable
renaissance among philosophers who were intent on securing a purely log-
ical foundation for mathematics—without any appeal to what Kant calls
"forms of intuition." Russell's *Philosophy of Leibniz* and Couturat's *Lo-
gique de Leibniz* are landmark achievements in this regard. From another
perspective the same can be said of the "Erkenntniskritische Vorrede"
(Epistemo-Critical preface) to Benjamin's *Ursprung des deutschen Trauer-
spiels* (Origin of the German mourning play), for it, too, is concerned
with the relation of philosophy to mathematics. Whereas mathematics
gains "genuine knowledge" by divesting itself of historical languages, ac-
cording to Benjamin, philosophy invests itself with the inner intention of
such languages, namely truth: "The more clearly mathematics documents
the fact that the total elimination of the problem of presentation [*Darstel-
lungsproblem*], which every proper didactic system claims, is the sign of
genuine knowledge, the more conclusively does its renunciation of the re-
gion of truth that languages mean [*die Sprache meinen*] present itself [*stellt
sich dar*]" (GS, 1: 207; O, 27). Languages mean truth—whatever human
beings wish to say. Benjamin is attracted to Leibniz for the same reason as
Russell and Couturat are: he does not ascribe any particular importance
to the human mind. For Russell and Couturat, the foundations of logic
and mathematics do not lie in the makeup of the mind but are, rather, to
be found in a limited set of principles; for Benjamin, truth, which "lan-
guages mean," is not a matter of the mind at all.

The self-enclosed character of the "metaphysical points" around which
Leibniz's thought revolves renders it unfit for psychologism—even for the
transcendental psychology of Kantian critique. And the same undisturbed
yet harmonious self-enclosedness expresses itself in his style of writing.
Leibniz, who is without a doubt the most consequential mathematician
among major philosophers, nevertheless—or perhaps for this reason—

knows how to write in a manner befitting philosophy. Not only does he refrain from presenting his thoughts *more geometrico* (GS, 1: 207; O, 27), he also renounces any intention of putting them into systematic form. No post-Cartesian philosophers of note—with the possible exception of Wittgenstein, whose work Benjamin did not know—conforms more fully to the four "postulates" of philosophical style that are listed at the end of the section of the "Epistemo-Critical Preface" entitled "Philosophical Beauty": "The concept of philosophical style is free of paradox. It has its postulates. They are: the art of interruption in contrast to the chain of deductions; the endurance of the treatise in contrast to the gesture of the fragment; the repetition of motifs in contrast to shallow universalism; the fullness of concentrated positivity in contrast to negating polemics" (GS, 1: 212; O, 212). If there are any doubts that the postulates of philosophical style describe and circumscribe Leibniz's work, Benjamin's brief note in the original draft of the preface puts them to rest: "Reference to Leibniz?—All systems are true in what they assert, false in what they deny" (GS, 1: 931).[9]

In the final version of the "Epistemo-Critical Preface," Benjamin decides against including the reference to Leibniz; but the Leibnizian character of the four postulates of philosophical style is nevertheless unmistakable.[10] The inquiry undertaken here into arresting language takes its point of departure from Leibniz's theory of historical languages and examines in detail Benjamin's theory of original languages for this reason: both practice the *art* of interrupting their own presentations while nevertheless representing extremes in relation to the *concept* of interruption. Having discovered a point of exit from the "labyrinth of the continuum" (G, 6: 29; T, 53)—one name of which is "metaphysical point" (G, 4: 482; L, 456), another "monad"—Leibniz never tires of delineating the "law of continuity," according to which "nature makes no leaps" (A, 6, 6: 56). Benjamin, by contrast, is concerned with nothing so much as the moment and structures of discontinuity—including the "leap" or "crack" (*Sprung*) in every origin (*Ursprung*). The concept of continuity is intimately connected to that of infinity, for the composition of a continuum requires an infinite number of actual or potential, real or fictional elements. Without a perspective from which to grasp such infinitude, no continuum can be conceived, constructed, or interrupted. Leibniz and Benjamin mark out the limits of this study, in sum, because they both discover perspectives from which to grasp the infinite as they seek points of exit from the "labyrinth of the continuum" in the course of perfecting the philosophical art of interruptive discourse. Whatever else may be said of the relation of Leibniz to Benjamin—and no extensive comparison between the two is undertaken here[11]—it is important to emphasize that they do not represent right and wrong "positions," much less a right perspective and a *linkisch* one. If Hölderlin is right, the *only* perspective from which to grasp the infinite tends to go wrong. And Benjamin, for his part, underlines the congruence between Leibniz's line of thought and the one pursued in the "Epistemo-Critical Preface" when he entitles the last of its philosophical sections "Monadology."[12]

At the end of this section Benjamin abbreviates his line of thought, summarizes Leibniz's work, and repeats Hölderlin's brief response to the question "what are poets for?": "And so the real world could be a task in the sense that it would be a matter of penetrating so deeply into everything actual that an objective interpretation of the world would disclose itself therein. Considered from the perspective of the task of such immersion, it does not appear puzzling that the thinker of the monadology was the founder of the infinitesimal calculus. The Idea is a monad—that means, in abbreviated form: every idea contains the image of the world. The presentation of an idea must do nothing less than designate this image of the world in its abbreviation [*Verkürzung*]" (GS, 1: 228; O, 48). The thought of Leibniz, Hölderlin, and Benjamin can be all be abbreviated, however imperfectly, in accordance with these summary remarks. In all three cases—philosopher, poet, and critic—something is called upon to present the world on an abbreviated scale: for the philosopher, the monad as mind, regardless of what kind of mind it may be; for the poet, the poem, regardless of its genre; for the critic, the Idea, which is neither something created, like a mind, nor something made, like a poem, but, rather, an "objective interpretation" of phenomena.[13] What distinguishes the Leibnizian monad from the Benjaminian Idea can be expressed in a few words: the essence of the monad lies in subjective representation, whereas the "essentiality" (*Wesenheit*) called "Idea" is an objective interpretation. What draws the two together and allows Benjamin to assert that "the Idea is a monad" can be expressed even more succinctly: monads and Ideas are *undisturbed*—even and especially by others of their kind. Leibniz and Benjamin invent corresponding images of this condition: every monad is windowless, every Idea a sun in its own solar system.[14]

The windowless condition of the monad is, for Leibniz, not at all privative—nor precisely monastic: it is the positive condition of not being "influenced" by anything in the world and yet corresponding with everything worldly nevertheless. On the basis of this monadic correspondence, the mind is in harmony with the body, phenomena as a whole are "well founded," and scientific knowledge is possible. The undisturbed character of the Idea is, for Benjamin, similarly nonprivative; more exactly, it is *paradisal*. For the Idea, which is neither created nor made, can be given only in language—not, however, in a language through which concepts are separated and recombined into judgments. Only in the language of paradise are Ideas given—as the sole elements of this language, which is to say, as uncombined, noncombinarity, hence totally isolated names: "Adamic naming-bestowing is so far removed from play and arbitrariness that, on the contrary, it confirms the paradisal condition as one in which there is as yet no struggle with the communicating meaning of words" (GS, 1: 217; O, 37). Philosophy is the heir to Adam, its "father," insofar as it "renews" itself by engaging once again in the "contemplation of a few, ever-recurring words—of Ideas" (GS, 1: 217; O, 37). Nothing is therefore more detrimental to philosophy than the introduction of new terminologies. Leibniz is even more emphatic on this point than Benjamin, as the first chapter of this volume shows: technical philosophical terms should be "shunned as worse than dog or snake" (A, 6, 2: 411; L, 123). The reason for this strict ban on the development of new terminologies—which both Benjamin and Leibniz sometimes violate, in the case of the term *monad*, for example—lies in the structure of Ideas themselves: they "exist in complete independence and untouchedness [*Unberührtheit*]" (GS, 1: 217; O, 37). Cognition, as the correspondence between a sentence and the state of affairs it represents, owes its origin to the "preestablished harmony" among isolated, solarlike, and thus heavenly Ideas: "Every Idea is a sun and is related to others of its kind just as suns are related to each other. The sonorous relation of such essentialities is truth [*Das tönende Verhältnis solcher Wesenheiten ist die Wahrheit*]" (GS, 1: 218; O, 37). No wonder philosophical style should not succumb to polemics: truth is the harmonious tone among those "things"—monads, Ideas, *Wesenheiten*, paradisal names—that have *de jure* and *de facto* nothing to do with one another.

Even if the undisturbed character of the monad and the Idea is in both cases nonprivative—even paradisal, heavenly, or redeemed—it is scarcely unproblematic. Nothing indicates the problem more clearly than the anachronistic character of Benjamin's comparison between suns and Ideas, for, if Newton, who disrupted Leibniz's life more than anyone else, is right, stars do relate to others of their kind in a nonmonadic and non-monastic manner: more exactly, they are all attracted to one another. Benjamin's comparison between stars and Ideas depends on the ancient conception of the harmony of the spheres—and so, too, does Leibniz's talk of "preestablished harmony."[15] If Ideas, like stars, are attracted to one another, they may exist "in complete independence" but not in complete *Unberührtheit*: "untouchedness" or "virginity." And Benjamin's theory of Ideas indicates the character of "ideal" touchedness. Ideas are like mothers who are touched by their children: "Just as a mother is seen to begin to live in the fullness of her power only when the circle of her children, motivated by the feeling of proximity, closes around her, so do Ideas come to life only when extremes are assembled around them. Ideas—or, to use Goethe's term, ideals—are Faustian mothers" (GS, 1: 215; O, 35).[16]

Adam as "father of philosophy," Ideas as "Faustian mothers": these two remarks make it impossible to undertake an inquiry into arresting language from Leibniz to Benjamin without consideration of sexual difference. The last chapter of this study therefore brings Benjamin into conjunction with Irigaray, and the end of the first chapter, which is devoted to Leibniz's study of language, seeks to reassess his thought in relation to his largely forgotten inquiry into the "fable" of a *mulier papa* or "woman father" named John-Joan who was reputed to have given birth in the midst of her first papal procession. Leibniz seeks to "explode the fable" of this papess (FS, 364); in the course of doing so, however, he recommends her story to future poets and gives them guidance for its retelling: the offended congregation could be so shocked by the sight of a pope giving birth that both papess and child are able to escape (FS, 342). Shock arrests the continuum of representations, allows for an escape from the "just order of time" (FS, 297), and delivers everyone it seizes into the condition of monads and Ideas: windowless and untouchable—at least for a moment.

The structure of such "epochal" moments is the object of Benjamin's thought from beginning to end. By converting Husserl's phenomenological *epochē*, the residuum of which is pure monadic consciousness, into an even more radical, paradisal *epochē*—which no one, strictly speaking, can carry out, least of all the lone philosopher—his lines of thought continually retrace those of Leibniz. Instead of defending divine justice by determining which infinite set of compossible monads is the best, however, Benjamin concerns himself solely with the construction of monadological structures. So close are their respective lines of thought, moreover, that in

Benjamin's last writings, the final two aphorisms of "On the Concept of History," they almost touch: monadological structures—crystallized by shock, evacuated of everything natural, including consciousness, and thus made into historical objects for the first time—are ordered in precisely the same manner as both messianic time and its model, the *Jetztzeit* (now-time): namely "enormous abbreviation [*ungeheurere Abbreviatur*]" (GS, 4: 703). This mode of ordering has nothing to do with the aristocratic principle of the best; on the contrary, under the enormous pressure of "enormous abbreviation," every element of the order is made almost equal—and altered in turn. Only an "awkward perspective," however, grants access to this possibility.

An awkward perspective cannot fail to go wrong, but wrongness cannot be the criterion of having attained the "right" perspective. Awkwardness, to paraphrase Spinoza, is the index of itself. The errors in this volume of essays are not therefore protected from error by virtue of its guiding intention: to grasp the infinite and the "spirit of states" from perspectives that go awry.

§ 1 Antonomasia: The Fate of the Name in Leibniz

> Time passed, and the young girl Antonomasia reached the age of
> fourteen and such perfection of beauty that nature could not raise
> it higher. And what can I say of her intelligence! She was as intelligent
> as she was fair, and she was fairer than all the world and is so still,
> unless the envious fates and hard-hearted Sisters Three have cut the
> thread of her life. But that they have not, for Heaven will not suffer
> so great a wrong to Earth as to pluck unripe the grapes of the fairest
> vineyard on its surface.
>
> —Miguel de Cervantes, *Don Quixote*

Philosophical Style

For Leibniz, there is nothing paradoxical about the idea of philosophical
style. On the contrary, philosophical discourse cannot hope to advance
the cause of knowledge unless it reforms itself, and an indispensable ele-
ment of its reformation lies in the development of its own style. Far from
being paradoxical, the idea of philosophical style gives direction to the de-
velopment of philosophical discourse that accords not only with tradi-
tional logic but also with a new "verbal" one. As Leibniz explains in the
extensive "Preliminary Dissertation" (1670) with which he introduces his
edition of a relatively obscure attack on medieval scholasticism written by
the late Italian Renaissance humanist Mario Nizolio, *De veris principiis et
vera ratione philosophandi contra pseudophilosophos*,[1] the study of philo-
sophical style is a hitherto unexplored dimension of logic that corresponds
to the verbal—as opposed to emotive—dimension of rhetoric:

> Under these conditions, I almost believe that just as there are two parts of
> rhetoric, one concerned with combining words elegantly, ornately, and effec-
> tively, the other with arousing emotions, so there are also two parts of logic,
> the one verbal, the other real: one concerned with the clear, distinct, and
> proper use of words or with philosophical style [*de claro, distincto et proprio
> verborum usu seu de stylo philosophico*], the other with the regulation of think-
> ing. (A, 6, 2: 420; L, 127)

Philosophical style is almost as important as the rules of thought—but only *almost*. Leibniz's hesitation is understandable: the space of an introductory "dissertation" to a relatively weak logician—and Leibniz concludes his introduction by delineating the poverty of Nizolio's account of logical terms—is hardly an auspicious place from which to disclose an entirely new dimension of logic, still less to discover a dimension of logic modeled on one of the two branches of rhetoric. For this reason, Leibniz oscillates between two positions. The *logica verbalis* that he proposes under the rubric of "philosophical style" prepares the way for the traditional discipline of logic, and it almost—but once again, only *almost*—also functions as an autonomous agent of discovery:

> Only truth remains to be discussed [having already discussed clarity and having bracketed elegance as of slight significance for philosophical style], but it is the logician's proper task to teach the rules concerning how truth is to be achieved and confirmed and all the devices for invention and judgment. For the logician, in turn, the otherwise necessary burden of examining and painstakingly discussing all his terms is wonderfully lightened if they are accurately clear. For if no word is used unless its meaning is clearly and accurately defined, all equivocations necessarily vanish, and with this a vast throng of fallacies will at once disappear. Hardly anything more will then be required for sound judgment than the senses be protected from error by means of the right constitution of the sense organs and their medium, and the intellect be protected by observing the rules for reasoning. (A 6, 2: 420; L, 126–27)

From his earliest philosophical writings to his last, Leibniz remains true to this vision of philosophical style. As long as the "logic of words" remains outstanding—and Leibniz is never quite sure how long this interim will last—this vision not only allows for a multiplicity of "styles" for philosophical discourse; it fully endorses and even enforces such a multiplication. Leibniz takes advantage of this endorsement by writing dissertations, commentaries, meditations, dialogues, pedagogical letters, and treatises—along with copious memoranda, notes, remarks, and fragments. The unity of philosophical style does not consist in a set of established principles of composition but in a single postulate: clarity. Since clarity is a function of the medium of transmission, different media require different modes of expression—on the assumption, of course, that a perfectly diaphanous medium is still outstanding. Responding to the postulate of clarity in the absence of such a medium, philosophical discourse multiplies its modes of expression, each of which serves at least two distinct functions: each discourse makes up for the lack of *the* philosophical style, understood as the "logic of words," and each likewise presents itself as one *possible* philosophical style, understood as a signature of sorts through which a discourse is recognizable as one of its kind: a work of a particular author, a manifestation of a particular "spirit," or a contribution to a particular line of thought. In 1670 Spinoza announces, "God does not have a peculiar style of speaking [*Deum nullum habere stylum peculiarem dicendi*]."[2] In the very same year, perhaps under the same inspiration, Leibniz develops in detail the dimensions of a discursive style that would be able to make up for the lack of a divine style and, in addition, make this lack comprehensible as something other than a sign that God cannot speak at all.

Nothing in discourse can secure its philosophical character other than its supple response to the postulate of clarity—which means that philosophical discourses should avoid at all costs those signs of "philosophicalness" through which they seek to certify their disputed status, namely *technical terms*. Leibniz is unambiguous about this matter in the manifesto on philosophical style that goes under the modest title "Preliminary Dissertation": technical terms are sinful; they signal the fall of discourse into the abyss of obscurity. Discourses claiming to be philosophical are particularly prone to obscure terms as long as philosophers seek to distinguish their discourse from that of the people, in the vain delusion that they are somehow different—or can make themselves *appear* different by virtue of an impenetrable "philosophical style." Philosophical discourse, according to Leibniz, not only can dispense with signs of its "philosophicalness," it *must* do so in order for it to be philosophical. In Leibniz's dissertation, therefore, "philosophical style" no longer means the style that philosophers have hitherto adopted; nor does it mean the style philosophers should henceforth adopt: it is a name for any mode of discourse responsive to the postulate of clarity. And for this reason, "philosophical style" is a technical term for diverse modes of discourse, the unity of which consists in avoiding—whenever possible—technical terms. A paradox is averted only under one condition: philosophical discourses cannot describe *themselves* in terms of philosophical style. Expositions of philosophical style belong, rather, to *preliminary* dissertations—preparations for philosophical works with pretentious titles like *De veris principiis et vera ratione philosophandi*. Leibniz's battle against technical terms in philosophical discourse thus takes the form of a commentary on Nizolio's polemical treatise; but its modesty, which is doubtless appropriate for a young philosopher eager to please his benefactor,[3] cannot hide the gravity of the offense it seeks to eradicate:

> We may thus regard it as established that whatever cannot be explained in popular terms is nothing [*usse nullum*] and should be expiated from philosophy as if by an incantation [*a philosophia velut piaculari quodam carmine arcendum*], unless it can be known by immediate sense experience (like many classes of colors, odors, and tastes). . . . [I]t is clear that the canon and measure for selecting terms should be *the most compendious popularity* or *the most popular compendiousness.* Hence *wherever equally compendious popular terms are available technical terms are to be avoided.* This is surely one of the fundamental rules of philosophical style, though often violated, especially by metaphysicians and dialecticians. For dialectical and metaphysical subjects frequently occur in the utterances, writings, and thoughts of uneducated people and are often encountered in everyday life. Instigated by this frequent demand, the people have as a result designated these subjects by special words that are familiar, very natural, and compendious. When such words are available, it is a sin [*peccatum*] to obscure matters by inventing new and mostly inconvenient terms. (A, 6, 2: 414; L, 124–25)

If new terms are incapable of resolution into "popular" ones, they are nothing more than arbitrary inventions, the nullity of which corresponds to the vanity of their inventors, all of whom have the audacity to create "things" in the absence of both nature and God. Without a basis in either a natural or a divine order, technical terms belong solely to the order of language, which, however, loses its defining function once it no longer represents either the world created by God or the exalted Word in and through which the world comes into being. And Leibniz is careful to emphasize that philosophical discourse does not escape the same judgment: since metaphysics and dialectics are matters of popular discourse, philosophers cannot legitimately claim that their discussions, like those of mathematicians, for example, make otherwise incomprehensible terms of the trade indispensable. The pathos of Leibniz's battle against technical terms—and neither the obliqueness of his manner of writing nor the niceties of his impeccable scholarly Latin can hide this intensity—indicates the degree to which his attempt to champion the cause of clarity corresponds to the spirit of the earliest German *Aufklärung,* as it simultaneously seeks to dispel the threat of satanic darkness: "The greatest clarity is found in commonplace terms with their popular usage retained. There is always a certain obscurity in technical terms" (A, 6, 2: 411; L, 123). Because technical terms can never shed their obscurity, they cast a shadow on any discourse in which they are used; and because of their opaqueness technical terms are vicious—so much so that Leibniz aligns them with beasts in which melancholia, death, and the devil assume earthly form: "Technical terms are therefore to be shunned as worse than dog or snake" (A, 6, 2: 411; L, 123). Against the vision of a fully developed philosophical style in which discourse leads to discoveries almost on its own, as if by magic, Leibniz presents a countervision: a discourse dominated by technical terms that are grounded neither in nature nor in God and that therefore appear in the guise of the great Adversary.

Leibniz's "Preliminary Dissertation" is thus inhabited by two countervailing visions of discourse operating on its own—without a human speaker: one in which such discourse yields new knowledge almost automatically, the other in which discourse plunges unsuspecting speakers into an ever expanding abyss of chatter, as new technical terms are "created" in order to "clarify" the obscurity of older ones. Neither of these two visions is, of course, unique to Leibniz. The preliminary—and profusely learned—character of Leibniz's dissertation make his indebtedness abundantly clear, especially with respect to the tradition of Renaissance rhetoric. Nizolio may not use the same theologically tinged language of sin and snakes when he speaks of scholastic "barbarisms," but the aim of his highly charged polemical treatise is the same: rid philosophy of the technical terms developed under the guise of scholasticism and return philosophical discourse to the vernacular language of the people. And Leibniz's plea for clarity is far from original, even if his exposition of clarity in terms of *stylus philosophicus* recognizes few precedents. The peculiarity of the program Leibniz lays out for himself in the "Preliminary Dissertation" does not lie in the two visions of discourse operating on their own but, rather, in the manner that they run counter to—and at the same time blend into—each other.

No terms could be less "popular" than the ones that Leibniz envisages for the language that he first outlines four years earlier in his groundbreaking *Dissertation on the Art of Combination* (1666).[4] Under the rubric of "universal language," "rational writing," "rational language," "exact language," "philosophical writing," or "alphabet of human knowledge,"[5] Leibniz thereafter proposes languages and systems of writing that will allow him to make good on his claim in the "Preliminary Dissertation" that discourse can be brought to such a high degree of clarity that "hardly anything more will then be required for sound judgment"—and thus for the continual advancement of knowledge—"than the senses be protected from error by means of the right constitution of the sense organs and their medium, and the intellect by observing the rules for ratiocination" (A, 6, 2: 420; L, 127). Inasmuch as these languages and systems of writing are artificially devised, all of their terms are "technical" in a precise sense: the *ars* of *ars combinatoria* constitutes the *technē* in which each term is defined in coordination with every other. All of Leibniz's proposals for—and experiments in—"universal characteristics" thus violate the rule that he lays down for philosophical style in the "Preliminary Dissertation": flee from technical terms as if they were snakes. And, ironically, these proposals violate the rule against technical terms for the very same reason Leibniz makes his "Preliminary Dissertation" into an essay on philosophical style in the first place: for the sake of clarity.

Only under the condition that historical languages are somehow akin to the "universal language" or "universal characteristic" that Leibniz seeks to develop can the opposing directions of the *Dissertation on the Art of Combination* and the "Preliminary Dissertation" be comprehended and fully contained. The affinity of universal languages, which are the product of rational calculation, to historical languages, which are not, should manifest itself in the development of the latter. Historical languages, in other words, must be able to clarify *themselves*, which means that they must develop toward clarity, and this development must constitute in some sense the very historicity of these languages. Yet this development is far from certain; it is always prone to breakdowns, and the signs of such interruption are precisely those *technical*—and therefore *unnatural*—terms through which philosophers have tried to secure the place for a distinct and recognizable philosophical style. In technical terms, therefore, the two programs for philosophical discourse that Leibniz elaborates from his earliest experiments onward interfere with each other. The invention of technical terms within particular languages is a (necessarily doomed) piecemeal attempt to do what his program for a "universal characteristics" seeks to accomplish all at once: replace popular words by invented ones. For the sake of clarity, then, Leibniz sets into motion two parallel programs for the reform of language. By presenting his effort at the reform of philosophical discourse in the guise of a polemical attack on the use of technical terms, Leibniz can avoid a tautological imperative: clarify one's discourse in order to speak clearly. The postulate to which the "Preliminary Dissertation" responds cuts across both philosophical programs: clarity must itself be clarified.

Only in light of a clarified clarity can the proximate aim of all Leibniz's efforts in the reform of philosophical discourse become apparent.

The Rhetoric of Clarity

The "Preliminary Dissertation" clarifies the term *clarum* with little ado: "*Clear* is that which is well perceived [Clarum *ist quod bene percipitur*]." Leibniz's immediate application of this definition to discourse is similarly succinct: "so discourse is clear if the meaning of all its words are known, at least to the attentive" (A, 6, 2: 408–9; L, 121). As the addition of "attention" itself indicates, however, this clarification of *clarity*—both the term and the phenomenon—cannot be entirely free of obscurity. Obscurity resides in the tropological character of the term to be clarified: "clear" in this case moves from the register of perception to that of discourse by means of metaphor. The perception of *this* movement requires a corresponding movement of the term *perception*, the perception of which requires *another* corresponding movement, *ad infinitum*. Only by paying attention to such potentially endless and therefore vertiginous movements of discourse from one register to another can Leibniz's own sentences become clear, for otherwise talk of "clear discourse" will be fully obscured—as though understanding a discourse were the same as perceiving an object. And Leibniz's clarification of *verum* leaves no doubts that the primary meaning of "perception" resides in the field of vision:

> An utterance is *true* whose meaning is perceived through a right disposition of both the percipient and the medium; for clarity is measured by the understanding, truth by sense. This is the unique and truest definition of truth. . . . But this must be explained elsewhere; here we will merely make it clear with an example. The sentence "Rome is situated on the Tiber" is true because nothing more is needed to understand what it says than that the sentient being and the medium of sensation be in a right relation. (A, 6, 2: 409; L, 121)

Throughout the "Preliminary Dissertation" Leibniz remains content with this clarification of *verum*; all of his attention is directed at defining the parameters of discursive clarity; for, unlike truth, clarity is traversed by unclarity, and the sign of the constitutive unclarity of the term lies in the trope through which it comes to be used in the context of speech. When Leibniz returns in later dissertations, meditations, and dialogues to the nature of truth, he doubtless departs from the "truest definition" of truth he proposes in the "Preliminary Dissertation," but the general motivation for this departure is indebted to the same line of argumentation: the problem of truth as correspondence between word and thing is subordinate to that of clarity, for the truth of any proposition should be—and, for the divine mind, is—as readily perceptible as the truth of "*A* is *A*." *Clarum* retains its place as the primary name for the problem to which philosophers must address themselves, and even if the "Preliminary Dissertation" dispatches with truth much more quickly than Leibniz's later discourses, none of them would dispute the priority that it accords to the postulate of clarity: "Certainty is nothing but the clearness of truth, so that it follows from the very concept of certainty that the properties of philosophical discourse, that is, of speech seeking certainty, are clarity and truth. Indeed, it is manifestly true that the truth of a proposition cannot be known unless the meaning of its words is known, that is, unless it is clear (by the definition of clear discourse)" (A, 6, 2: 409; L, 122).

The unclarity surrounding clarity is therefore of no small significance. The reason for this awkward condition is quite obvious, even if the remedy for its resolution is not: *clarum* can be applied to discourse only under the condition that it undergo a figural transformation. And in pursuit of this transformation, which generally escapes attention and opens up the prospect of vertiginous motility, Leibniz turns the central paragraphs of his "Preliminary Dissertation" into an investigation of the tropes through which historical languages develop. The aim of this investigation is not only to account for the obscurity of certain discourses, especially those of scholastic philosophy, but also—and more importantly—to uncover the ways in which historical languages clarify *themselves* by constantly enriching and diversifying their lexicons. The motor and means of this self-clarification of language is paradoxically the open assemblage of figures— or "army of tropes," to use Nietzsche's famous phrase.[6] Whereas Leibniz follows Nizolio in the first endeavor, he sets out on his own in the second. The comparison between the branches of rhetoric and the dimensions of logic that he seeks to disclose by developing a *logica verbalis* is therefore far from casual: the discipline of rhetoric is integral to the logical program Leibniz establishes for himself—not, to be sure, rhetoric understood as "the elegant combination of words" or "the arousing of emotions," but as a prolegomenon to a rigorous study of the self-development of historical languages. Or, to cite Leibniz's own definition, which he devised only a few years before writing his introduction to Nizolio and which serves as a constitutive element of the reformation of the principles of legal reasoning that he proposes under the title *A New Method for Learning and Teaching Jurisprudence* (1667), rhetoric is to be understood primarily as "the analysis of the tropes of speech, discourse" (A, 6, 1: 339).

In the course of the wide-scale methodological reflections that constitute *A New Method*, Leibniz underscores the importance of rhetoric, understood as an analysis of tropes, for the "art of interpretation" (*ars hermeneutica*) in general—especially the interpretation of antiquated legal documents, including the legal language of Scripture. Leibniz suggests that the discipline of jurisprudence would be greatly advanced if someone were to write a treatise *De tropis legum* modeled on Bartholomew Westhemerus's *De tropis scripturae* (A, 6, 1: 326).[7] And in his extensive notes for the revision of *A New Method*, which were written some thirty years after its publication, Leibniz goes even farther. Drawing on his own long-standing efforts to reduce the unruly plurality of Aristotelian categories to three fundamental categories of relation, he succinctly indicates how a treatise about tropes might progress if it could reduce the even more unruly plurality of tropes to three primary ones—metaphor, metonymy, and synecdoche:

> Since I was a young man, I have divided relations into two classes, those of comparison and conjunction. The relations of identity and diversity, of similarity and dissimilarity, of equality and inequality, are relations of comparison. Conjunction may be either *simple* (as whole and part, part and other part, place, time and other similar adjuncts) or a relation of *connection*, in which some influx and consequence is present, as in cause and effect and sign and signified. And as an aside, the three primary figures of rhetoric correspond to these three species of relation, to wit: *metaphor* to comparison, *synecdoche* to simple conjunction, *metonymy* to connection. In view of the fact that words correspond to things by means of fixed relations, they provide marvelous uses not only for whatever must be retained but also for whatever can yet be discovered. (A, 6, 1: 278)

In the paragraphs of the "Preliminary Dissertation" devoted to the "tropes of discourse," Leibniz does not venture so far; he makes no effort to correlate certain "primary figures of rhetoric" with the fundamental categories of his newly devised logic of combinatorial relations. Yet the "Preliminary Dissertation" almost exclusively concerns itself with the three "primary tropes" Leibniz identifies in these later texts. Even if it is not clearly formulated, something of this project of reduction expresses itself in the attempt of this "dissertation" to clarify *clarum* and thereby develop the parameters of a properly philosophical style. As Leibniz makes clear, it is certainly possible for someone to know all the words of a discourse and yet remain in the dark about its meaning, for each word of the discourse under discussion may have acquired more than one meaning—and acquired them by means of tropes that have gone unnoticed. In the "Preliminary Dissertation," in contrast to *A New Method*, Leibniz does not concern himself with any particular methods of interpreting a discourse and thus determining its overall meaning along with the sense of its individual terms; rather, he turns his attention to the means by which speakers could clarify their discourse to the point where the *ars hermeneutica* would be effectively rendered unnecessary.

According to Leibniz, who anticipates the philosophical inquiries of the later Wittgenstein—with whom he would otherwise seem to have little in common[8]—the meaning of a linguistic term consists primarily in the use to which it is put, and conversely, the use of a term is for the most part its meaning: "use [*usus*] is the meaning [*significatio*] of a word known in common by all those who use the same language" (A, 6, 2: 410; L, 122). The multiplicity of uses to which any given word may be put constitutes the fundamental problem of clarity. Clarification of words, including the word *clarum*, consists in the process of reducing the multiplicity of uses in a nonarbitrary manner. Simply imposing a meaning on a term by fiat cannot be considered clarification but, at best, nominal definition and at worst, the invention of a technical term. The problem of clarification is particularly important—and remarkably difficulty—because no principle for the reduction of the multiplicity of uses to which a word may be put is readily apparent, nor indeed do the philosophical, grammatical, and rhetorical traditions that Leibniz copiously documents throughout the "Preliminary Dissertation" give any reliable principle for the accomplishment of this task. Nor indeed are his own youthful attempts to reduce the categories of traditional logic of any help in this context. Only *in words themselves*—more precisely in their historicity—can Leibniz begin to make progress in his endeavor. The fact that words *are* historical and therefore leave recognizable traces of their development is the sole point of support for Leibniz's effort to reduce the multiplicity of uses to unity and thereby clarify terms —without having to stipulate a univocal meaning by an arbitrary act in which one simply announces "this means that," regardless of how a word is used. Under the premise that the multiplication of meanings is an historical process, the beginning of which can be sought in a univocal use, the process of clarification can distinguish itself from arbitrary stipulations of meaning and equally arbitrary inventions of technical terms. Each word bears its own complete history in itself, and under the condition that this history takes its point of departure from a state of unitary "rootedness," it can be an independent source of clarity—or more exactly, the resource upon which efforts at *clarification,* as opposed to sinful stipulation, can draw: "The clarity of a word arises from two factors: either from the *word in itself* or from its *circumstance in discourse.* The clarity of a word in itself, in turn, has two sources [*fontes*]: *origin and use* [originem et usum]" (A, 6, 2: 410; L, 122).

From the origin of a word flows its clarity. With this formula Leibniz articulates the premise upon which he can eradicate technical terms from philosophical discourse without thereby cutting himself off from the other —and diametrically opposed—program for the development of a philosophical language or system of writing. Origin is a source of clarity insofar as it sheds light on the path toward a nonarbitrary, rational, and at the same time *natural* reduction of the multiplicity of meanings. Origin, to repeat a famous saying of Karl Kraus, is the goal.[9] Or at least it is the goal of the program for the reformation of philosophical discourse Leibniz undertakes in the "Preliminary Dissertation": "one must make sure above all else to choose among the many uses offered that one which is nearest the origin of the word" (A, 6, 2: 411; L, 123). Only by referring each of its words to its origin can philosophical discourse secure the univocity of its vocabulary without relying on arbitrary acts of denomination. Only under two conditions, however, can historical languages function in a manner analogous to that of an *ars combinatoria*: at its origin, each word must have been used in only one manner, and no two words were used in precisely the same way. Some languages, according to Leibniz, are particularly apt for the development of philosophical style—those in which the roots of the word are readily apparent. Since German happens to be one of these languages, in Leibniz's eyes, he vigorously recommends its use for the "testing and examination of philosophical matters" (A, 6, 2: 414; L, 125).[10] Nothing is more important for Leibniz's project of exorcizing technical terms from philosophical discourse than the exposition of origin as a source of clarity. Insofar as every technical term proceeds away from its origin, it cannot escape a certain obscurity. And instead of inventing technical terms, philosophical discourse, according to Leibniz, should designate what he calls "formal meanings." *Significatio formalis* thus becomes the—

unavoidably obscure—*terminus technicus* with which Leibniz brings his clarification of *clarum* to a close and, by so doing, completes his preliminary delineation of philosophical style:

> This rule must be adhered to in applying words—if the origin disagrees with the use, we should follow the use in discourse rather than the origin; but if the use is either doubtful or does not forbid it, we should rather cling to the origin. If the word has multiple uses, one must either be careful to abstract some so-called *formal meaning*, that is, the meaning that includes all uses in it—a method employed by theologians, especially the interpreters of Hebrew Scripture (in this search for the meaning of words Samuel Bohl particularly distinguishes himself); or if this cannot be done, one must at least constitute some one use in which it itself flows from the origin [*ex origine fluxit ipse*], namely, through a canal of Tropes [*per canales Troporum*]. (A, 6, 2: 410-11; partially translated in L, 122)

Leibniz fails to spell out what he means by "formal meaning," and instead, takes refuge in the work of Bohl, who made this formula into a technical term within the general art of biblical interpretation.[11] But at least this much is clear about the puzzling if not wholly obscure phrase *significatio formalis*: as long as it is possible to discovery a "formal meaning" for a term, it is not necessary to draw on its origin to achieve a measure of clarity. The failure of historical languages to allow for the determination of "formal meanings" for all of their words testifies to the need for another source of clarity; otherwise, every one of these languages would have to be wholly abandoned for the purpose of philosophical discourse. Historical languages can be saved for such discourse under the condition that the twists and turns—which is to say, the tropes—through which words have passed can be traced back to their origin. Insofar as tropes multiply the uses of words, they run counter to the demands of philosophical style, and Leibniz makes clear that they are no more welcome in philosophical discourse than technical terms: "So far we have shown that technical terms are to be avoided as far as possible. Now we must note that whether terms are popular or technical, they ought to involve no *tropes* or *few and apt ones*" (A, 6, 2: 418; L, 126). But the study of tropes is something else altogether: by investigating the often unnoticed, even subconscious reasons for the alterations to which words are subject, Leibniz can legitimately propose that linguistic history is inherently rational, and this proposal, even if only in outline, prepares the way, in turn, for the development of a fully rational—which is to say philosophical—style.

Instead of elaborating a rhetoric within the context of his introduction to Nizolio—who, for his part, concentrates much of his energy in precisely this direction—Leibniz invents a trope: "canal of tropes." By means of this metaphor, which is a metaphor for the movement of a word from one context of application to another and therefore a metaphor for the very movement of metaphorization, Leibniz makes up for a lacuna in his exposition. And this, too, corresponds to the metaphor he makes up, for a canal has no other function than making up for a lack in nature. Just as the development of philosophical style in historical languages makes up for the absence of a fully functional *ars combinatoria*, the trope of "canals of tropes" makes up for the lack of a fully articulated analysis of the modes through which words depart from their origin. And just as literal canals compensate for a lack of navigable rivers, "tropical" canals are created for want of available words. The nonnatural character of canals does not, of course, imply that they are unnatural; rather, if the trope "canal of trope" captures the character of tropes themselves, then canals of tropes cannot fail to be technical. Their technicity does not, however, always manifest itself in the positing of technical terms. On the contrary, for the most part, the various twists and turns in the course of discourse are accomplished without anyone planning anything; for this reason alone historical languages are "natural," outside the "theses," conventions, or positings of self-conscious subjects. Coming to an awareness of the twists and turns of discourse has traditionally been undertaken under the rubric of rhetoric, especially its nonpersuasive dimension in which "elegant" combinations are defined, described, and catalogued. Breaking with this tradition, Leibniz assigns such awareness to the newly invented field of philosophical style. With the trope of "canals of tropes," Leibniz thus captures in two short words the coimplication of necessity and contingency in so-called natural languages: there is a reason for every turn in the course of discourse, but the reason for any given trope generally escapes notice, as if slight tropological alterations were in effect the "petite perceptions" (A, 6, 6: 53–55) of discourse: as hidden from the consciousness of both speaker and hearer as the minute rustlings that together make up the roar of the sea. Only by "turning" into and out of itself; only by twisting new terms from its lexicon; only, in short, by means of figural canals can historical language *develop* in the literal sense of this word—a sense that Leibniz will later exploit when he begins to interpret the idea of substance in terms of doubly infinite en- and de-velopment.[12]

According to Leibniz, who follows Nizolio more closely on this point than on any other, nowhere are tropes more deceptively used than in the dry discourses of the last generation of scholastic philosophers:

> Now we must note that whether terms are popular or technical, they ought to involve no *tropes* or *few and apt ones*. Of this, the Scholastics have taken little notice, for strange though this sounds, their discourse teems with tropes [*oratio tropis scatet*]. What else are such terms as *to depend, to inhere, to emanate,* and *to influx*? (A, 6, 2: 418; L, 126)

And of all these "barbaric" words, none is more misleading than the one Leibniz underlines last: *influere*. With this term, Francisco Suarèz sought to resolve the perplexities surrounding the relation of the body to the soul.[13] But the creation of *influere* by means of minor *flexus* interferes with the flux of discourse—for at least two reasons: *influere* interferes with the grammar of *fluere*; and *influx* merely redoubles the term it is meant to clarify, namely *causa*:

> The Scholastics before him [Suarèz] had been exerting themselves to find a general concept of cause, but fitting words had not occurred to them. Suarèz was not more clever than they, but more audacious, and introducing ingeniously the word *influx*, he defined "cause" as *what flows Being into something else* [*quod influit esse in aliud*], a sufficiently barbarous and obscure expression. Even the construction is inept, since *influere* is transformed from an intransitive to a transitive verb; and this *influx* is metaphorical and more obscure than what it defines. I should think it is an easier task to define the term *cause* than this word *influx*, used in such a monstrous manner. (A, 6, 2: 418; L, 126)

Instead of discovering a "formal meaning" for the term *cause*, the "barbarian" philosopher willfully creates a metaphorical monster. The flow of water from source to sea is comparable to the flow of Being from origin to goal, but neither Being nor language flows in this manner. *Influx* is such an unnaturally constructed version of *flexus* that under its influence philosophical discourse dries up.

Historical languages would flow more clearly from their sources if only philosophers were more attentive to the historicity of the languages they used. Almost on their own, regardless of their speakers, historical languages make up for their original paucity by diversifying their lexicons, and this diversification, which is the principle of linguistic growth, naturally takes place by means of artificially constructed channels leading away from the origin. Within the context of language, then, the categories of the natural and the artificial, *physis* and *thesis*, curiously envelop each other: "natural" languages grow by way of artificial twists, which, in turn, are the source of their flow away from the origin.[14] As a *flexus* of the flux, each trope artificially alters the course of the flow, but since no "rivers of discourse" wind their way downward, there would be no flux at all if it were not for a figural *flexus*. But the twists of discourse cannot for this reason be understood simply as natural; and some twists are downright *unnatural*, which is to say, wholly technical and for this reason sinful. According to an ancient doctrine that Leibniz adopts and adapts for his own theological, metaphysical, legal, and political purposes, "sins arise from the aboriginal limitation of things [*peccata oriuntur ex originali rerum limitatione*]" (A, 6, 4: 1657; L, 265). Applied to language, this doctrine yields the following principle: the origin of linguistic sin lies in the paucity of terms with which every historical language was originally endowed. And this possibility of sin is actualized whenever a trope doubles—rather than diversifies—the lexicon of a language. The creation of synonyms, in short, is sinful: canals of tropes turn into blind alleys, dead-end streets, or—to stay with the flow of the metaphor—channels of discourse that lead nowhere *new*.

Fatum

All of Leibniz's directions for philosophical style take aim at "monstrous" terms, like *influx*, in which the flow of discourse comes to a stop. As a solution to the threat posed by such terms, Leibniz encourages philosophers to abandon late-born languages that flow out of classical Latin and immerse themselves in those languages, like German, which are awash in "realities [*realibus*]" (A, 6, 2: 414; L, 125). And by charting the "canals of tropes" through which words wind their way into current usage, philosophers, according to Leibniz, can gain a perspective from which to clear discourse up—which is to say, dissolve and clear away ambiguous, perplexing, immobilizing, and therefore arresting terms. Philosophical style makes the flow of discourse more fluent. Leibniz, for his part, is not entirely guided by his own directives. Not only does he continue to employ Latin—and a particularly ornate Latin—but he also declines to undertake any sustained explorations of the "tropical" canals through which words flow away from their origin. Whereas his decision to write in Latin rather than German is fully comprehensible in terms of the editorial task he seeks to accomplish in his introduction to *De veris principiis*, his failure to elaborate the terms in which "canals of tropes" might be charted is less so. Perhaps he senses something dangerous here: the canals of tropes, potentially multiplied *ad infinitum* by the very effort to chart them, suddenly turn into a raging sea, overflowing with terms that are no longer *termina*. In any case, the only philosopher who, according to Leibniz, successfully navigated "tropical" canals—Julius Caesar Scaliger—died without leaving any record of his bold adventures, lost on the open seas of discourse. Not even his son, Joseph Justus Scaliger, was bold enough to follow him: "although we have greater erudition in the thought of the son, we have lost greater acumen and philosophy in the lost book of origins of the father" (A, 6, 2: 410; L, 122). With this memory of a double loss Leibniz undertakes his sole exploration of a "tropical" canal within the space of the "Preliminary Dissertation," one of the very few that he investigates in all his subsequent reflections on language: the canal of tropes that fatefully—and perhaps fatally—issues into the word *fate*.

The word *fatum* occupies an exemplary position in Leibniz's exposition of philosophical style. Under the condition that his choice of words was not itself fated, Leibniz could have concentrated his considerable analytic power on any number of other terms. The absence of this condition—which amounts to the postulate of authorial freedom—is, however, the very condition under which it makes sense to speak of style in the first place. Fate and style are in this sense antithetical and yet curiously intertwined. The analysis of *fatum* Leibniz proposes may even function as a replacement for a similar and silent analysis of *stilus*, which, as is well known, originally meant a stake in general, then a particular kind of stick, those used for inscribing waxen tablets, then by metonymy, the practice of composition in general, thereafter a particular mode of composition, and finally—outside of classical Latin and in competition with the last usage—a singular mode of composition, comparable to a signature: style par excellence, in other words, which, because it can never be entirely formalized, comes to be known, if it can be known in the exact sense of the term, in accordance with singular terms, that is, proper names. In any case, the fate of philosophical style rests in the torturous course of *fatum*. For this reason—among many others—*fatum* exercises a particularly powerful spell over the "Preliminary Dissertation," to say nothing of Leibniz's other dissertations, dialogues, correspondences, and meditations. What grants *fatum* an exemplary status is the manner in which the figural movement from its original to its current use gives an indication of the "natural" diversification of a language's lexicon.

As Leibniz notes elsewhere, historical languages—and particularly those at their earliest stages—are inevitably prone to homonymy: "the origin of homonymy is that the number of things to name is infinite, the number of names, by contrast, poor" (A, 6, 4: 1307).[15] By means of tropes, historical languages make up for the original scarcity of words. Synonymy at the origin, by contrast, poses a more perplexing problem—one that original speakers of Latin were forced to confront. For in its original state Latin suffered from a superfluidity of words for the act of speaking: both *fari* and *dicere* originally meant "to say." If a language is rich in names and poor in things to name, including the act of naming, then it should lend one of its names to another "thing." And this is precisely what Latin did: one of the names for "saying" turns into a name for something other than "saying," and this transformation is an unambiguous sign that the course of languages can be reconstructed and is, for this reason, rational. As long as synonymy frees one of the words for other uses, historical languages can be understood to operate on their own in the same manner as a properly instituted "logic of words"—and, for that matter, as a natural *ars combinatoria*:

> For example, the use or meaning of the word *fate* is necessity of events. In origin it is compounded from the use of the root and from analogy. The root is *for* or *fari*, the meaning of the root is "to say" [*dicere*]; the analogy of fate is *fatum*, the perfect passive participle of the designated verb in the Latin language, so that the origin of *fate* and *dictum* is the same. Mostly, too, use has arisen from origin by a certain *trope*, which appears in the example, since *fatum* is originally the same as *dictum* but means in use what will happen necessarily; let us see [*videamus*], therefore, whose *dictum* will happen necessarily; it is manifest that God's sayings alone [*Dei solius dicta*] fit this description. Thus by origin *fatum* is *dictum*, then by *antonomasia* or *kat exochen*, the saying of God [*dictum Dei*], then by *synecdoche* the saying of God concerning the future, or the decree of God [*decretum Dei*], and finally by the *metonymy* of cause, what will happen necessarily, which is the current use of the word. (A, 6, 2: 410; L, 122)

Freed to mean something other than "to say," *fari* becomes the name for the opposite of freedom, namely *fate*. The course of *fari* can thus be described as an ironic one: semantic freedom issues into a term for the rigorous necessity in which all freedom, including that of meaning, is eradicated. Leibniz does not arrive at this account of the movements undergone by *fari* on the basis of empirically verifiable philological data; nowhere does he cite examples of Latin usage. Rather, he reconstructs in retrospect the movement that *fari* must have taken for it to arrive at its current use: "Let us see, therefore, whose *dictum* will happen necessarily." From this perspective, Leibniz's preference for the work of Scaliger the father over that of the son is readily understandable: "acumen and philosophy," not assiduous research, are the prerequisites for inquiry into tropological transformations like that of *fari* (to say) into *fatum* (the necessity of events). The clarification of the manner in which the origin of word can serve as a source of its clarity dovetails with a fundamental principle that Leibniz first announces at the very moment he completes his edition of Nizolio's *De veris principiis*: "Nothing is without reason [*Nihil est sine ratione*]" (G, 4: 232).[16] With this principle, which easily assimilates itself to a doctrine of fatalism, all of Leibniz's thought—and indeed his life—will later be almost wholly identified. Just before Leibniz publishes this principle, he makes sure that it works, *mutatis mutandis,* for the course of discourse: *in curriculo orationis nihil est sine ratione.* The twists and turns of language, all of which seem quite disorderly, can render reasons for their existence. Only after the flow of discourse has been grounded and the flood of meaning averted can the principle of groundedness itself be safely articulated. And there is no better example of thoroughgoing grounding of all things—including words—in God than the word *fatum*, which, by way of antonomasia, functions as a pseudonym for the divine name itself.[17]

Only a single word can be true merely by virtue of its having been said: the word of the One God whose oneness is so incomparable that it cannot be conceived in terms of numeral unity. By antonomasia, *fari* comes to name the sole speaker who makes his word true simply by speaking, and the trope accomplishes this trick even if—and especially when—the speakers who use the "troped" word remain in the dark about *who* precisely this speaker might be. Leibniz says nothing of the Parcae in his accounts of the etymology of *fatum*.[18] Nor does he concern himself with Roman religious practices or beliefs. The god named *fatum* by virtue of antonomasia is God *tout court*—or God *kat exochen*. Such are the resources of antonomasia: as long as a common noun can function as a proper name, it is possible to speak of God without knowing his proper name—and without even knowing *that* he has a *proper* name. The independent "logic" of the language thus invents a replacement for the exalted Name without the speakers having any knowledge that they are missing anything at all. The trope of antonomasia accommodates—or better yet, accomplishes—the transformation of an abstract noun into a proper name, which, for its part, reflects the singularity of the unknown God by performing the function of singling something out. In the case of *fari*, the unique "thing" designated by means of antonomasia is the incomparable Being himself. *Fatum* can thus assume, if only for a moment, a self-reflective function: it singles out the singular God. And antonomasia is indispensable for the performance of this function insofar as the *absolutely* proper name of this God—the name God calls himself—remains forever hidden.

Under the condition that the absolutely proper name of God cannot be known—or cannot be spoken even if it is known—all names for the divinity are not so much pseudonyms as *figural* proper ones: names by way of antonomasia. And this is the initial course of *fari*. In its first turn away from the origin, it signifies an infinite language in which there is no distinction between saying-so and being-so. At the same time it reasserts the finitude of language by serving as a replacement for an unknown, unknowable, or in any case unspeakable name of the One whose speech is immediately reality. If it were possible to speak of style *kat exochen*, here would be the place. Yet the principles of such style, which run counter to fate in the current sense of the word, could not be formulated. For this reason, style *kat exochen* could never be repeated or even recognized as such. Spinoza's dictum, "God does not have a peculiar style," is therefore justified in absence of any hermeneutical study of Scripture: when God speaks, his singular style of discourse—the best—could never be known, which means in effect that he has none. If, however, it is appropriate to speak of speech—or, to use a term Leibniz later employs, the order of the symbol[19]—only under the condition that it be distinguished from reality, then the first turn of *fatum* away from its origin marks both the eclipse and the resumption of speech, properly speaking.

The further course of *fatum* takes it away from the precarious turn of antonomasia. The two tropes through which the "canal" of *fari* then travels on its way to fate are the ones that—along with the meta-trope of metaphor—form the basic schema through which the early-sixteenth-century Dutch rhetorician Gerard Jan Voss hopes to order once and for all the unwieldy catalogue of tropes and which Leibniz, in his wake, explicitly endorses: the tripartite schema of metaphor, metonymy, and synecdoche.[20] By taking only one temporal dimension of the *dictum Dei* for the whole, synecdoche breaks up the unity of saying-so and being-so; instead of being synonymous with *dictum*, *fatum* comes to occupy the place of another, more restricted, word for the act of speaking: *decretum*. Broken up in this manner, *fatum* abdicates its status as a name and becomes once again a common noun. And metonymy finishes off where synecdoche stops short: it takes *fatum* entirely away from its origin as a redundant term for the act of speaking and makes it into a term for the condition in which events follow one another necessarily—regardless of what anyone, including a god, might say. The act of speaking and the fate of things thus part ways, so to speak, and the exact place of this parting is designated by the rhetorical category: "metonymy of cause." Taking the consequence (what is predicted) for the ground (the act of saying), metonymy removes *fatum* from the sphere of speech altogether. Instead of referring to the One speaker whose word creates the things to which it refers or, in a diminished version, whose word decrees the character of the future, it expresses the outcome of this decree: the irrevocable—and unvocalized—course of events. By virtue of the "metonymy of cause," everything is understood to be caused—and thus "fated." *Fatum*, in turn, loses all association with *dictum*; instead, it comes to express the very category of relation that, according to Leibniz's later revision of rhetorical terms, corresponds to metonymy: "a relation of *connection*, in which some influx and consequence [*influxus quidam et consecutio*] is present, as in cause and effect and sign and designated" (A, 6, 1: 278). Leibniz's discourse cannot altogether escape the monstrosity of *influxus*. Exorcised from the "Preliminary Dissertation," it returns to his notes on *A New Method* at the precise point where he reminisces on his youthful attempts to reduce the number of traditional categories to three and, by so doing, as an unexpected bonus, discovers what Voss had earlier perceived: the three "primary" tropes. By the "metonymy of cause," *fatum* finally twists free of its previous semantic redundancy—and turns into a term for rigorous "influence." Understood in these terms, metonymy is the figural equivalent of the category of universal *connexio* from which nothing can ever escape. With the "metonymy of cause," the flux of the word *fari*—and by extension, the flow of discourse—is finally and fully arrested.

Antonomasia—Ancient and Modern

If *fari* can be understood as a synecdoche for the act of speaking as such—and the exemplary character of Leibniz's exposition of its "tropical" canal points in this direction—then antonomasia can be said to set speech into motion. The stakes around this trope are correspondingly high—and so, too, are the difficulties. Unlike synecdoche and metonymy, which are the other two tropes through which *fari* passes, antonomasia is generally underplayed in rhetorical manuals; if anything, it is a "minor" trope, one of the dozens that proliferate in rhetorical treatises from antiquity onward. Leibniz nowhere defines *antonomasia* in his "Preliminary Dissertation." The same is true of synecdoche and metonymy, but with these tropes the absence of any explicit definition poses few problems, for Leibniz could count on a certain consistency of usage from the inception of classical rhetoric to his own day. The case of antonomasia is entirely different, for the use of this term—like that of the words it sets into motion—changes in an unexpected, even dramatic manner. The deviation of the term *antonomasia* from its origin is particularly problematic given the context in which Leibniz employs it: in order to clarify the twin sources of clarity and thus contribute to the reformation of the philosophical discourse conducted in historical languages.

As a late Greek construction, *antonomasia* derives from a verb meaning "to name, nominate, or denominate instead." Quintilian, whose authority in rhetorical matters Leibniz generally acknowledges,[21] defines the trope in a deceptively simple manner: "something posited for a name [*aliquid pro nomine ponit*]."[22] Insofar as this definition could be understood to apply to all tropes—each one replaces a "name" with something else—the distinctiveness of antonomasia must lie in the kind of name that it replaces: a proper name rather than a common noun. True to the general procedures of his *Institutiones oratoriae*, Quintilian clarifies the trope by means of representative examples: "Antonomasia, which substitutes something else for a name, is very common in poets and may be done in two ways: by the substitution of an epithet as equivalent to the name which it replaces, such as 'Tydides,' or 'Pelides,' or by indicating the most striking feature of an individual, as in the phrase 'Father of gods and king of men.'"[23] Regardless of Quintilian's immense authority, however, his account of antonomasia does not remain fixed; it is subject to a radical revision in the first half of the seventeenth century, for the same term—"antonomasia"—is used to name an inverse operation. Instead of only meaning "naming instead," *antonomasia* comes to mean "instead of a noun" as well. The rhetorician who completes this reversal is Voss, whom Leibniz repeatedly mentions in his "Preliminary Dissertation" and whose revision of Quintilian under the title *Commentariorum rhetoricorum* (1630) gives direction to Leibniz's own tropological inquiries.[24] In his *Elementa rhetorica*, Voss offers a succinct de-

finition of antonomasia that includes the mode of this trope that has since
become associated with his own name—"Vossian" antonomasia:

> Antonomasia is a species of synecdoche in which a proper name [*proprium*] re-
> places a common one [*communi*]; or the contrary. For the first mode: an *Irus*
> for a pauper, a *Thersites* for someone deformed. . . . For the second mode: *the
> philosopher* for Aristotle, *the city* for Rome, *the poet* for Homer. . . . To this lat-
> ter, add unequivocal periphrasis, thus *the writer of the Trojan War* for Homer.[25]

From the perspective of Voss's account of antonomasia, certain aspects
of Leibniz's use of the term in context of the "Preliminary Dissertation" are
discernible—and discernibly puzzling. For Leibniz does not follow Voss in
reducing antonomasia to a species of synecdoche, even though he shares
with him the ambition of reducing the unruly multitude of tropes to a few
"primary" ones—and may very well have taken over this ambition from
the Dutch rhetorician.[26] And nowhere in his early work would he find a
more perfect place to undertake such a reduction than in the staunchly re-
ductionist introduction to Nizolio, the last pages of which include an en-
comium to the philosophical "genius" of Occam (A, 6, 2: 428; L, 128). In
his account of *fari* and, only a few paragraphs later, in his analysis of the
distinction between popular and technical uses of the term *square* (A, 6, 2:
412), antonomasia functions as a trope in its own right—with no indica-
tion that it should be reduced to synecdoche. The reason for Leibniz's re-
luctance to follow Voss on the path of reduction cannot be ascribed to any
unfamiliarity with the particular power, range, and scope of synecdoche,
for large parts of Nizolio's *De veris principiis* are concerned with nothing
else: synecdoche, according to Nizolio, is at the root of the "barbaric" lan-
guage of scholastic philosophy. By replacing plural terms like *homines* with
singular ones like *homo*—and then forgetting or repressing the tropologi-
cal character of this substitution—scholastic philosophers, according to
Nizolio, find themselves in a position to attribute reality to universals.[27]
Even as they scorn metaphorical discourse and warn against metonymical
substitutions of cause and effect, such philosophers constantly employ syn-
ecdoche and thereby presume that the complementary terms of part and
whole, species and genus, or singular and plural are of the same ontologi-
cal order. As Leibniz briefly remarks in an editorial footnote, synecdoche
generates the philosophical doctrine that nominalists have always sought
to challenge: "The apparent reality of universals beyond individual things
derives from figural speech" (A, 6, 2: 448).

Challenges to the doctrine of realism—and the style of philosophical dis-
course through which it comes to speech—cannot fail to draw on the re-
sources of antonomasia, even if the trope goes unnamed. For antonomasia
is a privileged way for individuals to enter into discourse without names of
their own. And individuals, as Leibniz's note to Nizolio's treatise clearly as-
sert, are the only "real" things, which is to say, the only things worthy of the
common name "thing." Voss orders the modes of antonomasia and reduces
the trope as a whole to a species of synecdoche according to an "analogy":
the replacement of a genus-term by a species-term (or vice versa) corre-
sponds to the replacement of a species-term by a term designating an indi-
vidual—or vice versa. Since both of the former forms of replacement are
covered by the term *synecdoche*, both of the latter ones should be given the
same name, which is to say, antonomasia, even if antonomasia "proper,"
from Quintilian onward, is applicable only to one mode of replacement:
species pro individuo.[28] The premise of Voss's procedure—which corre-
sponds to the same demand for systematicity that finds its greatest expres-
sions in Leibniz's programs for an *ars combinatoria* and Spinoza's *Ethics*—
can be succinctly summarized: individuals are comprehensible as species.[29]

Given this premise, antonomasia itself functions as a species: specifi-
cally, a species of synecdoche. The status of antonomasia corresponds to
that of the individual, and its function consists, accordingly, either in re-
placing the names of individuals by equivalent epithets (antonomasia
proper) or in making such names into generally applicable terms (Vossian
antonomasia). The original mode of the trope operates in accordance with
one of the principles through which Leibniz seeks to identify the charac-
ter of identity: "Those are the same if one can be substituted for the other,
saving truth [*Eadum sunt quorum in alterius locum substitutui potest, salva
veritate*]" (G, 7: 219). The Vossian mode of antonomasia, in turn, corre-
sponds to the converse of this principle—that of the identity of indis-
cernibles.[30] If no individuals are exactly alike, then every individual is its
own species, and proper names, in turn, must all be species-terms in dis-
guise. The principle of individuation cannot, therefore, be sought in any-
thing "proper" to the individual but only in the totality of its attributes or
predicates. And even if no one other than God is in a position to recog-
nize the true character of proper names—as common nouns—individu-
als are nevertheless incapable of doing anything but fulfilling the fate of
their names: to be the kind of thing—a John *X* or a Joan *Y*—under which
they fall. Voss's apparently innocuous ambition to reduce the disorderly

crowd of tropes both presupposes and reinforces a fateful decision—in favor of fate. Leibniz, for his part, silently acknowledges this decision, as he identifies the original trope through which *fatum* passes on its way to meaning "fate." And yet, Leibniz does not *say* "antonomasia is a species of synecdoche." The trope silently asserts its independence, and around this silence the fate of the name plays itself out.

Lucifer

From his youthful *Disputatio metaphysico de principio individui,* written under the direction of a professor of rhetoric, until his last attempts to communicate his thoughts by means of the technical term "monad," Leibniz never ceased to investigate the relation of individuals to the species of which they are supposedly members. One of the reasons this investigation sustained itself—and did not simply arrive at a final and complete answer—can be found in the doctrine toward which the "Preliminary Dissertation" is drawn, even as it recognizes the devastation with which it would visit all philosophical discourse: Hobbes's doctrine of "more than nominalism" (A, 6, 2: 428; L, 128). Individuals, without regard to "their" species, can doubtless be named; but the names for these unspecified things is wholly arbitrary, a mere matter of the will, never a well-grounded expression of their constitutive characteristics. As individuals are freed from species through which their essences would be determined, the names by which they are designated become more arbitrary, and as their names become more arbitrary, they become more "proper"—applicable to themselves and to themselves alone. For this very reason, proper names are the most unprincipled of all linguistic elements and thus come to represent the specter of arbitrariness in the field of discourse. That they were spoken—*fatum*, in the original sense of the word—is the sole "reason" for their existence. The ability to give something a proper name can thus be understood as a residue of that power to which the first twist in the fate of *fari* attests: the power to make something true merely by saying it. The "something" in this case is, however, only a name—not a *res*. The more proper a proper name becomes, the fewer reasons can be found for *any* name to be chosen over any other one. And an absolutely proper name— like that of God—would solicit antonomasia more than any other: the turn of *fari* into *fatum* is, from this perspective, anything but accidental.

In the "Preliminary Dissertation" Leibniz lightly touches on the problematic character of proper names whenever he mentions the operation of antonomasia, but he does not consider the problem in its own right. In an untitled dialogue of 1677, by contrast, the problem of the proper name receives a startling formulation. The dialogue is directed against a doctrine that Leibniz only names in the "Preliminary Dissertation": Hobbesian "more than nominalism." And the point of the dialogue is to show that the apparent arbitrariness of linguistic terms neither violates the integrity of truth nor implies that truth is wholly dependent on either the mere will of human beings or even on the supreme will of the One whose word makes things real. Although the dialogue remains almost completely silent regarding this incomparable One, the name of his arch-enemy makes a surprising appearance. Having repeatedly failed to strike up a correspondence with Hobbes, Leibniz invents a conversation in which he has a chance to reach an agreement with his adversary about the manner in which words can be understood to correspond with things. If *any* agreement can be reached by means of conversation alone, moreover, the dialogue succeeds, regardless of what doctrine its characters agree to support, for this is precisely its point: agreement about the nature of things can be generated solely by discourse under the condition that the latter can arrive at truth, and truth can enter into discourse under the condition that the relationship among linguistic terms corresponds to the underlying order of things—and does not, instead, simply respond to a willful command, regardless of whether it be human or divine.

The characters of Leibniz's dialogue, unlike the Platonic ones he was in the process of studying, are distinguishable only by their names—not by any "personal" characteristics. As is if to emphasize the characterlessness of his characters, Leibniz does not even assign them proper names; instead, they are designated by mere characters: *A* and *B*. Although wholly arbitrary, these names nevertheless stand in an ordered relation to each other that corresponds to the progress of the dialogue—from *A* to *B*, which is to say, from premise to conclusion. No wonder the question that interrupts the progress of the discussion between these two characters concerns the possibility of thinking without "characters." The resumption of the dialogue in the wake of this question takes place as *A* momentarily mentions its own name and then names, as if by accident, the great adversary of God:

> *B.* Only one thing makes me worry. I notice that no truth is ever known, discovered, or proved by me except by the use of words and other signs inhabiting the mind.

A. Instead, if characters were absent, we could neither think of anything distinctly nor reason about it.

B. Yet when we inspect geometric figures, we establish truths by accurately meditating upon them.

A. True, but we must recognize that these figures must also be regarded as characters, for the circle described on paper is not a true circle and need not be; it suffices if we take it for a circle.

B. Nevertheless, it has a certain similarity to the circle; this is surely not arbitrary.

A. Granted; figures are the most useful of characters. But what similarity do you think there is between ten and the character 10.

B. There is some relation or order in the characters that is also in the things, especially if the characters are well invented.

A. Perhaps, but what similarity do the first elements themselves have with things; for example, *0* with nothing, or *A* with a line? You have to confess, therefore, that in these elements at least, there is no need of similarity to things. This is true, for example, in the words *lux* and *ferens*; even though their compound *Lucifer* has a relation to these two words, *light* and *bearing*, which corresponds to that which the things signified by *Lucifer* has to the things signified by *lux* and *ferens*.

B. But the Greeks *phōsphoros* has the same relation to *phōs* and *pherō*.

A. The Greeks might have used another word than this.

B. True. Yet I notice that, if characters can be used for taking account of things, there is in them a kind of complex mutual relation or order which agrees with the things, if not in the single words (although this is better), at least in their combination and inflection. (A, 6, 4: 23–24; L, 183–84)

By proposing a language in which the internal elements of particular words are ordered in such a manner that they agree with the order of things that they are meant to express, *B* demonstrates the advantage of a properly constructed "universal characteristics" over historical languages like Latin: translations can be successfully accomplished element by element among the former, but not among the latter. And the sign of this failure is found in the father of lies. What is true of the Prince of Darkness is not also true of phosphorus: an element, the recent discovery of which Leibniz helped authenticate.[31] The ironic name of this prince corresponds to the paradoxical doctrine against which both *A* and *B* struggle: saying that truth depends on an arbitrary act of will—and even worse, on the elective will of finite beings—is as good as saying that there is no truth; and if it is true that there is no truth, then it is equally true that there can be no God. Satan reigns in a world of arbitrarily imposed names. As long as all the individual terms and compositional structure of an artificial linguistic system exhibit recognizable "similarities" with the order of things that they are used to express, such a language, although invented, is nonetheless *less* arbitrary than historical languages and therefore more closely approximates the language of God. Neither *A* nor *B* speak of divine language; but in a marginal note the author of the dialogue is less cautious: "When God calculates and thinks, the world is made [*fit mundus*]" (A, 6, 4: 22; L, 185).

Divine language resembles the language of arithmetic to the extent that the similarity between the structure of arithmetical propositions and the order of the things expressed by these propositions takes precedence over any putative resemblance between the characters of this language and things that it represents. The construction of the arithmetical world in the construction of arithmetical formulas resembles the creation of the world in the exercise of divine calculation. But the language of arithmetic is also one without proper names—or, more exactly, a language in which no distinction need be made between a proper name and a common noun, since each number refers without ambiguity to a single "thing," which, in turn, constitutes its own species. The differences between "things" expressed by arithmetical language can be completely captured by the order of its characters—which means that the expression of numerical properties have no need of any "proper" terms, for every properly constructed term is by the act of its construction necessarily proper. The translation of any given numeral based on any given numerical system into another numeral based on another such system is thus unlike the translation of "Lucifer" into *phosphoros*, for truth is "saved" in translation. Lucifer slyly insinuates himself into Leibniz's seemingly innocent dialogue as a trope for the proper name, which, as an ineluctably arbitrary element of language, proves itself least obedient to the order of reason—and therefore to that of God. To this extent, all proper names have something diabolical about them, and not a single one—except "Lucifer"—makes an entrance into the dialogue of 1677 or, indeed, with rare exceptions, into the other dialogues Leibniz would subsequently write.

"And in this Indetermination of Language . . . "

Instead of invoking proper names, Leibniz designates the characters of his dialogues by easily decipherable epithets. Not surprisingly "Théophile"—

"lover of God"—is the name by way of antonomasia that Leibniz uses for
the character in one of his early dialogues that represents his own views
about the nature of divine worship, "religion," and God.[32] Théophile is
without a proper name in the strict sense, for, as he insists in his opening
speech, he is so much a lover of God that he has nothing properly speak-
ing of his own, least of all a name. And the reason he loves God so much
is because of His infinite reason: God makes no arbitrary decisions or
tyrannical stipulations. As a sign of his love, the "lover of God" calls him-
self something that immediately recalls its impropriety, and he invites all
those endowed with a name to understand themselves as "théophiles."
This goes, first of all, for Leibniz, whose first name is, of course, Gottfried:
one who is at peace with God and whose pacification—Leibniz would call
himself Guilielmus Pacidius for the purposes of an all-encompassing and
comprehensive "Encyclopedia"[33]—presumably comes with requited love.

At the opening of his greatest dialogue—the misleadingly titled *New Es-
says on Human Understanding*—Leibniz indicates that he decides to re-
name himself "Théophile" on this occasion because he truly loves God;
more exactly, because he cured himself of an earlier inclination toward a
Hobbesianism in which God is rendered unlovable, for the predicate of
power predominates over those of perfection and wisdom. "Théophile" is
therefore a name of one who becomes a lover of God on the basis of "new
illuminations" (A, 6, 6: 73). All of these new illuminations are, however,
products of extensive research—not the result of some otherworldly inspi-
ration, still less of the "enthusiasm" that his Lockean interlocutor forcefully
attacks. At the beginning of the section of the *New Essays* called "Words,"
he applauds Philalèthe—whose name makes no reference to God—for re-
jecting out of hand Hobbes's doctrine. Unlike the other three sections of
the *New Essays*, "Words" thus begins with a point of agreement: "I am
happy to find you far removed from Mr. Hobbes's view. He did not agree
that man was designed for society, and imagined that we have merely been
forced into it by necessity and the wickedness of the members of our
species" (A, 6, 6: 273). But very soon disagreement ensues as Philalèthe of-
fers an economic justification for the general use of general terms: "since the
multiplication of words would have perplexed their use, if every particular
thing needed a distinct name to be designated by language, language had
yet a further improvement by the use of general terms, standing for general
ideas" (A, 6, 6: 275). Théophile, by contrast, insists on the fundamentally
derivative character of any word that is applied only to an individual:

General terms do not improve languages but are required for their essential structure. If by "particular things" you mean individual ones, then if we only had words that applied to them—only *proper names*, no *appellatives*—we would not be able to say anything. This is because new ones are being encountered at every moment—new individuals and accidents and (what we talk about most) actions. But if by "particular things" you mean the lowest species (*species infimae*), then, apart from the fact that it is often difficult to determine them, it is clear that they are themselves universals, founded on similarity. And then, since it is just a matter of more or less widespread similarity, depending on whether one is speaking of genera or of species, it is natural to mark all sorts of similarities or agreements, and thus to employ terms that have a degree of generality. Indeed those of greatest generality, although they have a wider spread over individuals with which they agree, carry a lighter load of ideas or essences; they were very often the easiest to form and are the most useful. Thus you will see children and people who are trying to speak an unfamiliar language, or to speak about unfamiliar matters, use general terms like "thing," "plant," "animal," in place of the more specific terms which they do not have. And it is certain that all proper or individual names were originally appellative or general. (A 6, 6: 275–76)[34]

The derivative character of proper names can be seen from two distinct perspectives—that of the individual speaker and that of the species of speakers as a whole. In a programmatic study completed a few years after he abandoned his efforts to publish the *New Essays*, Leibniz formulates the same principle in even more emphatic terms: "I take it as an axiom that *all the names that we call 'proper' were once appellatives*; otherwise they would not conform to reason."[35] An *original* proper name—or a proper name at the origin of language—would violate the principle of reason.[36] In the case of proper names, therefore, Leibniz does not even avail himself of his own directives for research into the manner by which often-repeated sounds "naturally" come to express common experiences. Words such as *strong, strength, strive, strike, struggle, stretch, strain,* and *strout*—to cite only one of the many strings of resonating words Leibniz sought to compile around the time of the *New Essays*—suggest that the experience of stress tends to express itself in the sound *str*.[37] The discovery of similar correlations among sonorous similarities might then issue into a more or less complete lexicon of the original language spoken by the first human beings. The point of such a proposal is not to discover an Adamic language or *Natursprache* along the lines of Jakob Böhme, whose work Leibniz briefly mentions in the *New Essays* (A, 6, 6: 281); rather, the proposal lends plausibility to the claim that it is possible to render reason for *all* things, including words.[38] Onomatopoeia creates words out of "natural" outbursts under the condition that the experiences to which these outbursts respond be *common* ones. The index of this commonality can be found in the proliferation of like-sounding words into which natural expressions are incorporated, and this proliferation, in turn, constitutes evidence for a "primitive" stratum of historical languages. For reasons of prudence, perhaps, Théophile does not insist on the "natural" origin of language and leaves open the possibility, sanctioned by Genesis, that the original language was based on an act of rational institution (A, 6, 6, 281). Théophile, however, also leaves room for the other possibility as well: that the original language—be it "Scythian," German, Hebrew, or Arabic[39]—could have arisen "naturally," without any appeal to wisdom other than the wisdom, of course, of the One whom Théophile loves. However it arose, the original language must have been radically insufficient; new words had to be created, and the manner of creation was by way of onomatopoeia:

> If we had the primitive language in its pure form, or well enough preserved to be recognizable, the reasons for connections—whether they were physical reasons or came from a wise "arbitrary imposition" worthy of the first author— would be bound to appear. But granted that our languages are derivative so far as origins are concerned, they have something primitive about them. This has come to them along the way, in connection with new roots created in our languages by chance but for physical reasons [*par hasard, mais sur des raisons physiques*]. (A, 6, 6: 281)

Historical languages constitute a place where chance and reason, so far from excluding each other, are curiously combined. Every element of language is thoroughly grounded and is for this reason, if *only* for this reason, "rational." The primitive trope of onomatopoeia, which, because of its primitiveness, cannot be considered a trope among others,[40] is grounded in the physiology of human beings, who, as a species, can be expected to respond in similar ways to similar experiences. And yet the physiology of this species by no means dictates the manner in which words, properly speaking, are generated out of inarticulate outbursts: each formation of a stable word is open to chance. Equally fortuitous, moreover, are the "canals of tropes" through which words imperceptively pass as they are used under slightly varying circumstances and for slightly different purposes. The repeatability of a word makes it into a word in the first place—and takes it out of the realm of natural outburst. But repeatability also opens words to easily overlooked tropological changes. When the twists and turns in these canals are "noticed," according to Théophile, they are called "synecdoche," "metonymy," "metaphor," and "irony." But he immediately adds: "they are rarely noticed." And because tropes tend to escape our attention, historical languages are doomed to an ineluctable indeterminacy:

> And in this indetermination of language [*dans cette indétermination du langage*], wherever one lacks a kind of law that rules the meaning of words, as there is something along these lines in the *Digest* of Roman law, *De verorum significationibus*, the most judicious persons, when they write for ordinary readers, deprive themselves of whatever gives charm and force to their expressions if they wish to abide rigorously to the meanings attached to their terms. It is only necessary that they be careful that their variation does not give birth to any error or false reasoning [*il faut seulement qu'elles prennent garde que leur variation ne fasse naistre aucune erreur ni raisonnement fautif*]. (A, 6, 6: 260)

With this *il faut* (it is necessary), Théophile makes up an ad hoc law of language that makes up for the lack of any such law. So important is this made-up law that it allows all authorized laws to be understood—and understood as laws. The *il faut* Théophile announces finds a single point of support: the "judiciousness" of those who submit to it. Since "judicious persons" are precisely the ones who, by definition, submit themselves to the rule of law, this point of support erases itself: the lawful follows the law, including—before any other law—the as-yet unwritten law of language. The point of this law does not consist in fixing the state of language once and for all; on the contrary, language constantly changes in response to—and in order to foster the growth of—new knowledge. When linguistic change occurs, however, it must be noticed. Tropes are not insidious because they alter the state of language but, rather, because they are generally ungoverned by consciousness: just as "little perceptions" do not rise to the level of consciousness,[41] little "tropical" variations escape the notice of both speaker and auditor alike. Because of these variations, language is in a perpetually unstable state of "indetermination." And for the same reason, the "canals of tropes" through which words flow away from their origin cannot always—or even in general—be charted.[42] The ad hoc law that Théophile proposes consists in the imperative to make these canals into self-consciously constructed ones, which is to say, make the "canals of tropes" *canal-like*. Only in this way can historical languages leave the indeterminate zone between nature and artifice. The indeterminacy of language—between *physis* and *thesis*—subtends the idea implied in all of Leibniz's discussions of "tropical" growth: the idea of a "natural canal," which, however, ought to be also recognized as an artificial construction. This zone of indeterminacy is the source of the "indetermination of language."

Only in the case of antonomasia does the interlocutor of the *New Essays* offer anything like an account of a tropological operation, however: not once, but twice—in preparation for, and in response to the excursus on the primitive process of onomatopoeia. Only after enough appellatives have been called into discourse by means of onomatopoeia can some of them be used for the relatively profligate purpose of referring to individual members of a species. And Théophile, in turn, returns to the derivation of proper names from common ones after his discussion of onomatopoeia. As primitive response and derivative trope, onomatopoeia and antonomasia—or, to use the corresponding Latin terms, *nominatio* and *pronominatio*[43]—constitute the two origins of linguistic terms: the former is the origin of general names, the latter of proper ones. By definition, *pronominatio* presupposes a prior process of *nominatio*. The "axiom" from which the section on words in the *New Essays* takes its point of departure—"all the names that we call 'proper' were once appellatives"—makes clear that proper names are the least "proper" words of all: without exception, they arise by virtue of an "original" trope, namely *pronominatio*. Proper names can be called "proper" only on the basis of a fundamentally improper use of the general terms generated by *nominatio*. And the principle by which proper names are improperly generated is, according to Leibniz, that of the best.

The principle by which appellatives are turned into names and the principle on the basis of which this world comes into existence are in this sense one and the same. Just as the essences that organize themselves into the best world can make good on their primordial and underivable "demand for existence," according to a line of thought Leibniz developed as early as 1677,[44] so, too, can the best—or better yet, *best known*—member of any given class lay claim to the class-term as its own. The most outstanding world of all possible worlds has a supreme claim to be called into existence; likewise, the most outstanding member of a species can legitimately claim the name by which the species as a whole comes into speech. From Quintilian onward, antonomasia is associated with the highest, most noble, most luminous, best. The author of the *Institutio oratio* first illustrates antonomasia by citing an epithet from the opening lines of the *Aeneid* in which the god par excellence is singled out by virtue of his superior lineage and outstanding power: "Divum pater atque hominum rex."[45] All of the examples that Voss proposes for his own "Vossian" mode of antonomasia in his *Elementa rhetorica* imply an operator through which the superlative member of a class is singled out: "the philosopher par excellence," contracted into "the philosopher" *simpliciter*, replaces the name "Aristotle"; and a similar operation yields *urbs* as a replacement for "Rome" and *poëta* as a substitute for "Homer."[46] In the "Preliminary Dissertation" Leibniz makes explicit this operation: in his account of the "canal of tropes" that issues into *fatum*, he speaks of "antonomasia or *kat exochen*" (A 6, 2: 410; L, 122), and in relation to the word *square*, he explains his figural use of the term *antonomasia* with reference to "perfectissimo" (A 6, 2: 412).[47] In all of these cases, antonomasia secures the "properness" of a term by applying the principle of the best to a class of things. Or, in reverse, the application of the principle of the best turns a common noun into a proper name. According to Théophile, who reiterates his account of proper names after his excursus on the origin of language, the principle of the best must have been the basis for the generation of proper names out of appellatives: "In fact I would venture to say that almost all words were originally general terms, since it will very rarely happen that a name will be invented just for one given individual without any reason for it. So we can say that individual names used to be names of species that were given to some individual either as a prime example of the species or for some other reason: for instance, one might give the name *Big-Head* [*grosse-tête*] to the one with the biggest head in the whole town or to the most eminent of the big-heads that one knew" (A, 6, 6: 288–89).[48] *Grosse-tête* is not only the proper name of Alexander's horse, Bucaphelus; it also an appropriate name for the one whose mind is the most capacious: among human beings, real or imagined, this is perhaps true of Théophile and Gottfried; among all beings, possible as well as actual, it is doubtless true of the One whom Théophile loves and with whom Gottfried is at peace.

Pronouns and Perspectives

Reflection on the operation of antonomasia thus issues into the central paradox of Leibniz's thought: individual things cannot be known by a finite mind, however big, and yet only such things are, properly speaking, *things*. Everything else is a "thing" only by virtue of a trope: "The apparent reality of universals beyond individual things derives from figural speech" (A, 6, 2: 448). Immediately after Théophile reiterates the "axiom" according to which proper names are derived from appellatives, this paradox finds a particularly lucid expression:

> I do not deny that abstractions are used in that way [ideas become general by separating from them time, place, and other circumstances that determine a particular existence], but it involves an ascent from species to genera rather than from individuals to species. For (paradoxical as it may seem) it is impossible for us to know individuals or find any way of precisely *determining* the individuality of any thing except by keeping watch over it itself [*à moins de la garder elle même*]. For any set of circumstances could recur, with tiny differences that we would not take in; and place and time, far from being determinants by themselves, must themselves be determined by the things they contain. The most important point in this is that individuality involves infinity, and only someone who is capable of grasping the infinite could know the principle of individuation of a given thing. (A, 6, 6: 289–90)

Whatever escapes notice, if only for a moment, cannot be determined as an individual and cannot, as such, be known: differences from one moment to the next can be so "tiny" that they approach the infinitely small, which, by definition, escapes the power of finite minds—even those able to represent infinitesimal rates of change in a *symbolic* manner. Only an infinite power of surveillance can keep watch over infinitesimal differences, and without such surveillance, the principle by which an individual can be rightly considered "this here" individual cannot be properly determined. Conversely, only those things that a finite mind can fully survey without interruption can be properly individuated. Mathematical objects are doubtless such things, but so, too, is the finite mind itself. There is, of course, a great difference between these two "things." Whereas mathematical objects are nameless insofar as each one is necessarily a *species infima* in which the difference between proper and general term disappears, "I" is a replacement for the proper name in the absence of a general term: in short, it is a *pro-noun.* Because I can survey myself—even if I cannot perceive all the tiny differences that are intimately associated with the phenomenon of myself—I can discover at least one principle whereby things are individuated and thus made into things in the first place. Leibniz calls such self-survey *apperception.* Antonomasia, understood as the replacement of a proper name by the first-person pronoun, makes it possible for us to arrive at a name—however improper it may be—for primary being: "the I."

In a famous passage of his *Meditationes de prima philosophia* Descartes makes the first-person pronoun through which he has hitherto conducted his practice of meditation into the very subject-matter of "first philosophy": "I know that I exist; I am asking who I be, as that I that I know [*Novi me existere; quaero quis sim ego ille quem novi*]."[49] By speaking of *ego ille*—"that well-known I"—Descartes removes the first-person pronoun from its pronominal function and turns it into a noun: he intensifies antonomasia, as it were, and thus guarantees its absence from the progress of the meditation. No individual named René Descartes, for example, can be wholly identified with the *ego ille* that asks about itself: everyone— and thus no one in particular—can undertake the same exercise and be *ego ille*. Leibniz, following Descartes, takes this substantialization of the first-person pronoun one step further, for he turns the "I" into the index through which the idea of substance as such—and not simply one of two substances—can be deciphered. The "I" is not merely, as with Descartes, an incidental term that prepares the way for a categorial distinction between two "realities"—*res cogitans* and *res extensa*—but is, on the contrary, a formal indication of the reality of the *res* and the substantiality of substance.

A pronoun replaces a proper name with an index whose significance is determined by the context of its enunciation.[50] By turning the "first-person" pronoun into a substantive term through which the idea of substantiality is itself indicated, philosophical discourse can exorcise the curse of arbitrariness that attaches itself to the proper name, and yet it can nevertheless retain a place for its function: that of bringing fully individuated things—which is to say, things in the proper sense—into speech. For all its inherent indeterminacy, "I," as the pronoun of properness, secures a place for itself in clear philosophical discourse as the name for primary being, and it does so by way of this redoubled and intensified antonomasia. A pronoun takes the place of a proper name, and then this singular term, "I," is replaced by a generalized one: "the I." In one of the more elaborate philosophical letters that Leibniz addresses to Sophia Charlotte of Prussia, he makes the replacement of the proper name by the pronoun of properness into the primary pedagogical principle for the edification of the princes and princesses of this world:

This thought of *I*, who apperceives sensible objects and my own action that results from it [*Cette pensée de* moy*, qui m'apperçois des objets sensibles, et de ma propre action qui en resulte*], adds something to the objects of sense. To think of some color and to consider that I think of it—these two thoughts are very different, just as much as color itself differs from the I who thinks it. And since I conceive that there are other beings who also have the right to say "I" [*le droit de dire moy*], or for whom this can be said, it is by this that I conceive what is called substance in general, and it is also the consideration of myself that provides me with other concepts in metaphysics, such as those of cause, effect, action, similarity, and so forth, and even those of logic and ethics. (G, 6: 502; L, 549)[51]

Apperception, which is colorless, allows me to perceive myself in such a manner that I can distinguish "the I" (*le moy*) from everything I perceive —and do so to a point where I can arrive at the general principle of individuation: every*thing*, properly speaking, is like me, which is to say, I-like and therefore colorless. Apperception likewise grants access to the basic relational categories: the relation of the I to itself lets the I understand what it means when it speaks of supposedly real relations like causality as well as ideal relations like similarity. But since apperception is neither perception nor surveillance, it cannot grant anything more than a general principle of individuation; its application to anything merely perceived remains indeterminate. The I, in turn, cannot know the principle on the basis of which it is *an* I—this particular I, *ego ille*—in the first place. All the I can know is that there are other I's to which it stands in some relation. Such is the presupposition of Leibniz's correspondence with the queen. But the fact that all the I's of the world stand in some relation to one is at the root of the paradox of individuation. Once again I cite the passage in the *New Essays* in which Théophile articulates this paradox— this time allowing the sentence to run to completion:

> For (paradoxical as it may seem) it is impossible for us to know individuals or find any way of precisely *determining* the individuality of any thing except by keeping watch over it itself [*à moins de la garder elle même*]. . . . The most important point in this is that individuality involves infinity, and only someone who is capable of grasping the infinite could know the principle of individuation of a given thing, which comes from the influence (if this is understood soundly [*sainement*]) that all things in the universe have on one another. (A, 6, 6: 290)

Prompted by the reflection on the derivative character of proper names, Théophile thus gives a résumé of Leibniz's "new system," but—paradoxically and thus in keeping with the movement of the reflection—the very term that this "new system" sought to banish from philosophical discourse returns with a renewed majesty: *influence*. According to "A New System of Nature and the Communication of Substances" (1695), "there is no real influence of one created substance upon another" (G, 4: 483; L, 457). And yet, there is nevertheless influence—everywhere and on everything. Universal influence without any "real" influence: such is the principle of the new system and an expression of its apparently paradoxical character. Once *influx* is no longer understood as a hopelessly incoherent trope, it can serve as a term through which the relation of every substance to every other one can be *properly* figured. Every I is "influenced" by all others insofar as every one represents the world as a whole. Understanding *influx* in a "sound" or "healthy" manner consists in recognizing its "tropical" character—not only as a trope, moreover, but as a trope through which the "tropical" character of the individual can be cast. Influx without "real" influx not only makes it impossible for any one to be known as such and, in turn, makes it necessary that every proper name in use be derived from an appellative; it also guarantees that the relation of individuals to the world as a whole is synecdochal.

Although the term *influx* is itself a case of "metonymy of cause," once it is properly understood—which means understood as a trope—*influx* designates a relation of part to whole: each part of the whole represents the whole to itself and can therefore be taken as a representative of the whole, which, for its part, exists only in the representations of every part; every substance stands in for every other one, and such standing-in can, in turn, be understood in terms of perspectival stances: "each substance," according to "A New System," "represents the entire universe accurately in its own way and according to a definite point of view" (G, 4: 484; L, 457). Once the relation of influence is understood as synecdochal rather than metonymic, it is possible to deny real influence and yet affirm at the same time that everything influences everything else—so much so that no mind other than an infinitely capacious one could determine the principle by which one individual is distinguished from all others. Without such a principle of individuation, in turn, proper names cannot fail to derive from general terms. Antonomasia cannot be a species of synecdoche as long as every individual is a species of its own; and yet as long as every individual represents the world as a whole, each of these species can be taken as a representative of every other one: all represent the whole from a different position, and this difference of perspective is precisely what makes each one special. The irreducibility of antonomasia to synecdoche ironically makes possible the "proper" interpretation of *influx* in terms of universal synecdoche.

Alexander, Caesar, and the Kaiser

As Leibniz rehabilitates the scholastic term "substantial form," he simultaneously makes use of the Cartesian strategy of making the first-person pronoun into a privileged guide for the elucidation of primary being. By virtue of its generalized individuality, the personal pronoun can take the place of all proper names and thereby give direction to the elucidation of the question, What does it mean to be? The prominence Leibniz thus accords to the pronoun is not, however, his only—or even most daring—response to the paradoxical function of proper names: since our sole access to individuality is found in the I that every I apperceives, only a proper name allows discourse to express something real, and yet for this reason no one other than God, who has no need of symbols, can be sure that any proper name, including my own, is properly used. And for precisely the same reason, proper names always verge on the arbitrary: there is never any reason for any "proper" name, properly speaking. Reasons for the choice of a name can only arise when a name is first common and then applied only to a single individual. Philosophical discourse, whose distinguishing postulate is clarity, must therefore devise methods, however artificial, to return proper names to their origin in general terms: every proper name of an individual substance must be convertible into an appellative.

Such is the project Leibniz first proposes for Antoine Arnauld's consideration in the so-called "Discourse on Metaphysics" (1686): not only will every name of every given substance be understood as a general term; every supposedly proper name of an individual can be replaced by an infinitely complex term composed of all the appellatives that can be properly applied to the individual in question. The first example of such an individual in the "Discourse on Metaphysics" is the substantial form named Alexander. The reason for this choice can perhaps be found in the name "Alexander" itself—or, more exactly, in the operator by which it is made into a proper one: "the Great." Alexander is the best Alexander of them all, which is to say, he is Alexander *kat exochen*:

> The quality of king that belonged to Alexander the Great, if abstracted from its subject, is not determinate enough to define an individual, for it does not include the other qualities of the same subject or everything that the concept

of this Prince includes. God, on the contrary, in seeing the individual notion or haeccecity of Alexander, sees in it at the same time the basis and reason for all the predicates that can truly be affirmed of him—for example, that he will conquer Darius and Porus. (A, 6, 4: 1540–41; L, 307–8)

The scholastic term Leibniz firmly ejects from philosophical discourse in his earlier exposition of philosophical style, *haeccecity,* returns in this discourse as a replacement for the proper name.[52] "This here" individual can be named by a common noun, the origin of which lies in the process of substantializing an indexical term. The general term can be appropriately applied only to "this here" individual under one condition: every individual happens to be the sole member of the species to which it belongs, and strictly speaking, the individual earns—as the best or, at worst, as a member of the best possible world—the common name of its species. All proper names for individual substances must return to their original status as appellatives, and yet every proper name is still supposed to fulfill precisely the same function: singling an individual out. Only if it is impossible for two or more individuals to be designated by the same infinite order of appellatives can both of these two requirements be met. Immediately after Leibniz explicates the example of Alexander, he articulates two of the "important paradoxes" that this example teaches, the first of which has come to be known as the principle of the identity of indiscernibles and the second of which is the synecdochal character of all relations among substances. Both Leibnizian principles are functions of antonomasia:

> It is not true that two substances can resemble each other completely and differ *solo numero,* and what St. Thomas assures [us] about angels or intelligences (*quod ibi omne individuum sit species infima*) is true of all substances. . . . Moreover, every substance is like an entire world, and like a mirror of God or of the whole universe which it expresses, each in its own manner, just as the same city is represented differently depending on the different positions from which it is regarded. (A, 6, 4: 1541; L, 308)

If all proper names can in principle be replaced by general terms composed of a doubly infinite series of appellatives—without remainder— then there is nothing "proper" about any substance other than the set of properties by which it is distinguished from every other possible thing, and there is nothing "special" about any individual other than the fact that it, like everything else in the created world, is the sole member of its species. The use of proper names instead of infinitely complex series of appellatives is merely an index of the finitude of the speaker. But the use of the proper name is also an indication that the "thing" named may enjoy a certain freedom: there is something "more" to an individual than the complex of predicates that can be legitimately applied to it. By denying this "more," Leibniz casts upon himself the charge that he is promoting fatalism. The correspondence with Arnauld inaugurated by the "Discourse on Metaphysics"—like many of Leibniz's subsequent discourses, correspondences, dialogues, and meditations on metaphysics—seeks to show that his reduction of all names to common nouns does not make him a fatalist.

The substantial form toward which Leibniz first turns in his endeavor to counter the accusation of fatalism is another warrior, Julius Caesar. Few proper names are as rich as this one—and as fully immersed in the sphere of fate. Not only did the name of the general become a general term after his assassination, but the act of calling oneself Caesar became a supreme sign of freedom: the caesar, as the prince par excellence, enjoys the authority of decreeing his own fate. But the name "Caesar" is even richer, for, as Leibniz emphasizes in the *New Essays*, it, like that of his principal assassin, is a particularly vivid and singularly violent demonstration of the axiom according to which all proper names were originally appellatives: "We know that Brutus was given his name because of his apparent stupidity [and] that Caesar was the name of a child delivered through an incision in his mother's abdomen" (A, 6, 6: 288).[53] The violence of Caesar's birth corresponds to the violence of his death. Between the two, at the turning point of his life, Caesar violently seizes power, names himself "dictator," brings an end to the republic, and establishes the imperial conditions under which his own name will henceforth turn into the general term for the prince of princes. The kaiser of the Holy Roman Empire, whom Leibniz ultimately serves, owes his title, if not his power, to the transgressive act of the exemplary dictator:

> Let's come to an example: since Julius Caesar is to become perpetual Dictator [*Dictateur perpetuel*] and master of the republic and will destroy the liberty of the Romans, this action is contained in his concept, for we have assumed that it is the nature of a perfect concept of a subject to include everything, so that the predicate is included in it, *ut possit inesse subjecto*. . . . [I]t is reasonable and assured that God will always do what is best, even though what is less perfect implies no contradiction. For it will be found that this demonstration of the predicate of Caesar [his crossing the Rubicon and winning the battle of Pharsalus] is not as absolute as that of numbers or of geometry but that it supposes

the sequence of things which God has freely chosen and which is founded on the first free decree of God [*le premier decret libre de Dieu*], which leads him always to do what is most perfect, and on the decree which God has made about human nature (following the primary one), which is that human beings shall always do (though freely) what appears to be best. (A, 6, 4: 1547– 48; L, 310–11)

"The first free decree of God" not only contrasts with the second divine decree—that human beings freely do what appears best—but also with the decrees on which the "perpetual Dictatorship" of Caesar is founded and through which it expresses itself. Leibniz's subsequent correspondence with Arnauld seeks, above all, to convince the Catholic theologian that the two eternal decrees of God are fundamentally different from the decrees issued by a perpetual dictator; in other words, God is not, for Leibniz, the Caesar of Caesars, even if everyone, including Caesar, is a "mirror of God" (A, 6, 4: 1541; L, 308). Arnauld would hardly have been satisfied with the parenthetical remark in which the "Discourse on Metaphysics" seeks to save the second divine decree—"man shall always do what appears to be best"—from the fatal implications of "always": "(although freely)." The correspondence initiated by the "Discourse" does not settle the matter, but it nevertheless does establishes the terms within which Leibniz seeks to address the old question of *fatum et libertas*. Leibniz's fullest expansion of this parenthetical remark takes place in the "essays" with which his own name soon became inextricably associated: *Essais de Théodicée sur la bonté de Dieu, la liberté de l'homme, et l'origine du mal.*

"The Arrest of His Wisdom"

The title of Leibniz's best-known philosophical discourse, *Essais de Théodicée*, is uncharacteristically ambiguous: not only is the word *Théodicée* a neologism, if not a technical term; the title as a whole can be read as though these "new essays" were written by a certain Théodicée—and indeed some of the initial readers of the anonymously published treatise read the title page in this manner.[54] A possible reason for this act of self-concealment under the pseudonym Théodicée can be found in the presumptiveness of the new name itself: who would presume *in her own name*—for "Théodicée," of course, is feminine—to "justify" God and thus absolve him of the accusation that he is ultimately responsible for sin? Who would be bold enough to put God on trial—perhaps for his life?[55] As if to forestall such questions, the title of the treatise emphasizes its "essayistic" character, and the preface proposes only modest goals: "Do your duty and be content [*content*] with what will come of it" (G, 6: 31; T, 55)—content, not happy, still less joyous. Just as "the best" is different from "the good," so contentment is distinguished from happiness. The *Theodicy* need not justify the command "do your duties," for this command is nothing other than the form of the imperative, which justifies itself in its very formulation and is, for this reason, entirely contentless: you must do your duties once you recognize that they are your duties. If such were the content of the treatise, it could end with the preface—or, perhaps, it could venture into the territory Kant began to explore in *Laying the Ground for the Metaphysics of Morals* (1785) and seek to show the ground on which one can recognize one's duties as one's own. Instead, the treatise sets out to show that those who do their duties can be content—not with their conduct *regardless* of what happens, which is the starting point of Kant's reflections on the "metaphysics of morals," but also with what *follows from* their conduct; content, in short, with the world as it appears to dutiful agents in the course of doing their duties: "Do your duty and be content with what will come of it, not only because you cannot resist divine providence or the nature of things (which may suffice for tranquillity but not for contentment), but also because you have to do with a good master. And this is what one could call *Fatum Christianum*" (G, 6: 31; T, 55).

Whereas Luther defends "Christian freedom,"[56] Leibniz defends "Christian fate." He can continue to be regarded as a Lutheran—and perhaps as a Christian as well—only under the condition that the terms *libertas* and *fatum* be in some sense synonymous. By examining the relation between these terms, he enters into one of the "two famous labyrinths in which our reason very often goes astray" (G, 6: 29; T, 53). Both labyrinths, like the original one, are sites of frustration rather than places of contentment. The point of entering into the labyrinth of freedom is, of course, to discover a way out—and thus, like Theseus, to recover his original freedom of action. Opposed to freedom, then, is not fate but, rather, the labyrinth in which the term *freedom* is caught. In accordance with a vertiginous movement that keeps the *Theodicy* in an unsettling motion among a set of traditional topics, the very existence of the labyrinth of freedom is itself a dimension of this labyrinth, for, unlike the labyrinth of the continuum, which is "important only for speculation," the labyrinth of freedom bears directly on "practice" (G, 6: 29; T, 54), which is to say, on freedom itself. This vertiginous movement gravitates toward the question of divine freedom: why does God choose to create a world in which reason so easily goes astray— and strays so easily, as a result of its "laziness," into sin? God would, of course, be absolved of all responsibility for the sins of the world if he could not create any other one; but if he could not create any world other than the one he created, then he would effectively be subject to fate. Such, in short, is the perplexity into which all branches of the labyrinth of liberty issue. Stoic tranquillity—but not contentment—may be possible under the condition that God, like the ancient gods, be subject to fate. And, for Leibniz, the distinction between stoicism and Christianity comes down to the distinction between tranquillity in the face of inevitable events and contentment with them.

The immediate instigation for Leibniz's entrance into the labyrinth of freedom is Pierre Bayle's labyrinthine construction, *Dictionaire historique et critique*.[57] Thinking through the consequences of Leibniz's "new system" in an article on Hieronymous (Sacred Name) Rorario's *Quod animalia bruta saepe ratione utantur melius homine* (1547), Bayle suspects that the premises of this system lead to an inevitable conclusion: "God would be subject to a kind of *fatum*" (G, 6: 229; T, 246). If God is subject to *fatum*, freedom can hardly be predicated of his creatures; indeed, the closer they are to their model, the further they are from freedom. In the final paragraphs of the second part of the *Essays of Theodicy*, Leibniz comes across a passage where Bayle draws an even stronger conclusion from the premises of the "new system." All qualifications are dropped, and its form of fatalism outstrips even that of the Stoa:

"There is therefore no freedom in God; he is compelled by his wisdom to create, and to create precisely such a work, and finally to create it precisely in such a way. These three servitudes form a more than Stoic *fatum* and render impossible all that is not within their sphere. It seems that, according to this system, God could have said, even before shaping his decrees: I cannot save such and such a man, nor condemn such and such a man, *quidde vetor fatis*, my wisdom permits it not."

I answer [Leibniz writes] that it is goodness which prompts God to create in order to communicate himself, and this same goodness combined with wisdom prompts him to create the best: a best that includes the whole sequence, the effect, and the paths. It prompts him thereto without compelling him, for it does not render impossible that which it does not cause him to choose. To call that *fatum* is taking it in a good sense, which is not contrary to freedom:

fatum comes from *fari,* to speak, to pronounce; it means a judgment, the de-
cree of God, the sentence of his wisdom [*il signifie un jugement, un decret de
Dieu, l'arrest de sa sagesse*]. (G, 6: 253–54; T, 268–69)

By reverting to the account of *fatum* he proposes in the "Preliminary
Dissertation," Leibniz seeks to show that *fatum* is not an antonym of *li-
bertas.* On the contrary, at its origin, *fatum* expresses the very exercise of
freedom. The *Theodicy* follows the methodological principles outlined in
Leibniz's earlier exposition of philosophical style: the original sense of a
word is better than its later uses, which, having been subject to unnoticed
"tropical" transformations under the auspices of a "barbarian" philosophy,
gives rise to dry canals, which is to say, linguistic and cognitive dead-ends.
No longer a term in which the free act of speaking is articulated—so free,
in fact, that speech institutes the conditions it announces—*fatum* be-
comes diametrically opposed to *libertas.* Yet the brief account of *fatum* in
the *Essays of Theodicy* deviates significantly from the more extensive one
in the "Preliminary Dissertation." Not only does the account in the *Essays
of Theodicy* fail to identify the "canals of tropes" through which the word
passes, it also considers *fatum* in isolation from the rest of the language:
Leibniz refrains from presenting the flow of *fari* as a response to a lexical
superfluidity—another word meaning "to say"—and thereby leaves the
subsequent course of the word unmotivated, if not entirely ungrounded.
Leibniz, by fiat, arrests the flow of the word at its first turn, stopped at the
trope of antonomasia. *Fari,* turned into *fatum,* functions as a name—or
anonym—of the mysteriously revealed God whose Word is supposed to
make the world. But such a God cannot be equated with the gods about
whom the Romans spoke—not even the god to whom Quintilian refers
when he cites one of Juno's speeches at the opening of the *Aeneid* as the
first example of antonomasia: "Divum pater atque hominum rex [father
of the gods and king of human beings]."[58] The incompatibility between
the Roman and Lutheran conceptions of divinity may inconspicuously
undermine the account of *fari* Leibniz proposes in the "Preliminary Dis-
sertation," but in the *Theodicy* the same incompatibility is unambiguously
subversive, for, as Bayle's well-chosen citation of Virgil quite clearly indi-
cates, Juno announces her subjection to fate: "quidde vetor fatis [because
the fates forbid me]."[59]

When Leibniz explicates the original sense of *fatum,* he concludes with
a phrase that registers this subversion in its very formulation: *l'arrest de sa
sagesse.* Without a doubt Leibniz means by *arrest* "sentence," as in *l'arrest*

du mort (death sentence); the word serves as a specification of *decret*, which, in turn, further specifies *jugement*. But *arrest* also means "arrest," "hold in place," "stop," or "interrupt." And as anyone trained in Latin knows, these meanings are closer to the origin than "sentence" or "decree": *ad-re-stare*.[60] Wherever a process stops, there is an arrest—regardless of whether the interrupted process is physical, mental, or juridical. In the term *arrest* both of the "famous labyrinths" are thus in play. Indeed, these two labyrinths run counter to each other, for freedom exercises itself in an act of arrestation, which is to say, in an interruption of a continuous motion—regardless of whether the motion is understood in physical, mental, or juridical terms. Only under one condition is the "arresting" noninterruptive: if it comes at the end of the motion, in both senses of the term *end*. Wisdom alone can guarantee this condition. According to another reading of Leibniz's formulation, however, wisdom could *itself* be under arrest: *l'arrest de sa sagesse*. Understood as "the sentence of his wisdom," *fatum* is the pronouncement of God that expresses the completion of the infinite process of intellection; understood as "the arresting of his wisdom," however, *fatum* is the announcement of God that silently marks the interruption of the very same process. The end of the *Theodicy* is therefore of no small importance for the treatise as a whole: only if it ends properly—and properly *ends*—can it demonstrate that the "arrest of his wisdom" is something other than its interruption.

Recapitulation

Leibniz, however, was unsure how to end his treatise. As he was preparing it for publication, he changed the order of its conclusion: the magnificent "fiction" (G, 6: 357; T, 365) with which the published version of the treatise concludes was originally placed in an inconspicuous location near the middle.[61] By concluding the treatise with an imaginary journey beyond the bounds of mortal vision, Leibniz aligns himself with an impressive tradition of philosophical conclusions. Cicero's *De republica* ends with an account of a dream in which a Roman warrior flies to the vault of heaven and, having reached a divine perspective from which to view human affairs, comes to understand the depths of their insignificance. And the model for Cicero's work—Plato's *Politeia*—ends similarly: Er's passage beyond the river of Lethe.[62] Whatever else Leibniz's *Essays of Theodicy* accomplishes, it resumes the line of thought that takes its point of departure from the conclusion of Plato's dialogue: *theos anaitios*, "the god is not responsible" (617e). Such is also Plato's conclusion in both senses of the word—and Leibniz's as well. And Leibniz leaves no doubt that the end of his treatise is supposed to be altogether conclusive, for he justifies his extravagant experiment in creating a "mythology of reason"[63] by claiming that a philosopher who aligns himself with the same tradition—Laurenzo Valla[64]—had failed to conclude his work on the problem of freedom properly and had thus failed to conclude, properly speaking, his work. Leibniz, by contrast, will complete his own treatise and cap off the Platonic tradition by completing the story of divine wisdom that Valla had unwisely interrupted:

> I planned on finishing here after having satisfied (as it seems to me) all the objections of M. Bayle that I could find in his works. But remembering Laurenzo Valla's *Dialogue on Free Will*, in opposition to Boethius, which I have already mentioned, I thought it would be opportune to quote it in abstract, retaining the dialogue form, and then to continue from where it ends, continuing the fiction it initiated [*en continuant la fiction qu'il a commencée*]—less with the purpose of enlivening the subject-matter than in order to explain myself toward the end of my discourse in the clearest and most popular manner that I possibly could [*la maniere la plus claire et la plus populaire qui me soit possible*]. (G, 6: 357; T, 365–66)

By "continuing the fiction"—from Plato to Cicero and from Boethius to Valla—Leibniz brings an end both to his treatise and to the entire tradition it summarizes. This end is eschatological *kat exochen*. Its content is the revelation of "last things." Its form, accordingly, conforms to the protocols of Pauline doctrine: with the "the fullness of time" comes a moment of *anakephalaiomai* or "recapitulation."[65] If there were ever any doubts about the Pauline shape of these final paragraphs, Leibniz puts them to rest by presenting God himself in the act of "recapitulating" the beginning of the world: "Jupiter," Athena announces, "having surveyed them before the beginning of the existing world, classified the possibilities into worlds, and chose the best of all. He comes sometimes to visit these places, to give himself the pleasure of recapitulating things [*récapituler les choses*]" (G, 6: 362; T, 370).[66] And the treatise as a whole, appendices and all, concludes with a Latin recapitulation of the argument, which, for its part, ends with an astounding reference: the "*bathos* of Paul" (G, 6: 459–60).[67] In these depths there are no grounds, and the principle of reason, in turn, seems no longer justified: Jupiter can do what he wills, without grounds, and can even—for no reason other than his own satisfaction—"recapitulate things."

Not only does the end of the treatise recapitulate its argument, in imitation of the Jove whom it represents; it also recapitulates the life of its author. For, as Leibniz attests in an autobiographical interlude at the end of the preface to the treatise, he began reflecting on the vexing problems treated by his essays—reason, faith, and the apparent ubiquity of evil—as he first entered the library:

> There are perhaps few persons who have toiled more than I in this matter. Hardly had I gained some tolerable understanding of Latin writings when I had the opportunity of leafing through a library. I flitted from book to book, and since material for meditation pleased me as much as histories and fables, I was charmed by the work of Laurenzo Valla against Boethius and by that of Luther against Erasmus, although I was well aware that they needed some softening. (G, 6: 43; T, 67)

In remembrance of his entrance into the labyrinth of the Latin library, Leibniz shows the point of exit from the labyrinth of the freedom. By "continuing the fiction" in the conclusion to his treatise, he brings together the three kinds of books toward which he was originally attracted—meditations, fables, and histories. For the fiction, which takes the form of a "little fable" (G, 6: 361; T, 369), concerns the historical act of founding a republic by expelling an evil king and serves as "material for meditation."[68] This recapitulation of both the content of the treatise and the life of its author—which amounts to *apokatastasis panton* in miniature[69]—obeys the principal postulate of philosophical style: it seeks the highest degree of clarity and thus chooses popular over technical modes of expression.

The recapitulation in the form of a completed fiction begins at the precise moment when Leibniz presents the last of Bayle's arguments against his "new system," as if it were no more than the dire complaint that God is incapable of committing suicide. Had Leibniz not decided at the last minute to conclude the treatise by "continuing" Valla's "fiction" until its proper end, the *Theodicy* would have ended with this: the suggestion of theocide.[70] For a writer as attuned to the play of sounds as Leibniz, the proximity of *theodicée* to *theocide* would have been disturbing—to say the least. *Essais de Theodicée* would approximate "essais de theocide": attempts on the life of God. Leibniz dismisses this thought without argument. Since God does not have enough power *not* to be and he cannot therefore overcome his own necessity, possibility—and therefore power—cannot be the dominant element of the divine attributes. Hobbes, in short, is refuted one last time. This last refutation is, however, silent: "To complain of not having such power [to will without rhyme or reason] would be to argue like Pliny, who finds fault with the power of God because God cannot destroy himself" (G, 6: 357; T, 365). Nothing more can be said: "I planned on finishing here" (G, 6: 357; T, 365). If power were the dominant attribute of God, then he would *have* to destroy himself in order to manifest himself *as* himself. For only an act of self-sacrifice reveals those whose principal attribute is power. Unless such a being conquers *itself*, it cannot show who it is. And this act of self-overcoming would likewise demonstrate the "arresting of wisdom."[71] *Arresting* this arresting of wisdom is then the task Leibniz assigns himself at the end of *Theodicy*: to show that it ends with something other than divine self-sacrifice; to demonstrate that it ends with a "sentence of wisdom" rather than its interruption. At the end of the treatise Leibniz therefore begins again, recapitulating his argument for the wisdom of God in the form of a fable, the central characters of which are a goddess and her pupil.

Antonomasia and the Fate of the Name "Sextus"

Leibniz's continuation of Valla's "little fable" is concerned with nothing so much as sacrifice, self-sacrifice, and suicide by default. It is not, however, God who sacrifices himself: it is, rather, Sextus Tarquinius, the last of the legendary kings of Rome, the mirror image, so to speak, of Julius Caesar. When Leibniz takes over the fable, he transposes its location from Delphi, home of Apollo, to the sacred space of the greatest of the gods, who, in his conversation with Sextus, implicitly declares himself master over the fates:

> Sextus, quitting Apollo and Delphi, seeks out Jupiter at Dodona. He makes sacrifices [*Il fait des sacrifices*], and he then exhibits his complaint. Why have you condemned me, O great God, to be wicked and unhappy? Change my lot and my heart, or acknowledge your error. Jupiter answers him: If you will renounce Rome, the Parcae will spin for you different fates, you shall become wise, shall be happy. . . . Sextus, not being able to resolve upon so great a sacrifice [*si grande sacrifice*], went forth from the temple, and abandoned himself to his fate. (G, 6: 361; T, 370)

Sextus, in short, is willing to make sacrifices, but he is not willing not to make a *sufficient* sacrifice that would satisfy the greatness of the "great

God." More exactly, Sextus is not willing to sacrifice his *power* for the sake of *wisdom*, and therefore he loses himself: "If you go to Rome, you are lost," Jupiter tells him. By choosing to proceed from Dodona to Rome after having spoken with a god who claims to be able to order the Parcae to cut him a different lot, Sextus in effect commits suicide.

Just as Jupiter is—to cite once again Quintilian's first example of antonomasia—*divum pater*, so Sextus Tarquinius seeks to be honored as *rex hominum*. By means of the trope of antonomasia, the relation between the two characters who first appear in Leibniz's continuation of Valla's "little fable" can be succinctly defined: Sextus would be "the Jupiter" of human beings; or, in reverse, Jupiter would "the Sextus" of the gods—if only Jupiter, like Sextus, were defined primarily by the attribute of power. And the "real" Jupiter of Roman mythology is defined in this manner, of course, and so, too, is the "real" Sextus of Roman legend. The question generated by the comparison between the rapist of Leda and the rapist of Lucretia gives shape to the recapitulation of Leibniz's argument. It is not posed by one who makes sacrifices in order to receive something back— divine favor, a happier life—but, instead, by one who, without a thought for himself, facilitates sacrifices and, as his name suggests, gives to the god without an expectation of return. Such is Theodore, *le grand Sacrificateur*, high priest, *pontifex maximus*, or pope *avant la lettre* (G, 6: 361; T, 370). The scene in which Jupiter condescends to converse with Sextus is, for this "sacrificer," a moment of crisis, for it makes the "*great* God" whom he honors appear as though he were a singularly powerful Sextus:

> Theodore, the great sacrificer, who had been present at the dialogue between God and Sextus, addressed these words to Jupiter: Your wisdom is to be revered, O great ruler of the gods. You have convinced this man of his error; he must henceforth impute his unhappiness to his evil will; he has not a word to say. But your faithful worshippers are astonished; they would hope to admire your goodness as well as at your greatness: it rested with you to give him a different will. JUPITER—Go to my daughter Pallas, she will teach you what I had to do [*ce que je devois faire*]. (G, 6; 362; T, 370)

With these words, the greatest of the gods, who alone has a right to use the general term *deus* as a proper name, departs from the treatise. Just as Sextus, according to Theodore, "has not a word to say," neither does Jupiter. The conclusion to the conclusion, which begins with the exit of Jupiter, thus intensifies the fact that the *Essays of Theodicy*, unlike the *New Essays*, does not appear in the form of a dialogue. Even the goddess of wisdom fails to enter into a dialogue with the one whom she is supposed to teach, namely Theodore. Instead, she merely annotates the vision with which he is now blessed: "You see the palace of the fates, over which I keep watch [*le palais des destinées, dont j'ay la garde*]. Here are representations not only of that which happens but also of all that is possible" (G, 6: 362; T, 370). Pallas guards the palace; her name echoes her function. Or the palace she guards echoes her name. In either case, however, she is neither the mistress of the fates nor one of the Parcae herself. Nor, indeed, according to her own instruction, does Jupiter have the power to create "the fates" by fiat; rather, he constructs the palace over which Pallas keeps watch, and, in addition, out of love, lets one of its rooms enter into existence. No one, strictly speaking, can make things come true by the power of speech alone—unless "truth" means "being-actual" (as opposed to "being-possible"), in which case the speech act is merely transformative, not absolutely creative. The "palace of fates" itself escapes *fatum* in the original sense of the term, for it can only be constructed. Far from being defined by power, Jupiter is essentially powerless—or, more accurately, powerless when it comes to the creation of the essences over which the goddess keeps watch. And because the "palace of fates" cannot itself be ascribed to *fatum*, Jupiter, according to the line of argument Leibniz illustrates with his fable, escapes the charge that he is responsible for evil; he cannot *make* anyone do anything: "Jupiter, having surveyed them before the beginning of the existing world, classified the possibilities into worlds and chose the best of all. . . . I have only to speak, and we will see a whole world that my father might have produced, wherein will be represented anything that can be asked of him" (G, 6: 362; T, 373).

By speaking, Pallas Athena does not make things happen; she only makes possibilities appear as if they were "real" appearances—"as in a theatrical representation" (G, 6: 363; T, 371). In the "palace of fates," Athena can transform possibility into virtual reality. But in order to make sense of what she does in that place, she must call on a "tropical" transformation that seems to escape both her notice and that of her dutiful pupil—the "tropical" transformation of a proper name into a common noun, namely Sextus into *a* Sextus:

> These worlds are all here, that is, in ideas. I will show you some, wherein shall be found, not absolutely the same Sextus as you have seen (that is not possi-

ble, he carries with him always that which he shall be) but several Sextuses approximating him, who will have everything that you know already of the true Sextus, but not all that is already in him imperceptibly, nor in consequence all that shall yet happen to him. You will find in one world a very happy and noble Sextus, in another a Sextus content with a mediocre state, a Sextus, indeed, of every kind and endless diversity of forms. (G, 6: 363; T, 371).

Athena could not fulfill her divinely sanctioned obligation of instructing Theodore in the ways of providence without drawing on the resources of antonomasia. She could doubtless make things appear—or appear to appear—but her pupil would be utterly unable to make sense of these virtualities. By calling different apparitions by the same name, the goddess allows Theodore to understand the *sense* of what she conjures into spectral existence. And Jupiter would be in no better position. "Sextus" cannot be a proper name: its generality is fully evident, however, only in the palace of fates. Outside of this palace—which is to say, in the world that Jupiter creates—the term "Sextus" reverts to its original status as a proper name; more exactly, it re-reverts to its derived status as a proper name, since, according to one of the fundamental principles of any Leibnizian inquiry into historical languages—"all the names that we call 'proper' were once appellatives"—the name must have originally been a common noun. The goddess thus *re*-restores the proper name Sextus to its original status. For this reason, the "palace of fates" is confirmed in its originality: all proper names are held in common. The return to the origin is not accomplished by tracing names back to their roots; rather, Athena treats a proper name as a common noun—without, however, making this common noun any more meaningful than a proper name: it still serves to single out individuals. There is, in other words, nothing "Sextean" about all the infinite class of Sextuses other than the extrinsic determination of being called by the same—improperly designated—"proper" name. Athena can draw on the resources of antonomasia to single out "a Sextus" in an infinite number of worlds; but the only property that all of the Sextuses have in common is their "proper" name, which, in reality, is nothing—or nothing in principle. Athena is not so much the name-giver as the one who guards the "proper" name against the twin threat of pure propriety, on the one hand, and of general applicability, on the other. In the last sentence of the *Essays of Theodicy* Leibniz reveals that Athena is supposed to serve as the mythological figuration of "simple intelligence (which regards all the possibles)" (G, 6: 365; T, 373); but it would also be possible to say, along the lines of Leibniz's own exposition, that she is, in addition, the allegoresis of antonomasia: she not only names all the Sextuses; she is herself only named by way of an epithet. The two modes of antonomasia thus come together in the one who guards "the palace of fates": Pallas, "the brandisher of the sword" (from *pallō*) or, more likely, "the maiden" (from *pallax*). Regardless of the tropological canal through which she passed—and Leibniz never chooses one over the other—the only term that Leibniz uses to name the goddess who guards the "palace of fates," guides Theodore, and "regards all the possibles" is itself wholly improper: it is a "proper" name, applicable to a single individual, only by virtue of antonomasia.

Replacing Proper Names with Identifying Numbers

The worlds Pallas conjures into existence for the purpose of edifying Theodore shine forth as though they are real. At her command, each of the halls in the "palace of fates" turns into a world *"solemque suum, sua sidera norat* [that has its own sun, its own stars]" (G, 6: 363; T, 371). But the world made visible by the word of the goddess does not fill up the hall; all its scenes are staged, and at the edge of the stage there lies a book:

> Theodore saw the whole life of [a nonbelligerent] Sextus in a blink of the eye and as in a theatrical representation. There was a great volume of writings in this hall: Theodore could not prevent himself from asking what that meant. It is the history of the world that we are now visiting, the Goddess told him; it is the book of its fates [*le livre de ses destinées*]. (G, 6: 363; T, 371)

The "little fable" would seem to require only halls or books—not both at once, still less halls in which a theatrical scene appears alongside a book that is open to the page in which the same scene is described. Leibniz, who champions clarity of exposition and celebrates the principle of parsimony, seems to abandon both causes, as he multiplies the media in which the possible worlds under Pallas's protection present themselves. And Leibniz does not stop with the book: it, too, gives way to another medium of representation in which book and stage are combined with each other. Having replaced the stage, the page turns into something like a tele-vision screen whose scenes can be manipulated at will. By placing his finger on a line of text, Theodore can make an image instantaneously appear, and this image can be just as swiftly reconverted into its corresponding textual expression. All of Leibniz's numerous attempts at constructing sophisticated calculating machines may have failed, but in the "little fable" of the *Theodicy* he nevertheless succeeds in imagining a medium of communication very much like the Internet:

> "You have seen a number on the forehead [*front*] of Sextus," Pallas proceeds to explain, "Look in this book for the place that it indicates." Theodore looked for it, and found there the history of Sextus in a form more ample than the outline he had seen. "Put your finger on any line you please," Pallas said to him, "and you will see represented actually in all its details that which the line broadly indicates." He obeyed, and he saw coming into view all the particularities of a portion of the life of that Sextus [*ce Sextus*]. (G, 6: 363; T, 371–72)

The movement from theater to book to Internet is supported by the *systematization* of antonomasia: proper names are all replaceable by identifying *numbers*. The site of this systematization is the palace guarded by Pallas: only in this place—not in the world Jupiter calls into existence—are individuals branded with "proper numbers" on their foreheads. This number allows the guardian (or warden) of the palace (or prison) to keep track of those uncreated "things" (or prisoners) whom she guards. And this number also associates these forever guarded "things" with another kind of uncreated being: the golem. For the golem, who owes its origin to an *ars combinatoria* that clearly resembles Leibniz's own, carries a name-number on its forehead as a sign of its distinction from creatures derived from God: אמת.[72] The advantages of a world in which the forehead of every individual displays a number over a world in which foreheads may have lines but no "proper numbers" are enormous—at least from the perspectives of its wardens. For the names of individuals are no longer "extrinsic denominations" but, rather, intrinsic properties. If all the Sextuses in the "palace of fates" did not have numbers on their foreheads, the term "Sextus" would be utterly ambiguous: it could apply to an infinite number of individuals, none of whom would have any "Sextean" property other than the purely extrinsic one of being called—entirely arbitrarily—"Sextus." A number on the forehead literally *de-nominates* the individual thus enumerated: it replaces an extrinsic denomination with an intrinsic "denumeration."[73] And this number carries out to the letter the principal postulate of philosophical style: disambiguation.

Sextus is well prepared for the replacement of his name by an identifying name, for his name is already a number: six. Leibniz, by contrast, is less well prepared to assign each of the infinitely many Sixes their own number, for the proper numbers in the infinite pyramid over which Pallas stands guard would have to be *infinite ones*. Such numbers, however, as he insists in an earlier passage of the *Theodicy*, are entirely fictitious:

> One gets into the same embarrassing situation with the series of numbers that goes to infinity. One conceives of a final end, a number that is infinite, or infinitely small; but these are nothing but fictions [*fictions*]. Every number is finite and assignable, every line is the same, and the infinites or infinitely small only signify magnitudes that one can take as big or as small as one wishes. (G, 6: 90; T, 113)[74]

Outside the "fiction" with which Leibniz concludes the treatise, infinite numbers can be considered mere fictions, *entia fictitum*; within the fiction, by contrast, such fictions must be ideal, *entia rationis*—like all the (finite) numbers in any possible world, including our own. Otherwise, all the Sixes buried in the pyramid could not be distinguished from one another. It is doubtless fictional, if not entirely fanciful, to suggest that the replacement of proper names by identifying numbers, as the perfection of antonomasia, leads Leibniz in the direction of Cantor: every Six must be assigned a transfinite number commensurate with its—uncreated, golemic—character: from א (the first Hebrew letter-number) through מ (the middle Hebrew letter-number) to ת (the last Hebrew letter-number).[75] אמת would then name the complete system of identifying numbers—or "truth." Leibniz, of course, nowhere indicates anything of the kind, although he, like Cantor, experiments with alephs as newly devised numerals (A, 6, 4: 206–8). In any case, he would have known that finite numbers are wholly inadequate to identify all the possible Sixes. The palace of possible worlds is ironically a place where the *actual* infinite must not only be acknowledged; it must also be expressed by a consistent system of enumeration—*if* a consistent system of enumeration *can* be developed, which is by no means certain. Otherwise, the process of replacing names with numbers cannot be acomplished. And this, too, Leibniz may have known: every Six has its own number, but neither Pallas nor Theodore discloses a single one. If, however, a consistent system of enumeration for the identification of all possible individuals in all possible worlds cannot be developed; if the last number of "truth"—call it ת—is fundamentally inconsistent, then so, too, perhaps are all the others. And so, too, is the palace that Pallas guards.

Leibniz, however, cannot do without infinite numbers to identify all the "Sixes" or "Sextuses." Or at least, Athena in her role as guardian cannot. And even if neither Leibniz nor Athena give any indication of the grave difficulties into which the systematic replacement of proper names by identifying numbers leads; even if neither admits, as Cantor will, that the numbers needed for the successful ordering of the "palace of fates" are "new irrationalities" (GA, 395),[76] an unmistakable atmosphere of nonnumeric irrationality pervades the entire operation. For no one—not even Jupiter—can render a reason for the assignment of any particular number to any particular Six. The numerals inscribed on the forehead of the golemic figures Athena calls into existence are not only without reason; they are virtual incarnations of irrationality. Every particular numeral that is inscribed on the forehead of these noncreatures is a sign of an absolutely arbitrary will. "Proper numbers" are even more groundless than proper names—*and are groundless for the sake of a perfectly rational system of ordering*. With the replacement of proper names by "proper numbers" the last vestige of arbitrariness is overcome: no longer is truth in any sense dependent on names. But the impossibility of grounding the choice of "proper number" gives evidence of an even more insidious and more subtle arbitrariness. It takes little imagination to see the great Adversary slyly insinuating himself into this scene—as 666 . . . Because all of the numbers on the foreheads of the phantoms of fate are "without rime and without reason" (G, 6: 357; T, 365), even if the general replacement of names by numbers is itself grounded in the very principle of reason, all of the numbers are signs of a tyrannical will. Or more exactly: these "proper numbers" are signs of a more than tyrannical will. A will whose arbitrary impositions are undertaken *for the sake of reason* cannot be considered simply tyrannical—or "Sextean"—any longer. Another term must be sought: "Jupiterean" might be one; "totalitarian" another. In any case, the worlds conjured into existence by Athena's command can be distinguished from the world outside the "palace of fates" by only one *legible* criterion: in the latter, numbers are not systematically branded into individuals' foreheads for the sake of ordering them. This criterion is not, of course, infallible: foreheads and other bodily surfaces can be inscribed with identifying, proper numbers. Only in one respect, however, does existence in the palace differ from existence "in the penal colony": whereas only some of the anonymous inhabitants of the penal colony are branded in Kafka's great fable, all the inhabitants of the palace are in Leibniz's little one.

Interrupting Consciousness, *La Langue*

The reappearance of the tyrant named Sextus is the climax of Leibniz's clarifying "fiction." Of all the Sextuses whom Theodore is allowed to observe as he passes through the "palace of fates," only the last one commits any unjust acts: the other Sextuses end their prosperous lives in a peaceful state—perfect figures, in other words, for the conclusion of "little fables." The last Sextus, who could also be called the least Sextus, occupies the eschatological position par excellence: the top of a pyramid. The "palace of fates" does not resemble a Baroque church; instead of an illusion of condescending grace—the *ponderacíon misterioso* with which Walter Benjamin concludes his *Origin of the German Mourning Play* (GS, 1: 406–9; O, 233–35)—there is endless and irreversible descent; and instead of signs of grace, there are suggestions of arcane knowledge. Earlier in the *Essays of Theodicy*, recapitulating some of his contemporaneous investigations into historical languages, Leibniz had associated Theut, the Egyptian god of cleverness and technical knowledge, with the "Tuitsche," Teutons, or Germans (G, 6: 193; T, 212).[77] The pyramid with which he concludes may be another reminder of this same line of descent:

> The halls rose in a pyramid; they became ever more beautiful as one mounted toward the apex, and they represented more beautiful worlds. Finally they reached the highest one which completed the pyramid, and which was the most beautiful of all; for the pyramid had a beginning, but one could not see its end; it had an apex, but no base; it went on increasing to infinity. That is (as the Goddess explained) because among an endless number of possible worlds there is the best of all, else would God not have determined to create any; but there is not any one which has not also less perfect worlds below it: that is why the pyramid goes on descending to infinity. Theodore, entering this highest hall, found himself ravished in ecstasy [*se trouva ravi en extase*]; he had to receive succor from the Goddess, a drop of a Divine liquor placed on his tongue restored him [*une goutte d'une liqueur Divine mise sur la langue le remit*]. He was insensate with joy [*Il ne se sentoit pas de joye*]. We are in the real true world [*le vray monde actuel*] (said the Goddess) and you are at the source of happiness. (G, 6: 364; T, 372)

Leibniz gives no reason for Theodore's ecstasy. It is, of course, associated with his arrival at the pinnacle of the pyramid, but nothing in the wording of the "little fable" indicates how this coincidence should be understood: he enters; he "finds himself" in ecstasy—which is to say, he does not find himself but, on the contrary, loses himself. This minor inconsistency in Leibniz's formulation may indicate the groundlessness of Theodore's ecstasy, or it may point toward a suppressed causal schema: Theodore is "in ecstasy"—and therefore out of his mind—because he "finds" something very much like himself; that is, he finds his mere possibility, the golemic figure whom he resembles in every detail. And if he exactly resembles this figure, he, like all the "Sixes" whom he has seen, must be inscribed with an unreadable, unbearable number on his forehead. As he finds himself—inscribed—he instantaneously loses consciousness. Or, in other words, he dies. Such is the price of "finding" oneself inscribed with a "name" all one's own. For, as Leibniz explains in the "Principles of Nature and Grace," each of the deaths that we supposedly witness is only a "long stupor [*un long etourdissement*]," whereas "a death in the rigorous sense [*une mort à la rigueur*]" is one in which "all perception would cease" (G, 6: 600; L, 638)—sheer *rigor mortis*. Use of the term *death* in the "real true world" cannot fail to be figural, for no reason can be given for the complete interruption of representation. Theodore is, however, an exception: at the very moment that he enters into the "real true world" he takes leave of every possible world, for he ceases to feel anything at all: *Il ne se sentoit pas*. And the source of this interruption of feeling is itself a feeling—one might say, the fundamental feeling, which, by virtue of its baseness, does not let itself be felt until all other feelings have been arrested. "Joy is a pleasure that the soul feels in itself" (G, 7: 86; L, 425).[78] The experience of entering the "real true world" as an adult—or, more exactly, as a noninfant, as one who can articulate the experience of entrance into the world—is, in colloquial terms, out of this world. And being in the "real true world" is subsequently being out of one's mind: *en extase*, dead for joy.

No mortal can stand to be in this state. How close Theodore's *extase* is to the "little death" of sexual ecstasy to which Leibniz alludes in his correspondence with Arnauld (G, 2: 124; L, 345) is difficult to say. Only this much is clearly known: Theodore would not recover from his ecstasy without a dash of the "Divine liquor" by means of which his ecstasy is redoubled: otherwise, "cold sober," all sensation would stop; his life in the "real true world" would really be death. This liquor is not the only one with which Leibniz conducts some philosophico-fictional experiments. In another startling allegory, which goes by the title "Leibniz's philosophical dream,"[79] Theodore's tale of "finding himself" out of his mind assumes an autobiographical form. The "I" of the narrative begins by noting that he is "content" with his place among human beings but is "not content with human nature" (LH, 108). His discontent makes him "melancholic" (LH, 108). Overcome with fatigue by the weight of his thoughts, he falls asleep and soon finds himself in a vast cave peopled by creatures that "strangely run around in the darkness after some errant fires, which they call honors or after little fireflies they call riches" (LH, 108–9). Unlike these lost creatures, however, the narrator cannot suppress the voice that constantly cries "stop [*arrestés*]," and he thus discovers a "little light" that commands his attention and that, according to an old man, is called "good sense and reason." Following his researches conducted under the guidance of this light, he reaches the one place in the cave "destined for those whom the divinity wished to remove completely from this darkness." Once again, however, he is overcome by the sight of the misery spread out before him. "But a moment later"—and this "but" marks the critical moment of the narrative—"a dazzling clarity surprised me" (LH, 110). As the narrator is on the verge of fainting, he feels himself "touched by a branch imbued with a marvelous liquor [*une liqueur marveilleuse*], which I would not compare with anything I ever felt before and which gave me the force necessary to sustain the presence of the celestial messenger. He called me by my name" (LH, 110)—a name, however, that the fragment never reveals. Transported to the pinnacle of a mountain, given telescopic vision to clarify his vision, and given instruction by the messenger so that he may likewise clarify his soul, the anonymous narrator fully recovers from his earlier melancholia and learns, in the words of the angel, "that [his] future perfections will be proportionate to the care that [he] takes to attain them here" (LH, 111).

The "marvelous liquor" by which the narrator of this "philosophical dream" sustains the presence of the "celestial angel" (LH, 110), like the "Divine liquor" with which Athena revives Theodore from his stupor, does not number among the elements of the "real true world," nor of any other one. Yet this liquor alone lets the lives of Theodores and Théophiles resume—as memorials to the moments of their interruption. In Kafka's great story "A Report to an Academy," an ape named Rotpeter (so named because of a gunshot wound on his thigh) recounts his passage out of "apeness" and into "humanity," the critical moment of which takes place when he is finally able to swallow a dose of Schnapps. By placing this liquor on his tongue, Rotpeter forms his first word: "Hallo!"[80] From then on, progress is assured, in ever-renewed forms of intoxication. Leibniz, who sought to found academies all across Europe and was the principal architect of the Prussian Royal Academy, would have doubtless welcomed Rotpeter's articulate report of his passage into speech. For there is only the slightest difference between this report and his own: Rotpeter must conquer his own disgust at the smell of liquor in order to pass into the permanently intoxicated—or ecstatic—state of potential speech; neither the unnamed narrator of "Leibniz's philosophical dream" nor the Theodore of the *Theodicy*, by contrast, can overcome himself, having fallen into a helpless stupor; instead, they both rely on what is radically unavailable to the great ape who wishes at all costs to find a "way out" of his imprisonment: an angel or a goddess.

The stupor into which Theodore falls and from which he recovers is reflected in the vertiginous structure of the "little fable." Nowhere does Pallas point to the "book of fate" for the world in which Theodore both finds and loses himself. In the presence of such a book, Theodore, like his romantic descendants,[81] would be in a position to read the story of his own life, including the story of himself reading the story of his own life, which, again, would include the story of himself reading the story of himself in the story reading the story of his life—ad infinitum. Without indicating as much, the narrative is nevertheless thrown into a *mise-en-abyme* structure as a result of Theodore's revival, for the high priest awakes from his stupor only to return to his dream, which, however, consists in a state of acute wakefulness. Such is the effect of the "Divine liquor": it counteracts vertigo by inducing vertigo to the second degree. This process of revival corresponds to the project of perceiving tropological currents. The intoxicant is the "cure" for the very ecstasy it would otherwise induce. Like the numbers on the forehead of the Sextuses whom Theodore has witnesses, this liquor is a supplement to the world—but a supplement of a completely different kind: whereas the numbers clarify the Sextuses, the liquor restores clarity to Theodore. And the foreheads of the inhabitants of the world that the "grand Sacrificateur" then sees do not appear to be numbered. In other words—those of Luce Irigaray—the foreheads of this world are "subtracted from the order of number" (EDS, 107; ESD, 110). The world as a whole is not subtracted, of course; but the last of the worlds Theodore witnesses, which represents the "real true" one, is mercifully free of identifying numbers. It also appears to be free of any "book of its fates." The two absences are in truth one: without a "book of fate," there is no need for the replacement of proper names with "proper numbers"—and vice versa. Of all the worlds represented in the "palace of fates," only the last one appears to be entirely a place of names. And perhaps for this reason alone—the absence of identifying numbers—it is the best of them all. For this absence is the sole legible criterion by which this world is distinguished from the other ones represented, and (to emphasize the obvious) the scenes of the tyrannical Sextus that Theodore witnesses are scarcely cause for joy: "Here is Sextus as he is, and as he will be in reality. He issues from the temple in a rage, he scorns the counsel of the Gods. You see him going to Rome, bringing confusion everywhere, violating the wife of a friend" (G, 6: 364; T, 372).

Witness to the sight of a rapacious Sextus, Theodore, like Jove before him, turns silent. His *langue* is restored to him—without *parole*. The reason for his silence can only be a matter of conjecture: perhaps the actualization of his language would betray the experience of reentrance into the world; perhaps he does not have the words to express the experience of coming out of the world of dreams and "theatrical representations" and into the world of *experience*. In any case, Theodore enters into a state of second infancy or infancy to the second power. Instead of speaking, Theodore only listens to Athena's half-hearted explanation of the dismal sight that greets him upon his recovery: "The crime of Sextus serves for great things [*grandes choses*]: it renders Rome free; it will give birth to a great Empire [*grand Empire*], which will give great examples [*grand exemples*]" (G, 6: 364; T, 373). Pallas's instruction thus relies on the term *grand*: greatness is all, after all. Jupiter assigned Theodore to his daughter so that he could learn of his goodness, having acknowledged his greatness (G, 6: 362; T, 370). Perhaps for this reason Pallas adds a final word to her lesson—a word introduced with a *but* that indicates the degree to which her recapitulation of the argument has been interrupted, if not entirely arrested, by her inability to make greatness turn into goodness by way of "great examples." Exemplification of greatness is not a sufficient reason for the praise of goodness, and so the daughter of Jupiter gestures toward another explanation, which, for its part, shows that her entire pedagogy is premature: "But that [the prospect of 'great examples'] is nothing in comparison with the worth of this whole world, at whose beauty you will marvel when, after a happy passage from this mortal state to another, the Gods will have made you capable of knowing it" (G, 6: 364; T, 373).

Only in the future, then, will Theodore marvel at Jupiter's goodness. At present, in the waking dream from which he will soon awaken, he remains in a state of astonishment, arrested by the greatness of what he witnesses, shocked, unable to understand how the god whom he serves can make good on his greatness. Even as his *langue* is restored to him, he is struck dumb. Having experienced a second infancy, he cannot make himself into another Pallas and turn from "grand sacrificer" to great teacher. Theodore has yet to learn anything: he is a "great example" of an *infans* who cannot say what he has seen. No wonder this vision appears in the form of a "little fable." His fate, which he cannot find in any book, consists in returning to the ultimate root of *fatum*: he appears as the representative of a sheer potential to speak, a fabulous figuration of *fari* arrested at its origin. In a future that itself seems to escape "the palace of fates," he will, according to Pallas's prophecy, know what to say of what he has seen. What he will say, perhaps, is this: here—thankfully—there are no numbers on our foreheads.

The Perhaps Impossible Papess

On April 30, 1709, Leibniz writes a letter to Bartholomew des Bosses and offers him two manuscripts for publication. As he makes this offer, Leibniz reflects on the reasons publishers decide to choose one manuscript over another. This choice cannot be without a reason; indeed, it mirrors the choice of Jupiter, as it is presented in the "little fable" that recapitulates the argument of the *Essays of Theodicy*. For Jupiter, too, must decide which of the infinitely many "books of fate" will be brought to light and which ones will remain solely in manuscript form, confined to the private halls of an ever descending archive of ever more inferior would-be books. Publishers in the "true real world" are, however, from at least one perspective, in a better position than God, for they can choose to publish more than one book. But they cannot publish all manuscripts, and so reason must still guide their choice. Unfortunately, according to Leibniz, the rational process of publishing is often arrested prematurely. The best of all possible books, from publishers' limited perspective, is a best-seller. Since, however, publishers cannot tell which ones will sell best, they are stuck in the unhappy position of permanent indecision, so that it is a wonder that any manuscript sees the light of day: "In the realm of book publication [*Bibliopolis*] there are two things that usually give rise to hesitation: one is the desire for profit; the other is ignorance. Thus they do not know what they should select" (G, 2: 369; L, 596–97).

Having outlined the principles of publication, Leibniz proceeds to describe a "dissertation" that he has completed in Latin and mentions, as an aside, that des Bosses's publisher might prefer another manuscript, one written in French and aimed at the renowned and recently deceased author Pierre Bayle. This book is, of course, the one published under the title *Essais de Théodicée*, which became the principal work through which Leibniz's philosophy was disseminated and with which it was, for centuries, almost wholly identified. The other manuscript remained unpublished until 1758, when it appeared in an obscure compilation of miscellaneous historical documents edited by Christian Ludwig Scheidt—and has never been republished since. This other manuscript concerns a woman named Joan who was said to occupy the throne of St. Peter during the obscure time between Leo IV and Benedict III. Having dressed as a man in order to become a scholar, Joan alias John ascended the summit of the Church's hierarchy—only to be revealed and reviled when she gave birth in public:

> I tried recently to publish a dissertation that I wrote some time ago and in which I examined some problems of the ninth century and became involved in chronological studies. I called it *Flowers Strewn at the Tumulus of Papess Joan*; in it I explode the fable of the papess [*fabulam Papissae explodo*], partly by new arguments, partly by confirming the old. I set the generally obscure chronology of the time in clear order, replying to the newest subterfuges of Friedrich Spanheim, a Leyden theologian, which he put in a book published some years ago in Holland. I have also dealt with some matters that have been overlooked, for I discovered a book on magic ascribed to the papess which has not yet been published, and I drew some other things worthy of readers' interest from manuscripts. Perhaps this little book would please your printer in Liége better, but I would willingly give him either one—the one in Latin about the papess as well as the one in French against Bayle. (G, 2: 369; L, 579)

In the first words of his other work—which, unlike the *Theodicy*, agrees with Bayle's conclusions[82]—Leibniz disqualifies himself as its best author; as an historian, he is not even a suitable author: "This illustrious woman [Papess Joan] pertains to poets, not historians, for the series of events and persons does not allow her any place in the just order of time [*in iusto temporum ordine nullum locum relinquit series rerum personarumque*]" (FS, 297). Whereas one manuscript Leibniz offers des Bosses demonstrates the justice of God, the other, which presupposes the "just order of time," could be titled *An Essay of Chronodicy*. Instead of arguing for the justice of the "just order of time," Leibniz only seeks to demonstrate the nonexistence of one particular individual in the "series of events and persons" that comprise this order: the papess. This demonstration could be done in two ways: by showing that she is impossible or by showing that she is possible but never came into existence; in other words—those of the "little fable" that concludes the *Theodicy*—by showing that she had no place in the "palace of fates" or by showing that she belongs to lower orders than the one Jupiter chose to bring into existence. Without considering whether she inhabits the "palace of fates" in the first place, Leibniz treats her as a possibility who "pertains to poets" and could therefore be made into the subject-matter of numerous little fables. "Papess Joan" is in this sense more—or less—than a proper name: it is a common noun that could serve as the basis for a series of stories. Leibniz, who knew how to create fine fables and meticulously crafted poems, gives future poets of the papess some directions: having dressed as man and given birth in public, Joan dies, but, since only a few trusted friends know the cause of her death, the child survives and becomes a great hero; or, alternatively, since the witnesses to the birth are so shocked by the apparently miraculous event, mother and child escape (FS, 342). The fables of Papess Joan that Leibniz examines and proposes function like the "theatrical representations" of Sextus which Theodore witnesses: shared traits allow for the (improper) use of the same "proper" name, which, in turn, makes possible the multiplication of representations of the "same" individual. In the case of Sextus the impropriety of this usage is figured as rape and plunder; in the case of Joan, it is figured as transvestism and "illegitimate" birth. In both cases, the witnesses to the fabulous events are—if only for a moment—shocked.

Leibniz, however, is not. He is certainly not shocked by the story of Joan, nor does he give an indication that he considers the "crimes" of which Joan is accused and through which she is defined—tranvestism and adultery—criminal. And this equanimity is no small accomplishment: it sets the treatise against a massive tradition, recapitulated by Spanheim, according to which Joan—real or fictional—appears as the figure of feminine falseness in a particularly self-evident form.[83] Instead of making Joan into the figure of pure impropriety, Leibniz presents her as one who, unlike the legendary Sextus, accepts Jove's advice: "If you will renounce Rome, the Parcae will spin for you different fates" (G, 6: 361; T, 370). For, as Leibniz suggests at the end of his treatise, the fable of the papess may have arisen as a consequence of the well-known phenomenon of women donning male attire in order to gain access to educational institutions and engage in scholarly pursuits: "what prohibits some woman dressed in bishop's clothing from having given birth in public? All bishops were then called by the

name 'pontifex' [*Pontificum autem nomine olim omnes Episcopi vocabantur*]"
(FS, 367). Joan, in other words, was dressed as a bishop—but not recog-
nized as the bishop of Rome. Like the possible Sextuses whom Theodore
observes, the actual Joan, according to Leibniz, stayed away from Rome; or
at least she stayed away from its throne. Perhaps she was not tempted by
the prospect of occupying the seat of St. Peter; perhaps she had no oppor-
tunity to seize it. In either case, the fable of the papess Joan arose as a result
of a linguistic change. The distinction between "overseer" (*episcopus*) and
"pontiff" (*pontifex*) had not been clearly delineated. "Pontifex" Joan, as she
would have then been called, may belong to the "just order of time," but
Pontifex Joan, as the name is now understood, does not: the generation of
a singular term by the addition of the operator *pontifex*—as the highest, if
not the best, of bishops—generates the fable of the papess.

By presenting the origin of the fable in terms of the ambiguity of *pon-
tifex* and *episcopus*, Leibniz silently passes over another account of the ori-
gin of the fable. According to Aventinus, whose book on the papess Leib-
niz lavishly praises in his own (FS, 321), the stories of a papessy in the ninth
century owe their origin to Theodora, "a noble and domineering whore,"
who subjugated Rome in the next century and made her lover into the
pope.[84] The "little fable"—this, too, is Aventinus' term, *fabella*—develops
from the association of the woman in power with the man whom she in-
stalls on the throne of St. Peter: since she is the governing potentate, she is
the real "papa" or "pope." Leibniz makes much of a fabulous Theodore,
loyal servant of a Jupiter who serves the same God whose presence later
pontifices of Rome are supposed to represent. But in the book on the pa-
pacy Leibniz makes no mention of the Theodora from whom the fable of
the papess, according to one of his trusted sources, originates. Since Pro-
copius's *Anekdota*, which records the sexual escapades of the empress Theo-
dora, this name ("gift of the god") has ironically served as a term of rebuke.
Yet the only Theodora whom Leibniz mentions—and honors—is the
transvestite scholar named Theodora Alexandrina Callistus (FS, 367).[85] In
the lengthy foreword to his edition of Leibniz's treatise, Scheidt, who was
one of the founders of the "Göttingen school" of scientific historiography,
admonishes Leibniz for offering "probably the most improbable account
[of the origin of the fable] that could ever have been provided."[86] The story
of a woman dressing up as a bishop and giving birth in public is as un-
substantiated as the story of a woman ascending the papacy and doing
the same. A more likely explanation, according to Scheidt—who seems to

be ignorant of Aventinus's proposal and therefore its silent repudiation in Leibniz's treatise—can be found in the Machiavellian machinations of Theodora.

Instead of ascribing the "little fable" of a pontiff to a "real" Theodora in the first manuscript Leibniz offers des Bosses, he invents in the other manuscript a "little fable" about a fictional Theodore. Theodore and Theodora are fabulous cousins: the former, although a fable, is equivalent to the pontiff of Rome; the latter, although real, is a master of dissimulation who gains the Roman throne in a "Sextean" manner. It is almost as though Leibniz invented the "little fable" of Theodore in order to avoid mentioning Theodora as the origin of the "little fable" that he demolishes: *Explosa Papissae fabula* (FS, 364). By "exploding" the fable, Leibniz doubtless hoped to contribute to a peaceful purpose: the unification of Christendom under one "catholic," but not Catholic, church.[87] The same is also true of the other manuscript he offers des Bosses, *Essays of Theodicy,* the original subtitle of which reads "Catholic Demonstrations Formed with Mathematical Certainty."[88] For the fable of the papess has become fodder for Protestant attacks on the legitimacy of the papacy, including salacious rumors that cardinals pass under every newly elected pope in order to assure themselves that he is indeed a "he."[89] Leibniz, however, refuses to blame anyone for anything: the Church is unblemished by a papess; Protestants are blameless in the invention and dissemination of the rumor; and—most telling of all—no woman is guilty of any wrongdoing. If some dressed up as men in order to study, and one of these gave birth in public, so be it: the fable has no "moral"—except perhaps that of *heroic scholarship,* which Leibniz in his own way emulates. Leibniz recommends the papess to poets of the future as a "heroine and lover" (FS, 297). If the word "lover" alludes, however lightly, to Theodora, "heroine" associates her with Theodore: a pontifex who courageously risks his life to read unwritten books. The books Theodore reads are those of the fates; among the books Joan dresses up to read is perhaps Boethius's *Consolation of Philosophy,* which prompted Valla to invent the "fiction" that Leibniz "continues" and concludes at the end of the *Theodicy* (G, 6: 357; T, 365). Because Leibniz leaves everyone blameless, his "explosion" of the fable is hardly explosive. The flux of an historical language alone is responsible for the fate of the fable: a word now produces a singular term or proper name, whereas long ago it did not. The papess is a fiction generated by inadvertent antonomasia.

Leibniz faults Descartes's proof for the existence of God on a sole point:

Descartes, according to Leibniz, fails to demonstrate that God is possible; if he is possible, then he is necessary, and if he is necessary, he clearly exists.[90] For the demonstration of the *non-existence* of anything, including papess Joan, the same procedure applies. If she *cannot* exist, the manner of her non-existence is radically different from all that of the "non-things" that do not exist because of God's justice: she cannot be found among the halls of the "palace of fates." And the papess—or *any* papess—does not belong in the infinitely capacious logical space, for, as a *mulier papa* (female father), she is a contradiction in terms: neither a transvestite nor a hermaphrodite; not a "two in one" but "something" that cannot even be considered *one*, much less two—or any ratio of these numbers. The fate of "the" papess lies in escaping from the "palace of fates," the guardian of which is Pallas, who, as supreme priestess of Jupiter, born from papa alone, can be seen as the papess in double disguise. She represents her absent father in Leibniz's "little fable," and she, more than any of the popes who followed her on the throne of St. Peter, deserves to be called "pontifex." As an escapee from the "palace of fates" or in the guise of Pallas "herself," the papess in either case is radically different from any of the possible individuals whom Theodore encounters in the pyramid; she *cannot* appear in this or any other world. She therefore *appears to appear* during "dark ages" only and *as* an interruption in the otherwise continuous line of papal succession.[91] By virtue of its continuity, time constitutes itself as a "just order" (FS, 297), an order, that is, in which everything is accorded its proper "place" along a linear continuum. With his chart of the "true computation [of time] against the papess" (FS, 364), Leibniz succeeds in representing time as an uninterrupted line of papal succession. The essay in "chronodicy" is thus complete and the fable of its interruption "exploded."

Once the fable of the papess is "exploded," she can be buried—but not in the pyramid of possibilities over which Athena stands guard. She has no place in this monument to divine wisdom and tomb for all unrealized possibilities. The title Leibniz gave to his little book on the papess—the one named Joan, not Pallas—is perhaps the most beautiful he ever devised: *Flores sparsi in tumulum papissae* (Flowers strewn at the tomb of the papess). The tomb in which she is buried is different from the pyramid in which the other manuscript Leibniz offers des Bosses culminates. For the tomb of the papess is not only finite, containing less than, or other than, a self-consistent "thing," it is also empty: a cenotaph, or a cenotaph to the second power, for it could never have been full in the first and last place.[92]

Whether the internment of the papess in her tomb is cause for joy or an occasion for sorrow is impossible to say: the ironic character of Leibniz's title points in both directions. Only this much is certain: flowers are strewn at her grave. The meaning of this gesture eludes determination, just as the papess escapes the "palaces of fates." The gesture, which generally expresses mourning, could instead—or also—signal the absence of anything left to mourn. Only at one place are flowers to be strewn: at the unlocalizable tombs dedicated to anyone who appears to interrupt the "just order of time." Only at this place is there reason for ambiguous gestures of ambivalent mourning. For all other tombs, according to Leibniz, are full of life.

§ 2 Language on a Holy Day: The Temporality of Communication in Mendelssohn

I.

Only those who have experienced the unreliability of language are able to communicate with one another.

Moses Mendelssohn does not quite say this in *Jerusalem; or, On Religious Power and Judaism* (1783), the book with which he wishes to put an end to questions about the extent of "religious power" and cut short inquiries concerning the depth of his commitment to Judaism. Although he does not quite say that communication cannot take place without a common experience of linguistic unreliability, he suggests it at the precise point where an outburst of inarticulateness—"O!"—interrupts an otherwise highly articulate statement about the limits of linguistic articulation:

> With my best friend, whom I believed to be ever so much in accord with me, I very often failed to come to terms about certain truths in philosophy and religion. After a long dispute and exchange of words, it would sometimes emerge that we had each connected different ideas with the same word. . . . Our ideas had to rub up against each other for a long time [*mußten sich unsere Begriffe lange Zeit an einander reiben*] before they could be made to fit themselves to one another, and before we could say with assurance: Here we agree! O! [*hierin kommen wir überein! O!*] I should never like to have for a friend anyone who has had this experience in his lifetime, and can still be intolerant, and can still hate his neighbor because he does not think or express himself on religious matters in the same way as he does; for he has divested himself of all humanity. (JubA, 8: 134–35; J, 67)[1]

If friendship is understood as the proper model of relations among human beings—and this is the conception of friendship developed by the eponymous hero of Lessing's *Nathan the Sage* and by its model, who would soon address a plea *To the Friends of Lessing* [2]—then the conclusion toward which Mendelssohn is headed in the first part of *Jerusalem* is unambiguous, even if it is allowed to languor in the interjection "O!": communication can take place only after a "long time," and this time is marked by the inability of language to serve as a reliable medium of communication. Communication during this time—and "this time" knows no fixed limits—comes close to being a paradoxical endeavor: those who communicate must let those to whom they communicate know that they cannot fully know what they wish to communicate and indeed cannot even know *that* they wish to communicate something other than what they otherwise, regardless of their wishes, do in fact communicate. No wonder Mendelssohn, who was generally adverse to rhetorical effects and opposed to expressions of sentimentality in principle, indulges himself and interrupts his remarks with an exclamation of interruptive negation: "O!"

Yet, for all his expression of distress over the lamentable state of human language in the concluding pages of the first section of *Jerusalem*, Mendelssohn maintains that he is not a skeptic. His carefully worded denial of skepticism amounts to a confession, however, as he himself comes close to admitting, and the skepticism for which he almost becomes a mouthpiece gains force to the degree that his disposition veers in the opposite direction from the line of argument that he seeks to communicate. Having said that language cannot do without the "artifice" of metaphor, Mendelssohn proceeds to demonstrate the truth of this familiar thesis of eighteenth-century reflection on the relation among word, thought, and thing by presenting his demonstration in terms of the very operation to be understood: namely, metaphor; more exactly, a metaphor that, like the word *metaphorein*, indicates a movement from one place to another: "We cannot illustrate the words by *things*, but must again take our recourse [*unsere Zuflucht*] to signs and words, and finally, to metaphors; because, with the help of this artifice, we reduce [*zurückführen*] the concepts of the *internal* sense, as it were [*gleichsam*], to *external* sensory perceptions" (JubA, 8: 134; J, 66).[3] When inner sense—the sole dimension of which is temporal—is supposed to announce itself in an outward manner, words cannot give way to the "things" about which one speaks; and insofar as words in particular and signs in general are indispensable for the purpose of communicating any modification of inner sense, especially communicating beliefs concerning "things" that cannot be perceived by the outer senses, the mind must take refuge in the resource of last resort: the "artifice" of metaphor. Metaphor, for Mendelssohn, is a sign of this flight—not from reality, to be sure, but from the frightful inevitability of signs for the externalization of what is essentially internal: beliefs about "things" that no one can publicly point out. By presenting inner sense in terms of some corresponding object of outer sense, regardless of how this correspondence is established, metaphor "reduces" words so that *something* may appear: not, of course, the "thing" of which the words are a sign, but its "correspondent," which is then taken for its meaning. Or at least metaphors are supposed to accomplish this trick by offering intermediate zones within which inner and outer senses are momentarily made compatible with each other. Mendelssohn does not so much illustrate the meaning of *metaphor* with the metaphor of "leading back" or "re-duction" (*zurückführen*) as indicate that metaphor runs counter to the movement suggested by the term *metaphorein*. A metaphor does not carry the sensible over into the supersensible but, in reverse, allows objects of inner sense to be sensed by others, who would otherwise have no access to them. Because metaphor never truly reduces words to things, however, "reduction" can be only a metaphor, and even the friendliest forums of communication remain precarious. Far more precarious is any other forum of communication, including the agonistic and impersonal one in which Mendelssohn finds himself, as he describes the artifice of metaphor to his ironically named "dear readers." So precarious is the forum offered by the form of his treatise that communication verges on the impossible, articulation breaks down, and Mendelssohn himself appears addicted to doubt:

> Whoever you may be, dear reader, do not accuse me of addiction to doubt [*Zweifelsucht*: skepticism] or of employing some evil ruse in order to turn you into a skeptic. I am perhaps one of those who are the farthest removed from that disease of the soul, and who most ardently wish to be able to cure all their fellow men of it. But precisely because I have so often performed the cure on myself, and tried it on others, I have become aware of how difficult it is, and what little chance one has of success. (JubA, 8: 134; J, 66–67)

By attempting again and again to cure himself of an addiction from which he would not otherwise suffer, Mendelssohn has become a skeptic about the very performance of this cure: the ability of language to communicate the objects of inner sense from one person to another by means of signs available to the outer senses. The awkwardness of Mendelssohn's situation cannot be underestimated: since "atheism" and "Epicureanism" (JubA, 8: 181; J, 62–63) are inimical to pacific society, atheists and Epicureans can be legitimately exiled from a duly constituted political order. Mendelssohn's doubts about communication do not issue into either of these afflictions, to be sure; nevertheless *addiction* to doubt, *Zweifel-sucht*, tends in this direction—which means that, by confessing to doubts about the efficacy of communication, Mendelssohn runs the risk of effectively excommunicating *himself* from the legal order he seeks to legitimate in the opening section of *Jerusalem*. And these doubts are themselves expressed in an effort to demonstrate that legal orders alone, not religious ones, have the power to ban those members who confess to doubts deep enough that they can be considered "atheists" or "Epicureans." As he explicitly argues against the religious power of ex-communication, Mendelssohn simultaneously casts himself into the role of potential ex-communicant: one who is *already* exiled from the community insofar as he cannot communicate with his fellow citizens—or cannot do so *in time*.

Mendelssohn's doubts about communication lead him into a sphere where he is in danger of ex-communicating himself. Not only does language interfere with the relation among friends, even ones who relate to each other as ego and alter ego; it also interferes with and interrupts the relation of the self to itself. Language allows one to maintain one's thoughts over time; but the duration that language grants to thoughts, to the mind, and thus to the self opens the self to the same uneasiness that afflicts the relation among close friends. Language, in other words, grants the self time, as it simultaneously robs it of any certainty about what it thinks and therefore about who it may be. It is hardly surprising that a self-proclaimed antiskeptic like Mendelssohn should publicly worry about the accusation that he is addicted to doubt: "I may feel sure of something right now, but a moment later, some slight doubt of its certainty may sneak or steal its way [*schleicht oder stiehlt*] into a fold of my soul and lurk there, without my being aware of its presence [*lauert in einer Falte meiner Seele, ohne daß ich ihn gewahr worden*]" (JubA, 8: 134; J, 66). Mendelssohn, moreover, who is scarcely alone among his contemporaries when he exposes the unreliability of language, is bolder still. The "fold of the soul" can refuse to unfold itself; it can remain, in every sense of the term, *implicit*. This is the troubling topology of the Mendelssohnian soul: it can doubt without being aware "in" inner sense that it entertains doubts. Inner sense, in short, does not grant full access to the innermost recesses of the self, which, as every good Leibnizian knows, are found in its folds.[4] By stealing away and folding itself up into a fold, doubt can disrupt the soul's self-explication, which is to say, the communication of itself to others—and even the communication of its beliefs to itself. At best, the soul, folded into itself, takes time to explicate itself: "Many assertions for which I would suffer martyrdom today may perhaps appear problematic to me tomorrow" (JubA, 8: 134; J, 66). Under more adverse circumstances the recesses of the soul remain implicit: twisted by doubt, it nevertheless communicates conviction. At worst, the soul vociferously communicates its convictions precisely because, unknown to itself, it remains wrapped in doubt.

Almost against his will, Mendelssohn's meditation on communication makes him confess that he suffers from an addiction to doubt after all; but this illness has little to do with the kind of skeptical doubts that Descartes entertained when he sought to give philosophy an absolutely firm and solid foundation. True to its author, there is nothing hyperbolic about the skepticism that gains ascendancy in *Jerusalem*. Mendelssohn does not deny the existence of the external world, nor does he conjure up an evil genius who torments him with illusions of reality. Mendelssohn's doubts are not about the world but, rather, about the language through which beliefs are expressed, and his doubts are less about language per se than about the length of time it takes for human beings to express themselves about those states of inner sense that are unrelated to potentially perceptible objects. And these doubts are tempered by a recognition of their limitations; under no condition do Mendelssohn's doubts go so far as to proclaim a corruption in the soul that makes human beings incapable of communicating their genuine convictions. Only under artificial conditions are the doubts he expresses of any significance, for in general—or by nature—language does not serve as the medium for the expression of beliefs that are not about objects of outer sense. Skepticism, for Mendelssohn, is thus enlisted in a critical function: to distinguish legitimate from illegitimate conditions for linguistic communication. Of the latter Mendelssohn mentions only one, but it is the fulcrum of his exposition of *both* the limits of "religious power" *and* the reasonableness of his religious conviction. The "O!" in which his doubts gain inarticulate expression can thus be understood to articulate the two parts of *Jerusalem, or, On Religious Power and Judaism*.

The primary condition that calls for doubt even among those who assiduously avoid skepticism is the artificial condition of being forced to swear in the name of the Eternal about what one believes *now and forever* to be the nature of the Eternal.[5] Skepticism does not, for Mendelssohn, serve as a prolegomenon to "first philosophy," nor is the critical potential of skepticism used to justify such doctrines as naturalism or fideism. On the contrary, Mendelssohn feels himself forced to be what he is not by nature or by conviction—a skeptic—because he recognizes that the condition in which communication takes place runs counter to the medium of communication and can never entirely free itself from the exercise of illegitimate force. Mendelssohn is not only *not* tortured by doubts when he announces his inability to cure himself of skepticism; rather, he is troubled by those who advocate oath-taking as a *tortura spiritualis*. Discussion of imperceptible things takes up so much time, according to Mendelssohn, and the topography of the soul is so uneven, that any attempt to make one swear *now and forever* the articles of one's faith brings every conscientious speaker to the edge of articulation. The "O!" with which Mendelssohn interrupts himself is not merely an indication of linguistic unreliability and a sign of a certain emptiness but is, above all, an expression of compassion for the loss of language:

> It is obvious that human beings can be made to take oaths only about things that affect their external senses, things of which they are able to maintain the truth with the conviction which the evidence of external senses carries with it, and concerning which they can say: This I *heard, saw, said, received, gave,* or *did not hear,* etc. But we are putting their conscience to a cruel torture when we question them about things which are solely a matter of the internal sense. Do you believe? Are you convinced? Persuaded? Do you think so? In case there still remains any doubt in a corner of your mind or heart [*einem Winkel deines Geistes oder Herzens*], indicate so or God will avenge the misuse of his name.—For Heaven's sake, spare the tender, conscientious innocent! Even if he had to state a proposition from the first book of Euclid, he would, at that moment, hesitate and suffer inexpressible torment [*unaussprechliche Marter leiden*]. (JubA, 8: 133; J, 65–66)

The pathos of Mendelssohn's presentation corresponds to the thesis he proposes: language cannot secure reference to the exalted things about which people, under artificial conditions, are supposed to swear. And if Mendelssohn is successful in generating pathos, he has—ipso facto or, better yet, *ipso patho*—made his point: the soul is seen to have a geometry of its own; convictions and doubts cannot be determined in the same way as the world available to outer sense; and therefore the conditions under which one is supposed to swear in the name of the Eternal about the time-bound complexities of one's own soul are always artificial, forced, and violent. Mendelssohn's reluctant skepticism takes issue with these conditions alone—not with the "human condition." And the issue of swearing is the precise point where the scope of "religious power" is determined, for every act of swearing is nothing less than a sacramental sign in which the sphere of religion attests to and tests out its power.[6]

Mendelssohn does not go so far as to call swearing a curse, which, regardless of the oath sworn, makes oath-taker and oath-administrator alike into blasphemers of the divine name. Nor does he draw on the linguistic resources of German and present swearing (*beschwören*) as a mode of conjuring ghosts (*beschwören*), which, for their part, would be less matters of belief or faith (*Glauben*) than of irreligious superstition (*Aberglauben*). Mendelssohn pursues none of the lines of attack broached by the linguistic ambiguities that gather around the words *Schwur* and *beschwören*—and for good reason: as one whose overall argument in the first section of *Jerusalem* is directed against the "religious power" of excommunication, Mendelssohn would hardly wish to invoke the act of cursing through which accursed ones are banned from community and communication alike. And as a philosopher whose overall project encourages the promotion of greater enlightenment in conjunction with broader culture, it would be highly uncharacteristic of him to enter into a consideration of conjuring, even if he only wished to conjure away—*beschwören* once again—the ghosts supposedly conjured up in certain linguistic acts. In each of these cases of *beschwören*—swearing, cursing, conjuring up, and conjuring away—not only is language, understood as a medium of communication, considered reliable, it is made into something immediate, which is to say, magical. Words have the power to create certain things or, better yet, uncertain "nothings," especially ghosts and specters; but they also have the awesome power to create the very conditions in which the speaker speaks. On this point swearing is distinguished from promising and therefore from the basic act that all contractarian theories of society consider initial, inaugural, and decisive: whereas promising creates nothing more—but also nothing less—than a debt, an obligation, or, as Mendelssohn puts it, a "perfect duty,"[7] swearing creates the very world in which the swearer henceforth lives: a blessed or cursed one. Or, according to one possible interpretation of the Third Commandment, swearing immediately transposes the one who swears into a cursed world. For *any* use of the divine name for the purpose of vouchsafing one's *own* word takes this unique name out of its proper context—God giving his word—and thus cannot fail but take the name of God "in vain."[8] By virtue of the name that it invokes, regardless of the conditions under which it is spoken, every act of swearing is not simply serious, still less playful, but rather "solemn"—in German, *feierlich*.[9] The phrase "to solemnly swear" is at best an explication of what is implied in the idea of swearing, at worst a pleonasm. If, as Wittgenstein famously proclaimed, "philosophical problems arise when language goes on a *holiday* [*philosophische Probleme entstehen, wenn die Sprache* feiert],"[10] then swearing testifies to a preeminent philosophical problem, even if it has rarely been treated as a point of "first philosophy." In swearing, speech is invested with a solemnity (*Feierlichkeit*) that robs it of its everyday conditions and therefore makes it either hyperactive—capable not only of magical conjurations but also of creating the world in which a speaker speaks—or curiously empty: "in vain."

Mendelssohn decides for the latter position: to solemnly swear that one believes a doctrine, the content of which is entirely a matter of inner sense, does not *do* anything; it is both idle and vain. Under certain limited conditions, according to Mendelssohn, swearing can doubtless have a limited function: when speakers are conscientious but nevertheless prone to temporize, especially when it comes to telling the truth, and when, in addition, something available to the outer senses is at stake in their speech. The act of swearing in the name of the Almighty that "such is the case" cannot by itself institute either of these conditions, however, especially not the condition of conscientiousness. And a sentence like "I solemnly swear that such is the case" is idle for at least one reason that has nothing to do with moral psychology: the utterance means exactly the same as "such is the case," even if, under appropriate circumstances, it makes the speaker accountable—or accountable in another way—for the truth of the utterance. If, finally, one must also make explicit what is implied in sentences like "I solemnly swear that such is the case"—that I understand the distinction between a solemn and a nonsolemn occasion—then the act of swearing ends up in an infinite regress: one must swear that one understands what it means to swear and what it means to swear that one understands what it means to swear, and so forth ad infinitum.

Swearing, then, would do precisely the opposite of what under the best of circumstances, it can do: remind speakers that *now* is a solemn occasion—not a holiday, but, rather, a holy time. At issue in any meaningful act of swearing is the threat of *indefinite delay*:

Perhaps the good spirit [*der gute Geist*] that contends with him for justice is put off from day to day until it is tired out and succumbs. One must therefore hasten to his assistance and, first of all, transform the case that is liable to delay into an action that takes place now when the present moment is decisive and excuses no longer allowable; then we must summon, in addition, all the solemnity [*alle Feyerlichkeit*], and gather up all the force and emphasis, with which the recollection of God, the all-righteous avenger and retributor, can act upon the mind. (JubA, 8: 133; J, 65)

If, as Mendelssohn proceeds to explain, "the purpose of an oath" is misunderstood, and some authority seeks to make the institution of oath-taking do more than it can, especially if it tries to force speakers into revealing what they believe *now and forever* about their own beliefs—not about things to which other speakers can testify—then this institution can only serve the diabolic purpose of pointless torment: forcing someone to do what cannot in principle be done.

All of this is, therefore, reason for skepticism. Language is not well adapted to the solemnity of the occasion that the act of swearing demands. Consideration of the institution of oath-taking establishes the context in which Mendelssohn comes close to confessing that he is addicted to doubt because it leads him to conclude that language is too coarse or too clumsy a medium to facilitate *quick* communication about the One in whose name swearing takes place and whose presence, if only in name, makes an occasion solemn. If the temporality of solemnity is of the moment, then nothing should be less solemn than a speech about what one believes to be the nature of God, for, owing to the unreliability of language, genuine communication (as opposed to forced and enforced confession) takes time, perhaps even more time than any human being has on this earth. The irresolvable temporal mismatch—solemnity is momentary, communication about the nature of God a matter of duration—is at the heart of Mendelssohn's critique of swearing. This contretemps demands, moreover, a resolution unless, or until, *either* solemnity can do without speech *or* society can do without solemn occasions. Mendelssohn clearly does not subscribe to the latter proposal, since it would be tantamount to "atheism" or "Epicureanism," and he considers the former suggestion impossible: solemnity cannot do without some form of communication, even if it consists of a simple invocation of the divine name. Invocations of this name are, however, fundamentally questionable: even those who are inclined against skepticism tend, for good reason, to raise questions like "what is the nature of the One named?" Solemnity and communication, therefore, cannot remain at odds with each other, and the question Mendelssohn must address to himself is: How can the temporality of solemnity correspond to the temporality of communication?

Mendelssohn's response is contra-Leibnizian. Every other doctrine for which he argues in his philosophical works may be ultimately attributable to Leibniz or Wolff, but not this one. For Mendelssohn implicitly but resolutely rejects Leibniz's proposals for an "exact" language, "universal characteristics," rational language, or system of writing that would, if it ever came into existence, make possible an almost instantaneous solution to every conceivable problem.[11] Whereas a Leibnizian would attempt to speed up language to the point where it would replicate the timeless calculus of God, Mendelssohn sets out to slow solemnity down.[12] Instead of carrying out Leibniz's program for the construction of a rational language or system of writing, Mendelssohn promotes a peculiar mode of symbolic practice. The function that Leibniz assigns to a "universal characteristics" is fulfilled, for Mendelssohn, in characteristic, hence symbolic "ceremonies." The response to the question "how can the temporality of solemnity correspond to the temporality of communication?" is contained, in other words, in the second term of the subtitle to *Jerusalem*: "Judaism."

II.

For, according to Mendelssohn, Judaism slows down solemnity, and thereby creates the conditions within which the temporality of communication can match that of solemnity. More exactly, Judaism makes it possible for the longevity of conversations about the nature of the Eternal to come into line with the swiftness of occasions consecrated in and by the divine name. Nothing will make communication any quicker or language any more reliable; language, for Mendelssohn, is so fundamentally faulty that no effort at reform—not even Leibniz's—will do any good in matters of metaphysics. And for the same reason, "divine wisdom" would never bother communicating itself in speech, relying, rather, on speech in a figural sense—more exactly, on the fixed "speech" of creation:

> It seems to me that only where historical truths are concerned does it befit the supreme wisdom to instruct human beings in a human manner, that is, through words and writing. . . . Eternal truths, on the one hand, insofar as they are useful for human salvation and felicity, are taught by God in a man-

ner more appropriate to the Deity; not by sounds or written characters, which are comprehensible here and there, to this or that individual, but through creation itself, and its internal relations, which are legible and comprehensible to all human beings. (JubA, 8: 160; J, 93)

This familiar restatement of natural theology serves to support the most famous thesis that Mendelssohn proposes in the second section of *Jerusalem*: "I believe that Judaism knows of no revealed religion. . . . The Israelites possess a divine *legislation*" (JubA, 8: 157; J, 89–90). This legislation as a whole has the specifiable purpose of solemnifying the occasion of its execution. And it accomplishes this solemnification by making the execution of certain prescriptions—to use the term Mendelssohn rescues from Daniel Ernst Mörschel, the man who most recently challenges him to defend his decision to remain a Jew or promptly to convert[13]—into "ceremonies." In response to Mörschel's talk of "onerous ceremonies [*lästigen Zeremonien*]" and of a "true divine service [that is] bound neither to Samaria nor Jerusalem" (JubA, 8: 154; J, 86), Mendelssohn calls his response *Jerusalem* and reclaims the non-Hebraic and non-Germanic term *ceremony*. The reclamation of a familiar term of abuse follows upon an exact description of the language with which challenges like that of Mörschel are issued: "solemn and pathetic [*feyerlich und pathetisch*]" (JubA, 8: 154; J, 87).

The occasions for the execution of "ceremonial law" are, for Mendelssohn, entirely absorbed in language. More exactly, each of these occasions should be understood as a linguistic moment in its own right, and the act of understanding them in this manner constitutes the orientation of thought toward Jerusalem: "the *prescriptions* [*Vorschriften*] *for action and rules of life* [are] in large part to be regarded as a mode of script [*Schriftart*] and have as *ceremonial laws* significance and meaning [*Bedeutung und Sinn*]" (JubA, 8: 193; J, 128).[14] Ceremonial law thus allows the temporality of solemnity to agree with that of communication, and the locus of their agreement is writing in an unconventional sense. For writing both temporizes speech and is speech held in place. Before proceeding to propose a history of writing that accounts for the disadvantages of both its hieroglyphic and alphabetic forms,[15] Mendelssohn emphasizes that writing is distinguished from speech on the basis of its temporality: above all, writing *arrests* speech, and by so doing, makes it last longer. Because of its longevity, moreover, writing not only "has" a history but is preeminently historical. Mendelssohn goes even further in this direction, for he suggests that writing may be the hidden fulcrum upon which human history as a whole ultimately turns. At the very least, religious ideas—the beliefs of "inner sense"—are as much functions of the particular historical condition of written communication as expressions of independent and free reflection:

> It seems to me that the changes that have occurred in different times of culture with regard to written signs have always had a very important part in the revolutions of human knowledge in general, and in the manifold alterations of human beings' opinions and concepts in matters of religion. . . . Scarcely does a human being cease to be satisfied with the first impressions of the external senses . . . when he becomes aware of the necessity of attaching them to perceptible signs, not only in order to communicate them to others, but also to hold fast [*festhalten*] to them himself. (JubA, 8: 171; J, 104–5)

As arrested speech, writing exacerbates the difficulty of verbal communication. Regardless of the mode of writing, hieroglyphic or alphabetic, more time is required to comprehend written signs than verbal ones. For better or worse—at best in the case of biblical study, at worst in the idolatrous worship of hieroglyphic characters—writing can occupy an entire lifetime. Each of the two modes of writing in the conventional sense gives evidence of the faultiness of communication: hieroglyphic script becomes the origin of idolatry because it is based on the "artifice" of metaphor through which states of inner sense, like courage and fear, are associated with corresponding perceptual signs, especially the images of animals; and alphabetic writing isolates human beings because it gives the vain illusion of rapid and general comprehensibility: there are few things human beings can do more rapidly than translate letters into verbal sounds without comprehending what is being said. But writing in the metaphorical sense, as the execution of ceremonial and solemn (*feierlich*) prescriptions, resolves the very same difficulty, for it holds out no prospect that its complete and final meaning can be determined.[16] Least of all can the meaning of these prescriptions be found in, or derived from, any doctrine or "belief" to which one could legitimately swear permanent allegiance in the name of the Eternal. This general absence of *doxa* gives rise to the paradoxical character of Mendelssohn's proposals.[17] Frozen in place, arrested until the solemn and glorious day when God publicly says otherwise, ceremonial script is released from the horizon of *fixed* meaning and is, for this very reason, at once completely *fluid* in its meaning and forever *overflowing* with significance: "a living mode of script, awakening mind and heart, which is full of meaning [*eine lebendige, Geist und Herz erweckende Art von Schrift, die bedeutungsvoll ist*]" (JubA, 8: 169; J, 102).

Mendelssohn's defense of Judaism devolves onto this last phrase: "which is full of meaning." Ceremonial writing is so meaning-full that it overflows the fragile vessels of finite communication. This overflow means that the medium of meaning cannot be confined to whatever is conventionally understood as language. Mendelssohn continues: "full of meaning, ceaselessly awakening contemplation and giving occasion and opportunity for oral instruction" (JubA, 8: 169; J, 102–3). Theory is not, for Mendelssohn, practice; rather, practice gives rise to theory, which, however, is incapable of justifying the very practice of which it is the theory.[18] The contemplative life cannot take precedence over the active one; on the contrary, contemplation owes its origin and its solemnity—if not its specific *gravitas*—to these practices, regardless of which "exalted" object is under consideration. And speech, which, like contemplation, is occasioned by ceremonial practice, comes last, after the act. Since, however, the act is supposed to be regarded as a "mode of writing," it is possible to arrive at the surprising, if not paradoxical, thesis that speech comes after writing not only in a temporal sense but also in terms of priority. Such a thesis would scarcely be surprising, of course, if it were found among the writings of a Kabbalist,[19] and in the previous paragraph Mendelssohn had in fact echoed the words of certain "modern Kabbalists [*neurere Kabbalisten*]" whom he had recently cited: "In our teaching," according to the doctrine of the Lurianic Kabbalah, "everything is fundamental" (JubA, 8: 167; J, 101).[20] But Mendelssohn can hardly be considered a Kabbalist, even if he is not merely a spokesman for "the Enlightenment" either. The difference between Mendelssohn and Isaac Luria can be stated in an exact manner: whereas Luria understands the letters of the Torah as the ultimate a priori and therefore as the elements of creation that precede any vocalization, including the command "let there be light" (Gen. 1:1), Mendelssohn considers speech to be antecedent and ancillary only to one particular mode of writing—the mode of "*living* writing" that, unlike both hieroglyphic and alphabetic script, never gains independence from speech.

Just as Mendelssohn mentions the Kabbalistic a priori only in passing, he only touches for a brief moment on the doctrine that underlies his exposition of natural religion in the first part of *Jerusalem* and, accordingly, his interpretation of ceremonial script in the second—namely, the Platonic doctrine of anamnesis: "The instruction that we may give others is, in Socrates' apt phrase, merely a kind of midwifery [*einer Art von Geburtshülfe*]" (JubA, 8: 158; J, 91–92). More important to *Jerusalem* than the account of anamnesis in the *Meno* is the consequence Socrates draws from this account of the origin of the geometric knowledge in the closing passages of the *Phaedrus*. Indeed, Mendelssohn, who was often called—by way of antonomasia—"the Socrates of Berlin,"[21] excoriates the tendency toward writing he finds among his contemporaries in the same terms as the Socrates of Athens attacks his own compatriots. Both Socrateses express their fear of becoming merely "litterati" (JubA, 8: 170; J, 104). Following the venerable example of the earlier Socrates, Mendelssohn laments the temporal inversion that results from alphabetic writing: "hoary age has lost its venerableness, for the beardless youth knows more from books than the old man from experience" (JubA, 8: 170; J, 103). Yet, once again like Socrates, Mendelssohn does not simply condemn writing; another and more originary mode of script comes to the rescue of speech that would otherwise be helpless in the face of this perverse transformation of youth into old age and old age into youth. According to the older Socrates, this protoscript consists of "writing in the soul."[22] And the younger Socrates says the same thing: "eternal truths" are "legible" to and therefore inscribed in every human soul (JubA, 8: 160; J, 93).

Yet, for Mendelssohn, psychic inscription does not spell the end of the story. To be sure, it leads to "human salvation and felicity" as long as the soul learns to decipher its innate script; but every soul, from the moment of its birth, still needs to learn *how to learn*, and so every one is in want of something other than itself; indeed, souls cannot rest content with isolated and accidental "midwives," for every "midwife" similarly stands in need of other ones—ad infinitum. The need for learning in the secrets of learning cannot be fulfilled by any process of indoctrination. It can only be fulfilled *by time*—more time than anyone can reckon. The inversion of youth and old age serves as the trope of the revolutionary perversions that owe their origin to alphabetic modes of writing, which, regardless of their enormous advantages over transient speech and immobilized hieroglyphs, make theorems and techniques too readily available. Learning that learning needs time itself needs an historical—or, to use a more appropriate term, a *counterhistorical*—correlate: a continuous community of "midwives" that, for its part, serves to preserve the *discontinuity* between the linear temporality of individuals and the cyclical history of social and political orders. When Mendelssohn attacks Lessing's idea of an "Education of the Human Race,"[23] he operates on the same ground as his critique of religious oaths: just as human beings need time to say what they believe, they need time to develop themselves. And nothing—neither the ancient demand that one swear in the name of the Eternal nor the modern claim to a purely temporal perspective—has the power to cut this time short. Mendelssohn, like his friend, is interested in the "education of the human race," but the *basis* of this education must be secured—education is needed in the ways of education. And this basis is never secure enough to support anything "higher."

Ceremonial script is the basis for a nonindoctrinating and nondoctrinal process of learning how to learn, for it arrests speech for the right amount of time, long enough for it to do what it is supposed to do—communicate—but not so long that it produces purely visual mementos of forgotten metaphorical reductions. By virtue of its meaning*ful*ness, ceremonial script exceeds every effort to delimit and thereby determine its meaning once and for all. It thus functions as a constant reminder of the irreducible faultiness of human language. Whereas writing in the conventional sense replaces experience, ceremonial script repeatedly grants access to a "transcendental" experience: not an experience of the conditions under which communication is possible but, rather, the experience of linguistic unreliability. In his renunciation of religious oaths, Mendelssohn presents this experience in terms of a trope—the friction that makes movement possible: "Our ideas had to rub up against each other for a long time before they could be made to fit themselves to one another, and before we could say with assurance: Here we agree! O! I should never like to have for a friend anyone who has had this experience in his life. . . . " (JubA, 8: 134; J, 67). No one can say once and for all time what ceremonial script means to say—which means that such "living writing" is destined to be understood by those who stake their faith in the reliability of language as completely meaningless, mere ceremony, or, to use Mörschel's word, an "onerous" duty. By granting the experience of linguistic unreliability, ceremonial script makes it possible for communication both to take place *and* to be interrupted: it occasions ever-renewed conversations about its meaning, and yet it also guarantees that every conversation, especially ones devoted to the nature of the Eternal, are understood in advance to be incomplete. The imperfect and constantly interrupted character of these conversations cannot be understood in terms of progress toward a goal, moreover—not even in terms of an asymptotic approach toward the infinitely distant telos of discovering *the* meaning for the script that occasions conversation in the first place. For this metaphorical script does not have *a* meaning. The absence of *a* meaning does not mean, however, that its meaning simply succumbs to mere indeterminacy and that the symbolic "ceremonies" are empty after all. Such is the force of the term *bedeutungsvoll* (full of meaning) as the defining attribute of ceremonial script: it forestalls, without sublating, the conventional alternative between fixed meaning and indeterminate nonsense. Forever preliminary, incapable of coming to their appointed end, the ceremonies that should be regarded as a mode of writing cannot be considered practices in any sense: no deed is done, no task accomplished. Rather, these performances constitute a form of transcendental *poiesis*: time is *made*. Making time for—discussion about—the Eternal is, for Mendelssohn, "divine service." The time made for the Eternal never issues into a finished product: a "perfect" time, *kairos*, *Augenblick*, or "moment of truth." On the contrary, the unfinished character of this time brings the temporality of communication finally into sync with the solemnity surrounding the divine name.[24]

III.

Mendelssohn's conception of ceremonial script had no future. None of his loyal followers among the Maskilim developed or even adapted his exposition of the character and function of Jewish commandments.[25] And there is little doubt that *Jerusalem*, like *Morning Hours*, the other magnum opus Mendelssohn hastily wrote down in the last years of his quickly diminishing life, remains silent about many of the more pressing philosophical and doctrinal questions with which he was confronted. Both of these late works are less summations than lengthy admissions that their author is no longer in a position to produce the requisite treatise: he, too, has become untimely. Although *Jerusalem*, unlike *Morning Hours*, does not explicitly issue a plea for someone to come and rescue the fragile structure of thought Mendelssohn spent his life constructing—which has, in any case, been put to rest by the "all-destroying Kant" (JubA, 3, 2: 71–72)—it subtly marks its own status as a preliminary effort; it cuts short conversation about the meaning of Jewish commandments, as it simultaneously proposes a thesis according to which the fulfillment of these "prescriptions" is the occasion for discussions about their meaningfulness.

Mendelssohn's arguments in *Jerusalem* do not address any of the embarrassing problems of scriptural interpretation that Spinoza had posed to posterity in his *Tractatus theologico-politicus*,[26] and his mode of argumentation leaves the door open for those, like Hamann, who accuse him of abandoning the steadfast beliefs of his ancestors for an "atticism" that is indistinguishable from atheism.[27] Mendelssohn, moreover, underestimates the timeliness of Lessing's talk of the "education of the human race," as he delivers what amounts to his own confession of disbelief: "I, for my part, cannot conceive of the education of the human race as my late friend Lessing imagined it under the influence of I-don't-know-which historian of humanity" (JubA, 8: 162; J, 95). No less an authority on the limits of reason than the "all-destroying" Kant will attack *Jerusalem* on this point in the conclusion to his essay of 1793 "On the Old Saying: That May Work in Theory But Not in Practice" (Ak, 8: 307–12).[28] And the future was with these three: Spinoza, Hamann, and Kant, who laid the groundwork for German idealism. The German idealists—not Mendelssohn—gave direction to philosophies of Judaism and to Jewish philosophers in the coming centuries.

And yet, something of Mendelssohn's conception of a "living mode of writing" nevertheless did outlive *Jerusalem*. Although Mendelssohn ironically prefaces his exposition of divine legislation with an attack on writing in the ordinary sense—"we are all *litterati, letter people [Buchstabenmenschen]*" (JubA, 8: 170; J, 104)—all of the characteristics he attributes to ceremonial script will come to describe the critical performance of an extraordinary, non-everyday, playfully solemn language that calls itself "literary." Full of meaning, fluid in its meaningfulness, and thus transcending the horizons of fixed meaning; preliminary and yet always containing its own internal telos; executed with the utmost conviction and yet not undertaken in accordance with any doctrine to which one could now and forever swear allegiance; interrupted so as to present indirectly what infinitely recedes from representation: all these traits are applicable not only to the "living mode of script" as it was understood by Mendelssohn but also to "literature," as this term was beginning to be understood by the early German romantics. And for Friedrich Schlegel and his friends, "literature" is supposed to become the form of communication that Mendelssohn envisages: a *living* mode of writing, the purpose of which is to be sought in preliminary, endless—and therefore endlessly interrupted—conversations conducted by a community of writers. When one of Mendelssohn's daughters renames herself Dorothea, "gift of the god," and marries Friedrich Schlegel, prince of the early romantics, she doubtless abandons the tradition to which her father devoted his entire life; but in accordance with an irony that would perhaps amuse her father, however bitterly, more than her husband, she secretly carries on and carries out the otherwise arrested development of *Jerusalem.*

§ 3 "The Scale of Enthusiasm": Kant, Schelling, and Hölderlin

I. Magnetic Chains and Ionic Swarms

Ever since Plato deployed the word *entheos* in battle with the Homeric gods, it has played a critical role in a wide variety of attempts to define the relation between thinking, knowing, and speaking. The word *enthousiasmos* is of service to philosophy whenever a discussion turns toward something that cannot be understood as a particular case of a general rule and must therefore be considered singular. *Enthousiasmos* does not so much explain the singularity under discussion as mark the place of its inexplicability: a god is said to be responsible for something, but this god does not respond to any inquiries and cannot therefore serve as the basis of an unambiguous explanation. In the case of Ion—the flighty and, one might say, "ionic" rhetor whom Socrates encounters—the word comes to mark the singularity of his excitement: Ion is thrilled *only* when Homer is the topic of conversation, and he has things to say *only* about Homer; for this reason, nothing he says about Homer accedes to the generality of *technē* (know-how).[1] Socrates proposes the term *enthousiazein* as an explanation of the singularity of this "rhetorical" excitement. Ion is *ekphrōn*, "out of his mind," whenever he comes into contact with the Homeric poems. He is not alone, however, when he is *ekphrōn*: just as the god communicates to the poet his ability to communicate, the poet communicates to the rhetor this ability to communicate, and the rhetor communicates to his auditors this "enthusiasm" alone—no know-how, no *technē*, and no further ability to communicate. Whenever Ion comes into contact with the Homeric poems, he takes part in this paradoxical community: a community of singularities, each of whose ecstatic members is unaware of its very existence.

Yet the *Ion* does not conclude with Socrates' apparently "enthused" explanation for Ion's excitement[2]—apparently "enthused," because, as Ion concedes, Socrates' speech, like the poems about which he speaks, communicates something about which he is not in a position to speak: "somehow you touch my soul with your words" (535a). Socrates interrogates Ion a second time and in almost the same terms after this "touching" speech, for the rhetor rejects Socrates' explanation for the singularity of his excitement: he knows himself to be entirely *emphrōn*—sober, collected—at the very moment he turns his audience into an ecstatic collective. As long as he maintains that he remains "in his right mind," he cannot make good on the promise with which the dialogue begins—the promise to say what he knows, what he does, and therefore who he is. This is no small failure: the very possibility of an ordered community in which each member has a proper function rests on the ability of its members to make good on an original promise to say what they do (for the community) and, by so doing, define who they are, beyond their apparently arbitrary names. Ion, whose name may not be so arbitrary,[3] can abrogate this promise only if he admits to being an "enthusiast." The term *entheos* in the *Ion* does not so much explain anything as excuse an inexplicable singularity by making it part of a new multiplicity: the audience, the rhetor, the poet, and even the god are all held together in a "Heraclitean" or "magnetic" chain. Those who are able to communicate only the ability to communicate are unable to fulfill their promises; but they nevertheless belong to an ordered community. "Enthusiasm" thus becomes an ironic term of excuse—ironic at the very least because the "ionic" community to which the "enthusiasts" belong is always only a momentary assemblage, the origin of which is nevertheless supposed to be divine.

Because Ion cannot find the general term under which his activity falls and because he cannot therefore say what he is, he could be anything in the world. As Socrates says in the final discussion of the dialogue, Ion resembles no one so much as Proteus. As long as he rejects Socrates' interpretation of his excitability, Ion is not a being (*on*) but is, rather, a movement (*ion*) that—before, outside, or beyond *on*, understood in terms of constancy, standing still, or permanence—represents nothing in particular, nothing in general, and therefore *anything whatsoever*.[4] By speaking of Ion in terms of *entheos* Socrates places him in a well articulated "chain," grants him a certain distinction, and thereby assigns him a function after all: an unpromising and futile function, to be sure, but a function nevertheless. As long as Ion presents himself as one who does indeed represent—or acts as the spokesman for—the god, he no longer is anything whatsoever. A god who controls the "magnetic" chain of enthusiasm gives distinction to those who participate in the "ionic" communities of poetry and rhetoric; "anything whatsoever," by contrast, is a term for complete nondistinction. The ontological—or perhaps iontological—problem of enthusiasm can thus be stated in the following terms: *entheos* is a word by which an ion that would otherwise represent the greatest possible nondistinction is understood as an entity that stands for the greatest possible distinction: that between the divine and human.

Because Ion concedes to Socrates' interpretation of his singularity in the end and thus allows himself to be designated a spokesman for the god, the *Ion* is drawn toward an ironic solution to the question of how singularity comes to speech: it does so in the performance of a poem, that is, in the re-presentation of something "made" by a god. Nothing *about* which one speaks would be singular; indeed, everything about which a poem speaks, according to the premise of Socrates' interrogative procedure, belongs to a particular kind of general "know-how." The question remains, however: can singularity come to speech outside of a poetic performance? This question gains greater significance whenever it is assumed that the unnamed god about whom Socrates remains silent in the *Ion* does not have a Homeric provenance but is, instead, God, the absolutely unique and incomparable One from whom everything else originates, so incomparably unique that its proper name is as unpronounceable as its ultimate attributes are hidden. Speaking about this One, predicating something of the single God, and making statements concerning his nature would also bring singularity into speech, but those who speak about the One cannot escape the predicament in which, according to Socrates' interpretation, Ion finds himself whenever he touches on the Homeric poems: even when the Singular one is only the subject of predication, not the "maker" of the speech, the act of speaking is nonetheless singularized, for no *technē*, no body of knowledge, and no discursive faculty could offer a solid foundation upon which a true statement about the One could be made. Only the One could grant a basis upon which to speak in a positive manner about the One.

Ungrounded and therefore false statements about the One, by contrast, could have a variety of sources. If singularity cannot be predicated without the performance of this predication finding a ground in—or, as Socrates ironically proposes, a magnetic link to—the unique One about whom one speaks, whoever speaks in this way will be open to the accusation leveled against Ion: the speaker cannot disclose the basis for the speech in reality. Once "ideality" is no longer seen as the fundamental character of "what is" and, instead, is understood in terms of "mental contents," then it is possible to draw this conclusion: speakers who cannot ground their speech in something real—whether it be the One or the multiplicity of created things —can find a foundation for their speech only in something altogether "ideal": illusions, fantasies, creatures of the imagination. Those who speak about the One on the unstable basis of the imagination can no longer be interpreted as singularities who participate in an exalted community during the time of a poetic performance; on the contrary, such speakers are singular, not in the sense that they are more than a "natural" kind, but in the sense that they are *less* than a kind: oddities, aberrations, or monstrosities.

Numerous words designate those constitutively inconsistent pluralities that are less than a natural kind and something other than a well-ordered set. A particular importance accrues to one of these words because it points toward the natural—which is to say, nontranscendent—origin of "enthusiasm": *Schwarm,* "swarm." The members of a swarm are not only impossible to distinguish from one another but cannot, for this reason, even be called *members* of the swarm: instead of belonging to a stable collective according to which they would be recognized and named, each one is a temporary participant in an act of "swarming" or *Schwärmerei.* Whereas the term "enthusiasm" refers without ambiguity, although not without irony, to something more than humankind, *Schwärmerei* points toward something more and less than humankind—less than human because animals, not human beings, aggregate into swarms and more than human because the only animals whose pluralities turn into swarms are those that, like the gods, are able to take leave of the earth. A desire to depart from the earth, if only in a *Fischschwarm* (swarm of fish), is implied in every use of the term *Schwärmerei,* just as, *ordine inverso,* the descent of a god to the earth is implicated in Socrates' use of the term *entheos.* And "swarmers" associate with one another precisely because they desire something more than terrestrial society. According to Lessing, "*Schwärmer, Schwärmerei* comes from 'swarm,' 'to swarm,' particularly as it is used for bees. The desire to make a swarm is thus the definitive mark of the *Schwärmer.*"[5] By disassociating themselves from civil society, swarmers collect into noncivil, if not uncivil, nonsocial, if not antisocial, nonnatural, if not unnatural, and always temporary collectives.

The "swarmer" exists only in the swarm, just as the poet, the rhetor, and the audience of a poem exist only in relation to the god; but the relation of the "swarmers" to one another is not an *ordered* relation; no "magnetic" or "Herculean" chain holds them together, and so each "swarmer" is out of order, disorderly, odd, or, to use an already familiar word in another way, singular. *Schwärmerei* names the unstable condition of a coordinated disorderliness. *Schwärmer* may want to distinguish themselves from everyone else—and the origin of the word *Schwärmerei* in accusations of radical sectarianism points toward this desire—but the word itself says the opposite: the swarm allows for no distinctions within its ranks. The disorder of the swarm is reflected in the disorderly vision of the *Schwärmer*, and insofar as the term "world" already indicates a certain principle of ordering, the *Schwärmer* is not "otherworldly" or "spiritual," but not yet worldly.

Schwärmerei is therefore one of the terms by which the German *Aufklärung* sought to define itself. If those who champion *Aufklärung* speak of something singular—and in the context of the *Aufklärung*, this only means the One God—they speak of him only as something superlative: all "perfections" can be predicated of him. But if, as the *Critique of Pure Reason* sets out to show, this talk, too, is illegitimate; if nothing positive can be said of God, not even the statement "He exists," then it becomes impossible to avoid this question: under what conditions am I, or is the self, in a position to speak *of* singularity, especially when the self, too, is singular by virtue of its freedom? This chapter concerns two responses to these questions from the last years of the eighteenth century: one from the side of philosophical criticism (Schelling), the other from the side of critical poetology (Hölderlin). Both of these responses can be understood to develop the implications of Kant's sole definition of *Schwärmerei* within the space of the three *Critiques*, and both responses undertake a "critique" of critical thought that refines, redefines, and in the end finishes off Kant's definition. If the self-definition of the *Aufklärung* depends on the definition of a particularly unclear word—*Schwärmerei*—then the attempts to define this term can show the limits of the self upon which the appeal for "clearing up" finally depends. Because they leave no room for a God *about* whom one could speak, Schelling and Hölderlin together execute the Kantian legacy. Whereas Schelling seeks to save *Schwärmerei* as a term against which critical thought can define itself, Hölderlin allows for no such defensive self-definition: the principle of subjectivity—the principle upon which the critical project of a self-critique of reason rests—is shown to be nothing short of *Schwärmerei*.

II. "If in Its Most General Meaning *Schwärmerei* Is . . . " (Kant)

Enthousiasmos can be translated in many ways. The multiplicity of possible translations for this word would not of itself pose a problem if it would be possible to determine an experience through which its sense and meaning could be secured once and for all. But it is the point of Kantian critique to dispute the possibility of the experience named in the word "enthusiasm": something "holy," according to Kant, may make itself known to us in the announcement of an unconditioned law—we will come back to this—but a god cannot be said to *appear* as long as "god" refers to something unconditioned, for appearances are necessarily conditioned. "Enthusiasm" cannot therefore mean what it says. As long as something "holy," if not divine, makes itself known, however, the term "enthusiasm" does not have to be either ironic or "ionic." From his earliest writings onward, Kant is drawn into the critical project of distinguishing an empowering enthusiasm from a debilitating *Schwärmerei*. This project becomes all the more important when, following the publication of the three *Critiques*, the very act of reading Kant—especially a Kant who assumes the divine function of "lawgiver and patron of peace"—is itself considered a cause for enthusiasm. No one expressed this enthusiasm better than Hölderlin, who, in a letter to his brother, calls Kant "the Moses of our nation" (SW, 6: 304).[6]

In an early text, "Essay on the Sicknesses of the Head," Kant proposes to distinguish enthusiasm from *Schwärmerei* on the basis of an impressive but nevertheless indefinite criterion: the former gives rise to great action, whereas the latter remains within the inactive sphere of imagined intimacy:

> This ambiguous appearance of fantasy [*Phantasterei*] in moral sentiments that are in themselves good is enthusiasm [*Enthusiasmus*], and nothing great in the world has been done without it. Things are altogether different with the fanatic (visionary, *Schwärmer*). The latter is actually a lunatic with a supposed immediate inspiration and great intimacy with the powers of heaven. Human nature knows no more dangerous delusion. (Ak, 2: 267)

When fantasy appears "in" moral sentiments, they acquire a degree of power, converted from mere sentiments into "great" actions "in the world." Since, however, fantasy is not itself grounded in these sentiments, it cannot be judged altogether good. Fantasy makes up for a failure on the part of "moral sentiments" to ground action on their own, and the phenomenon of enthusiasm is supposed to bear witness to this phantasmagoric function. "Enthusiasm" names the condition under which moral feeling turns into worldly action; but it is not a *pure* condition of conversion. "Essay on the Sicknesses of the Head" seeks empirically recognizable causes not only for the sicknesses that it identifies but also for the ambiguous state of health in which great things are done in the world. Enthusiasm must therefore have an empirical cause, and Kant has no better name for this cause than the rather fantastic term *Phantasterei.*

This term is a monument to one of Kant's earliest attempts to address a problem whose solution will ultimately disclose the pillar on which the critical metaphysics that he projects will henceforth rest: under what condition does the possibility of morality make moral action necessary? In "Essay on the Sicknesses of the Head," the possibility of morality is understood in terms of "moral sentiment," moral action in terms of those things that are "great in the world," and the ambiguous condition of conversion from possibility into actuality in terms of an "enthusiasm" that stands opposed to *Schwärmerei.* By the time Kant comes to write his groundbreaking exploration of the principle of morality in *Laying the Ground for the Metaphysics of Morals* (1785), each of the terms of the schema changes, but a radicalized version of this schema still structures his thought: no empirical cause serves as a condition under which the possibility of morality is translated into moral action; the possibility of morality, being able to be moral, is itself the condition for morally sanctioned conduct *under the ambiguous condition* that the agent regards itself as altogether free. Transcendental freedom thus takes over the function of enthusiasm: "nothing great in the world has been done without it" (Ak, 2: 267).[7] And the entire project of laying the ground not only for the metaphysics of morals but for metaphysics as such rests on the principle that the actions of human beings can be and therefore, from a certain perspective, *must* be regarded as free. Because this freedom is unconditional, however, it is impossible to construct a general rule under which a particular case of free action could be recognized. No one who is free, in turn, can be treated as a particular case that falls under a general rule, and so everyone must be regarded as singular. As long as the singularity implied in the claim to freedom is grounded in the universality of the law under which those who claim to be free must act, it remains a *well-ordered* singularity, and those free beings who submit themselves to the order of an absolutely universal law do not so much aggregate into a *Schwarm* as constitute its exact inversion: an active order of singularities, a nonnatural, immediate, and thus magical chain of moral enthusiasts—or, to use the critical vocabulary developed in the *Critique of Pure Reason*, a *"corpus mysticum* of rational beings" (A, 808; B, 836).

From *Laying the Groundwork for the Metaphysics of Morals* through the *Critique of Practical Reason* and *Religion Within the Limits of Reason Alone* to the *Metaphysics of Morals*, Kant laid out the same fundamental and irresolvable circle: transcendental freedom is the condition under which an agent can respond to a categorical, apodictic, unconditional—which is to say, moral—command *as* a command addressed to the agent; but according to Kant, the freedom of the agent can be recognized only in the experience of being commanded to act without regard for empirical conditions. But this "experience" of being commanded is so unlike any other experience that it threatens to undo the unity of experience. Saying "I am free" does not amount to *Schwärmerei* only if this statement is understood to mean I recognize "in myself" unconditional commands. But, once again, this is the recognition of something singular—a unique "fact of pure reason." To the extent that this fact is singular, it cannot be said simply to fall under the concept "fact" but must, instead, present itself as a "fact, as it were [*gleichsam ein Faktum*],"[8] and the recognition of this fact can itself be understood only as a recognition "as it were." The supreme point of Kantian criticism, *das Faktum der reinen Vernunft*, cannot escape an association with the operation by which "Essay on the Sicknesses of the Head" describes the generation of *Schwärmerei*: moral commands may do without "inner vision," but the *exposition* of the basic principle on which all of the *Critique*s will come to rest—the principle of autonomy—cannot do without certain *Gleichnisse* (likenesses, images). Saying "I am free" cannot be justified unless the statement includes at least one *gleichsam* (as it were).

Yet there is an even more compelling reason to associate the supreme point of Kantian criticism with enthusiasm: the very fact that moral commands are unconditional brings them into the vicinity of *Schwärmerei*. The definition Kant proposes for this term in the section of the *Critique of Practical Reason* (1788) devoted to the "driving springs [*Triebfedern*] of pure practical reason" is therefore of no small significance for the entire critical project. It is not only the *sole* definition of *Schwärmerei* within any of the *Critique*s, it is also a definition about which Kant seems to hold certain reservations, for he proposes it in the form of a conditional judgment: "If in its most general meaning [*in der allergemeinsten Bedeutung*] *Schwärmerei* is a transgression of the limits of human reason undertaken according to principles . . . " (Ak, 5: 85). This definition of *Schwärmerei* is conditional for at least one reason: it does not correspond to the general tendency of Kant's other definitions of this word. The last word Kant would associate with *Schwärmerei* in his many anthropological reflections on "sicknesses of the head" is "principles" (*Grundsätze*). In these lectures and writings, as in most contemporaneous attempts on the part of those engaged in the project of *Aufklärung* to explain the supposedly irrational character of *Schwärmer*, the word is defined in terms of vision, fantasy, imagination, figurality, "symbols"—or *Phantasterei*.[9] The remarkable character of the definition that Kant proposes in the *Critique of Practical Reason* can perhaps be judged by citing Lewis White Beck's otherwise meticulous translation: "If fanaticism in its most general sense is a deliberate overstepping of the limits of human reason . . . "[10] The word "principles" drops out. If *Schwärmerei* is "principled," it cannot be wholly irrational, and if its principle is freedom—from limits, conditions, natural causes—it moves in the direction of the very doctrine Kant is in the process of defining. Defending this doctrine against *Schwärmerei* demands that the latter be defined in the first place; that is, it must have limits, even if this consists of taking a stand against limits. The conditionality of Kant's definition, for this reason, deserves more attention. The limit on the use of the term *Schwärmerei*, its "definition," is predicated on the definition of another, and even more problematic term: *moralische Schwärmerei*. The fate of enthusiasm within the context of Kantian thought is inscribed within these paragraphs of the *Critique of Practical Reason*.

There are at least two further reasons—the first developed later by Schelling, the second by Hölderlin—for the conditional character of Kant's only definition of *Schwärmerei* within the space of the *Critiques*.

A.

Kant may have placed the definition of *Schwärmerei* in conditional terms because the definition on which it is predicated—that of "moralische Schwärmerei"—is itself problematic from the perspective of reason's self-critique. The moral law, by definition, commands unconditionally, and as Kant explains in the very first words of the second *Critique*, he has therefore chosen not to write a *Critique of Pure Practical Reason*, but, rather, a *Critique of Practical Reason*: pure practical reason requires no critique; on the contrary, it is precisely what ought to be *promoted*, for it is morality itself (Ak, 5: 3). One can, of course, transgress the limits of pure practical reason—this would be the most general definition of immorality—but it appears entirely problematic, if not impossible, to transgress these limits in the direction of being "too moral" or "too virtuous." Kant's renunciation of the classical ethics of the "just mean" supplies sufficient proof of this: "to be too virtuous—that is, to be too attached to one's duty—would be almost equivalent to making a circle round or a straight line too straight" (*Metaphysics of Morals*, Ak, 6: 434). In the *Religion Within the Limits of Reason Alone* Kant defends his "rigorism" against Schiller's polemical remarks in "On Grace and Dignity" (Ak, 6: 23), and it is this defense, perhaps more than anything else, that imparts to Kant the image of a "moral *Schwärmer*" in the eyes of certain of his readers—in those of Goethe's brother-in-law, Johann Schlosser, for example,[11] who, by attacking Kant during the 1790s, instigated one of the last scenes of mutual accusations of *Schwärmerei* in the eighteenth century. Schlosser takes offense at Kant's unorthodox conception of religion and attacks the "inhuman" doctrine of moral conduct upon which this conception is founded.[12] Because critical philosophy does not recognize "human" limitations, Schlosser presents it as a version of moral *Schwärmerei*, and Kant responds in kind by accusing Schlosser—and an unnamed nobleman who had recently translated Plato's *Ion*[13]—of theoretical *Schwärmerei*. Only a univocal definition of *Schwärmerei* could bring these reciprocal accusations to an end, but the definition of this term presupposes a definition of human limits as such, and this, in turn, demands an answer to the question to which, according to Kant, all questions of philosophy "in its cosmopolitan sense" ultimately refer: *was ist der Mensch?*[14]

Kant's definition of moral *Schwärmerei* is meant to forestall the accusation that his moral rigorism amounts to an excessive and, at least to this extent, *schwärmische* morality, an accusation that is not altogether unjustified, since moral demands, according to Kant, exceed terrestrial conditions: when one experiences the singular feeling of *Achtung* (respect, attention) and thus attends to one's duty, one must no longer pay any attention to natural limitations. Making oneself too virtuous should therefore be considered exactly equivalent to making a circle round, which is to say, doing what is demanded if there is to be a circle—or virtue—in the first place. Moral *Schwärmerei* must therefore be defined in such a way as to disregard the concept of virtue: a moral *Schwärmer*, according to Kant's initial treatment of the term in the *Critique of Practical Reason*, does not seek exceptional virtue but, rather, claims to "possess" an inviolable "purity." Instead of attending to "holy prescriptions" from which everyone re-

mains at a certain remove, moral *Schwärmer* regard themselves as holy and
thus deceive themselves into believing that moral action can be done au-
tomatically, as it were, on the basis of their successfully secured holiness.
All action that is not grounded on moral commands alone is, according to
Kant, based on certain pathological inclinations, and moral *Schwärmer* are
therefore those who have worked themselves into a position where they
confuse their pathos with holiness. But Kant does not conclude his dis-
cussion of moral *Schwärmerei* with a diagnosis of this "confusion of feel-
ing." Instead, he undertakes a definition of the term and in the course of
defining it does not so much erase the distinction between the clarity of
his own doctrine and the confusion of moral *Schwärmer* as inscribe the
"holy prescriptions" to which his doctrine appeals within *another*, this
time "critical" enthusiasm: an enthusiasm in which absolutely nothing is
communicated—no philosophical knowledge, no technical "know-how"
other than the ability of the law to communicate itself. The law thus oc-
cupies the place Socrates assigned to the god in his interpretation of the
singularity of Ion's excitability:

> If in its most general meaning *Schwärmerei* is a transgression of the limits of
> human reason undertaken according to principles, then moral *Schwärmerei* is
> this transgression of the limits that pure practical reason poses to humanity
> through which it forbids us to place the subjective determining ground of du-
> tiful actions, that is, their dutiful driving spring, anywhere else than in the law
> itself, and to posit the disposition [*Gesinnung*] that is thereby brought into the
> maxims elsewhere than in the respect for this law [*Achtung für das Gesetz*]; it
> commands that we make the thought of duty, which strikes down all *arro-
> gance* as well as idle *philautia*, the supreme life-principle [*Lebensprinzip*] of all
> morality in man. (Ak, 5: 85–86)

This definition of moral *Schwärmerei* would follow directly from the
conditional definition of *Schwärmerei* if it were not for one unresolved
problem: pure practical reason poses limits on human *action*—*not* on
"humanity" (*Menschheit*) itself. The latter is doubtless "limited" (finite),
but no human being *ought* to respect any natural (pathological) limita-
tions in determining a course of action. Kant's definition thus takes a cu-
rious direction: whereas it is supposed to draw a boundary between his
own doctrine and *Schwärmerei*, it concludes by speaking of morality tak-
ing up residence "in man." And since the moral law, as Kant emphasizes
again and again, not only is "holy" but is our only access to a justifiable

concept of God and is therefore in its own way "divine,"[15] its ability to inhabit, if not possess "man" gives rise to something like a critical *enthousiasmos*. In order to defend his doctrine from the accusation of enthusiasm, Kant gestures toward a distinction for which he has no clearly defined terms, an otherwise impossible distinction between a criminal transgression and a noncriminal, if not altogether innocent, overstepping of the limits imposed on humanity.

The first term by which he wishes to install this distinction is "novel writing" (*Romanschreibung*). Writing novels runs counter to critical reflection insofar as it fails to recognize any limit to the possibility of moral perfection. But novelists, rather than being alone in this failure, are its representatives. Anyone who entertains the idea of moral perfection as something other than a *sheer* possibility—a possibility without the possibility of its actualization—engages in a version of novel writing. Failure to recognize the necessity of this sheer possibility gives rise to the fictional discourses of novelists, educators, and Stoic moral philosophers. The massive discourse of "aesthetic education" unleashed by Schiller's *Aesthetic Letters*—to say nothing of the less conspicuous but nevertheless significant burst of edifying novels inspired by Kant's *Critique*s[16]—takes its point of departure from this association of literature with education in the context of a rigorous doctrine of moral practice. Another "if" seals the definition of "moral *Schwärmerei*" and begins the next paragraph:

> If this is so, then not only novelists [*Romanschreiber*], or sentimental educators (even though they may be zealously opposed to sentimentalism [*Empfindelei*]), but also philosophers and indeed the most rigorous of them, the Stoics, have introduced moral *Schwärmerei* instead of a sober [*nüchtern*] but wise moral discipline, although the *Schwärmerei* of the latter was more heroic, while that of the former is more shallow and pliable. (Ak, 5: 86)

"Sober *but* wise": the definition of *Schwärmerei* comes down to this phrase, for it captures the criteria by which Kant distinguishes his own doctrine from the discourse of novelists. Sobriety by itself is not wisdom, as the "but" indicates; and wisdom, as the Stoics demonstrate, is not always sober. "Sobriety" does not simply mean being aware, staying awake, opening one's eyes, or even waking up from "dogmatic slumbers."[17] It also means acknowledging the possibility of a sheer possibility, a possibility—and indeed the most necessary of all possibilities, moral perfection—which nevertheless cannot under any condition be understood to have been realized: "the sage (of the Stoics)," according to the *Critique of Pure Reason*, "is an ideal, that is, someone who exists merely in thought" (A, 569; B, 597). As long as the aim of novel writing is to make pure possibilities—"ideals," fictional beings—appear to be realiz*able* by integrating them into spatial-temporal frameworks, anyone who claims to be able to realize the possibility of wisdom takes part in a "novelistic" failure: each one converts a sheer possibility into an apparently real one. Sobriety, by contrast, consists in a recognition of an impossibility that is nevertheless possible—by virtue of being demanded unconditionally. Those who are sober know that they are supposed to be wise but acknowledge, with regret, that wisdom is never more than a possibility and that the sage is never more than a *pure* fiction. Any claim to have realized this fiction, even if this realization takes place only in the fictional form of the novel, does violence to its purity and likewise robs a sheer possibility of its power. The *Critique of Practical Reason* could therefore be called the *Critique of Impure Fiction*.

The *Critique of Practical Reason* is nevertheless, from its inception, dedicated to the principle that pure reason *can* be practical. This "can" must be kept "sober," and this silent "must" is as significant an imperative as the categorical one. No one can secure the condition under which the ability to be moral turns into the actuality of moral conduct—or, to cite the "Essay on the Sicknesses of the Head" once again, something great is done in the world. It is therefore no small matter to understand what Kant means by "sobriety": it names the affective condition for the possibility of the effectiveness of pure practical reason. The term "sobriety" thus replaces the one Kant elsewhere favors, namely "critique." The *Critique of Practical Reason* could be given the more active and thus more effective title: *Sobering Wisdom*. And yet, according to an irony that accords with the topic of enthusiasm, nowhere does Kant appear less sober than in the subsequent paragraph of the second *Critique*, where he interrupts the exposition of his argument by naming the singularity in whose favor the very discourse and style of argumentation is undertaken in the first and last place:

> *Duty!* You sublime great name that embraces nothing charming or insinuating but requires submission and yet seeks not to move the will by threatening aught that would arouse natural aversion or terror, but only holds forth a law which of itself finds entrance into the mind and yet gains reverence [*Verehrung*] against my will (though not always obedience), before whom all inclinations are silenced. . . . What origin is there worthy of you, and where to

find the root of your noble descent, which proudly rejects all kinship with in-
clinations . . . ? (Ak, 5: 86)

Kant does not simply address duty in this rare rhetorical outburst to a
noble patron: duty makes possible the apostrophe to duty, hence to *itself*,
by silencing all other voices, including Kant's. Only when all these voices
have fallen silent can anyone act as the spokesman for the abstract term
duty. Kant's apostrophe does not so much speak the language of duty—it
is an address, not an imperative—as communicate the ability of the law to
communicate on its own, without any prior condition other than the un-
recognizable condition of transcendental freedom. Inasmuch as duty is
here called a *name*, not a concept, it designates some*one*, not something;
inasmuch as it is a *sublime* name, it rises above every common name or
noun; thus ennobled, without earthly kinships, swarming finally removes
itself entirely from the order of generality; and inasmuch as it is singled out
in the address, it comes forth—or perhaps, like Astrea, withdraws (Ak, 6:
190)—as a You through which the I itself is defined: a You by virtue of
which the "authentic self" (Ak, 5: 118) *is* a self in the first place.[18] By inter-
rupting the course of a philosophical "analytic," the apostrophe may not
associate Kant's program with "novel writing," but it nevertheless shows
that the discourse by which human reason justifies its practices is itself
grounded in a prior discourse, the language of hymnic address. Duty, con-
verted into a heroic demigod by virtue of antonomasia, is not only singu-
lar; it founds the universal order of singularity Kant generally calls "the
kingdom of ends." This kingdom, without a prince, realizes—without ever
coming into existence—the idea of the swarm: infinite and therefore in-
consistent pluralization. The conditional definition of *moralische Schwärm-
erei* thus draws Kant toward a question from which he shies away: under
what condition can one speak not of critical enthusiasm but of a *sober* one?
This is the question to which Hölderlin will turn when he presents the re-
lation between poetry, knowledge, and *Schwärmerei*.

B.

Kant may have presented his definition of *Schwärmerei* "in its most gen-
eral meaning" under the sign of conditionality for another reason. He had
only recently published his contribution to the so-called *Pantheismusstreit*,
"What Does It Mean: To Orient Oneself in Thinking?" (1786), and it is
in view of Spinoza—not just his exceptional thought but his exemplary

life—that debates around the idea of enthusiasm took another turn. Unlike Swedenborg, for example, Spinoza could hardly be accused of allowing himself to be swept up in his own imagination, "symbols," or *Phantasterei*. And yet, in a certain sense, "enthusiasm" is found in the very heart of Spinoza's speculative system: God is not "in us," to be sure, but, in reverse, we are all "in" God or nature. If Kant wants to enlist Spinoza into the ranks of *Schwärmer*, then he cannot define *Schwärmerei* in terms of imagination, fantasy, or figuration, for, as Kant knows—although he may know very little else about the legendary "atheist"—Spinoza makes no use of these in the explication of his system and indeed condemns them as sources of error. One definition of *Schwärmerei*, however, could be understood to include the author of the *Ethics*, since this work postpones talk of "human reason" until the second book: "If in its most general meaning *Schwärmerei* is a transgression of the limits of human reason undertaken according to principles . . . " The principle on which Spinoza transgresses the limits of *human* reason is the principle of principles—the principle of reason, or, as Lessing says, *a nihilo nihil fit.*[19] The conflict over Spinoza did not simply erupt because Jacobi had divulged a secret about Lessing and, by doing so, caused great discomfort to Mendelssohn, his friend, but because Jacobi proceeds to present Spinoza's *Ethics* as the ineluctable outcome of all philosophical speculation: under the principle of reason, every doctrine turns into an expression of "nihilism," a term Jacobi invented,[20] which is tantamount to a furious denial of freedom.

However complicated the swarm of controversy unleashed by Jacobi's publication of the most famous *Aufklärer*'s alleged allegiance to Spinoza, the question around which it turns always remains simple: can anyone, or anything, be said to be free? Whatever is said to be free is singular; but all talk of singularity—regardless of whether it is the singularity of Spinoza's "substance" or the singularity of Jacobi's *salto morale*—implies a certain enthusiasm, if not *Schwärmerei*. To the extent that the term *Schwärmerei* arises out of an experience of disorderly swarming in which the *Schwärmer* loses all sense of direction, it calls for a radical reorientation, and the only point of reference for an orientation of thinking that does not depend on the dogmatic assumption of "right thinking" will be the principle upon which all thinking about movement, motives, and motivation—or, in short, practical reasoning—is based; namely, the principle of freedom. "What Does It Mean: To Orient Oneself in Thinking?" thus gravitates toward Kant's impassioned plea for freedom *of* thought. This freedom is endangered, according to Kant, whenever self-proclaimed "geniuses" exempt themselves from the generality of law, including the laws of thought, and thereafter seek to demonstrate their exceptionality. And the freedom of thought cannot do without a certain freedom of speech, as Kant himself insists in the closing paragraphs of "What Is Enlightenment?" (Ak, 8: 41). The paradox of transcendental freedom, the very possibility of which cannot be comprehended, comes into its own whenever "free thinking" is brought into conflict with "free speech." Only a self-restrained speech—more precisely, speech that refrains from expressing "free thinking"—allows for a space and a time in which there can be *self-sustaining* freedom of speech. Kant orients his thought toward such a space-time: it is the multidimension of "openness" or "publicity." Spinozism demands a renewed encounter with *Schwärmerei* once it becomes public. Whereas novelists are *Schwärmer* insofar as they present the sheer possibility of moral perfection as a fictional reality, Spinozists are enthusiasts insofar as they suppose they are in a position to proclaim that an independent, perfectly moral being is *impossible*:

> The *Critique* [*of Pure Reason*] shows that, in order to assert the possibility of a being which is itself an object of thought, it is not nearly enough that its concept should be free from contradiction (although it remains permissible to assume this possibility when there arises a case of need [*nötigenfalls*]). Spinozism, however, proposes to have perceived the impossibility of a being, the idea of which consists solely of pure concepts of the understanding that have only been detached from all conditions of sense-experience, and in which it is therefore impossible ever to discover a contradiction; yet it is altogether incapable of supporting this excessive demand [*Anmaßung*], which goes beyond all limits. For precisely this reason Spinozism leads directly to *Schwärmerei*. (Ak, 8: 143)[21]

Spinozism and criticism agree on a least one point: the possibility of an entity completely detached from sense-experience does not go without saying. But something, according to Kant, can be said in favor of this sheer possibility: such an entity cannot be known, to be sure, since knowledge is grounded in the possibility of sense-experience. Whenever there is an emergency (*nötigenfalls*), like the strife unleashed by Jacobi's publication, this pure possibility comes to fulfill a need (*Bedürfnis*), more exactly, "the need of reason" (Ak, 8: 140–41). Spinozism, by contrast, leaves no room for the mere possibility of a "detached" being to whom all other beings would nevertheless owe their origin. According to Spinozism, a self-sufficient intellect is not simply unpresentable; it is altogether impossible. For Kant, this amounts to a denial of a God in whose existence one can have a rational faith. But the denial could also mean, on second thought—or for another Kant—that reason has no place for an *agent* who detaches *itself* from "all conditions of sense-experience" for the tautological reason that the agent consists solely in acting. A *radical* criticism, according to which all talk of "things in themselves" is itself an *Anmaßung* (unwarranted demand), develops on the basis of the distinction between these two explications of this detachment. Spinozism leads toward *Schwärmerei* insofar as the being about which it speaks is so singular that everything different, including the one who speaks about it, is only its modification, and so everything, including the self, subsists in God or nature. "There is no more secure means of eradicating *Schwärmerei* at the root [*mit der Wurzel*]," Kant concludes, "than the determination of the limits of the pure faculty of reason" (Ak, 8: 143). But this still leaves the question: what is the root of all possible *Schwärmerei*? Under what condition does one say, "I am not free," which is to say, "I do not act" and therefore "I do not exist"? It is toward these questions that the young Schelling turns in his belated contribution to the Mendelssohn-Jacobi controversy, *Philosophical Letters on Dogmatism and Criticism* (1795).

III. "The Middle-Point of All Possible *Schwärmerei*" (Schelling)

Instead of recommending a medicine (*Mittel*) to eradicate *Schwärmerei*, the young Schelling seeks out its middle point (*Mittelpunkt*)—a position in which he finds himself when he reaches the eighth of his "philosophical letters": "By speaking of the moral principle of dogmatism, I believe that I am at the middle point of all possible *Schwärmerei*" (HKA, 3: 85).[22] Once he has reached this point, he can overcome the distance demanded by the epistolary form of communication and join his addressee: "Here, my friend, we stand at the principle of all *Schwärmerei*" (HKA, 3: 90). The plurality of enthusiasms converges on this "moral principle," which is not *itself* a kind of *Schwärmerei*—not even of "moral *Schwärmerei*"— but, rather, the law of its generation. From this point of view Schelling's *Philosophical Letters* presents itself as a universal solution to the problem of *Schwärmerei*. Once the "friend" whom Schelling addresses is able to meet him at the point from which enthusiasm originates, he will have distanced himself from every kind of enthusiasm.[23] But the radicality of his analysis drives Schelling to the point where *any* self-expression is necessarily nonenthusiastic: I cannot under any condition mean what I say when I say, "I am a *Schwärmer*." The meaning of *Schwärmerei* thus lies in the impossibility of meaning to be a *Schwärmer*.

As Schelling announces in the preface, the *Philosophical Letters* aims to set out the terms of a distinction, between dogmatism and criticism, that is not sharply enough drawn in the *Critique of Pure Reason*. This distinction is of decisive significance to philosophy, since dogmatism and criticism do not simply hold conflicting opinions about something, they name completely opposed systems about everything—or, more precisely, about the nature of the unconditioned, the absolute or, to use a misleading word, God. Conflict cannot take place about the absolute unless one has already established a distance from it. Criticism and dogmatism are, according to Schelling, the two possible positions from which to stand with respect to the absolute: "Anyone whose task consists in settling the dispute [*Streit*] of *philosophers* must proceed from precisely the point from which the dispute of *philosophy* itself, or, to say the same, the original conflict [*Widerstreit*] in the human *spirit* [*Geist*], proceeds. But this point is none other than the departure from the absolute, for we would all be one concerning the absolute if we never left its sphere" (HKA, 3: 60). In the simplest of terms— and Schelling promises clarity, if not simplicity, in the preface—criticism proposes to found a system in which the absolute is understood as the subject (the I, or the self), whereas dogmatism proposes to establish a system in which the absolute is understood as the object (the not-I, Spinoza's substance, or the thing-in-itself). The singularity of the absolute, its ability to escape the schemata of subsumption whereby a particular falls under a generality, guarantees that it—the absolute—will always be absolutely ambiguous: it can be systematized in two ways, and neither of these two systems can say what it means to say; each system can only announce, in two different versions or two opposing tonalities, "I demand . . . "

Although there is little doubt that *Philosophical Letters*, like Schelling's other contemporaneous writings, is meant to elucidate and thereby promote "criticism,"[24] it does not simply reject dogmatism; on the contrary, it seeks to show that the latter, like criticism, is *theoretically* irrefutable. The same cannot be said of what Schelling calls "dogmaticism," and the opening letters consist for the most part in the refutation of the apparently critical systems developed by Schelling's more orthodox teachers in the Lutheran Theological Seminary in Tübingen—*apparently* critical because they constantly cite Kant's *Critique*s and, in particular, make use of their gestures toward an apology "without hypocrisy" for Christianity (Ak, 5: 86), but they are nevertheless uncritical for the simple reason that they rely at every point on a thing-in-itself; they still consider it acceptable to speak *about* God without having to inquire into the freedom upon which the act of speaking is itself based.[25] For Schelling, there is only one representative of genuine dogmatism, Spinoza, whose major work not only represents a thoroughgoing dogmatic system but points toward the *practical* resolution of the dispute within philosophy by presenting this system in terms of an "ethics." In order for the dispute to be settled with a *theorem*, either the subject or the object would have to be shown to be absolute; but an absolute subject is no longer a subject, and an absolute object is no longer an object: "If the conflict between subject and object stops, then the subject must no longer have the need to step outside itself; both must become absolutely identical, that is, either the subject must lose itself in the object or the object must lose itself in the subject" (HKA, 3: 64). For the subject to win the dispute, it would have to lose itself, and for the object to win, it would have to do the same. No wonder *Philosophical Letters* veers toward a definition of *Schwärmerei* and ends up with an unprecedented discussion of tragedy.

"One or the other must happen. Either no subject and an absolute object or no object and an absolute subject. How can this dispute be settled?" (HKA, 3: 65). The dispute can be decided, according to Schelling, only by converting a theoretical statement about the nature of the absolute into an ethical postulate to make good on this theorem: "Here philosophy passes into the domain of *demands* [*Foderungen*], that is, into the domain of practical philosophy, and here must the principle that we established at the beginning of philosophy and that was dispensable for theoretical philosophy if it was to constitute a separate domain decide the victor" (HKA, 3: 65). Every assertion about the absolute is, therefore, as Schelling remarks, "proleptic" (HKA, 3: 80): it does not solve the unique problem of philosophy—"the riddle of the world" (HKA, 3: 78), the enigma that there *is* a world of finite things after all—but, instead, anticipates a solution in lieu of its practical realization: "No philosopher will imagine having done *everything* merely by setting up the highest principles. For those principles themselves have as foundations of his system only subjective value; that is, they are valid *for him* only insofar as he has anticipated *his* practical decision" (HKA, 3: 81). One may want to say something about the absolute—and this desire, for Schelling, gives rise to the word *philosophy*—but every assertion about the absolute is at bottom a self-assertion: each one says not precisely *what* the speaker will decide to be but *if* the speaker will decide *to be* at all: "'To be or not to be'" (HKA, 3: 89; quoted in English) is the question every genuine system of philosophy (theoretically) answers in advance of *the* (practical) decision.

From this perspective Schelling not only comes to the resolution of a theoretically irresolvable problem, the nature of the absolute, but also approaches the root of all *Schwärmerei*. According to the seventh letter, the *Critique of Pure Reason* and the Jacobi-Mendelssohn dispute result in the same demand: the two genuine philosophical systems—unlike "dogmaticism," which still speaks of a creation *ex nihilo*—join together in demanding that there be absolutely no passage from the infinite to the finite: "Philosophy cannot, to be sure, pass from the infinite to the finite, but it can nevertheless pass from the finite to the infinite" (HKA, 3: 83). Both criticism and dogmatism "postulate" this passage, but they do so in opposite ways: criticism demands that the I strive to be infinite, whereas dogmatism demands that the I "collapse [*unterzugehen*] into the infinitude of the absolute object" (HKA, 3: 84). Dogmatism thus comes down to the command "annihilate yourself [*Vernichte dich selbst*]!" (HKA, 3: 84), and it is in the command of self-annihilation that Schelling finally finds the "middle point of all possible *Schwärmerei*" (HKA, 3: 85). There is no limit to the number of different modes of *Schwärmerei*, but all modes of *Schwärmerei* make the otherwise unbearable thought of nonbeing into an uplifting, lighter-than-air notion:

> The holiest thoughts of the ancients and the monstrosities of human insanity come together. 'Return to the divinity, the primal source of all existence, unification with the absolute, annihilation of oneself'—is the principle of all *schwärmerisch* philosophy, which has only been laid out, interpreted, veiled in images by different people in different ways, according to their cast of mind and thought. The principle for the history of all *Schwärmerei* is to be found here. (HKA, 3: 85–86)

But this, the principle for the history of all *Schwärmerei*, is not yet the principle of *Schwärmerei* itself. The thought of self-annihilation can be made bearable if the self "outlives" (HKA, 3: 84) its own annihilation, and it can do so only because of something "we" all do: we "translate" (*über-*

tragen) the word "being" from its literal, or "proper," sense to an improper, or metaphorical sense (HKA, 3: 87). The origin of *Schwärmerei*—which is now tantamount to the command "annihilate yourself!"—can henceforth be sought in a fundamental failure of nonphilosophical language: nonphilosophers mean "appearances" or "nonbeing" when they say "being"; every nonphilosopher is therefore a philosopher of nonbeing—and a potential *Schwärmer*. The *Übertragen* of "being" from the I to the not-I makes it bearable (*erträglich*) to demand that the passage (*Übergang*) from the finite to the infinite result in an absolute not-I, for "being," properly understood, outlives this annihilation—and *I is being in the proper sense of the word.*

About this Schelling has no doubts: they would arise only when an intuition is lacking, but it is impossible, according to Schelling, for one to lack self-intuition and still be oneself. Schelling's exposition of the principle of *Schwärmerei* depends on a self-intuition in which the self reveals itself to itself: "A secret, marvelous capacity [*Vermögen*] dwells within all of us: to withdraw ourselves from the alteration of time into our greatest inwardness, to withdraw ourselves from everything that comes from the outside, and there, under the form of immutability to intuit the eternal in us" (HKA, 3: 87).[26] Schelling considers himself justified in using the term "intuition" for this revelation of the self to itself because Kant had defined "intuition" at the very opening of the first *Critique* as a singular, immediate, and hence nonderivable relation. What corresponds to this definition better than the relation of the self to itself? This relation (*Beziehung*) can then be seen to consist in a withdrawal (*Zurückziehung*) from everything outside the self, and since this withdrawal leaves no room for sensation, self-intuition must be considered "intellectual": "This intellectual intuition comes on stage where we stop being objects for ourselves, where, withdrawn into ourselves, the intuiting self is identical with the intuited" (HKA, 3: 88).[27] Once this intuition has been secured in a moment of world-consuming withdrawal in which everything disappears other than the self securing itself, Schelling can at last join the one to whom he addresses his remarks, his friend, who is himself perhaps a *Schwärmer*,[28] and who, if he outlives his friend's self-intuition, does so only *in* being addressed by his friend. The friends finally meet when they are apparently most apart:

> Here, my friend, we stand at the principle of all *Schwärmerei*. It originates, when it turns into a system, through nothing other than objectivized intellec-

tual intuition, whenever one takes an intuition of oneself for an intuition of an object outside oneself, the intuition of the inner intellectual world for the intuition of a supersensible world outside oneself. (HKA, 3: 90)

More than anything else, the discovery of a "secret capacity" for self-intuition distances Schelling from Kant, if not from his friend. For one of the decisive "facts" to which the first *Critique*, like Hume's *Treatise*, returns is a radical absence of self-intuition: I never encounter myself as such. To account for this "fact" is one of the all-important tasks of any critique of reason; to discount it, by contrast, amounts to engaging in "dreams of spirit-seers." From the perspective of this basic doctrine of Kantian critique, Schelling would arrive at the origin of *Schwärmerei* by falling into one of its versions. But Schelling's talk of a "secret, marvelous capacity" also runs counter to everything previously argued, for criticism *does* seem to be in a position to offer a strictly *theoretical* refutation of dogmatism. What is more "theoretical," what is more closely connected to *theorein* ("looking"), than *Anschauung* ("looking at")? The ability to refute dogmatism in a theoretical manner lies in the "secret, marvelous capacity" itself: the secret of this "capacity" is that it *can* be actualized, and because the actualization of this capacity obeys no causal law, it can be only considered a marvel. Having arrived at "the principle of all *Schwärmerei*" by virtue of this capacity, Schelling then finds another kind of *Schwärmerei* in its very actualization. There is always one more kind, an excessive kind that escapes the "principle" by which each kind is defined as one, and Schelling comes across this other kind of *Schwärmerei* at the end of the ninth letter: it is, as one might expect, the *Schwärmerei* of criticism, a mode of swarming that corresponds to what Kant called "moral *Schwärmerei*." If all objective causality is negated by my own causality, "I would be absolute.— But criticism would fall into *Schwärmerei* if it also represented this last goal only as *attainable* (not as *attained*)" (HKA, 3: 106). The dash points toward an elision and a paradox: Schelling should have written in parenthesis "even if not yet attained," but this would make the thesis of the I, the thesis of "intellectual intuition," into . . . a paren-thesis.

Schelling could therefore arrive only at an aporia, a nonpassage from the infinite to the finite: "criticism would fall into *Schwärmerei* if it also represented this last goal only as *attainable* (not as *attained*)." What is represented as attained cannot be represented as possible "only" to attain: it is, and it is impossible. Just as Kant places his doctrine of pure practical reason under the sign of a "sobriety" in which one remains aware of the impossibility of attaining the moral perfection that one must nevertheless be able to attain, Schelling thrusts any criticism that represents the goal it demands of itself into the hands of the *Schwärmer*: the possibility of the self absolving itself of all relations other than those that it institutes is supposed to be—this is the law—a sheer possibility, a fiction so pure that it corresponds to no representation, no image, and no idea. By doing so, Schelling is no longer in a position to claim that he has found a single "principle of all *Schwärmerei*." But this is by no means the only disadvantage of his disclosure of a critical *Schwärmerei*. Criticism can keep itself sober only under the ambiguous condition of a radical foreshortening of its vision: it cannot represent the goal of its activity, which is "itself," and this prohibition on making an image of itself *as* the absolute, even as it demands of itself that it *be* the absolute, makes it impossible for the activity of criticism to imagine the goal of its progress. Critical activity, the act of the I as it posits itself in relation to something other than itself, cannot therefore distinguish itself from the meandering, disorderly, disoriented, aimless buzzing of the "swarmer." By defining a *Schwärmerei* of criticism, Schelling comes close to confessing that criticism, which takes the principle of subjectivity as the foundation of knowledge, action, and being, is itself *Schwärmerei*. Sobriety—or the troubled knowledge that one cannot act as one can, should, and must act—would have to be sought in something other than this principle.[29]

Schelling can save himself from confessing that his presentation of the *Schwärmerei* in the *Philosophical Letters* is less than critical, if not hypocritical, only on the condition that he justify the hypercritical thesis of self-intuition. And this is precisely what he proceeds to do in the essays he published in the *Philosophisches Journal* after the completion of the *Philosophical Letters*. One of the methods by which he justifies his thesis—that the self is the sole ground on which philosophy stands—consists in showing that Kant, too, builds his architectonic on this basis, regardless of what he says to the contrary. Schelling thus quotes Kant to refute Kant's own self-representation, first citing the recently published polemic against Schlosser, "On a Newly Arisen Superior Tone in Philosophy," and then the well known but, according to Schelling, little read *Critique of Pure Reason*. In the essay, Kant speaks of freedom as the "Archimedean point" on which reason can move the world (Ak, 8: 404), and in a section of the book that denies the possibility of intuiting oneself, he describes the I as a "purely intellectual representation" (B, 423). Schelling draws the following conclusion from these two quotations: "This constant activity of self-in-tuition and transcendental freedom on which it maintains itself is alone what makes it such that *I myself* do not drown in the stream of representations, and it is what carries *me* over [*fortträgt*] from act to act, from thought to thought, from time to time (on invisible wings, as it were)" (HKA, 4: 128–29).

The "carrying over" (*Forttragen*) by which the I maintains itself runs directly counter to the "transfer" (*Übertragen*) in which *Schwärmerei* is grounded: the "translation" of the word "being" from one sphere—that of the I—to another. But this "carrying over" on which the entire exposition of idealism rests is itself a "transfer," "translation," or "metaphor," and is, moreover, an *Übertragen* whose every word calls out for an elucidation of the relation of philosophical to nonphilosophical and especially poetic language: the "as" (*wie*) of the phrase "as on invisible wings" marks a metaphorical moment; the word "invisible" (*unsichtbarm*), especially within a discussion of "intuition" (*Anschauung*), inscribes this moment into one of the foundational metaphorics of Kantian thought; and the generally poetic term for "wings" (*Fittige*)—which is, furthermore, a term poets apply to their own flights of fancy[30]—enlists this metaphysical metaphorics in a poetic movement that makes it impossible to decide on the metaphorical character of a term. For "wings"—especially the often invisible ones of bees—constitute the condition for the creation of a swarm in the original sense of the term. By disclosing "the principle of all possible *Schwärmerei*," Schelling returns to its root.[31]

The I carries itself over the stream of representations "as on invisible wings." On the basis of this image Schelling finds himself in a safe position not only to define *Schwärmerei* but also to defend himself against the accusation that he, like the hapless Schlosser, is a *Schwärmer* after all.[32] Schelling's definition of *Schwärmerei* accords with Kant's but for two related details: he drops the term "human" from Kant's talk of "human reason" and he accordingly abandons the term by which he has hitherto explicated the critical system, namely "the I." Instead of speaking of the I, Schelling finds it necessary to determine *Schwärmerei* in relation to "the spirit" (*der Geist*). The image by which Schelling reaches safe harbor thus resolves into a primordial one—spirit hovering over the surface of the primal seas (Gen. 1:2): "All *Schwärmerei* transgresses the limits of reason. Spirit itself, we maintain, draws these limits, for it gives itself its sphere, intuits itself in this sphere, and out of this sphere there is nothing for it. It is ridiculous to find *Schwärmerei* in *that which* forever makes all *Schwärmerei* impossible" (HKA, 4: 129). By drawing its own limits, "spirit" withdraws into itself. "Spirit" is not the same as the I, and yet it is no different from it either: it is the *philosophical* I, and only insofar as the I is properly philosophical can Schelling authorize his definition with a "we maintain." But even more to the point: "spirit" is the name for the I as it *actualizes* the "secret, marvelous *capacity*" for self-intuition. Philosophers, for Schelling, cannot acknowledge the sheer possibility of self-intuition without at the same time actualizing this possibility, for philosophy consists in precisely this actualization of "the secret, marvelous capacity."[33]

Schelling does not present "spirit" in quite this way. Or, more precisely, the assertion that spirit is the actualization of the capacity for self-intuition goes without saying and therefore says *nothing*: spirit is not something about which a philosopher, properly speaking, is able to speak—even to other philosophers. Philosophy, in other words, presupposes philosophical spirit in which philosophical language will be comprehensible *as* philosophical. In a footnote appended to his remarks about "invisible wings, as it were," Schelling rejects the possibility of a properly philosophical explanation of the term *Geist*, and suggests that this rejection of philosophy's ability to explicate its own spirit keeps it sober:

> After what Herr Professor Fichte in volume 5, no. 4, of the *Philosophical Journal* has said about this, there remains nothing more to add.[34]—The entire investigation, properly speaking [*eigentlich*], belongs in *aesthetics* (where I will also return to it). For this science first shows the entrance to all philosophy because only in aesthetics can it be explained what philosophical spirit [*philosophischer Geist*] is. Wanting to philosophize without such spirit is no better than wanting to endure outside of time or to write poetry without imagination. (HKA, 4: 129)

This footnote displaces Schelling's entire exposition, including his definition of *Schwärmerei*, for, insofar as the exposition constitutes an introduction to the idealism of the *Wissenschaftslehre* and at this very moment directs its readers to Fichte's "Second Introduction," it ought to take place, properly speaking, within the parameters of an "aesthetics." Without "philosophical spirit" there can be no philosophy, no actualization of the capacity for self-intuition; only a "science" that treats this actualization as a poetic act—or a pure fiction—can teach philosophy what it means to philosophize. Without this supplementary science, the capacity for self-intuition cannot be distinguished from its actualization, and philosophy, in turn, cannot keep itself from falling into *Schwärmerei*. Although aesthetics should come first, it is not even last, for Schelling never makes good on his promise to return to this topic within the context of his elucidation of critical idealism.[35]

IV. "In Good Times There are Seldom *Schwärmer*" (Hölderlin)

The same cannot be said of Hölderlin, who, in the course of repeating Schelling's footnote, does not so much propose "the principle of all possible *Schwärmerei*" as offer a critical genealogy of the *Schwärmer*. This repetition of the footnote in which Schelling proposes "aesthetics" as a solution for the otherwise intractable difficulties of "criticism" takes place in Hölderlin's sole experiment in writing prose fragments—a collection of seven fragments, aphorisms, or even anecdotes to which later editors have attached the title "Reflections." Each of the seven prose texts is concerned with the nature of *enthousiazein*, and together they constitute one of the most concentrated confrontations with the tradition inaugurated by Plato's *Ion* in modern European thought. By opening the collection with the bold statement "There is a scale of enthusiasm [*Es giebt Grade der Begeisterung*]" (SW, 4: 233),[36] Hölderlin associates his reflections with those of Renaissance neo-Platonism, especially Ficino, and in some of the later fragments, particularly in the third and fourth, he takes up, takes to task, and transforms certain remarks of Pseudo-Longinus in praise of enthusiasm that had been understood throughout the eighteenth century as programmatic statements for poetic productivity.[37] Later fragments go even further and challenge the very foundation on which every critical venture—Schelling's no less than Kant's—seeks to distinguish something like a heroic or critical *Enthusiasmus* from a debilitating illness or self-annihilating *Schwärmerei*. The second half of the penultimate fragment pursues this challenge by repeating Schelling's statement: "The entire investigation, properly speaking, belongs in *aesthetics*." But this repetition is only a preparation for the shocking assertion that *Schwärmerei* is *good*:

> All knowledge [*alles Erkennen*] should begin with the study of the beautiful. For, the one who can understand life without mourning [*ohne zu trauern*] has gained much. Moreover, even *Schwärmerei* and passion are good, devotional

prayers [*Andacht*], which life does not touch and may not know, and then despair, when life itself breaks forth from its infinity. The deep feeling of mortality, of change, of his temporal limitations enflames man so that he attempts much; [it] exercises all his powers, and does not allow him to fall into idleness, and one struggles so long with chimeras until finally something true and real [*etwas Wahres und Reelles*] is again found for knowledge and creative occupation [*Erkenntniß und Beschäfftigung*]. In good times there are seldom *Schwärmer*. Yet when man lacks great, pure objects, then he creates some phantom out of this or that, and [he] closes his eyes in order to be able to take an interest in it and live for it. (SW, 4: 235–36)[38]

Knowledge—which means, above all, the science of philosophy[39]—begins with aesthetics, or the "study of beauty," for it alone allows us to understand life without mourning. Since mourning is itself related to life as the experience of its loss, the reason Hölderlin proposes aesthetics as the foundation of knowledge can be expressed in another manner: the study of beauty allows us to understand life without experiencing the loss of the very thing to be understood. Aesthetics therefore allows us to study something without having to add "and it has been lost"—without, in other words, casting ourselves into the role of mourners and memorialists. Since, however, anyone who studies is also alive, the "object" of study cannot be really distinguished from its "subject." Without a study of beauty, neither subject nor object are themselves, which is to say, alive. All of the concepts to which Hölderlin then turns—*Schwärmerei*, passion, devotional prayer, and despair—are from this perspective specific modes of mourning: life has lost its unity for the one who, having succumbed to despair (*Verzweiflung*), is now two (*zwei*); life never even touches the one who is devoted to memorial prayers (*Andacht*); passion (*Leidenschaft*), as the condition of suffering (*Leiden*), is by definition removed from the pure activity of life; and finally—or, more precisely, at first—there is *Schwärmerei*, which, however, unlike the others, does let itself be so easily deciphered as a specific mode of mourning.

   Schwärmerei distinguishes itself from the other modes of mourning insofar as the word does not indicate the manner in which life has been lost. *Schwärmerei* is different from despair, devotion, and passion also in that these three can be understood as forms of *Schwärmerei*. And all four, Hölderlin insists, are "good." This apparent approbation of *Schwärmerei* doubtless corresponds to a revaluation of the term in the last decades of the eighteenth century. What better way to express a general dissatisfaction with the image of reason promulgated by the *Aufklärung* than by extolling its polemical opponent?[40] But Hölderlin's fragment cannot simply be understood as an "Apologie der Schwärmerei," to use Novalis's phrase.[41] For the goodness of *Schwärmerei* is not unconditional: "In good times there are seldom *Schwärmer*"—which means at the very least that the goodness of *Schwärmerei* lies in its relation to bad times. Hölderlin, furthermore, specifies the character of these times: there is nothing "true" for "knowledge" and nothing "real" for "creative occupation." *Schwärmerei* is good, in short, as long as there is neither philosophy nor poetry, and since philosophy, or "knowledge," should begin with the study of beauty, one comes back to the formula: *Schwärmerei* is good "for the remainder" (*übrigens*)—as long as life, in other words, cannot be understood without mourning.

Every action based on mourning is thus brought into the orbit of *Schwärmerei*. Whereas Kant defined *Schwärmerei* as a "principled" overstepping of all boundaries, and Schelling sought the "principle of all possible *Schwärmerei*" in the almost unbearable demand of the self to pass into the infinitude of the nonself, Hölderlin presents it as the very experience of limitation—and, above all, the experience of a limited, defined, and thus principled life: "The deep feeling of mortality, of change, of his temporal limitations enflames man so that he attempts much; [it] exercises all his powers, and does not allow him to fall into idleness. . . . In good times there are seldom *Schwärmer*. Yet when man lacks great, pure objects, then he creates some phantom out of this or that, and [he] closes his eyes in order to be able to take an interest in it and live for it."[42] *Schwärmerei* is defined by the feeling of being defined and the corresponding demand to define oneself. Seeking to discover one's "identity" is a meaningful activity only in "bad times"—and only among *Schwärmer*. For the act of defining oneself converts the indeterminacy of "idleness" into a less than fully alive activity. By defining *Schwärmerei* as the experience of being defined, Hölderlin is in a position to determine its provenance: *Schwärmerei* arises whenever those "objects" that, by virtue of their purity and greatness, are "true" and "real" have been lost. But only "true" and "real" objects are objects in the first place. "Something true and real" cannot be understood as some-one-thing among other things; rather, it is thinghood—or "being"[43]—as such. No one can define this "something." It can show itself only in, and *as*, the infinite rupture of the very deed by which the *Schwärmer* comes into existence: the—suicidal—deed of self-definition. The name for "infinitude" in the context of this fragment—

and this act of naming is itself a "creative occupation"—is, therefore, "life." The loss of "living objects" makes *Schwärmerei* possible, and this possibility is realized whenever this loss goes unnoticed and is thus lost yet again. Losing sight of the loss of his loss, the *Schwärmer* "closes his eyes," and in this tragic act of self-blinding, he survives his suicide by creating for himself a "nothing"—which is to say, a "phantom," not "something true and real," but a phenomenon he can admire and a task to which he can dutifully devote himself. The self's making for itself a phenomenal world that it oversteps in pursuing its "infinite task" is, however, the fundamental operation Kantian critique ascribes to the self as a whole. By the time Hölderlin has completed this fragment, the word *Schwärmerei* has become equivalent to the term *subjectivity.* "In good times there are seldom subjects."

But *Schwärmerei*—and, one may now add, subjectivity—is nevertheless good. When *Schwärmer* lose sight of the loss as such, they mourn for something about which they are unaware, and this very unawareness keeps the loss "pure." To this extent, *Schwärmerei* distinguishes itself from the other modes of mourning that Hölderlin mentions: passion, devotion, and despair, each of which names an experience of suffering, commemoration, or division. Not so with *Schwärmerei*: insofar as it is associated with an experience of flight, it points in the opposite direction—toward *Freude* (joy), more precisely, toward the hyperbolic hermeneutic imperative with which the fragment begins: "It is from joy that you must understand the pure in general [*das Reine überhaupt*], human beings, and other kinds of being, grasp 'everything essential about and characteristic of' these beings, and know their relations to one another" (SW, 4: 235).[44] *Schwärmerei* is a mode of mourning after all: *Schwärmer* mourn in joy. They are able to mourn in joy because they do not know that they are "in" mourning. Because they are unaware of the loss of which they mourn, *Schwärmer* themselves—not the "phantoms" in which they take an "interest"—*represent* this loss: they are the very "objects" with which to begin understanding life without mourning. In a letter to his friend Immanuel Niethammer, Hölderlin indicates that he would soon begin work on a series of "New Letters on Aesthetic Education."[45] To this, one might add: aesthetic education begins *here*—with the study of the *Schwärmer*.

Schwärmerei is a riddle whose solution lies in poetry. For the structure of the poet corresponds to that of the *Schwärmer*. Just as the *Schwärmer* mourns joyfully, the poet is soberly "enthused" (*begeistert*). Determining the meaning of this paradoxical *Begeisterung* is the initial task Hölderlin assigns himself. Instead of defining *Geist*, he shows what it means to be *begeistert*. *Begeisterung*, as the fundamental condition for the possibility of poetry, cannot simply be translated as "inspiration." Since *Geist*, for the theologians under whom both Schelling and Hölderlin studied, stands for "God,"[46] *be-geistern* could be equally well understood as a literal translation of *enthousiazein*. The definition of *Begeisterung*, however, lies in "sobriety" (*Nüchternheit*): "Wherever sobriety forsakes you, there are the limits of your *Begeisterung*" (SW, 4: 233). The sober enthusiasm of the poet corresponds to the mournful joy of the enthusiasts, and at the very point at which the aphorisms turn away from their original concentration on the task, nature, and feeling of the poet, which is also the point at which the principle of "aesthetic education" is laid down—"All knowledge should begin with the study of beauty"—Hölderlin turns toward the definition, provenance, and principle of *Schwärmerei*. The two belong together, poets and *Schwärmer*—not because poets are *Schwärmer* but, on the contrary, because poets, who do not devote themselves to phantoms and are not therefore subjects, bring to speech what *Schwärmer* represent: the loss of life.

Life, for Hölderlin, can show itself only in an infinite, inconsistent or "aorgic" way (SW, 4: 153)—*not* in the form of an infinite, substantial, and self-consistent being. *Begeisterung*, in turn, is always limited: "Wherever sobriety forsakes you, there are the limits of your enthusiasm." Yet *Begeisterung* is also infinite: "there is an infinite ladder" (SW, 4: 233). The infinitude of *Begeisterung* consists in degrees, or—to use an old term that Kant, for one, revives—in intensive magnitudes.[47] The "infinite ladder" of *Begeisterung* can thus function as a continuous scale. What this scale measures is neither finite nor infinite, neither self-defining subjects nor infinite gods. Rather, the scale of enthusiasm measures those who escape this alternative: namely, poets. Poets neither define themselves, nor are they undefinable, chaotic, or "aorgic" life. And the scale of *Begeisterung* does not rate their relative value; rather, poets apply the scale to themselves *as a whole*—and are for this reason poets, which is to say, those who escape the alternative: self-defined subject or limitless life. Poets *are* poets whenever they apply themselves to the scale of enthusiasm—whenever, in other words, the intensity of their self-relation does not make them withdraw into themselves and create something through which they define themselves but, on the contrary, allows them to measure something else altogether: "There is a scale of *Begeisterung*. From joviality, which is surely the lowest, up to the *Begeisterung* of the general who in the midst of battle maintains control of his genius through concentration [*Besonnenheit*], there is an infinite ladder. To climb up and down this ladder is the calling and bliss of the poet" (SW, 4: 233).

The freedom of poets consists in their ability to move up and down the "infinite ladder" of enthusiasm. By doing so, they liberate themselves from the particular and limited perspectives disclosed by each of its rungs. Nowhere does Hölderlin indicate that a higher perspective is of greater value than a lower or middling one; still less does he imply that the freedom from particular perspectives gives rise to a general point of view, which, because of its generality, would sublate and encompass the lower ones. At the highest level of the ladder of enthusiasm there is indeed a general (*Feldherr*); but the viewpoint of the general is still of a very particular kind of field: the field of slaughter. From this, the highest perspective, life is seen to be lost.

At the end of the *Ion*, the "ionic" rhetor whom Socrates has relentlessly pursued finally claims a *technē* for himself: the general "know-how" of the general (*strategos*). Socrates demands that Ion make a decision: explain why the Athenians have not chosen him as a general or enlist himself into the ranks of "enthusiasts." To this decision, which Ion wishes to delay, Hölderlin finally responds: poets can indeed rise to the enthusiasm of generals, but poets distinguish themselves from generals—and distinguish themselves in their poetry—because they not only observe the loss of life but also see that life is lost.

§ 4 On a Seeming Right to Semblance: Schiller, Hebel, and Kleist

By the end of the eighteenth century, appearances were emancipated from reality. If, as the grammar of the word suggests, appearances still have to be appearances *of* something, it became possible at the end of the eighteenth century to contest the metaphysical and theological prejudices that took root in this grammatical theorem—prejudices according to which the things that give rise to phenomena are more durable, higher, and more valuable than mere appearances. The decisive moment of this challenge to the grammar of the word "appearance" takes place in Kant's first *Critique*. Although the first readers of the *Critique of Pure Reason* tended to interpret the term *phenomenon* as merely subjective representation, no attentive reader of its second edition could do the same: phenomena are the things we encounter, and if, as the grammar of the word suggests, they are still to be understood as the appearances of something else altogether, which, for its part, does not appear, this grammatical theorem has no theoretical consequences. The transcendental deduction of the categories of the pure understanding has the function of challenging and overcoming this prejudice, and by doing so, indeed as the first step in this direction, Kant begins to emancipate *Erscheinungen* from the things of which they are appearances.

But the complete emancipation of appearances from reality is not a project Kant himself undertakes. Appearances do not deceive, to be sure, but they are still appearances of something we have no right to discuss in a determinate manner or a confident tone. And this "something" is simply the thing as such—the thing considered without respect to the forms of intuition in which it appears. In some of his late reflections Kant began to investigate the status of appearances as such—or "the appearance of ap-pearance"[1]—but these reflections did not themselves appear in public un-til the end of the nineteenth century, and by then, the course of post-Kantian critique had long been established. The successors of Kant sought to succeed where Kant had supposedly failed by ridding philosophy of the "thing-in-itself" once and for all. In this way, appearance would be eman-cipated from reality. The course of this emancipation not only constitutes the history of German idealism; it also gives direction to its dissolution under various rubrics—from materialism and pessimism to Dionysus and fundamental ontology. When Nietzsche famously announces that "with the true world we have also abolished the apparent one,"[2] he expresses in a particularly dramatic fashion the aporia to which Fichte laboriously re-turns in an effort to initiate a thoroughgoing critique of the thing-in-itself. And the same aporia continually unsettles the philosophical inquiries that understand their point of departure as critiques of this critique of the Kantian *Critique*s: there are only appearances, nothing "beyond," and every apparent "beyond" is only the world of appearances seen in a par-ticular—exalted or diminished—manner. The "essence" of appearance can consist in nothing other than appearing as such. This "appearing as such," for its part, cannot *itself* appear as anything other than an event in which appearances are emancipated from—or *robbed* of—reality.

I. Schiller: Proclaiming the Right to Semblance

One of the first to register an oblique awareness of this robbery is the au-thor of *The Robbers*, Friedrich Schiller. None of the scenes and accounts of robbery in *The Robbers* suggest that appearances are somehow robbed of reality, but in the figure of Franz Moor—more so than in that of his brother, the hero of the drama—something like this robbery is brought on stage, for the treacherous Franz seeks to gain control of the family property by casting himself in the part of the loyal son. Motivated by a desire for mastery, Franz forsakes everything supposedly real solely for the sake of ap-pearances. Schiller never fully acquits himself of the nihilistic implications of what might be called Franz Moor's theatrical mission. The baroque hy-perbole toward which much of the discourse of *The Robbers* is drawn cor-responds to one of Schiller's unmistakable traits—his attraction to the "sensational": conspirators, frauds, charlatans, robbers, and other assorted outlaws. Insofar as it presupposes a well-ordered course of the world from which each sensational episode is only a shocking exception, sensational-ism offers a certain solace. By placing his account of the genesis of an ex-emplary robber in his contra-*Robber* narrative "The Criminal from Lost Honor" within the framework of what might be called forensic psychology, Schiller gains some ground in his effort to discover a convincing response to the threat of world-consuming nihilism that takes shape in Franz Moor, and the same might be said of the other "legal cases" he edits from 1792 to 1795, under the unremarkable title *Remarkable Legal Cases as a Contribu-tion to the History of Humanity*.[3] These cases serve a purpose beyond that of sensationalism as long as they are indeed contributions to the history of humanity—in both senses of the term *history*: contributions to historiog-raphy, as Schiller, relying on Kant, had outlined in his *Antrittsvorlesung* (first lecture) at Jena,[4] and contributions to the history of humanity itself, *res gestas*, insofar as they contribute in reflection to the progressive refine-ment of the law (*das Recht*).

Schiller's "remarkable legal cases" are largely forgotten (even among Schiller scholars, who tend to emphasize his medical over his legal train-ing, which is doubtless justified, since he gave up law for medicine). The opposite is true of the *other* project that occupied Schiller's attention dur-ing the tumultuous years between 1792 and 1795—the writing and rewrit-ing of his letters on the aesthetic education. The full title of the *Aesthetic Letters* is reminiscent of the *Remarkable Legal Cases*, which is hardly sur-prising, since the letters, like the legal cases, are meant to contribute to the history of humanity in both senses of the term. And something else brings together aesthetics and jurisprudence in an era marked by the critique of Kant's *Critiques*: both the study of art and the study of law seek to distin-guish themselves from moral philosophy with which they are nevertheless intimately bound. The basic criterion of this distinction is, moreover, the same: both aesthetics and jurisprudence are concerned solely with appear-ances—with "externality," to use Kant's preferred term, rather than with the interiority, essence, or noumenal character of the agents in question.[5] The *Aesthetic Letters* go one step further in this direction, for they are, as a whole, an epistolary plea for the total emancipation of appearances not only from reality but also, as a consequence, from moral imperatives. Once appearances are fully freed, if only for a certain duration and only under certain conditions, human beings can finally become what they are supposed to be—namely, free. Freed from essence and moral imperative, an appearance is no longer an appearance but is, rather, sheer semblance:

not *Erscheinung*, but *Schein*. All of Schiller's considerable exegetical energy is concentrated into the exposition of the conditions of, and moment for, the appearance of semblance, *die Erscheinung des Scheins*. If Schiller's determination of these conditions and this moment is open to certain ambiguities—and a bewildering proliferation of antithetical terms—this is hardly surprising, for every appearance of semblance takes place in a zone of indetermination that resolves into a figuration of complete determinability. In view of *schöner Schein* or "lovely-looking semblance"—which is another name for *Schein* emancipated from essence and imperative—the transition of the human being from a determined being to a self-determining one can be *gently* accomplished.

The appearance of semblance marks a new beginning—without, however, itself *being* in fact a new beginning: no radical break, still less a dissolution of the order of things and a return to a state of nature in which an appeal to something like natural rights would be fully justified. The semblance of a new beginning obviates the demand for a complete break or even only a return to a primordial condition, and it simultaneously establishes the conditions under which the very same demand can be satisfied and a new beginning will have been initiated after all. The transition to freely self-determining subjectivity ironically—or comically—will have taken place, if it takes place, only in retrospect, without any plans for its institution. Little wonder, then, that Schiller does not make good on his promise to furnish a constitution for the "aesthetic state": keeping his promise would compromise the integrity of the transition, since a publicly proclaimed constitution of a nonexistent state is nothing if not a self-conscious inauguration of a *novum* according to the temporal schema of revolution: immemorial and obscure *Recht* made into the openly proclaimed *Gesetz* of the land.[6] For the same reason, it is surprising that Schiller nevertheless enters into the arena of legislation and proclaims an inviolable right—the right to semblance: "Since all actual existence derives from nature considered as an alien power, whereas all semblance originally derives from the human being as a representing subject [*aller Schein aber ursprünglich von den Menschen als vorstellendem Subjekte, sich herschreibt*], he is only availing himself of the absolute right of ownership when he reclaims semblance from essence [*den Schein von dem Wesen zürucknimmt*] and disposes over it according to its own laws" (NA, 21: 401).

The right to semblance derives from the absolute right of ownership, and semblance itself derives—or, better yet, "gets its official papers," *sich herschreibt*[7]—from the representing subject. Even if the right of ownership is natural—and Schiller does not enter into this complicated question[8]—the right derived from it, as a right to dispose over the ownmost property of the representing subject, is not; nor, of course, can it be considered a matter of an unnatural, instituted, or "positive" law, since it pertains to the representing subject as such—not to the membership of a subject in some political order, however vaguely outlined. Regardless of how this right is determined, however, this much remains clear: the subject has been robbed; essence has captured what belongs to the subject; and *now* is the time for the proclamation of a rightful reclamation, a *Züruacknehmen* in which the representing subject restores its original property to itself.

As Schiller insists, however, the right that he proclaims in the penultimate letter does not proceed beyond "the essenceless empire of imagination [*dem wesenlosen Reich der Einbildungskraft*]" (NA, 20: 401). Only in the "world of semblance" can "this human right of sovereignty [*dieses menschliche Herrscherrecht*]" legitimately find a field upon which to exercise itself. In every other world, which is to say, in the world of appearance, a claim to this right amounts to usurpation, and since only those who can freely distinguish "real" appearances from those appearances that are freed from reality and therefore accede to semblance are in position to adjudicate this matter, it is by no means clear how a court of review could be established. Unclarity in this regard in no small matter. The shadowy existence of a critical-juridical authority charged with the review of potential violations of the right to semblance—on both sides, as it were—gives the whole matter a vaguely conspiratorial air. The juridical authority may be a branch of the legal order, or a supposedly independent coterie of art critics, or both in a tense tandem. In any case, however, the paragraphs on the right to semblance in the penultimate letter of the series cannot fail to raise their own series of questions, the first of which would doubtless be whether or not the right to semblance is itself a matter of semblance, a sham right or *Scheinrecht* by means of which a legal order grants a place for the sovereignty of the subject in general without conceding any real rights to the subjects over whom it rules. By granting its subjects a right to semblance, a regime without rights can appear in a very different light—so different in fact that it may even be able to legitimate itself in the eyes of its subjects, who have seen (or imagined they have seen) a regime founded on the idea of universal human rights. With the enactment of a right to semblance, a legal order could thus allow thoroughly dominated subjects a chance to experience not only the pleasures of domination, which are doubtless considerable, but also the far greater satisfaction of having a *right* to dominate something—even if this something is, after all, nothing. Semblance would be ironically freed of reality, for the enactment of the right to semblance—not the world of semblance it is supposed to protect—would be a sheer act, *a coup de théâtre* by means of which an unjust state could impersonate a just one.[9] This would be a "remarkable legal case" indeed.

Schiller betrays no awareness of this reversal, and yet it is entirely in spirit with the compositional principle of his aesthetic theory as a whole, if not his entire corpus, for both his theoretical and poetic writings are replete with chiastic figures, and nowhere more so than in the central sections of the *Aesthetic Letters*. By the time his readers reach the penultimate letter, they have become so accustomed to the mobility of such figures that the reversal of the right to semblance into the semblance of right would be, as it were, *de rigueur*. That Schiller does not himself move in this direction cannot simply be ascribed to political timidity, moreover. With the declaration of the right to semblance he touches on a paradox that disturbs the feasibility of this reversal; and it likewise casts doubts on the efficacy of the demystifying gesture through which the "truth" of Schiller's discourse on the right to semblance would otherwise be brought to light. The paradox arises at the precise moment the conditions are stipulated under which semblance accedes to the status of a right: *Schein* must "expressly renounce . . . all claim to reality [*sich von allem Anspruch auf Realität ausdrücklich lossag[en]*" (NA, 20: 402). With its emphasis on the act of speaking, this formulation verges on the Cretan Liar's paradox: semblance uprightly speaks out "I do not dissemble"; but since it is, after all, *semblance* that speaks in this manner, its speech is discredited and unbelievable—even if it is true. The paradox, for Schiller, is generated out of the *wesen-loses* character of *Schein*, its essential lack of essence: semblance cannot purely and simply say "get lost" to reality (*los-sagen Realität*), since it is, from its inception, at a loss when it comes to *Wesen*, and this loss, and this loss alone, guarantees that it originally belongs to the representing subject, who, for its part, is subject to the nihilistic improprieties of a Franz Moor precisely because it may be, *like* its original property—and *as* its original property—*wesenlos*.

From Schiller's perspective, the appearance of a figure of total determinability promises to resolve the split in the subject between "person" and "state" (*Person* and *Zustand*) that, for Schiller, corresponds to the distinction between reality and appearance. A right to semblance may be nothing other than the semblance of right; but the very seemingness of this right falls prey to—or takes advantage of—the same indetermination that characterizes both the formal paradox of semblance renouncing *all* claims on reality and the moment of resolution Schiller seeks to capture under the rubric of "lovely-looking semblance." The right to semblance cannot, therefore, be one right among others; it cannot be a real right, univocally declared and straightforwardly acknowledged, and yet, even if it is therefore consigned to the category of sham rights—piously declared and incapable of being put into effect—its very fakeness may strike back at the matter of right as a whole: at the discourse of rights, which, represented by Schiller's declaration of a *Herrscherrecht* (sovereign right) over an imaginary empire, seems both to presuppose and produce a sovereign subject who, certain of its absolute right to property, can only exist *alone*, as an "individual," sentenced in advance to a world all its own; and it may strike even deeper—at the seeming character of *Recht* in general, which is to say, the law understood as something other than the absolute *Gesetz* of reason. From the "awkward perspective" of a right to semblance, the legal order whose justification lies in its guardianship of *das Recht*, may only *appear* legal; and rights, which would serve as the measure and guarantors of the lawfulness of a legal order, would only be functions of fictional personae who are made into semblances of themselves once they are cast—or magically cast themselves into—the role of rights-bearing subjects.

Schiller's apparently straightforward plea for poetic license in the penultimate letter does not explicitly participate in any of the contemporaneous debates concerning the codification of law, the relation between and relative value of natural and positive law, or the supposed right to revolt against a regime that violates the terms of an original contract.[10] But his nonparticipation does not amount to nonintervention. Presented in the most high-minded, "idealist"—one might even say, Schillerian—language, the declaration of sovereign right over the "empire of the imagination" registers something disturbing, even "unreal" about rights, legal orders, and *das Recht* in general. And it does so precisely because the declaration of this, the most insubstantial of rights, cannot be purely and simply—which is to say, honestly and uprightly—declared. Schiller, against his own intentions, or strangely in accord with some of his more "sensational" ones, may allow the truth of right and rights to be spoken: an incredible truth, to be sure. Nothing is perhaps better evidence for this than a well attested phenomenon that one might call the Schiller effect: a rejection of all things Schillerian, especially his high-minded declarations, even a hint of abjection that expresses itself in merciless parody, cries of incredulity ("this man could be paired with an authentic poet like Goethe or a genuine philosopher like Kant?"), and dramatic gestures of separation—from Friedrich Schlegel to Paul de Man (along with many others besides).[11] The incredulity into which Schiller's Schillerian declamations have regularly fallen corresponds to and resonates with the structural incredulity of semblance's declaration of right: "I, semblance, am honestly not dissembling, for I am in truth only semblance."

II. Hebel: The Legal Limits of Semblance

Personifying the concept of semblance in the explication of the conditions under which it is supposed to secure its legitimacy is neither accidental nor fully justified. *Schein* must be granted an "I" so that it can, once again, "explicitly renounce all claim to reality."[12] But granting an "I" to semblance for the sake of self-renunciation is itself paradoxical from the perspective of the Fichtean problematic with which Schiller seeks to associate himself, for only the "I" can legitimately claim reality—and vice versa. Schiller, true to the spirit of the quickly evolving *Wissenschaftslehre* and at the same time faithful to the letter of Kantian critique, never allows semblance *explicitly* to speak of itself. The only "I" in the *Aesthetic Letters* is that of the letter writer, whose identity remains unproblematic to the extent that it stands in a relation of dependence on a "you" who is in fact and in principle princely: a highness or higher instance that has the power to guarantee the existence of the persona and to support the existence of the legal person named Friedrich Schiller alike. Such is Prince Friedrich of Augustenburg's function. Insofar as the letter writer identifies himself and is identified with Schiller—and, of course, in Fichte's Jena, these acts of self-identification are anything but unproblematic—the paradox of emancipated semblance are kept at a distance; in reverse, the paradox is likewise kept at a distance if it turns into a compositional principle, and the "I," in turn, comes onstage to announce that it is only one of an infinite plurality of fictive "I's": the real one is unpresentable—or the stage itself. The right to semblance arises as a problem in its own right only under the condition that semblance not be made into an absolutely autonomous process, even if this process is by virtue of its absoluteness forever broken off. The question does not so much concern the ambiguous status of the "I" as that of the *proper name*, the insignia by means of which a legal person is constituted and that which "I" replaces. The right to semblance then comes into its own in the vicinity of those sentences in which the "I" claims its name—not as a right to personify, which is perhaps the "right of the poet" par excellence, but as a right to *impersonate*.

Even as they casts their analysis of the human being in terms of the ineluctable opposition between the "person" and "state," the *Aesthetic Letters* never concern themselves with personification or impersonation, still less with the status of the proper name. The same cannot be said of the articles, anecdotes, and stories Johann Peter Hebel regularly publishes in the name of the Baden Elector and under the strange name, pseudonym, or anonym, *der Hausfreund*: "the family friend," more exactly, "the house friend."[13] In the absence of any explicit theory of selfhood or self-constitution, the friend of the house nevertheless poses again and again the problem: "Who am I?" And the question is posed by the problematic persona of the *Hausfreund*—neither, therefore, by an "I" nor by the legal person named Johann Peter Hebel, whose family name suggests an instrument controlled by others' hands (*Hebel* means "lever"). Few writers have been less willing to write "I." The continuity of the *Hausfreund* does not quite lie in a constitutive act of self-positing, nor does it quite lie in the already constituted power of the legal order that he serves with apparent loyalty. *Wer ist dieser, der Hausfreund?*—"Who is exactly *this* one, the house friend?"—is not only a question posed by a philosopher whose relation to the Allemannic official borders on identification, namely Martin Heidegger.[14] It is also a philosophical question that hovers around the house friend as long as he remains precisely that: not Johann Peter Hebel, not a neighbor, not even a friend of any human being, a *Menschenfreund* (to use the common term of the *Aufklärung*), but, rather, a nameless friend of an equally unidentifiable house. In the strange name for a figure of official familiarity, the *Hausfreund* enters into the problem of the right to semblance without any of the assurances that, after all, semblance can secure this right by purely and simply, in its own person, renouncing all claims to reality. And his point of entrance for this problem is the practice of aesthetic *instruction*.

The calendars that appeared under Hebel's editorship are instructional; at the very least, they inform the subjects who are required to buy them about the order of official Lutheran time, if not about the Baden legal order that forces its subjects to buy its calendars. In an essay Schiller wrote in conjunction with the letter on aesthetic education where he proclaims the right to semblance, he describes the "contract" that "popular instruction [*der populäre Unterricht*]" makes with freedom: the imagination is never allowed to forget that "it acts merely in the *service* of the *understanding*" (NA, 21: 8). "Aesthetic instruction" would therefore be a contradiction in terms; but it is in the service of something like this contradiction that Hebel enlists his calendar when he takes over and refashions its economically failing predecessor: everything in the calendar need not immediately serve the understanding nor indeed illustrate a moral principle. One of Hebel's few explicit formulations of this program appears in an unsuccessful plea he addresses to the Baden consistory after it had objected to some of the stories he intended to publish in his first issue: "A calendar that wants to win many friends among its multitude of readers should without a doubt contain . . . next to the main article, which is meant for everyone, a supplement made up of many things, for the invitation and satisfaction of different humors."[15] The "addition," *die Zuthat*, does what the main article cannot: it momentarily interrupts the instructional service that the calendar is established to perform. This interruption is far from unambiguous: it could solidify this regime by showing that it is strong enough to allow for a certain relaxation—and this argument goes in the direction of Hebel's plea—but it could also show its "soft spots." The question, then, of Hebel's aesthetic instruction comes down to this: can an official calendar *mark* or even *make* such "soft spots": places where the legal order *cannot* solidify itself?

Of all the supplementary material appearing under the insignia of the *Hausfreund*, none responds to this question more directly, or more economically, than the stories about those "rogues" (*Gauner*) who invade the domestic spaces he promises to protect by virtue of his name. The family name of the "rogues," the brothers Zundel—Heiner and Frieder—whose adventures the *Hausfreund* regularly recounts (as if they were also calendrical phenomena), suggests fires or sparks.[16] Appearing for the first time in a story of 1809 called "The Three Thieves," the Zundel brothers are shown to threaten every sort of economy—not only human houses but also those of animals (hen stalls and nests). The *Hausfreund* takes over the story of the thieves from Johann Heinrich Voss, and transforms it entirely.[17] Whereas Voss, who calls his poem a "romance," leaves the conditions and consequences of criminality aside, the friend of the house insists on the pervasive presence of the legal order: at the opening of the story the narrator emphasizes that the Zundel brothers "murder and attack no human being." They are not, however, exempt from extreme legal violence: the brothers inherited their "trade" (*Handwerk*) from their father, whose own abstention from violence did not prevent him from having "copulated" with the "ropemaker's daughter, that is, with the noose" (H, 2: 153). Once they are caught, the sons are spared this violent copulation and are, instead, placed at the end of story in a "house of correction" (H, 2: 156). *Zuchthaus* is the last word of "The Three Thieves." To which a reader might well ask, "Wer ist dieser, der Zuchthausfreund?" (Heidegger does not ask such a question, of course, and his most ferociously loyal colleague among the law faculty at Freiburg, Erik Wolf, in an address of 1941 "On the Essence of Right in the Fiction of Johann Peter Hebel," assumes it has already been answered.)[18] The Zundel brothers are clearly no friends of the *Zuchthaus*, however familiar they may be with its operations; but the same may not be true of the *Hausfreund*. A *Zuchthaus* completes the story in which the Zundel brothers first appear: like father, like sons—with an alteration in the mode of punishment. Since, moreover, this alteration can easily be integrated into a narrative of the progressive humanization of the penal code, imprisonment replacing execution as sons replace fathers, the friend of the house may also, or even primarily, function as "der Rheinländishe Zuchthausfreund."[19]

Yet the same conclusion cannot be reached when Zundelfrieder returns to the calendar two years later. In "How Zundelfrieder One Day Escaped from Prison and Happily Crossed over the Border," the friend of the house fails to make good on the promise of his title: instead of relating how the thief escapes from the *Zuchthaus*, he simply notes in the opening line of the story that Zundelfrieder "found his way out of the *Zuchthaus* alone." If a title constitutes a promise of sorts—and particularly a title beginning with the word "how"—then the narrator is guilty of a breach of promise at the precise moment when the subject of his narrative breaks out of prison *alone*—without help or companionship. It is as though the *Hausfreund* joins Zundelfrieder as the latter finally goes solo. And the direction of their joint journey is *over the limit*: "über die Gränzen." The method Zundelfrieder develops for the transgression of these limits is, in turn, transcendental: he anonymously poses a question concerning the nature of the self. After having reproached some passing geese for their lack of discipline (*Zucht*) and their failure to come inside (*ins Haus*), he steals one, hides it under his coat, and approaches the *Schilderhaus* of the town closest to the border. He then presents himself *as* the question of selfhood: "three steps from the guard house, as the soldier inside started to stir, Frieder cried with a hearty voice: 'who goes!' [*wer da*] The soldier answered good-naturedly: 'good friend!'" (H, 2: 255). Thus the brief narrative concludes—with Frieder, fugitive from the *Zuchthaus*, as an ironically "good" friend of the guard house and with the *Hausfreund* . . . as the enemy of both houses? Or at least as a false friend of these houses, one who indicates *that* the former can be evaded and shows *how* to outwit the latter? This is hardly a proper conclusion, but neither is one in which the *Hausfreund* is represented simply as a friend of these houses who, like a lever, allows the legal order to exercise its power with minimal application of force. The inconclusiveness of this story corresponds to the anonymity of its narrator; it does not illustrate a moral or legal principle on the basis of which things can be assigned their rightful place, nor does it serve to exemplify specific points of practical reason, which, in this case, would have to be the narrow-minded wisdom of general distrust. The point of this story, like that of many others, including the next two ("The Recruit," about the function of the *Schilderhaus*, and "The Lightest Death Sentence," which consists, needless to say, in the perpetual postponement of its execution), cannot be made independent of its recounting—which is perhaps what Walter Benjamin meant when he describes Hebel in terms he reserves for very few other writers, most notably Goethe and himself: "everything factual is already theory."[20]

This proposition could be made more specific in the case of the stories about Zundelfrieder as he goes it alone: everything factual is already both aesthetic and legal theory—in tense competition. By the time Hebel publishes "How Zundelfrieder Got Himself a Horse to Ride, with an Illustration," the penultimate story of the irregularly appearing series, the thief has completely emancipated himself from all interest in gain, made con-artistry into an art form, and indeed freed swindling from utilitarian purposes to such an extent that it becomes a pure practical or poetic activity, the end of which—if it can be said to have an end outside of its exercise— would consist in a preparation for equally nonutilitarian, nontechnical knowledge. Even if Hebel had never glanced at a single representative of Kantian aesthetics,[21] which is unlikely, something of the formula for aesthetic judgment first proposed in the *Critique of Judgment* and unevenly developed in Schiller's *Aesthetic Letters* migrates into his summary description of Zundelfrieder's craft: "he does not steal out of need, nor for the sake of profit [*Gewinnsucht*], nor out of wickedness [*Liederlichkeit*], but from love of the art and for the sharpening of the understanding [*aus Liebe zur Kunst und zur Schärfung des Verstandes*]" (H, 3: 374).

No occupation is in a better position to throw light on the place where aesthetic semblance enters into the sphere of the legal order than con-artistry: where, to use Schiller's words, semblance fails to renounce *all* its claims to reality and, for this reason, delivers itself over to the critico-legal order for sentencing. Only under one condition would it be possible for more light to be cast on this murky place: if the con-artist acts "for love of the art and for the sharpening of the understanding" and is therefore upright after all. Such a condition obtains in "How Zundelfrieder Got Himself a Horse to Ride": "Now for once," he says to himself, "I want to test how far one comes with honesty [*Jetzt will ich doch auch einmal probiren, wie weit man mit der Ehrlichkeit kommt*]" (H, 374). The weight of this decision falls on "one" (*man*)—not on how far Zundelfrieder can go with honesty but how far it is possible for any given subject to travel under the imperative not to dissemble. Instead of crossing the border illegally, this time the thief seeks to discover the limit of the legal order, and asks himself: at what point does it *demand* dissemblance? At such a point, there would naturally arise a right to semblance.

When Zundelfrieder is brought in front of the judge for stealing a goat from under the eyes of the constable and thus demonstrating the failure of the civil authorities to do what they are supposed to do—protect the household—he soon learns not so much the distance one covers with honesty as the method and rationale of punishment: "twenty-five or so [lashes] for remembrance" (H, 3: 374). To this sentence, which perhaps serves as a reminder of his father's "copulation" with the noose, Zundelfrieder responds: "I have not yet been honest enough." More honesty means more stories, if not about himself, then about a certain persona whom he develops for the sake of his experiment—the persona, more exactly, of a split personality. Zundelfrieder informs the judge that he has always been a "half cockroach, that is, a human being who almost sees better at night than during the day" (H, 3: 374). This confession of inhuman insight occasions a change of sentence: instead of corporeal punishment in the open light of day, condemnation to the obscurity of the *Zuchthaus*.[22] And this confession likewise brings Zundelfrieder, who seems to have stolen his brother's stories,[23] into confederacy with the *Hausfreund*, for the wily thief and playful narrator are both intimately associated with the reflective light of the moon.

"[The moon] is the actual friend of the house [*der eigentliche Hausfreund*]," the *Hausfreund* announces in the opening article of next year's calendar and thereby acknowledges that he only impersonates the real *Hausfreund*, which, in any case, cannot appear on its own. As the authentic and proper *Hausfreund*, the moon combines two functions that, for the improper or fake *Hausfreund*, remain ineluctably distinct: "[the moon is] the first calendar maker of the earth, the highest general-nightwatchman, when others sleep" (H, 3: 410). Measuring time by means of its phases, the moon makes the calendar; casting light on an otherwise dark world, it watches over those who are unaware of its presence—as a remembrance of and preparation for something other than *stolen* light. The other *Hausfreund*, the fake one, by contrast, carries out only the first of these two functions; the second is delegated to others, whom Zundelfrieder, for one, slyly subverts. Under the protection of the reflected light of the moon, with insect eyes, Zundelfrieder takes advantage of a general unawareness. Each of them, Zundelfrieder and the *Hausfreund*, is in his own way—to borrow a biblical phrase Hebel interprets in a lecture whose point of departure is a comparison between the eyes of the biblical interpreter and those of the cockroach—a "thief in the night."[24] And to this line of shadowy and shady figures—*Hausfreund*, Zundelfrieder, cockroach, interpreter—two more might be added: the Jew and the Messiah. As Hebel writes in an epistle (*Sendschreiben*) of 1809: "Concerning Isaiah, however, this much I can say: whoever can read it from the fortieth chapter onward and never feel an impulse of a desire [*Anwandlung eines Wunsches*] to be a Jew, a beggar Jew, even if it means encamping with all the vermin of Europe [*europäischen Ungeziefers*], has not understood it. As long as *the moon* still shines on a single Israelite who reads this chapter, the belief in the Messiah does not die out" (H, 3: 611).[25]

As Zundelfrieder progressively frees his craft from utilitarian purposes and develops it into pure con-artistry, he, the arch-enemy of houses and economies, becomes progressively assimilated to the figure of the *Hausfreund*, who comes to admit that he is not *eigentlich* (authentic, proper) after all. Or, in reverse, the improper *Hausfreund*, who, like the moon, must always steal light in order to appear, presents the principle of impersonating house friendship in the figure of Zundelfrieder. And the thief turns into a storyteller as he approaches the *Zuchthaus*: "On the way [there]," the

Hausfreund continues, "he told the city soldier that he, too, had been a military man" (H, 3: 375). If Zundelfrieder is impersonating a former soldier—and every sign indicates this is so—his impersonation would not be legally culpable: the character whom he impersonates is out of work, no longer in service to the state, and his self-presentation is for the entertainment of his companion, a nail maker who, because of "hard times," is forced into the unhappy role of a "city soldier" or policeman. Zundelfrieder does not even precisely lie; rather, he only asks questions about himself, each of which is an explication of his earlier "wer da" (who goes, who is there): "Have I not been in infantry-service for six years in Klebeck? Couldn't I show you seven wounds from the war on the Schelt that Emperor Joseph wanted to lead with the Dutch?" (H, 3: 375). To use a Kantian vocabulary, Zundelfrieder supposes a right to lie out of *Menschenliebe*: the nail maker thinks better of himself and takes pride in the degraded position into which he has unfortunately fallen—the position, that is, of serving the civilian authorities: "a city soldier," Zundelfrieder goes on to say, "is more respectable to me than a field soldier [*Feldsoldat*], for the city is more than the field" (H, 3: 375). The unemployed nail maker is unaware of what Zundelfrieder means when he says in all honesty (*Ehrlichkeit*) that neither he nor his enemies have much honor (*Ehre*) in the fact that he remains alive; on the contrary, the nail maker is simply moved by the "honorable comparison [*ehrenvolle Vergleichung*]." With this remark the nail maker unwittingly completes the comparison between the honesty of Zundelfrieder and that of his closest literary relative, Christian Wolf, the solar-associated poacher in whose honor Schiller writes "The Criminal from Lost Honor."[26] In the hands of the *Hausfreund*, honor is doubtless lost—and more generally lost than in Schiller's account of an inept poacher turned into unhappy leader of a criminal gang. But the criminality of Zundelfrieder cannot be understood in terms of such psychological motivations. If there is a motive for his criminality, which is by no means certain, it is *critical*: not the loss of *Ehre* (his father's "copulation" with the noose, for example) but, rather, a sober inquiry into the legal-aesthetic limits of *Ehrlichkeit* (honesty). Fraud is to be freed from every material motivation and made into a matter of pure form—so pure, in fact, that the honest guardian of the law begins to look like a fraud himself. From the perspective of the great impersonator, Zundelfrieder, his companion appears to be impersonating a guard—not out of dishonor or indeed any psychological motive but, on the contrary, like Christian Wolf, because of general economic deprivation.

Impersonation so completely permeates the scene of reconciliation be-tween outlaw and agent of the legal order that the latter appears as the brother whom the former has seemingly lost—the nail maker calls his companion "Herr Bruder"—and the outlaw, in turn, casts himself in the role of storyteller, otherwise reserved for the *Hausfreund*. Not surprisingly, the storyteller is displaced from his role and replaced by an anonymous artist. Added to the title "How Zundelfrieder Got Himself a Horse to Ride" are the words "with an Illustration," and the image of Zundelfrieder at precisely this point in his story—which is the sole image of this, the most regularly appearing of the calendar's cast of characters—catches the criminal in the act of narration: open, carefree, and apparently uninhib-ited, Zundelfrieder brings his official auditor to tears, or bores him to death, or simply eases him into sleep by telling him tales, while all along a writ for the arrest of a certain Friedrich Zundel, renowned thief, is perhaps posted in the background.[27] "And," the *Hausfreund* continues, "Frieder continued to tell his war-stories [*immer fort erzählte von seinen Kriegsäf-fären*]" (H, 2: 377).

Yet, for all the effortless outpouring of Zundelfrieder's stories, not everything he says goes unopposed. When Zundelfrieder calls himself "a half cockroach," the judge accepts it as grounds for resentencing; when the thief then calls himself a soldier, the nail-maker-turned-guard accepts it as grounds for an estimation of his own worth. But when Zundelfrieder rids himself of his companion and sets out on a path "as far as the moon shed light on him [*so weit ihm der Mond leuchtete*]" (H, 3: 377), he finds out how far (*wie weit*) one can go with honesty. Presenting himself alone to "the administrator of the house of correction" (*der Zuchthausverwalter*), Zundelfrieder's aesthetic-legal experiment comes to an end:

> The administrator read and read and finally looked at Zundelfrieder with big eyes: "Good friend," he said, "this is in order [*das ist schon recht*]. But where then do you have the prisoner? You are supposed to deliver over a prisoner [*Arrestanten*]." Zundelfrieder answered entirely amazed: "Well, the prisoner, that is I myself [*Ey, der Arrestant, der bin ich selber*]." The administrator said: "Good friend, it seems that you want to make a joke. One does not joke here. Admit it, you let the prisoner escape. I see it from everything [*Ich seh es aus allem*]." (H, 3: 378)

The last agent of the legal order, who could legitimately be called *der Rheinländische Zuchthausfreund*, does not claim to be able to see or over-

Anonymous Holzstich illustration in the *Kalender auf das Jahr 1813*, probably the work of Hans Kaspar Hegi; from Hebel, *Sämtliche Schriften*. The source for the (merely probable) identification of the artist is Rohner, *Kommentarband zum Faksimiledruck der Jahrgänge*.

see everything: this is no panopticon. Rather, the prison administrator claims only to be able to see *it*—whatever "it" may be—from everything else, which is to say, to distinguish reality from appearance. This is the premise of the administrator's authority; without it, he could not find sanction for his power. The exercise of force can be justified only with reference to this intended object, which, for its part, must be *real*: "one doesn't joke around here." The ambiguity of the word "here" is vertiginous. The warden "reads and reads and opens his eyes," but instead of seeing, he *reads* appearances without seeing that he is still reading. And what else but a joke could he seem to see "here" when he still reads? He reads appearances as a joke because no one would present himself as a prisoner *alone*: no one would go this far with honesty. Truthfulness is trickery: this is the suspicion under which the agent of the legal order operates, and it marks out the *limit* to honesty: one cannot be honest enough—*not* because of human fallenness, according to Lutheran dogma, nor because it

is an infinite task, according to Kantian critique, but because the legal or-
der at some point *demands* that it and *it alone* be the one to distinguish
being from appearances.

Just as Zundelfrieder lies out of concern for the downtrodden agent of
the legal order in the first part of the story, he refuses to deny the premise
on the basis of which the representative of the *Zuchthaus* makes its sen-
tences come true in the second—its ability to distinguish reality from
semblance by virtue of its "big eyes": "If you see it from everything," he
replies, "I do not want to deny it" (H, 3: 378).[28] He thus arrives at the
limit to honesty: the warden's judgment that he is not himself but some-
one else—which is to say, another agent of the state. The warden does not
precisely see *himself* when he sees "it" from everything, but this "it"—
which, of course, cannot be seen—is the semblance of himself: a debased
semblance, to be sure, a "simpleton" as opposed to an "administrator," but
nevertheless a semblance of the administrator who can be trained to be
the real thing. (This is a *Zuchthaus* after all.) As he enlists him in the
search for himself, the administrator asks the simpleton, "Can you ride?"
To which Zundelfrieder replies with a question that his supervisor, like
the nail maker who honestly impersonates a guard, seems to see through:
"'Was I not with the Württemberg dragoons for six years?'—'Good,'
replied the administrator, 'someone will saddle up a horse for you as
well.'" Zundelfrieder once again does not lie: the question he poses may
have its origin in the stories he told the "city soldier," but as a question it
makes no claims; and even as a question it cannot be understood simply
as (empty) rhetoric, for it asks nothing less than "Who am I, who is the I
that speaks?" To which the administrator aptly replies "good"—good be-
cause he already "sees" who he is: the semblance of himself. Zundelfrieder
seems to have the right to appear as someone else—the "simpleton" from
whom he slips away—on the condition that the recognized and recogniz-
able agent of the legal order can see him only as himself in training.

This condition seems to be a *limited* one: limited by the particular
"blindness" of a particular warden of a particular penitentiary and limited,
as the house friend emphasizes in the final sentence of the story, to *other*
jurisdictions: "something like this could not happen in this country [*so et-
was könnte hier zu Land nicht passiren*]" (H, 3: 379). This sentence, which
is set off from the rest of story, reads like the conclusion it is supposed to
illustrate, its maxim or moral. But it can hardly be understood in this way,
for it is not a general statement; indeed, it is not a statement of principle

but of *impossibility*, as if Hebel, suddenly reminded of his official function, had to reassure his readers that this condition was *indeed* limited: to reassure them not only that prisoners cannot impersonate agents of the legal order who, for reasons of economic deprivation, are forced to impersonate "city soldiers"; not only that thieves cannot induce widespread panic by showing writs proclaiming their presence; but also that the reason for the release of the thief has *only* to do with the peculiarities of a particularly blind administrator in a particularly poorly administered land. More generally, it reassures his readers *e contrario* that it is possible to appear before some administrators *as* oneself. For if there is no right to impersonation *and* no warrant to present oneself "in person," if this contradiction stands at the foundation of the legal order, regardless of its specific form, one—Zundelfrieder's *man*—cannot speak *to* or appear *before* it at all. Or everything one says to the legal order and every form in which one appears before it can be understood only as if one were already its agent, or agent in training. And the only remaining house, indeed the only place in which one can reside, is the space defined by the *Zuchthaus* out of which Zundelfrieder, this *Hausfeind*, not only once found his way on his own, but alone—with only a stolen horse—again finds his way out.

III. Kleist: Arresting Disorder by a Fake Arrest Order

Zundelfrieder presents himself without any dissemblance and is accused of playful impersonation—which may be appropriate for a play but not for life, still less for somber houses where the legal order demonstrates the extent and intensity of its power: "here one doesn't joke around." The arrest warrant for the very one who broadcasts the warrant comically reveals the fallibility of the legal order, to be sure; its tragic version would be Oedipal. In either case, however, the circulation of the arrest warrant gives proof of both the pervasiveness and the invasiveness of the legal order: it remains in force regardless of its fallibility. The right to semblance seems to lie at the point or borderline where the legal order reveals its "soft spot" while nevertheless demonstrating its overall solidity.

If, however, the constituted legal order were unable to demonstrate its power; if it were to collapse, dissolve, or even only suffer a moment of suspension, then the right to semblance would appear in a very different light. And such is the case with Heinrich von Kleist's first published story— from its opening sentence, set in a prison, until its final paragraph, which, in miniature, captures the labyrinthine complications of freedom that Leibniz explicates and reduplicates in his *Essays of Theodicy*: "when Don Fernando compared Philipp with Juan"—which is to say, his natural son, who was murdered by an enraged mob, with his freely adopted son whom he saved—"and how he had acquired both, it seemed to him almost as though he had to rejoice" (SWB, 2: 59).[29] As Kleist sat in prison, unsure of the law under which he was being held, he entrusted a friend with a manuscript entitled "Jeronimo and Josephe, a Scene from the Earthquake in Chili." Taking the manuscript out of the prison, the friend had it published in the *Morganblatt für gebildete Stände* (Morning paper for educated classes).[30] When Kleist later republished the story in the first volume of his *Erzählungen* (Tales) he simplified the title to "The Earthquake in Chili." He could also have complicated the title to the point where it would be appropriate for a Rhenish house-friendly environment: "How Jeronimo One Day Escaped Prison, Josephe Execution, and Together *Almost* Came Happily over the Border." The accent, of course, falls on the *almost*.[31] How they escaped is easy to answer, even if the answer—by accident—merely begs the question.[32] And with the accident of the earthquake comes not only the collapse of the prison in which Jeronimo sets out to hang himself but also the downfall of the pseudo-juridical procession into which Josephe, his beloved, falls after she, like the papess at whose tomb Leibniz throws flowers,[33] gives birth in public. The procession is pseudo-juridical to the extent that the legal order under which Josephe is tried is divided among competing authorities: civil, ecclesiastical, and perhaps (for this is only suggested) inquisitorial; it cannot in any case *honestly*—and without embarrassment—present its sentence as *the* verdict of a wholly legitimate order of law.[34]

Just as with the corresponding story of Zundelfrieder, the story of Jeronimo and Josephe is less concerned with the details of escape than with their (in this case, failed) effort to get across the border. For reasons of economy, only the last scene of this failure will be considered here: it is a scene to the second power, a scene of mise-en-scene, which may be the very "scene from the earthquake in Chile" to which the original title of the story refers. In any event, the mise-en-scene fails, and the failure of the drama is far more consequential than any failure of "philosophical attempt at theodicy,"[35] for it precipitates the violence in which Josepha and Jeronimo are consumed. The violence doubtless owes its origin to the Dominican priest's theodicical interpretation of the earthquake as an act of divine vengeance, which, in turn, generates a spirit of prelegal or extralegal revenge among his swarming auditors. But the scene of theological exegesis and popular retribution turns violent only after a certain "marine officer" hesitates to play the part assigned to him in a spontaneous legal theater. "Popular justice" is never less just than in this unrehearsed mise-en-scene:

> The cobbler asked: Which of you, citizens, knows this young man? [Note the absence of both verbs and quotation marks: the scene is written as if it were a play, with lines and stage directions.] And several of the bystanders repeated: Who knows Jeronimo Rugera? Let him step forward! Now it happened at this moment that little Juan, frightened by the tumult, began struggling in Josephe's arm and reaching out to Don Fernando. Immediately: He *is* the father! a voice cried; and another, He *is* Jeronimo Rugera! And a third: These *are* the God-forsaken people! And the whole assembly of Christendom in the temple of Jesus: Stone them! Stone them! To this Jeronimo: Halt! You inhuman ones! If you seek Jeronimo Rugera, here he is. Free that man who is innocent!—
> The furious mob, confused by Jeronimo's utterance, cut short; several hands released Don Fernando; and then in the same instant a marine officer of significant rank rushed forward and, pushing himself through the tumult, asked: Don Fernando Ormaz! What is happening to you? The latter, now completely freed, with true heroic sobriety [*wahrer heldenmütiger Besonnenheit*] answered [and he alone is given quotation marks]: "Yes, you see, Don Alonzo, the murderous villains! I would have been lost had this worthy man not quelled the raging crowd by giving himself out as Jeronimo Rugera. Arrest him, if you would be so kind, along with this young woman, for their own security; and this worthless one," [he said] grasping Master Pedrillo, "who hatched the whole uproar." The cobbler cried: Don Alonzo Onoreja, I ask you on your conscience [*auf Euer Gewissen*], is this girl not Josephe Asteron? Since now Don Alonzo, who knew Josephe very well, hesitated with the answer [*mit der Antwort zauderte*], and several voices, enflamed once again into a rage cried: she is it, she is it and, kill her. So Josephe placed both little Philippe, whom Jeronimo had hitherto been carrying, and little Juan in Don Fernando's arm, and said: Go, Don Fernando, save your two children and leave us to our fate! (SWB, 2: 156–57)

The only place left for Jeronimo and Josepha to hide is *in language itself*, more exactly, in the *name* and, more exactly still, in the *stage name*. As long as they appear to be pretending to play the part of themselves for the sake of other "God-forsaken people," they can hide from the crowd and escape their "fate." But it is impossible for them to appear to be pretending to be themselves all by themselves; rather, they need another, who, as impresario, makes it possible for them to take refuge in their "own" names. Don Fernando—whom only very few seem to recognize, whose self-confidence has already been shown to border on self-deception, who will later show himself to be a master of dissemblance or "false pretense" (*falsche Vorspiegelung*),[36] and who, for all these reasons, may very well be an impostor—is this impresario: he spontaneously stages a play by casting Jeronimo in the role of an anonymous actor who has spontaneously cast himself in the role of Jeronimo, whose name means, of course, "sacred name." In the mise-en-scene of this deadly serious play, Don Fernando is not entirely dishonest, for Jeronimo does in fact give himself out as Jeronimo, but his arrest order is the first of his "false pretenses," since Jeronimo *is* Jeronimo after all. By giving Jeronimo out as the one who gives himself out as Jeronimo, he transforms Jeronimo's honest, upright, and self-sacrificing self-impersonation— "If you seek Jeronimo Rugera: here he is!"—into sheer semblance.

"Fully freed" from the crown, isolated but not alone, Don Fernando emancipates semblance from reality—not, however, in order to exercise the rights of a sovereign in a world of semblance, not even to demonstrate his own autonomy, but to feign for the first and perhaps the last time a *truly* legal order: a legal order distinct from that of the Church; a legal order not founded, therefore, on shaky interpretations of worldly events as ordered, justified, or even justifiable; an order of law, in sum, whose existence lies in *an arresting act of language alone*, not in the violence or threat of violence through which arrest orders are sanctioned and carried out. Such an arresting sentence cannot fail to be fake, and here, in this mock command issued by a supposed descendant of *the* Commandant, *would be* the origin of a truly legal order, one founded neither on violent acts of heroism nor grounded in self-sacrificing passivity. And here—not in a peaceful valley beyond the city where pomegranates hang down, where the human spirit miraculously rises up, and where everyone appears as if they were "*one* family" (SWB, 2: 152)—would be an eschatological site without a theologically sanctioned *eschaton*. A legal order *appears to appear*, but this order *only* appears *in order to* appear—not in order to establish a stable and self-consistent order through which its threats could be made effective and its sentences carried out.

This legal order appears nowhere outside of Don Fernando's fake order to arrest his company and hold them in an equally fake prison. Something holds back the marine officer to whom this order is directed. Although the sailor later says that "several circumstances . . . justified" (SWB, 2: 158) his "inactivity" (*Untätigkeit*), only one of these circumstances makes its way into the story: an appeal to the "voice" in which all stances and circumstances are consigned to rigorous judgment; an appeal, that is, to conscience.[37] The one who speaks in the name of conscience is Master Pedrillo, the cobbler, otherwise known as "the prince of the satanic horde" (SWB, 2: 158), and he is also the one who expresses his outrage at those who dissemble: "why do they lie to us!" (SWB, 2: 158), he cries, and thereby imputes blame to the liars, not the "satanic horde," for the murder of the one completely blameless bystander, Donna Constanza, whose name conjures up not only images of constancy but also the figure of the inconsistent Benjamin Constant, the victim of Kant's famous polemic "On a Supposed Right to Lie Out of Love for Human Beings."[38] Master Pedrillo may be satanic, but Satan here is not the father of lies; rather, he dwells in the appeal to conscience. And his accomplice is the name of the father: "A voice from the raging crowd that had pursued them cried: 'this is Jeronimo Rugera, citizens, for I am his own father' and struck him to the ground on Donna Constanza's side with an enormous blow" (SWB, 2: 158).[39] The appeal to conscience in conjunction with the naming of the father strikes down the last vestiges of the inconspicuous, almost invisible mise-en-scene of an unjustified legal order through which the explosion of violence would have been held in check. The appeal to conscience does so *not* because it makes "cowards of us all," or even makes cowards only of upstanding naval officers, but because conscience wants to know nothing of semblance. For there to be a truly legal order, it must distinguish itself so completely from conscience and the violent voice of the father that it cannot appear in good conscience, certain of itself; nor can it appear in the name of justice; rather, it appears, if it can appear, only in order to appear. Such a legal order, the true one, would, however, only be the semblance of legality.

§ 5 Anecdote and Authority: Toward Kleist's Last Language

> History is a great anecdote.
> —Novalis

> The constructions of history are comparable to instructions that
> commandeer the true life and confine it to barracks. By contrast: the
> street insurgence of the anecdote. The anecdote brings things nearer
> to us spatially, lets them enter our life. It presents the rigorous
> antithesis to the kind of history that demands "empathy," which
> makes everything abstract. Newspaper reading winds up with this—
> "empathy." The true method of making things present to us: to
> represent them in our space (not ourselves in theirs). Only anecdotes
> can move us in this direction. Thus represented, things tolerate no
> mediating constructions from "larger contexts."
> —Walter Benjamin

The daily circulation of anecdotes belies their name, for anecdotes, as
an-ekdota, are "not given out." Anecdotes can make good on their easily
deciphered etynom only if they somehow hold themselves in reverse and
refuse to give something away. What anecdotes generally withhold—and
this makes them into anecdotes in the conventional sense of the term—is
evidence. Instead of giving evidence, they pass along hearsay. Whoever re-
counts an anecdote knows of the things under discussion only by way of
the anecdote itself—and therefore does not really know these things at all.
At the limit of the anecdotal, speakers would not only *not* be witnesses to
the event about which they speak; they *could* never have witnessed the
event, for it would be, in the original sense of the term, an-ecdotal, not
given out. Which is to say that it could not be made into the subject mat-
ter of "eyewitness testimony"—or any other form of self-evidence. If, how-
ever, a subject-matter cannot be "given out," it cannot be "taken in" either:
it cannot be per-ceived and, accordingly, withdraws into a zone of indeter-
mination that subtends and suspends both givenness and takenness, both
evidence and perception. Anecdotes of this order would be sheer hearsay:
what they "give out" is the withdrawal of language into this zone of inde-

termination. Once it is thus withdrawn, language cannot be understood, even *as* language. And so the only event that such anecdotes could pass from one speaker to another is the passing on of language "itself."

Anecdotes, however, are not purely and simply "not given out." From the inception of the word, the *an* of *anecdote* serves as an expression of determinate negation, not as an indication of a zone of indetermination. What the *an* of *anecdote* negates is authority. Under no condition can *auctoritas* express itself anecdotally. Anecdotes may wax and wane, but their growth does not "augment" (*augere*) the foundation of the founders. "Authority" cannot, in turn, accrue to anecdotes.[1] On the contrary, from Procopius's *Anekdota* onward—and Procopius's work serves as the starting point for the development of the term—anecdotes have run counter to the order of imperial authorization. They can afford to do so, however, only because they are for the most part without identifiable authors. The source of anecdotes is unknown or unnamed. As the first book to bear the title *Anekdota*, Procopius's collection of stories about the imperial household of Justinian has an exemplary status: the work constitutes a broad challenge to the very emperor who codified Roman law, oversaw the creation of the Corpus Iuris Civilis, and authorized the publication of the great Digesta on whose basis legal authority was determined in large parts of Europe for centuries to come.[2] At the very moment when Justinian publishes the law, Procopius gives out what should remain unpublished: the stories, in particular, of the untrustworthiness of Justinian and the faithlessness of his wife, the empress Theodora. By giving out his "anecdotes," Procopius exposes the limits of imperial authority: Justinian may be able to make his word into law and thus bring the chaotic field of legal formulas into a semblance of order, yet stories about his household—"anecdotes" in the original sense of the term—can nevertheless circulate without any legal mandate. Procopius not only shows that Justinian, the great codifier of the law, was unable to control the goings-on in his own house; with even greater precision, the *Anekdota* shows that this inability resides in narrative, one of the constitutive features of legal reasoning. The *an* of an *anecdote* runs counter to the "no" of codified law, and both forms of negation express themselves in judgments based on narrative accounts of alleged wrong-doing. Procopius's *Anekdota* shows that the ultimate jurist, the emperor, is not himself just, and this demonstration of the unjust jurist perhaps gives direction to every subsequent anecdote that does justice to its name.

But only "perhaps": an account of anecdotes cannot easily sustain a conclusive or even preliminary thesis for the simple reason that anecdotes are too varied, too indistinct, and too widespread to constitute a recognizable genre. Since anecdotes are often used to keep their subjects in place, they can contribute to the solidification of a particular legal order just as easily as they can challenge the justice of its preeminent jurists.[3] Even if the "not" of anecdotes indicates that they somehow withdraw from the order of law and, to this extent, move in the direction of a "popular" justice, this movement is far from unambiguous. Never is the direction of anecdotal justice less so than when "the people" are understood as a solid and unified body, the existence of which lies outside of the generally recognizable order of law. Under these conditions the unregulated circulation of anecdotes can give "popular" sanction to representations of "essential" traits not only of "the people" but of all those who are outside of its provenance and protection. By running counter to the legal order, anecdotes can then establish in miniature a "popular" court of appeal in which judgments are made and executed in secret. Justinian's *Anekdota* is often translated as "Secret History," and a conspiratorial atmosphere envelops those anecdotes that serve as "popular" challenges to a more or less open sphere of legal reasoning.

The concept of popularity is therefore of little use in defining the function and significance of anecdotes. As long as the effort to arrive at an idea or form of something constitutes the fundamental feature of theoretization, the category of the anecdotal will remain an embarrassment to theoretical endeavors—perhaps more of an embarrassment than the category of literature. Whereas the literary, as "the lettered" in the widest sense, always implies a principle of exclusion—the first exclusion being the "unlettered," thereafter the insufficiently sophisticated or educated—the anecdotal hardly excludes anything at all; by comparison, it is utterly unprincipled. This lack is captured by the "an" with which the word begins, and it accordingly makes itself apparent in the almost undifferentiated mass of anecdotes that are published in ever expandable compendia. In terms of sheer length, the 2,371 pages of Fernando Palazzi's *Enciclopedia degli anedotti* is comparable to the fifty volumes of Justinian's *Digesta*; but, whereas the latter seeks a rigorous ordering of its sections, which are themselves articulated according to a principle of application, the former joyfully abandons any such search.[4] The nontheoretical character of Palazzi's "encyclopedia" expresses itself in the sole principle of its organization: disparate themes. Since anecdotes are without a form of their own, they can be cat-

alogued only in terms of their subject matter. To the extent that the sub-
ject matter of anecdotes is compromised by their unregulated circulation
—for who knows any longer what they are about?—even this principle is
unequal to its task, and anecdotes fall into the indistinct "categories" of
gossip, hearsay, or chatter.

Even as it fails, however, the theory of the anecdote might nevertheless
have the function of anticipating in abbreviated form the embarrassment to
which theories of literature succumb. The anecdotal can be seen to antici-
pate the literary, and the origin of this anticipation is the unauthorized—or
not yet authorized—character of everything anecdotal. Once it has been
authorized, which does not simply mean assigned an author, an anecdote
can assume the exclusivity and selectivity to which the word "literature" at-
tests. Anecdotes are of such great significance to the "historization" of the
literary that efforts to show the relation of literary works to the epoch of
their formation often touch on the anecdotal—from early romanticism to
"new historicism."[5] As unauthored and unauthorized accounts of odd, un-
usual, or singular events, anecdotes can serve as the link between a "lived"
experience and its literary representation, for they appear to give evidence
of something outside of or in between solid systems of regulation, circula-
tion, and representation. For anecdotes to perform this historicizing func-
tion, however, they must nevertheless be "edited" in some manner, which is
to say, arrested in their "free flow," solidified, and made public. It is not dif-
ficult to date when anecdotes began to appear in published forms: during
the end of the eighteenth and the beginning of the nineteenth century. Col-
lections of anecdotes are serialized; almanacs with assortments of anecdotes
are published; calendars with quotidian stories are distributed; newspapers
run anecdotes alongside the "news," and a few extraordinary attempts are
made—by Isaac D'Israeli and Novalis, for example[6]—to discover the char-
acter of the anecdote as a form in its own right.

Of all the many regular manifestations of anecdotes in print during this
time two deserve special attention—not simply because they have already
been accorded much attention but because they constitute temporal ex-
tremes. On the one hand, the stories with which Johann Peter Hebel filled
up his calendar, *Der Rheinländische Hausfreund,* testify to the rhythm of the
official year of a minor state in the years immediately following the dissolu-
tion of the last vestiges of the Holy Roman Empire. Not only do things reg-
ularly return to the calendar Hebel edits under the anonym of the "friend
of the house" or "family friend," but the retelling of this return makes the

act of narration all the more familiar, even if the conditions under which this act is itself effective are progressively undermined by the enforced form in which it appears. On the other hand, the anecdotes Heinrich von Kleist published in the *Berliner Abendblätter*—which was the first daily paper published in German-speaking lands[7]—correspond to the frenetic rhythm of daily publication. In both cases, anecdotes appear on a regular basis and mark the passing of day into evening; but the mode of appearance could scarcely be more different: nothing new makes its way into a calendar, whereas the daily paper is, of course, dedicated to nothing but "the news." The pairing of Hebel's stories and Kleist's anecdotes has one further advantage: some of these anecdotes were immediately published by their respective authors, fixed into widely recognizable literary forms, and thus made into the matter of "literature." The transformation of anonymous anecdotes into authored "ecdotes" doubtless abstracts both author and story from the demands of quotidian publication, whether in the form of a calendar or that of a daily newspaper; but the demands of a calendar are different from those of an "evening paper," and this difference can be seen in the naming of their respective anecdotes. Hebel, like Kleist, draws some of his stories from such regular anthologies as Johann Adam Bergk's *Sammlung von Anekdoten und Charakterzügen*, but he sees no need to distinguish "anecdotes," which are unauthorized accounts of events, from "news items," which claim a certain objective validity. For this reason, Hebel avoids the term "anecdote" altogether: everything is an "ecdote" insofar as its "giving out" is ultimately authorized by the Baden regime. The "anecdotal" must therefore go underground and appear in those personae—"rogues," swindlers, and other dissemblers—whose stories give evidence that the legal order is not entirely in the right.

All of the Baden Lutheran calendars published under the auspices of the *Hausfreund* begin with accounts of meteorological phenomena in the widest sense of the term: from the stars and the sun to the moon and atmospheric changes. The regularity of these phenomena correspond to the reliability of the calendar, and in one of these prefatory essays in service of popular enlightenment, Hebel compares his own function to that of the moon: "[the moon is] the first calendar maker of the earth, the highest general-night-watchman, when others sleep" (H, 3: 410). Baden and Brandenburg are almost at opposite ends of the German-speaking areas of Europe, but this geographical separation is scarcely sufficient to explain the vast difference between the meteorological conditions recounted in the

Rheinländisches Hausfreund and those that occasionally make their way into the *Berliner Abendblätter*. One of the first anecdotes to appear in the *Abendblätter* concerns a wholly unpredictable meteorological phenomenon: "God's Stylus," the story of a freak accident. A bolt of lightning melts the bronze monument erected to honor a wealthy woman who, after having "led a wicked life" (BA, 1: 21), donates all her money to a convent as a dying plea for exoneration from her sins. The predicate "unpredictable" cannot, however, capture the character of this event, for the lightning erases some of the letters on the monument and leaves only those that—when taken together, gather, co-llected, or read in the original sense of the word—spell out a verdict: "sie ist gerichtet! [she is judged]" (BA, 1: 21).[8] Whereas Hebel's prefatory expositions of the cosmos accustom the Lutheran populace of Baden to one of the basic presuppositions of modern experimental sciences—the regularity of natural phenomena—Kleist's anecdote of the divine writing tool proceeds in the opposite direction: toward the exposition of the singularity of an event that, without violating any of the canons of Enlightenment principles, nevertheless suggests either the doings of Zeus or those of a just God—or both at once, in a tense relation of divine antipathy.

"What this Berlin paper reports," the editors of the *Berliner Abendblätter* announce in a proclamation "To the Public" at the conclusion of the number containing "God's Stylus," "is the newest and the truest" (BA, 1: 24). Whenever the paper publishes something other than the "newest," it violates its original promise to the public. Such is the case, however, with a large share of the anecdotes, including "God's Stylus," which, as its conclusion attests, is far from being news: the age of the inscription on the gravestone attests to the truth of the story. The two superlatives, "newest" and "truest," cannot therefore always be considered counterparts, especially if tradition is supposed to be a reservoir of truth. The tension between "newest" and "truest" animates the relation between the two kinds of articles published in the paper: news and stories. Anecdotes in the *Abendblätter* run counter to the news in both senses of the term—alongside articles about recent events, and against the quotidian comprehensibility through which the "newest" is understood. If both kinds of stories are subject to a third imperative implied in the announcement "to the public"—the imperative of popularity—they nevertheless part ways in the manner of their subjection: the news informs all of the classes, whereas anecdotes, as Kleist explains to a nobleman who objects to an anecdote about a drummer who bares his anus to a French firing squad, entice "the people" to "read over" the items that it might otherwise ignore.[9] The irregular appearance of anecdotes thus sets the entire enterprise of printing a "popular" paper into relief. The reliability of the editor, the imprimatur of the Prussian authorities, and the conventions of authorship make anecdotes, as "popular" items, into sites of conflict over the nature of authority, and therefore over the relation between novelty and truth. If authority resides in a tradition of truth, then the publication of the "newest" *as* the "truest" strikes at the heart of authority. This strike is of little consequence as long as novelty is only a matter of fact: truth can then be understood solely in terms of already established principles. When, however, novelty is a matter of law—or judgment, especially *last* judgments—then its tense relation to truth cannot be so easily stabilized. And the anecdotes published in the *Berliner Abendblätter* gravitate toward these moments of instability. Their "truth" cannot simply be judged in terms of their representation of reality, for estimations of truth depend upon the juridical terms—including the very term *law*—that are themselves being judged.

The relation of novelty to law is the subject matter of the first article in the *Berliner Abendblätter* that calls itself an anecdote. As printed on October 4, 1810, this story complements a news item that makes its way into the paper on the same day. Both stories concern a "rogue" (*Kerl*); unlike the anecdote, however, the article submits itself to the rules of representing a *novum* and describes the process of condemnation as a matter of course—not as an occasion for judicial embarrassment:

Event of the Day

A statement of a recently caught military deserter, which has already become well known in the city, demonstrates how often the public is made uneasy for no reason: "he ran into a band of arsonists that offered to take him into their group," and so forth. This rogue [*Kerl*] has since confessed under interrogation that this entire report was an invention [*Erfindung*] through which he tried to free himself from the imposed sentence. (BA, 1: 17)

The *Abendblätter* contributes to the equanimity of Berlin by showing the story of the rogue to be just that: mere invention, not "information." Such inventions may be produced independently of any authority, but the author of these deceitful inventions remains responsible for them. Such is the function of juridical authority in this case: it makes the deserter—as a representative of anyone wishing to flee the jurisdiction of martial law—into an author, who, under the pressure of interrogation (*Vernehmen*), is liable for the crimes to which he confesses. The newspaper thereafter announces to the public that its fear of arson is irrational (*grundlos*). Even if the arsonist remains on the loose, the "invention" of the rogue never brings either the Berlin authorities, or the paper in which their interrogations are reported, into question.

The "invention" of the rogue recounted in the anecdote published on the same day, by contrast, throws a magistrate, as the representative of the legal order, into an unpleasant quandary. The state of anxious self-questioning is described as "embarrassment" and consists in a momentary displacement, *Ver-legenheit*, from an otherwise secure position. The source of this uneasiness is the possibility that the judgment of the magistrate may be, or only appear, unjust. His sentences would in either case become indistinguishable from arbitrary violence. The condemned "rogue," in turn, would appear no worse than the one who condemns him. Or, what is worse, the law under which the magistrate is supposed to make his judgments will be shown to desert what it generally claims to protect: justice. As a "feeling of right" (*Rechtgefühl*), embarrassment distinguishes the order of law from the demands of justice, and it is only in this feeling of displacement from an upright stance of rightness that justice still has a claim over legal decisions:

The Embarrassed Magistrate: An Anecdote

A militiaman from H——r not so very long ago, without the permission of his officer, deserted his sentry post. According to an age-old law, an offense of this kind, which, because of raids by the nobles, was of great importance, is actually punishable by death. Without the law having been canceled in so many words, however, no use has been made of it for several hundred years: with the result that, instead of a death sentence being passed, anyone found guilty of violating it is, according to established custom, condemned merely to pay a fine that goes to the city treasury. But the aforementioned rogue [*Kerl*], who had no desire to give up the money, declared, to the great consternation of the magistrate, that under these circumstances, in accordance with the law, he wished to die. The magistrate, supposing some misunderstanding, sent a deputy to the rogue so as indicate to him how much more advantageous it would be for him to pay a few coins rather than be executed by a firing squad. Yet the rogue stuck to it, saying that he was weary of his life [*müde seines Lebens*] and wanted to die: with the result that the magistrate, who did not want to shed blood, had no choice but to release the rogue from

his fine and was even glad when he declared that, in view of the changed cir-
cumstances, he wished to remain alive. rz [author's initials] (BA, 1: 16)

The power of the prisoner lies in his ability freely to renounce his own
life, which does not mean, however, that he "actually" (*eigentlich*) wishes
to die. On the contrary, his self-renunciation is improper, figurative, *un-
eigentlich*: he only *says* that he no longer wishes to live. But in a court of
law, saying is meaning, regardless of what is actually meant. According to
a Hegelian inversion, the account of which had recently been published,
the ability to put one's life on the line gives rise to mastery, and the ability
of the vassal to turn the negativity of death into work overthrows every-
thing that the master achieves in abandoning himself to death, "the ab-
solute master."[10] According to the Kleistian version of this inversion, by
saying good-bye to his life without meaning anything of the kind, the pris-
oner gains an advantage over the magistrate. The prisoner in Kleist's anec-
dote, unlike the vassal in Hegel's treatise, confounds the master because of
what he says, not because of what he does—and certainly not because of
any work he accomplishes. As a particularly lazy soldier in a town no
longer in need of his services, he is the figure of out-of-workness. And the
outcome of the anecdotal inversion is also different from the result of the
Hegelian scenario: the prisoner risks death, but he does not thereby be-
come the master; nor does he overcome the master by virtue of the nega-
tive character of his labor. Rather, the prisoner escapes death and impris-
onment by casting himself in the role of the pure renouncer, and the
master, in turn, finds himself displaced, *verlegen*, embarrassed, without be-
ing removed from his awkward position.

The embarrassment of the magistrate stems from his impotence: he
cannot bring the sentence demanded by the "positive" law into confor-
mity with his sense of justice. Such a concern would not arise if justice
were not something other than legality and were not, in addition, re-
moved from the sphere of temporality. The novelty of the political situa-
tion—towns no longer menaced by marauding bands of nobility—is the
source of the magistrate's embarrassment, for such novelty makes the pre-
scribed legal remedy for the abdication of sentry duty unjustifiable. As the
modern state gains power, its territory is homogenized: nobles are put into
their place, cities are protected, and—at least in the case recounted by the
anecdote—the legal statute enforced by the agent of the new legal order
turns into a memorial to a time when the legal order was much weaker, if
it had any power over the mighty at all. The magistrate is then ironically

placed in the position of the deserter whom he sentences: his post consists in imposing the sentence demanded by law; if he were to do so, however, he would unwittingly reveal that the source of the law's authority—its age—is also the reason for its divorce from the demands of justice. And so in a state of embarrassment he releases the prisoner and, to his relief, the prisoner regains his desire for life. His embarrassment, in other words, remains just that: *Ver-legenheit,* momentary displacement. Everything returns to its proper place. The magistrate is not upset from top to bottom, horrified, or, to use a term Kleist favors, *entsetzt.* However much the magistrate may desert the law that he is supposed to protect, the inversion of magistrate and deserter does not succeed, and the reason for this failure is clear: the magistrate retains his power to exonerate the deserter. Because of this power to the second power—the power not to exercise power—the sentence of the magistrate can retain a semblance of justice.

If, however, another dimension of the situation were to be reversed, and the magistrate, as a prisoner of his own making, were to express his weariness with life, the law could not be so easily brought into line with justice, and the price of exoneration would not be so cheap.[11] The prisoner's declaration of a desire to die would not amount to a prudent strategy in which he exploited the difference between saying and meaning so as to save himself a momentary monetary loss; it would in its own way constitute the only justified sentence the authorities could impose: death. If the rigidity of the law were to latch hold of the one who can make his word come true, the anecdote would no longer show the success of "unedited" and unauthorized speech, but would instead relate an impossible effort on the part of the authorities to bring language firmly into its domain. *Verlegenheit* (embarrassment) would then turn into *Entsetzen* (horror).

Such a situation obtains in an anecdote published in the *Berliner Abendblätter* a week after "The Embarrassed Magistrate." Like "The Embarrassed Magistrate," "The Beggarwoman of Locarno" first appears under a cryptogram. While the former carries the signature "rz," the latter is signed by "mz." The same signature appears at the end of an anecdote that can be understood as the revision of "The Marquise von O . . . "—or as the recursion of the story to its original status as anecdote.[12] "The Beggarwoman of Locarno" revises "The Embarrassed Magistrate" by taking its unstable situation to the limit: the authority of the magistrate over his courtroom turns into the authority of the nobleman over his household, and the condemned "rogue," who retains the right to speak in court, appears as a speechless beggarwoman. The sexualization of the conflict makes the woman appear as the manifestation of the hidden dynamic of the master: undisputed authority confronts sheer obedience, until one turns into the other, with no one left "on top." Both risk death and both die. And the nobleman is not embarrassed, *verlegen*; rather, he is horrified, *entsetzt*. Like the magistrate, his word is law; like the prisoner, however, he suddenly becomes "tired of his life" (BA, 1: 42). Every position is therefore displaced, and only at the end, with the disposal of the nobleman's bones in the place originally assigned to those of the beggarwoman, do things return to the original—but now lifeless—order.

The story of the beggarwoman is displaced in addition from its original status as an anecdote. Alone among the anecdotes Kleist publishes, it turns almost unaltered into an "ekdote" upon its entrance into the second volume of his *Tales*. This anecdote has since been counted among the most perfectly fashioned works of the German literary tradition.[13] The anecdote thus abbreviates the temporal displacement that published anecdotes already display: an unauthorized story, after it has been "edited," turns into a not-yet-authorized story, which, in turn, is reedited, acknowledged, and authorized as a literary invention in its own right. And the transformation of an anonymous anecdote—or widely circulating rumor—into a tightly controlled story is a concern of the anecdote itself. For the marquis, too, wants to "publish" an authorized account of his property. "The Beggarwoman of Locarno" thus brings into play the story of its own production: it shows the efforts on the part of a master to turn an unauthorized account of his household into an "ekdote," which, in this case, would amount to an advertisement for its sale. In the otherwise empty spaces of daily newspapers, advertisements will later take the place of anecdotes. The displacement of anecdote by advertisement is no accident: both forms of publication draw attention to other forms of novelty than those of "the news." Kleist's anecdotes stand between the tale and the sale, and nowhere is the status of the tale in relation to that of the sale more unstable than in "The Beggarwoman of Locarno."

From the opening sentence of the anecdote onward, authority resides in ancestral property and power in the ability to command. When language is then used to get rid of the property in which its authority is lodged, the unheard-of event around which the anecdote is organized begins: "At the foot of the Alps, near Locarno in northern Italy, there once stood an old castle belonging to a marquis [*einem Marchese gehöriges Schloß*], which can now be seen lying in rubble and ruins when one comes from St. Gotthard" (BA, 1: 39).[14] The castle belongs (*gehört*) to the marquis, which means that he must be heard, *er muß gehört werden*. The boundaries of his ancestral property are defined by his ability to make himself heard. As undisputed lawmaker and magistrate of his property, the marquis proceeds to do what masters of the legal situation have always done: put things back in order.[15] By doing so, the anecdote is set into motion. The beggarwoman—whose very anonymity reveals the extent of her powerlessness—is in no position to question or refuse his orders; still less can she, with sovereign presence of mind, ask that she be put to death out of "weariness of life," although she, much more than the "rogue" who appears in the previous week's anecdote, is defined by overwhelming fatigue:

> A castle with lofty and spacious room in which once an old, sick woman, who was found begging at the door, for reasons of compassion was bidden by the lady of the house to lie down on straw that was placed under her. The marquis, who, on his return from hunting, accidentally entered the room, where he was accustomed to place his gun, ordered with indignation [*befahl mit Unwillen*] the woman to get up from the corner in which she was lying and settle herself down behind the stove. (BA, 1: 39)

The marquis's order may be groundless, a matter of momentary *Unwillen* (indignation); but the beggarwoman proceeds to do *exactly* what he says. What he apparently wants her to do is *disappear*, which she does with supernumerary precision, as though she were a ministering angel and he not a lord but the Lord. She disappears *from sight* for good, or for his sake. And she reappears, if *she* can be said to reappear, only in the medium through which he originally exercises his authority: sound. For the voice of the marquis is the law. In his household his authority is incontestable and the power of his command irresistible. Whereas the antiquity of the castle is the source of his authority, his ownership of the property gives him power over its disposition. The coupling of authority and power in a single figure gives his words incontestable force. So forceful is his command that it seems magically to resurrect a crippled woman—until the precise moment when his order has been carried out in full:

> The woman, as she stood up, slipped with her crutch on the smooth floor and she fell, dangerously injuring her back; as a result, although she did manage with unspeakable effort [*mit unsäglicher Mühe*] to cross the room from one

side to the other, as it was prescribed to her [*wie es vorgeschrieben war*], she collapsed behind the stove, moaning and groaning [*unter Stöhnen und Aechzen*], and expired [*verschied*]. (BA, 1: 39)

The owner of the ancestral property makes his words come true; the beggar, by contrast, has no say at all. Between the two stands the housewife, who "bids" the beggarwoman to lie down. Not only is the degree of articulateness proportional to the status of ownership: so, too, is the power of speech. The marquis "prescribes," the housewife "bids," and the beggarwoman inarticulately obeys the former after having silently followed the latter. The peculiar character of the marquis's castle consists in the incomparable force of his command; in executing the prescribed action, the beggarwoman accomplishes the impossible. The sign of impossibility is the "unsayability" of her effort. Only an immediately effective speech could turn the impossible into something possible. Just as the source of its authority is immemorial, the duration of its power is immeasurable. And the command of the owner never lets go. Yet for this very reason, the "real" owner of the property is the *command*—not the one through whom it is issued. The supposed "owner" cannot absolve himself of the "prescription" that he once articulates. However "new" it may be— and what law would be newer than one directing incidental subjects to lie behind accidental objects?—it nevertheless applies as though it were as long-standing as the castle itself. The "owner" is thus owned by "his" speech. Ownership under these stringent conditions is something of a trap. Nietzsche, who preferred to live in hotels, once wrote, perhaps in memory of a trip through the St. Gotthard Pass, along a path that passed by the ruins of the marquis's property, "It is even part of my good fortune not to be a home owner."[16] The misfortunes of home-ownership are amply demonstrated in Kleist's anecdote of an intemperate marquis.

Wishing to rid himself of the authority enshrined in the home with which he is identified, wanting to convert land into mobile capital, perhaps even intent on ridding himself of the "von" by which his name is rooted in the ancient command to augment the ancestral possession, the marquis unexpectedly encounters a forgotten ancestor—or at least an "*X* von Locarno." Once he lets known his desire to sell his home, it becomes apparent that he does not really own it: his speech does. And this speech, which no longer can be said to be "his," *has to be heard.* Like the "power of music" (*Gewalt der Musik*) in another and closely related anecdote that Kleist transforms into an "ekdote,"[17] the speech "of" the marquis exercises its force, its *Gewalt*, in the erasure of the distinguishing marks by means of which character, individuality, and personality are secured. Disowned speech takes over the marquis's auctioned castle, as music invades the embattled church in Kleist's other anecdote. And the speech that overpowers the castle, like the music that overwhelms the church,[18] is wholly inarticulate—in this case, mere "moaning and groaning":

> Several years later, after the marquis had fallen into worrisome financial circumstances, due to war and bad harvest [*Mißwachs*], there was a Genoan knight at his house, who wished to buy it because of its beautiful location. The marquis, who held great store for this transaction, ordered his wife to accommodate the stranger in the above-mentioned, empty room, which was made to be very beautiful and comfortable. But how shocked was the couple when the knight came down to them in the middle of the night, disturbed and pale, assuring them by everything high and dear that the room was haunted [*in dem Zimmer spuke*], since something invisible to the eye, with a noise, as if it rested on straw, got up in the corner of the room, with perceivable steps, slowly and feebly, went across the room and collapsed behind the oven, moaning and groaning [*Stöhnen und Ächzen*]. (BA, 1: 39–40)

The language of "moaning and groaning"—which cannot be unambiguously called "language"—begins to dominate the castle at the very moment that the marquis makes it into disposable capital. And the marquis begins to conceive of his castle in this way—*as* his property rather than as a legacy through which he comes into his own—because of *Mißwachs* (bad harvest, misgrowth), which is to say that he does not "augment" the inheritance that has been entrusted to him, and he therefore begins to lose his *auctoritas*. His speech, however, loses none of its power, and the index of its strength resonates in the room where the sale of the house is supposed to be secure: in this room the property has to be heard. That such speech can *only* be heard—while its source remains hidden and its meaning indecipherable—constitutes the terror of ownership: no exertion of the will can release this owner from his position as owner. The marquis, in particular, cannot release himself from the order he absentmindedly and with indignation once, and only once, prescribed. The marquis does not then turn into a beggar, but the principal mode of his speech consists in bidding an accidental passerby to buy his property. His word is no longer authoritative, his position no longer powerful, and his command without authority. Even as he orders his wife to fix up the room, he comes to occupy in effect her original position, with a slight twist of fortune: he "bids" a knight occupy the same room as the beggar-woman, although not out of compassion, like his wife, but from a desire to rid himself of his house. The knight, who seeks to occupy the previous position of marquis, is similarly transformed: after hearing the "moaning and groaning," he beseeches the couple to let him spend the night in the safety of the master bedroom—as if the castle were suddenly truncated into a two-bedroom apartment in war-torn Berlin. His infantilism emphasizes the degree to which the "moaning and groaning" robs everyone in the house of a magisterial voice and likewise turns everyone into mere bidders, if not outright beggars.

After the failure of the sale, the institution of ownership enters into a crisis, the voice of which is rumor, for the circulation of rumors about the property runs counter to circulation of disposable capital. Whereas rumors run wild, commodities are tightly controlled; whereas rumors appear to grow on their own, commodities can grow only in relation to other commodities. Ownership demands the control of rumor, and this demand can be answered in at least two ways: in advertisements and in anecdotes. As controlled rumors, advertisements are, for the marquis, the key to unloading his property. Against the very story that makes its way into the *Berliner Abendblätter*, the marquis marshals all his forces. He attempts to undo the "an" of his servants' anecdotes and to give out instead an authorized account of the property he wishes to sell: "This incident, which caused extraordinary attention, scared off a number of buyers, to the marquis's extreme displeasure; with the result that, when his own servants, in a strange and incomprehensible manner [*befremdend und unbegreiflich*], raised the rumor that a ghost emerged at midnight in that particular room, he resolved to investigate the matter himself the next night in order to strike down this rumor with a brief procedure [*mit einem kurzen Verfahren*]" (BA, 1: 40).

The ability of the marquis to prescribe laws for the house does not imply a further ability to control descriptions of its contents. Prescription and description stand in no essential relation to one another, and this distinction gives rise to the crisis. With the spread of unauthorized descriptions of the house a reversal takes place: no longer is it the marquis who has to be heard; it is, rather, the house—in stereo. Inarticulate noises have to be heard, on the one hand, and the "household" tells tales about the house, on the other. The relation of language to power similarly changes. The servants, who have no say *in* the house, spread the rumor outside the house, and this rumor alienates the owner from his household. In order for the marquis to forestall this reversal, he must capitalize on another and more recent mode of authorization. Unable to rid himself of his own prescriptions or control the descriptions of his property, he must deliver himself over to a methodical procedure that allows "the things themselves" to appear. Scientific knowledge serves as the medium within which the crisis of ownership can be resolved. The gain in knowledge makes up for a loss in ancestral authority, and can then be used to dispel the doubts of the wary buyer. Knowledge, however, requires a measure of self-control—something for which the marquis has hitherto not been prepared. After he hears "sighing and gasping" (*Geseufz und Geröchel*) at the stroke of midnight, it takes more self-control than he can muster to maintain a scientific attitude and discover the source of the "incomprehensible" sounds. Only the sight of another begging woman—his wife—makes him return to the scene of his original encounter with the beggarwoman:

> The next morning the marquise, when he [the marquis] came down, asked him how his investigation had gone, whereupon he looked about him apprehensively and uncertainly, bolted the door, and assured her that the thing with the ghost was correct: at this she was more terrified than ever before in her life, and begged him, before he let the matter be published, once again, in her company, to subject it to a cold-blooded test. (BA, 1: 40)

Because master and mistress have an interest in the outcome of the investigation to which they jointly have enjoined themselves, the objectivity of their findings is compromised. A disinterested party must be present, and so they beseech a servant to help them disprove the anecdote that has made their house unsellable. All three thus conduct a controlled experiment, the aim of which can be described in Kantian terms: can the diverse elements of perception be made into a unified experience? In his essay "What Does It Mean: To Orient Oneself in Thinking?" Kant considers the possibility of disorientation in an otherwise familiar room: "In the dark I orient myself in a room that is familiar to me if I can take hold of even one single object whose position I remember . . . and if someone as a joke had moved all the objects around so that what was previously on the right is now on the left, I would be entirely incapable of finding anything in a room whose walls were otherwise completely identical" (Ak, 8: 135). Kleist takes the joke one step further—to the point where it is, at least for the marquis and his wife, a grave matter indeed: every object in the darkened room is familiar, including the sounds, but they cannot be integrated into a unified experience of the room as a whole, even if they light candles in every corner. While the couple and their servant conduct an experiment, so, too, does the narrator—in *pure sonorousness*, sound isolated from the other senses, especially that of sight. Anyone entering into this room, regardless of rank, is necessarily infantilized, for it is a room where sound and sight are no longer—or not yet—integrated with one another. The Kleistian joke is then this: instead of turning the furniture around, the narrator turns the room into a playroom for this childless couple, and they, too, are infantilized once they enter its space. Two modes of experimentation thus confront each other: one takes its point of departure from the unity of experience, whereas the other tears this unity apart.

As the "moaning and groaning" return once again, there is no question of which experiment takes precedence; the couple abandons any hope that they will see what they hear, and they therefore take refuge in a future: some day, as a matter of course, sound will cease to be isolated; it will be integrated with the other senses; the source of the purely sonorous will be seen, and all the elements of experience will once again be brought into unity. The vocabulary of science does not serve the purposes of knowledge in this case; rather, it gives the couple a chance to enact a spontaneous *theater*, the sole spectator of which is their servant:

> They heard, however, on the next night, together with a loyal servant whom they had taken along, the same incomprehensible, ghostly noise; and only the pressing desire to get rid of the castle no matter the cost, allowed them to suppress in the presence of the servant the horror that gripped them, and to impute the incident to some indifferent and accidental cause [*gleichgültige und zufällige Ursache*] that must somehow be discoverable. (BA, 1: 41)

If the anecdote were to end at this point, it would demonstrate the triumph of well-trained, scientific self-discipline. By fashioning an acceptable "ekdote" about their household, the aristocratic couple would finally make it disposable; they, in turn, could rid themselves of their hereditary property and join the ranks of the upwardly mobile bourgeoisie. Like the authorities in Berlin—and like the editors of the *Abendblätter* itself—the aristocratic couple could quell the anxieties of those upset by a "groundless" rumor. Both master and mistress would thus show themselves to be the finest of actors, and the purpose of the play performed for the benefit of their servants would be comically ironic; it would allow them to get rid of the stage on which their performance takes place. Yet the anecdote does not end with a dramatic fulfillment of this theatrical mission. At the very moment in which the marquis gives up any pretense toward science and throws himself into a drama of his own making, the anecdote alters. The index of this alteration is the sign of alteration as such: the verb form. Having begun in the preterit, the story suddenly changes into the present tense. As Emil Staiger notes in an acclaimed essay on "The Beggarwoman of Locarno," the alteration in tense does not come at a point of intensified human action; rather, it arrives when the couple sits down to talk and, in a more telling way, when a dog lies down to nap. But the alteration of tense does not necessarily imply that the story achieves its realization in drama, as Staiger proceeds to explain.[19] The presence of the present tense constitutes an anacoluthon in the story as a whole—an anacoluthon that thwarts the telling of "the whole story" and leaves no room for a "completed action." Insofar as the story happens now, in the present, it never comes to an end. All of what follows after the change in tense is drawn into this disruptive event of "nonfollowing," which repeats at the level of the narrative the disruption of comprehensibility that follows from the eruption of the purely sonorous:

> On the evening of the third day, when both of them, in order to get to the bottom of the matter, with pounding hearts once again climbed the stairs to the guest room, their house dog, which had been let off its chain, chanced to be in front of the door of the room; so that the marquise with the involuntary intention [*in der unwillkürlichen Absicht*] of having beside her husband a third thing, something living, took the dog with them into the room. The couple, two lights on the table, the marquise fully clothed, the marquis with sword and pistols, which he had taken from the cupboard, by his side, sit down about eleven o'clock on their separate beds; and while they try to pass time in conversation, as best they could, the dog lies down in the middle of the floor and, all curled up, goes to sleep. (BA, 1: 41)

Husband and wife return to the abandoned room in order to get to "the bottom of the matter"—no longer driven by a desire to rid themselves of the house but by a drive to get at the "ground" of things at all costs. This "ground" (*Grund*) is something other than the lands on which their castle rests, which is a lost cause in any case. And the *Grund* is something other than the "cause" (*Ursache*) of the pure sound: it is, rather, the groundedness of a "matter" for which they have no defining terms—and an apparently linguistic "matter" at that. The search for a ground of the phenomenon coincides with a lack of self-knowledge: the wife does not know why she brings the dog along. The marquise—or in the version that Kleist publishes in *Tales*, the couple (SWB, 2: 198)—invites the dog out of an *unwillkürlichen Absicht*: an "involuntary intention" or, more paradoxically but no less accurately, an "unintentional intention." The contradictory character of this phrase could then be understood as a sign of a hidden intention—hidden from the marquise, the couple, the reader, and even perhaps from the storyteller. And the search of reader and storyteller for this intention would replicate the search of the marquise and her husband for the "bottom of the matter." At the bottom, then, would be an intention: the reason for their compulsive repetition of a scene, the details of which they themselves seem to have forgotten. Since the content of this scene is the "moaning and groaning" of a woman begging in a bedroom, the "bottom" of the matter—and the reason for the slippage between marquise and couple—could be explicated as follows: the forgotten scene is "primordial," an *Urszene*, and the sounds overheard are those of a then incomprehensible and later reconfigured, if still misunderstood, sexual or sexualizing event. Instead of engaging in the time-passing activity of empty talk, the couple might then benefit from the presence of a third person—neither a servant nor a dog but, instead, the intersection of the two, which is to say, an analyst, who, in a Kleistian version of couple's therapy, would solicit from both husband and wife the reason why they asked him—analyst or dog—to join them. By analyzing their otherwise inexplicable desire to invite a third "person" into their second bedroom, they could perhaps get to the "bottom of the matter," discover what forces them out of bed at night, and thus resolve their compulsive complex. The title of this case history might then be "The Dog Couple." Instead of empty talk, the couple would finally arrive at "full speech"—which might be word-for-word the same as their idle conversation but would nevertheless spell the end of the purely sonorous, integrate their senses with one another, and make their second bedroom available for other purposes, including—but this is only one possibility among others—the conception of the infants whose playroom it already seems to be.[20]

The dog, however, remains only a dog, less an analyst than a catalyst. Or, if the dog is an analyst, it is because he undertakes his own investigation, which, like the "investigations of a dog" Kafka dutifully records, perhaps after having reread this very anecdote, does not recognize the desires, anxieties, or drives of its supposed masters.[21] And the dog in Kleist's anecdote may act as a catalyst rather than an analyst because it, unlike its owners, can apparently "see" the purely sonorous. Like the fencing bear who appears in an article Kleist anonymously published in three consecutive issues of the *Berliner Abendblätter*—"On the Marionette Theater"—the dog is able to do what human beings cannot: while the bear apparently can read the soul of his opponent, the dog can evidently see the invisible source of the sounds.[22] The dog, whose name might as well be Fido, enters the scene as a replacement for the couple's most loyal servant: its loyalty is supposed to be beyond dispute, and the same is true of its obedience. Yet the loyalty of the dog is altogether different from the loyalty of the servant or the obedience of the beggarwoman, for it exercises itself in a sphere at the margins of language—in gestures, barks, moans, and maybe even groans. If the dog is able to pass on any rumors about the house in which he finds his home, it would in all likelihood only be to other dogs, all of whom would be without authority and barred from the sphere of ownership, even if the house ends up "going to the dogs." Which it does:

> Then, at the moment of midnight, the terrible noise can be heard again; someone, invisible to the human eye, gets up, on crutches, in the corner of the room; one hears the straw that rustles under him; and at the first step: tap! tap! the dog wakes up, gets up suddenly from the floor, its ears pricked, growling and barking, just as if a human being [*ein Mensch*] were walking toward it, the dog backs away toward the stove. At this sight the marquise, her hair standing on end, rushes out of the room; and while the marquis, sword in hand, cries out, "who's there?" [*werda*], and since no one answers him, like, a madman, he cuts through the air in every direction, she has a carriage yoked with the intention of driving toward town. (BA, 1: 41)[23]

The marquis sees the "thing" only second-hand—or second-paw. And the insight into his inability to see the "thing" drives him out of his mind: he is in every sense of the word *dispossessed.* Once the marquis sees that the object he hears can be seen—but not by him—he recognizes that hearsay is irreducible. The "horror" (*Entsetzen*) of the marquis repeats the "embarrassment" (*Verlegenheit*) of the magistrate, but it takes the displacement to its limit: the marquis is so completely upset that the very form of intuition that generated the magistrate's embarrassment—time—collapses. The collapse of time in the space of the room expresses itself in the only language that remains. How does a master respond to the experience of a room that appears to interrupt the unity of experience? With a question, of course, which corresponds to the inarticulate "language" that brings nothing to light. The marquis does not ask "who is there?" (*wer ist da*). Nor even, for lack of time, does he revert to military parlance and ask "who goes?" (*wer da?*).[24] Without the leisure to return even to military forms of address, infantilized in the extreme, the marquis asks—if this can be translated—"whog's?" (*werda*)?

Not only is the "is" missing in this question—which would be appropriate in the context of a guard demanding a password—but so, too, is the space between the *wer* (who) and the *da* (there, now). There is no time for an "is," and no space for it either. Without the time-space for the third-person present tense of the verb "to be," without the security of "being there-now" (*Dasein*), without a "there" that is not at the same time a *wer*—without, in short, spatial-temporal articulation in general, the question, which takes to the limit the alteration of tenses by doing away with tense at the moment of the greatest tension, almost changes into an unconditional command to change unconditionally: "werda?" becomes the graphic and acoustical displacement of the absolute imperative—"werde!" (become). Rilke's famous "Du mußt dein Leben ändern" (You must change your life)[25] is far less radical than the question-command of the infantilized marquis: "become I-know-not-what," "become something other else altogether," "become"—*without being anything*. The marquis has no time to be, no place to live, no space to articulate his "lived" experience, and so, in shock, he, like the prisoner in the previous anecdote, enters into the sphere of life weariness. Completely unlike the prisoner, however, he *is* "weary of his life" and is for this reason robbed of the wherewithal to *say* so: "The marquis, overcome by horror [*Entsetzen*], had taken a burning candle and set fire to all four walls, weary of his life [*müde seines Lebens*]" (BA, 1: 42). The marquis disappears into the purely sonorous and becomes—what else?—the matter of an anecdote that does not even bear his name.

~

The regular return of a "language" over which no one seems to have any authority—not even the authority to say whether or not it is language in the first place—leaves no time for the "stretching" of one now-point into another. And nothing—no time, no space, no thing, no act—replaces the "is" of the question through which speakers first gain unambiguous access to language: "who's there now?" This "nothing" constitutes the "matter" (*Sache*) of the anecdote. There is no measure for such bottomless "matter," and its bottomlessness sets the anecdote on its erratic course—until it finally reaches the pages of the *Berliner Abendblätter*, as if these regularly appearing, rustling "evening leaves" were a place of refuge for the purely sonorous. In the spaces of this evanescent paper the last language of those weary from life—which corresponds to the first grumblings of the excited infant—can be distributed to the opining public under the watchful eyes of a judging regime. Whereas the "evening leaves" (*Abendblätter*) bring things into the light of a dying day, the anecdote of the disappearing beggarwoman brings to light the conditions under which the act of bringing things to light is itself brought to light and thus withdraws from the sphere of clarity, lucidity, sight, and human-all-too-human insight. Instead of first-hand knowledge of the "matter at hand," two pages of the evening paper bring to light a barking dog in retreat from something— perhaps a ghost, perhaps an angel—that appears to appear to it alone. In the appearance of this appearance, which itself appears in the autumnal mood of the last leaves, an anecdote in the original sense of the word gives itself out—and away.

§ 6 The Paradisal *Epochē*: On Benjamin's First Philosophy

Kant and the Multicolored Self

"I was not one who sees, I was only seeing. And what I saw were not things, Georg, only colors. And I myself was colored into this landscape" (GS, 7: 19). With these words, Margarethe describes a dream from which she has recently awoken—a dream that serves as the point of departure for one of Walter Benjamin's early writings and his last dialogue, "The Rainbow: Dialogue on Fantasy."[1] Margarethe's dream is that of "pure seeing" (*das reine Sehen*). Isolated from all other senses, seeing is so pure that, strictly speaking, no one sees anything: instead, colors are seen, and see in return. Not only do the colors of Margarethe's dream "look" (*Aussehen*) beautiful, they also "look out" and "look at" (*sehen aus*) each other. Only by being colored into the colorful scene can Margarethe "herself" see— and see "herself."

In the *Critique of Pure Reason* Kant describes the condition and consequence of the "revolution in thought" that he is in the process of executing: "Thoughts without content are empty, intuitions [*Anschauungen*] without concepts are blind" (A, 51; B, 75). Benjamin's "Rainbow" is an extended response to Kant's memorable apothegm. A thought without content is doubtless empty, especially if emptiness is defined as the absence of content; an unconceptualized intuition is not, however, blind. On the contrary, as a pure *An-Schauung* (intuition, looking at), it sees a landscape of color. Only if blindness is understood as the inability to distinguish one thing from another is "pure seeing" blind; under this condition, moreover, it is even more blind than Kant suggests, for it does not distinguish seer from scene. And no one sees this better than Kant, who only a few pages later, after reflecting on what it means "to think *red* in general," takes into consideration a—perhaps imagined, perhaps dreamed—counterfactual condition: "only because I comprehend their manifold in a consciousness do I call them all together my representations; for otherwise I would have as multicolored, diverse self [*vielfärbiges verschiedenes Selbst*] as I have representations of which I am conscious" (B 134). The quickly repudiated fantasy of a "multicolored, diverse self" allows Kant to identify "the ground of the identity of apperception": it lies in the spontaneity of the pure understanding, which is to say, the merely formal, unifying, and decidedly *colorless* "I." Having accomplished its self-defeating purpose, the multicolored self disappears from Kant's exposition for good.

The "multicolored, diverse self" of Kant's imagination reappears, perhaps for the first time, in Benjamin's dialogue: "I was not one who sees, I was only seeing. And what I saw were not things, Georg, only colors. And I myself was colored into this landscape." The distinction between self and world disappears in this dream; but this disappearance does not appear as sheer indifference—"the night in which all cows are black," to use Hegel's equally famous apothegm[2]—but, rather, as an infinitely nuanced scene of dappled differences, all of which are themselves different from the differences by which things are spatially, temporally, and conceptually determinable. The colors of Margarethe's dream are pure properties—not properties of any substance in which they inhere and to which they therefore belong. Her dream cannot, in turn, be considered properly *hers*. As she indicates at the beginning of the dialogue, she falls—or rises—into a state of "self-forgetting" (GS, 7: 20). By doing away with both substance and self-subsistent subject, the dream multiplies ad infinitum the number of "objects" and "viewers," for the "look" of color is doubled: subjective and objective at the same time, and never fully either.

Upon hearing Margarethe's description of her dream, Georg therefore concludes, "They were the colors of fantasy" (GS, 7: 19), to which Margarethe readily agrees. With the term *fantasy* Benjamin addresses one of the central discoveries, or inventions, of the Kantian "revolution in thought": the discovery of the "transcendental synthesis of the imagination." Without a careful delineation of this hitherto unknown synthesis, Kant could never have carried out his critical project, for only the imagination "in its transcendental use" makes it possible for the two otherwise heterogeneous "stems" of the human mind—the receptivity of the senses and the spontaneity of the understanding—to co-constitute a world of appearance in which a self-conscious "I" can recognize itself as such.[3] Without the discovery of the transcendental synthesis of the imagination, moreover, Fichte would not have been able to explicate the manner in which the absolutely self-positing self would have been able to open up space, make time, and thus stabilize itself as solid under-*standing*.[4] And if Kant and Fichte had not made the transcendental imagination into a central theme of their respective work, Schelling and Hegel, each in his own way, would not have been able to demonstrate that their predecessors on the path to systematic philosophy had sown the seeds for something greater: a genuinely speculative philosophy, from whose perspective the transcendental imagination discovered by Kant and radicalized by Fichte appears as a proleptic index of an absolute substance appearing as absolute subject.[5] In all of these cases, regardless of otherwise insuperable differences, the synthetic character of the imagination is constantly emphasized. By presenting the imagination "in its transcendental use" as a productive power, in contrast to its (merely reproductive, associative, or Humean) counterpart, Kant initiates this tendency; for his successors, the productivity of the imagination surpasses even Kant's imagination, since it can be shown to synthesize the very self who constitutes the world of which it becomes aware. The doctrine of "intellectual intuition," which Kant denies to human beings and reserves for a problematic God can then be shown to be justified after all, for, as the self constitutes its world by virtue of the transcendental imagination that it itself "is," it intuits itself as it thinks of itself. This act of self-constitution owes nothing to the receptivity of the senses; on the contrary, it is wholly spontaneous, hence "intellectual." And so, even if, as Hegel argues, intellectual intuition sees nothing but undifferentiated darkness, the very vision of this night *as* night heralds a speculative daybreak in which spirit appears to itself as it is: as absolute substance turning into self-absolving subject.[6]

Benjamin, however, will have nothing of this: "Pure fantasy . . . creates nothing new. Pure fantasy is therefore not a power of invention [*erfindinde Kraft*]" (GS, 6: 117). And colors, for their part, are never invented, even if as yet unseen ones can be made by mixing. As if it were the leitmotif of his remarks on color, Benjamin thus repeatedly emphasizes this fact: "colors must be seen" (GS, 6: 109, 119; W, 1: 48). As a distraction to those interested in the truth of substance and subjects, color is of little importance in the line of thought from Kant to Hegel,[7] and for the same reason—because of its inherent distractiveness—it occupies the center of Benjamin's attention. Unlike Goethe, moreover, against whom Benjamin can be seen to measure himself throughout his work,[8] Benjamin does not present his

Farbenlehre (theory of color) as a scientific inquiry into the true nature of color. Nor does he diagram the relation among various colors in an effort to determine which ones are pure or primary.[9] Benjamin may share with Goethe a suspicion of Newtonian science; but this suspicion does not lead him to invite his readers, as Goethe does, to conduct their own experiments, reclaim the experimental sciences from the petrified world of professionalized disciplines, and thus make these sciences once again conform to what the word *experiment* promises: life-enhancing experience. Benjamin's *Farbenlehre* is everywhere concerned with the status of experience; but instead of seeking to reclaim experience by "personal" observation and experimentation, he makes his *Farbenlehre* into a confrontation with the tradition in which the modern *concept* of experience takes shape. This tradition receives its canonical formulation in Kant's *Critiques*.

Nowhere does this concept of experience more effectively move in the direction of doctrine than in the sole place in the *Critiques* where Kant writes of rainbows. The purpose of Kant's reflections on the rainbow may be diametrically opposed to those of Benjamin's, but this very opposition indicates a commonality of concern. According to Kant, the phenomenon of the rainbow is a "mere appearance," and so, too, from a transcendental perspective, is everything we can experience. The rainbow can thus be seen as an appearance in which the merely apparent character of things comes to light. As an appearance to the second power, the rainbow is completely devoid of substance, and since the purely relational character of the "substances" we know is one of the fundamental teachings of the critical "revolution in thought," the rainbow can even illustrate the doctrine of transcendental idealism as a whole. The point of the project first broached in the *Critique of Pure Reason* can then be formulated in terms of the rainbow that graces the last pages of the "Transcendental Aesthetic." Every appearance appears as if it were a rainbow—or, more exactly, a *pure* rainbow, a rainbow produced by drops about which we know nothing:

> We would certainly call a rainbow a mere appearance in a sun shower, but we would call this rain the thing in itself [*die Sache an sich selbst*]—all of which is correct, as long as we understand the latter concept in a merely physical sense, as that which in universal experience and all various positions relative to the senses is always determined thus and not otherwise in intuition. But if we consider the object in general and, without turning to its agreement with every human sense, ask whether it (not the raindrops, since these, as appearances, are already empirical objects) represent an object in itself, then the question of the

relation of the representation to the object is transcendental, and not only these drops are mere appearances, but even their round form, indeed even the space through which they fall are nothing in themselves, but only modifications or foundations of our sensible intuition; the transcendental object, however, remains unknown to us. (A, 45–46; B, 63)

With these words, Kant, perhaps against his own intention, makes the rainbow into an emblem of transcendental idealism as a whole. If we see seeing properly, we see everything as rainbowlike. Benjamin, whose treacherous loyalty to the program initiated by the first *Critique* is evident throughout his early writings and finds an explicit formulation in his "Program for the Coming Philosophy," makes the rainbow into the "emblem [*Sinnbild*]" (GS, 7: 24) of intuition fully freed from the tendency of the mind to substantialize the objects it sees—even if substances are recognized as purely relational or functional. For this reason, Benjamin arrives at a peculiar radicalization of the critical project, the most succinct expression of which occurs midway in "The Rainbow": "only in intuition is there the absolute [*nur in der Anschauung gibt es das Absolute*]" (GS, 7: 21). However much this affirmation of intuition's absoluteness may resemble some of the young Schelling's remarks about "intellectual intuition," it could scarcely be more different.[10] For, as Benjamin notes in conjunction with the idea of "pure seeing" (*das reine Sehen*), "the nature of reception [is] unintellectual" (GS, 7: 563). At one stroke he disassociates himself from any tradition of German idealism that takes its point of departure from the idea of an intuition that spontaneously generates the "things" it intuits, including—if not exclusively—itself. According to Kant, we are completely unaware of what a purely spontaneous mode of intuition would be like; intuition, as far as we know, is always only receptive. "Going beyond" Kant, from Fichte onwards, consists in demonstrating the falseness of this restriction and, in general, disparaging receptivity in favor of spontaneity. In this regard, Benjamin does not wish to go "beyond" Kant, or "back" to him either: eschewing both programs, he seeks instead his own version of radicalization in which intuition is made absolute—without being conceived as conceptual in any manner whatsoever.

Benjamin's *Farbenlehre* thus opposes every "logical" reinterpretation of the Kantian program. Like Schopenhauer, who also wrote on colors but whom Benjamin rarely mentions, and like Heidegger, whom Benjamin may have known as a student in Freiburg and whose philosophical career he observed from a distance long before the publication of *Being and*

Time,[11] Benjamin takes his point of departure from the exposition of the receptivity of intuition in the "Transcendental Aesthetic" rather than the analysis of the spontaneity of the understanding in the "Transcendental Logic."[12] But Benjamin neither repeats the procedures of Schopenhauer, nor anticipates those of Heidegger, for, unlike both, he follows Kant by granting the possibility of an original mode of intuition. He deviates from Kant, and from all those who sought to outdo Kantian critique, on one point: *intuitus originarius* does not, according to Benjamin, consist in the spontaneous generation of the thing intuited; on the contrary, *intuitus originarius* not only remains receptive but receives its originality by being purely so. Pure receptivity (*reine Aufnahme*) is absolved of every synthesizing tendency. Instead of synthesis, there is creation (*Schaffen*). Creation from pure reception—without reliance on spontaneously generated forms and without the detour of discursivity in general—is the original mode of intuition, and it does without the "I" on the basis of which, according to Kant, appearances are formed into the phenomena through which the "I" secures its constitutive self-consciousness. This absence of this "I" appears in the "multicolored, diverse self" of Margarethe's dream. Creation from pure reception is the formula by which Benjamin maintains his treacherous loyalty to the Kantian project: receptivity takes precedence over spontaneity to the point where the very act of creation—which is generally understood to be the sign and seal of spontaneity—is completely nonsynthetic. Intuition is thus purified of every conceivable discursive detour, even the one imagined in the act of a divine "I" who is conscious of itself as it creates a world it then declares to be good. When intuition is pure, it does not intuit anything but is, instead, indistinguishable from—indeed identical to—pure fantasy. The creativity of fantasy does not therefore consist in an ability to form models—not even the primordial models (*Vorbilder*) of sensible intuition Kant calls "schemata." Nor does fantasy produce what, according to Kant, a divine intellect would create: archetypes (*Urbilder*). Creation from fantasy has nothing to do with images (*Bilder*) of any kind, all of which depend upon the distinction between itself and the thing of which it is an image. For this reason perhaps, Benjamin uses the term *Phantasie* rather than "imagination" (*Einbildungskraft*). The Kantian name for that which remains completely free of both images and imagination is "the law." As the sole rational datum of which we are aware,[13] the law is higher than any image or archetype. Creation must be purely receptive—with no admixture of "creativity." And the only manner in which creation can occur, if it can occur, is from, and not merely in accordance with, absolute laws:

> *Margarethe*: A poet wrote: "If I were made from material, I would color myself [*Wäre ich aus Stoff, ich würde mich färben*]."
>
> *Georg*: Receptively to create is the perfection of the artist [*Empfangend zu schaffen is die Vollendung der Künstlers*]. This reception from fantasy is not a reception of a model [*Vorbild*] but of the laws [*Gesetze*] themselves. It would unite the poet with the formations [*Gestalten*] themselves in the medium of color. To create entirely out of fantasy would be called divine. It would mean to create entirely from the laws, immediately and free from the relation to these laws through forms. God creates entirely from the emanation of his essence, as the neo-Platonists say, since this essence would be nothing more than the fantasy from whose essence the canon emerges. Perhaps the poet recognizes this in color. (GS, 7: 24)

Benjamin is drawn toward the neo-Platonic idea of emanation because it is the image of creative receptivity: an overflowing fountain receives its source from itself, and the overflow from this self-sustaining source *is* the "created" world. Whereas Descartes sought to make the "I" into the guiding thread of "first philosophy"—and Kant follows him in this endeavor—Benjamin goes in the opposite direction: toward the "I"-less source that purely receives itself. This source is the focal point of Benjamin's "first philosophy." Ever since Aristotle first introduced the term *protē philosophia* in book Epsilon of the *Metaphysics*, it has been vitiated by an ambiguity: it is both the study of being as being and the study of the most noble being or God.[14] The same ambiguity is captured in the sole sentence of Benjamin's dialogue that embarks on theology: the essence of God is fantasy, and the essence of fantasy, which would be the essence of essence, is the source of the "canon" for all nondivine, merely synthetic creativity. For anything to enter into this canon, however, it must be radically transformed—from thingliness to "colorliness" (*Farbigkeit*). Such is the point of the line that Margarethe cites; the author of it is Friedrich Heinle, a friend of Benjamin, who had committed suicide a few months before "The Rainbow" was written. The dialogue is dedicated to Grete Radt, who perhaps appears under the pseudonym Margarethe; but it can also be understood as an undedicated memorial to Heinle—or, more modestly, as a commemoration of this line, which opens a vista onto the landscape of paradise. In the counterfactual conditional of Heinle's line, the self distances itself from all synthetic acts: instead of producing itself in thought, it colors itself in fantasy, and can do so only after it has been magically materialized. Whatever else may be said of this material-ization—and Benjamin leaves everything unsaid—at least this much is known: it has nothing to do with projects of self-realizations or "becom-ing who you are."

The unity of spontaneity and receptivity in the act of a "fantastic" syn-thesis takes place under the aegis and direction of the latter. For this reason Heinle's line—with its dream of a material self that colors itself—is illus-trative. And for the same reason Benjamin distinguishes between law and form: forms are a matter of choice, whereas laws are not. However strongly the idea of fantasy suggests the concept of transcendental imagination, Ben-jamin sends this idea in another direction altogether, toward the section of the first *Critique* entitled the "Canon of Pure Reason": a canon is the com-plete collection of prescriptive laws.[15] Canonical creation means creating from these laws, which, however, as laws, cannot appear *in* any form but must, instead, appear only as the destruction of form—as, to use a term Benjamin introduces a few years later, *Entstaltung* or "de-formation":

> The German language possesses no word of its own for the forms of phantasy. Only the word "appearance" [*Erscheinung*] can in a certain sense be consid-ered an appropriate one. And in fact fantasy has nothing to do with forms [*Gestalten*] or formation [*Gestaltung*]. To be sure, fantasy gains its appearances from them, but they are as such so little subordinate to it that one can even designate the appearances of fantasy as the de-formation of that which is formed [*Entstaltung des Gestalteten*]. (GS, 6: 114; W, 1: 280)

Whereas, for Kant, the transcendental synthesis of the imagination is the power of the mind in which spontaneity and receptivity are brought to-gether—if they do not, as Heidegger concludes, both owe their origin to this original temporalizing synthesis[16]—receptivity under the sign of fan-tasy, according to Benjamin, engages in an irresolvable conflict with spon-taneity, which, in turn, gives rise to form: receptivity appears only under the condition that spontaneity recede, and the recession of spontaneity takes place as the undoing of forms. Since, however, phenomena are al-ways somehow formed, the undoing of forms can appear only as the dis-appearance of appearances—that is, as night—not, however, as the night in which all cows are black but as the night of "uninformed" motley. Not surprisingly, this night seems "negative":

A moment of the constructive [*ein Moment des Kunstruktiven*] is proper to all phantastic formation [*allen phantastischen Gebilden*]—or (spoken from the perspective of the subject) a moment of spontaneity. Genuine phantasy is unconstructive, purely de-formative [*rein entstaltend*]—or (spoken from the perspective of the subject) purely negative. (GS, 6: 115; W, 1: 280)

"The Rainbow" makes no mention of *Entstaltung*, nor does it consider in any greater detail the neo-Platonic idea of divine emanation. In various other early writings, most notably in "The Program for the Coming Philosophy" and in notes "On Perception," this thought resonates with the project of transforming an "empty" and "shallow" concept of experience (GS, 2: 160; W, 1: 102–3) into one commensurate with the possibility of artistic and religious experience. Outside of its reference to neo-Platonism, "The Rainbow" says little of the religious and is, rather, primarily concerned with the artist. Benjamin's studies of color are attempts to develop a concept of experience other than Kant's—without departing from the general "typic" of the critical program.[17] The direction of all these inquiries is succinctly stated in a fragment entitled "The Rainbow or the Art of Paradise," the aim of which seems to be the elucidation of the like-named dialogue: "color in its artistic significance is a form of appearance [*die Farbe in ihrer künstlerischen Bedeutung ist eine Erscheinungsform*]" (GS, 7: 563). This proposition could be reformulated in terms of the dialogue it seeks to elucidate: within the sphere of the canon, or in canonical terms, color is a form of appearance. Outside of the canon and therefore disregarding its artistic significance, color can only be, as it is for Kant, the material of sensation. As such, it has no relation to form whatsoever; it is neither a condition of possible experience nor a concept through which appearances are "informed" to the point where they can be matters of experience or learning (*Erfahrung*).

In a curious passage of the *Critique of Judgment* Kant reverses himself on the question of whether there is anything formal about color: the first edition denies form to color altogether, whereas the second edition erases a "not," identifies colors with imperceptible forms, and thus maintains that they can be considered beautiful after all.[18] In neither edition of the third *Critique*, however, is color taken to be "a form of appearance" in its own right. This is reserved, according to Kant, for the nonderivable and thus original, nonconceptual and therefore noncategorial forms of intuition: space and time. The program of the Transcendental Aesthetic consists in "isolating [*isolieren*]" receptivity from conceptuality, then "separat-

ing [*abtrennen*]" sensibility from the senses "so that nothing remains ex-
cept pure intuition and the mere form of appearances [*reine Anschauung
und die bloße Form der Erscheinungen*], which is the only thing that sensi-
bility can make available a priori" (A, 22; B, 36). In the case of time, the
"thing" that appears to us is always only the "I" as it appears to itself; in
the case of space, the reverse is true: space is the pure medium in which
things outside of the "I" appear. In both cases, the form of appearances is
an infinite given whole, and each of these infinitudes makes possible its
own pure science—in the case of time, the science of arithmetic, in that
of space, the science of geometry. "Color in its artistic significance," by
contrast, gives rise to no science—not even, for Benjamin, a Goethean
science of lived experience. And yet, for Benjamin, it retains its indepen-
dence from the two forms of intuition presented in the "Transcendental
Analytic": in other words, color is neither temporal nor spatial. Few
would worry about the nontemporality of color; space is another matter,
insofar as colors appear to appear in the medium of space. But this ap-
pearance of color "in" space is, for Benjamin, a function of a failure: a
nonisolation of *Anschauung* from conceptuality and a nonseparation of
Schauung from the other senses. Those who do not fail in this regard are
either artists who, by definition, see color in "its artistic significance," or
children, who, by nature, have not yet learned how to integrate their
senses to the point where they attribute and thus subordinate color to spa-
tially delimited relational or functional substances.

"Seen from itself," Benjamin writes of color, "in its own region, it is en-
tirely directed toward and absorbed into the spiritual essence of things
[*geht ganz auf das geistige Wesen der Dinge*]; it is not a matter of substance"
(GS, 6: 118). Because color is not made into a property of substances, even
purely relational ones, it opens onto the region of "spiritual essence,"
which is to say, if only in an approximate manner, it gives access to pre-
verbal sense. Such sense is accessible only to those who are, in the Kantian
sense, *disinterested* in the things they see. According to the *Critique of Judg-
ment* (Ak, 5: 211), disinterest in the positive existence of an object is the
conditio sine qua non of all pure aesthetic pleasure. Because the colors of
fantasy cannot be integrated into any purpose whatsoever, not even that
of symbolization, according to Benjamin, they are not merely beautiful
but are the canon of beauty (GS, 7: 24). Benjamin thus develops the con-
cept of spirit in his *Farbenlehre* by radicalizing the "Critique of Aesthetic
Judgment" of the third *Critique* to the point where it revises the "Tran-

scendental Aesthetic" of the first: not only are the souls of those who see color "in its artistic significance" wholly disinterested in the positive existence of the objects they see; their senses are *unaffected* by anything as well. What Benjamin says of children could also be predicated of artists: "Because they see purely, without letting themselves be psychically disconcerted [*ohne sich seelish verdutzen zu lassen*], color is something spiritual: the rainbow does not refer to a disciplined abstraction but to a life in art" (GS, 6: 111; W, 1: 51).

Drawing on the "Transcendental Aesthetic," Benjamin presents color "in its artistic significance" as a form of appearance: it is neither the material of sensation nor a conceivable form. Drawing on the "Critique of Aesthetic Judgment," he presents children's vision of colors as wholly uninterested in the positive existence of the objects seen. Colors are the canon of beauty once they are seen in the medium of colorliness. In the phenomenon of the rainbow, finally, the purely apparent character of appearance appears in the rainbow as the "emblem" to which everything beautiful returns (GS, 7: 24). And this emblem is the signpost to paradise. Benjamin, who has no aversion to the thought of divine violence, neither mentions nor even alludes to the biblical interpretation of the rainbow, which commemorates the most spectacular occurrence of such violence: "I have set my bow in the clouds," God says, "and it shall serve as a sign of the covenant between Me and the earth" (Gen. 9:13). Perhaps the idea of a renewed covenant suggests to Benjamin no hope for anything other than the reconstitution of previous forms of life after a disaster—not a transfiguration of life in the midst of its constitutive disastrousness. In any case, the rainbow, for Benjamin, does not signal the dispersion of the clouds in which heaven was thought to have its home; instead of being a sign of a new or renewed covenant, it appears as a counterimage to those guardians of paradise—"the cherubim and the fiery ever-turning sword" (Gen. 3:24) —whom God stations around the Tree of Life. The "life in art" to which the rainbow refers is life lived in the shade of this tree: "The order of art is paradisal because there is as yet no thought of melting in the object of experience from excitation [*noch nirgends an Verschmelzung im Gegenstand der Erfahrung aus Anregung gedacht ist*]; rather, the world is colorfully in a state of identity, innocence, harmony" (GS, 7: 111–12; W, 1: 51). The conversation depicted in "The Rainbow" follows the same path—from reflections on children's experience of color as a spaceless medium in its own right to the exposition of its proximity to paradise. Margarethe captures the sense of the entire dialogue when she says of children: "Their fantasy is untouched [*unberührt*]." To which Georg responds, in turn: "By way of color, the clouds of paradise are so close" (GS, 7: 25).[19]

All of Benjamin's reflections on color gravitate toward this paradise, which, however, conceals a corresponding paradox. It takes little effort to see why Benjamin would have chosen to develop his *Farbenlehre* in a dialogue: the motley of its form—where philosophical theorems present themselves in a fictional vehicle and a fictional setting is formed in accordance with the movement of philosophical motifs—corresponds to the motley of its subject matter. Yet it would be difficult to imagine a dialogue less like the "Socratic" ones with which Plato began his inquiry into the nature of things than "The Rainbow." Whereas each of Plato's youthful dialogues issues into an aporia, Benjamin's dialogue is completely porous: everything Margarethe says is confirmed by Georg and vice versa, until they conclude by recapitulating the journey they have jointly taken. Benjamin's early polemic against Socrates—with his fake questions and even more deceptive eroticism—gives some indication of why Benjamin would divert from Plato's precedent.[20] Nevertheless, Benjamin's youthful dialogue issues into an aporia as intractable as the ones encountered by the participants in Plato's early dialogues. For color neither affects those who see it, nor does it disturb them, but they are nevertheless—here is the paradoxical point—still *receptive*. According to the *doxa* to which Kant pays homage at the opening of the "Transcendental Aesthetic," receptivity consists in being affected: "The capacity (receptivity) to come by [*bekommen*] representations through the manner in which we are affected by objects is called sensibility" (A, 19; B, 33). However disinterested viewers of beautiful forms may be in the positive existence of the objects they intuit, they are still, according to Kant, "affected" by them. For Benjamin, by contrast, receptivity is not only *not* the capacity to be affected; it is the very opposite: an *inability* to be affected or touched, sheer impassiveness.

At the end of his contemporaneous study of Hölderlin, almost in passing, Benjamin names this condition "sobriety" (GS, 2: 125; W, 1: 35).[21] Children are sober insofar as they are—to use Margarethe's word once again—"untouched" (*unberührt*). The ecstasis of drunkenness (*Rausch*), according to Georg, grants artists a similar sobriety: receptive impassiveness. And Margarethe's dream of the multicolored self colored into a landscape of sheer color is the clearest vision of this dis-affected ecstasis: the self is utterly receptive, completely open to ever new colorations, and yet in no sense is it ever affected—much less disturbed—by the colors it sees. Affectivity the disturbability: these are "faculties" or deficiencies of subjects whose experience consists in being excited and disconcerted. Benjamin does not seek to resolve the paradox of unaffected receptivity; on the contrary, he seeks out guides who can help him delineate the points of entry into the paradisal condition defined by this paradox. An indispensable guide to this terrain is Hermann Cohen, who does nothing less than eliminate the trace of affection from Kant's concept of experience, while nevertheless maintaining its tripartite "typic."

Cohen and the Detour Through Nothingness

The central problem around which "The Rainbow" and related writings revolve can be stated in a succinct manner: how to free the critical program of its reliance on affectivity without thereby going "beyond" Kant and doing away with receptivity in the same stroke. Benjamin's "Program of the Coming Philosophy," written three years later, addresses the same problem. Insofar as Kant's concept of experience is inextricably rooted in the image of subjects being affected by objects, it is, according to Benjamin, mythological. However much Kant may have wished to overcome this image—and the progress of the *Critique* from the opening sentence of the "Transcendental Aesthetic" onward is evidence of this desire[22]—he cannot do so, for it accurately expresses the "worldview" of the Enlightenment: "It simply cannot be doubted that the notion [*Vorstellung*], sublimated though it may be, of an individual mental-bodily ego that receives sensations by means of its senses and forms its representations [*Vorstellungen*] on the basis of them plays a role of the greatest importance in the Kantian concept of experience. This notion is, however, mythology" (GS, 2: 161; W, 1: 103). Or, as Benjamin writes more dramatically in his earlier "Dialogue on the Religiosity of the Present Time," "to naturalize spirit [*Geist*], to consider spirit as if it were self-evident [*selbstverständlich*], conditioned only by causality, [is] to commit the cardinal sin" (GS, 2: 32). Those who conceive of spirit as affected by the senses, as if it, like everything else, could be subsumed under the category of efficient causality, are sinners against spirit and, for this reason, unpardonable. According to the "I" of Benjamin's dialogue, who issues this damning verdict, mysticism is as guilty of this sin as naturalism. And even if the Kantian "I" escapes the same sin—for, as pure spontaneity, it is neither affected by nor receptive to anything whatsoever—his concept of experience does not: undetermined objects still are at the basis of experience, and so the mind must still be affected by something in order to experience its appearance.

Benjamin's renunciation of this image is by no means unprecedented. On the contrary, it conforms to the general philosophical climate of "antipsychologism." From Hermann Cohen and Heinrich Rickert to Frege and Husserl—to name four vastly different personalities with whose work Benjamin was familiar—antipsychologism serves as the starting point for a wide range of contemporaneous philosophical projects. For Cohen, whose groundbreaking inquiry into *Kants Theorie der Erfahrung* (Kant's theory of experience) informs all of Benjamin's reflections on Kantian thought, antipsychologism can be successfully pursued only under the condition that the Transcendental Aesthetic be absorbed into a transformed Transcendental Logic. To this end, Cohen boldly proposes to do away with the distinction with which the *Critique of Pure Reason* begins: that between forms of intuition (space and time) and forms of thought (categories). Benjamin's "Program for the Coming Philosophy" does not so much assent to Cohen's famous proposal as interpret it as a sign of the problematic character of Kant's concept of experience and, in addition, as a hint toward a possible solution:

> From the development of philosophy demanded here and considered appropriate for the matter under consideration a sign [*Anzeichen*] can already be observed as neo-Kantianism. A major problem of neo-Kantianism has been to remove the distinction between intuition and the understanding—a metaphysical rudiment that occupies a position like the entire theory of faculties—from the place it takes up in Kant. With this—therefore with the transformation of the concept of knowledge—a transformation of the concept of experience also immediately got underway. For there is no doubt that Kant does not intend to reduce all experience so exclusively to scientific experience, however much it may belong in some respects to the historical Kant. In Kant there certainly is a tendency against dividing and fragmenting experience into the realms of the individual sciences, and even if later epistemology [*Erkenntniskritik*] has to deny recourse to experience in the usual sense, as it occurs in Kant, on the other hand, in the interest of the continuity of experience, its presentation [*Darstellung*] as the system of the sciences, as can be found in neo-Kantianism, is still lacking, and the possibility must be found in metaphysics of forming a purely systematic continuum of experience [*ein reines systematisches Erfahrungskontinuum zu bilden*]; indeed, the proper meaning of experience seems to be sought therein. (GS, 2: 165; W, 1: 105)

Even if these remarks are highly critical of Cohen's achievement—and the following ones even more so[23]—they nevertheless conform to the program for the transformation of Kantian thought that Cohen develops from his work on *Das Prinzip der Infinitesimal-Methode und seine Geschichte* (The principle of the infinitesimal-method and its history) to his major revision of the Transcendental Analytic, *Logik der reinen Erkenntnis* (Logic of pure knowledge). *Erkenntniskritik*—the critique of knowledge or epistemocriticism—must purify knowledge, and the method of purification lies in the reformulation of the *Critique of Pure Reason* in terms of the "infinitesimal-method" first secured by the Leibnizian calculus.[24] Because Kant did not employ this method, the Transcendental Analytic split asunder into a Transcendental Aesthetic and a Transcendental Logic: "Had the infinitesimal principle found its appropriate place in the *Critique*, sensibility would not have been able to take precedence over thinking; pure thinking would not have been weakened in its independence [*Selbständigkeit*]" (LRE, 32). By giving this principle its proper place in philosophy, Cohen eliminates affection altogether: pure thinking is entirely independent, and "first philosophy" turns into a "logic of origin." The space and time of knowledge—which is to say, scientific systems—are derived from the principle of origin, and so, too, is the material of sensation, including color: "All pure modes of knowledge [*Erkenntnisse*] must be modifications of the principle of origin" (LRE, 33). The origin of this logic lies in the absolutely original judgment through which all others are legitimated: "the judgment of origin." For Cohen, judgment is "discursive" in the Kantian sense: unlike intuition, it never relates immediately to something; rather, judgment must always take a detour through something so that something else can be presented. The "something" through which the judgment of origin, as the origin of judgment in general, originally "discurses" in presenting something else is, however, nothingness: *das Nichts*. And what judgment originally presents by virtue of its detour through nothingness is "something in general," *das Etwas*. Only this "something in general" is a matter of thought, which is to say, it is the origin of everything conceivable:

> Judgment is not allowed to shy away from an adventurous detour, if it wants to track down something in general [*das Etwas aufspüren*]. This adventure of thinking presents *nothingness*. By the detour of nothingness judgment presents the origin of something in general [*Auf dem Umweg des Nichts stellt das Urtheil den Ursprung des Etwas dar*]. (LRE, 69)

The detour through nothingness is Cohen's method. The "infinitesimal-method" is based on this detour as a dimension of its application. In Kantian terms, "intensive magnitudes" are represented "through approximation to negation = 0" (A, 168; B, 210).[25] Whereas the first detour—through nothingness—allows judgment to present "a something," the second one allows it to present "reality." In terms of Cohen's revision of the Kantian program: the judgment of origin replaces intuition, and the judgment of reality replaces sensation. Instead of saying "replacement," however, it would be more accurate to say "realization," for, according to Cohen, there is in a strict sense *nothing* beyond that which presents itself in judgment to pure thinking. The presentation of "a something" by way of nothingness is therefore the very origin of being, and the presentation of reality by way of "approximation to negation = 0" is, accordingly, the realization of thingliness.

For all its daring, however, the detour through nothing and the approximation to negation cannot be done without certain laws of thought, the first of which is continuity: "The adventuresome path toward the discovery of the origin needs a compass. One such compass is offered in the concept of *continuity*. . . . Continuity is a law of thought" (LRE, 76). By identifying the compass of continuity, Cohen completes the "judgment of origin." Judgment presents "a something" by way of nothingness under the guidance of continuity as the archaic law of thought: "continuity, as a law of thought, means the connection of something with nothingness, as its origin" (LRE, 115). Because continuity is a law of *thought*, it has absolutely nothing to do with sensation. If, as Kant famously asserts, neither necessity nor universality can be sensed, the same is true of continuity—and the truth of this principle is even more original insofar as necessity and universality are themselves unthinkable, according to Cohen, without the compass of continuity. Whereas something in general is presented by way of nothingness under the guidance of continuity, reality (*Realität*)—which corresponds to the sensation—is itself "realized" by the detour of the infinitesimal under the guidance of the same law of thought. Everything knowable is thus entirely immanent to thinking: "As a law of thought, continuity becomes *independent* from sensation for which there is only discretion or even only the unity of a heap. Thinking produces unity and the connection of unities. . . . *By virtue of continuity all elements of thinking are produced from the origin insofar as they are supposed to be valid as elements of knowledge*" (LRE, 76). The conclusion to Cohen's exposition of the "judgment of origin" reveals the *Sprung* (leap) in *Ur-sprung* (origin): "relative nothingness is the springboard [*Schwungbrett*] with which the leap [*Sprung*] through continuity can be carried out" (LRE, 77).[26]

Everything knowable originates, according to Cohen, by springing from nothingness into "something" under the guidance of continuity. Knowledge, therefore, cannot fail to be continuous—and so, too, experience. By making experience continuous, Cohen secures its immanence: there is no "affection" of the senses and no "disturbance" of the soul. The only disturbance—if this is the right word—is the original "leap" from the "springboard" of nothingness into being. But the law of continuity, as Cohen presents it, likewise deprives experience of its immediacy, which is to say, in Kantian terms, its immediate relation to *objects*. With the transformation of the concept of experience in conjunction with the transformation of the concept of knowledge, this version of immediacy is completely eliminated. Experience, for Cohen, is always discursively constructed. Not, for Benjamin, however: the proper sense of immediacy must be found, so that the concept of experience can immediately relate to something. The "something" to which this concept will relate in "the coming philosophy" is no longer an object, still less an appearance, understood as "the undetermined object of an empirical intuition" (Kant, A, 20; B, 34), nor even Cohen's "something in general" (*das Etwas*) but, rather, "being-there" or "existence" (*Dasein*). At the conclusion to the "Program for the Coming Philosophy," Benjamin introduces this term in order to specify the missing element of the *Logic of Pure Knowledge*:

> It must be said: philosophy in its questioning can never hit upon the unity of existence but only upon new unities of various conformities to laws, whose integral is "existence". . . . The source of existence lies in the totality of experience, and only in doctrine [*Lehre*] does philosophy encounter an absolute, as existence, and thereby encounter the continuity in the essence of experience, the neglecting of which can be suspected as the lack in neo-Kantianism. In a *purely* metaphysical respect, the original concept of experience in its totality is transformed in a sense quite different from the way that it is transformed in its individual specifications, the sciences—that is, immediately, where the meaning of this immediacy with respect to the former mediacy remains to be determined. (GS, 2: 170; W, 1: 109–10)

For all its appeal to the original law of continuity, the *Logic of Pure Knowledge* neglects the "continuity in the *essence* of experience," which makes the relation of experience to the "thing" experienced immediate—

without any discursive detours whatsoever. This "thing" cannot be anything other than that which is "absolved" of all mediate relations and is, therefore, recognizable *as* absolute only under the condition that the *concept* of experience have an immediate relation to something. Otherwise, *Dasein* is missed. The danger in making room for immediacy in the development of a new concept of experience is immediately evident: the mythological notion of affection, which neo-Kantianism successfully eliminated from the sphere of knowledge, may return. Benjamin's studies in color are all directed toward the development of a concept of experience that allows for immediacy without representing this trait in affective terms. Near the end of "The Program for the Coming Philosophy" Benjamin adds a note of caution: "All of this is only a sketchy indication" (GS, 2: 171; W, 1: 110). Nevertheless, the outlines of the program are unmistakable. Cohen's attempt to do away with the mythological notion of affection by way of the "springboard" of nothingness and the "leap through continuity" are to be radicalized to a point where this detour finally arrives at its destination: "existence," which is immediately related to the fully developed, systematic, and thus continuous concept of experience. But the concept of experience cannot be transformed unless experience is likewise transformed. For the concept of experience to make room for an immediate relation to *Dasein*, experience must be capable of being immediately related to the "object" of experience. A concept of experience must therefore be developed in which the elimination of affection does not in the same stroke do away with the immediacy of experience. Benjamin is not without help in this matter, moreover. Even if Cohen's neo-Kantianism can provide no guidance, he can look toward phenomenology.

Husserl, Hölderlin, and the Annihilation of the World

The pure vision of color goes after the "spiritual essence" of the things seen. Whoever sees in this manner has a different "attitude" than those whose vision is impure—which is to say, those whose *Schauung* (vision) is not properly isolated and detached, unaffected and undisturbed. Benjamin's studies in color are exercises in the "intuition of essences," which may differ significantly from Husserl's contemporaneous exercises but are nevertheless directed toward the same goal—the development of a concept of experience that insists on immediacy without representing it in terms of affection: "Intuiting essences [*Wesensschauung*] conceals no more difficul-

ties or 'mystical' secrets than does perception. When we bring 'color' to full
intuitive clarity, to givenness for ourselves, then the datum is an 'essence'"
(HGW, 25: 32; PRS, 110–11). Thus Husserl writes in a famous manifesto
published in the first volume of the newly founded journal *Logos*, "Philos-
ophy as a Rigorous Science" (1911), which Benjamin read a few years after
it was first published (GB, 1: 144; C, 43). The "essence" of color is available
to a pure "vision" (*Schauung*), according to Husserl, and only by virtue of
a pure vision—not by way of systematic construction—can philosophy se-
cure its independent sphere of knowledge. Husserl's program for the re-
newal of philosophy dovetails with Benjamin's at two points: both em-
phasize "receptivity" or "givenness" over synthetic construction, and both
reject any representation of spirit (*Geist*) in causal terms.[27] But the refuta-
tion of psychologism, for both Husserl and Benjamin, is of no conse-
quence unless it makes possible a completely nonpsychological inquiry
into the *sense* of experience. In the central paragraph of his "Program for
the Coming Philosophy," Benjamin indicates the point at which his pro-
gram comes into contact with the one launched by Husserl:

> An objective relation between empirical consciousness and the objective con-
> cept of experience is impossible. All genuine experience rests on pure episte-
> mological (transcendental) consciousness, if these terms are still usable under
> the condition that they be stripped of everything subjective. Pure transcen-
> dental consciousness is different in kind from any empirical consciousness,
> and the question therefore arises whether the application of the term "con-
> sciousness" is allowable here. How the psychological concept of consciousness
> is related to the concept of the sphere of pure knowledge remains a major
> problem of philosophy, one that perhaps can be posed with recourse to the
> time of scholasticism. Here is the logical place for many problems that phe-
> nomenology has recently raised anew. Philosophy is based on this—that the
> structure of experience lies in that of knowledge and is developed from it. . . .
> The task of future epistemology [*Erkenntnistheorie*] is to find for knowledge
> the sphere of total neutrality in regard to the concepts of both subject and ob-
> ject; in other words, it is to determine the autonomous, ownmost [*ureigene*]
> sphere of knowledge in which this concept in no way continues to designate
> the relation between two metaphysical entities. (GS, 2: 162–63; W, 1: 104)

By disclosing "the sphere of total neutrality," philosophy can overcome
the "empty" and "shallow" concept of experience Kant inherits from the
Enlightenment. According to this concept of experience, subjects gain ex-
perience of phenomena by being affected by the objects of which these phe-

nomena are representations. Even if Kant makes every effort to rid his work of precritical conceptions of the mind, according to which it is causally determined by transcendent things, he cannot fully do so, for this conception is the very starting point of the first *Critique*, as the critics of Kant from Jacobi onward have never failed to emphasize.[28] Cohen, Husserl, and Benjamin—along with everyone else who rejects psychologism—turn decisively against this conception. But Cohen's *Logic of Pure Knowledge* cannot go any further than the delineation of the structure of knowledge: the concept of experience folds into that of knowledge, just as the forms of intuition are absorbed into the forms of thought. By transforming the concept of experience—and not simply that of knowledge—Husserl's phenomenology surpasses neo-Kantianism in the depth of its questioning, even as it—unlike Plato and Kant, according to the opening paragraph of "The Program for the Coming Philosophy"—dismisses the desire for "depth" in philosophy.[29]

Nothingness is the element in which Cohen transforms the concept of knowledge: from the "springboard" of *das Nichts* (nothingness) *das Etwas* (something in general) springs forth and thus originates. The element in which Husserl transforms the concept of experience is, by contrast, the fiction of total annihilation. As he writes in *Ideas Toward a Pure Phenomenology and Phenomenological Philosophy* (1913)—which Benjamin accurately describes as "Husserl's difficult, principal groundwork [*schwere, prinzipielle Grundlegung*]" (GB, 1: 302)[30]—philosophy cannot even begin unless it immerses itself in the element of fiction: "if one is fond of paradoxical phrases, one can actually say, and if one means the ambiguous phrase in the right sense, one can say in strict truth, that *'fiction'* [Fiktion] *constitutes the vital element of phenomenology as of every other eidetic science*, that fiction is the source from which the cognition of 'eternal truths' is fed" (HGW, 3: 163; I, 160). Whereas Kant argues for the primacy of practical reason, Husserl proposes the "primacy of free fantasy [*freien Phantasie*]" (HGW, 3: 163; I, 157). And the primary fiction of first philosophy is that of world-annihilation (*Weltvernichtung*). The residuum of this annihilation is the "object" of phenomenological research: namely, "absolute consciousness," which is to say, the world no longer *posited* outside of its sheer coming-into-appearance. The method of phenomenology, its detour, thus consists in disposing of this "position" so that the world can—once again or for the first time—*immediately* make itself accessible.[31] Husserl's "annihilation of the world" takes Cohen's detour through nothingness one step further, without doing away with immediacy in the same stroke:

> The being of consciousness . . . would be necessarily modified by an annihilation of the world of things [*eine Vernichtung der Dingwelt*], to be sure; but in its own existence it would not be touched [*in seiner eigenen Existenz nicht berührt würde*]. Therefore modified, certainly. For the annihilation of the world means [*besagt*] correlatively nothing else but that in each lived experience (the full stream—the total stream, taken as infinite in both directions, which comprises the lived experience of the I), certain ordered complexes of experience [*Erfahrungszusammenhänge*] and therefore certain complexes of theorizing reason that orient themselves to those complexes of experience would be excluded. But that does not mean that other lived experiences and other complexes of lived experience would be excluded. Therefore *no real being* [*kein reales Sein*], no being that presents and proves itself in consciousness through appearances *is necessary to the being of consciousness.* (HGW, 3: 115; I, 110)

Whatever else may be said of this fantasy of total annihilation in 1913, it exactly conforms to Benjamin's criterion that spirit be *unberührt* (untouched). The "fantasy" of children, as Margarethe announces near the end of "The Rainbow," "is untouched [*unberührt*]" (GS, 7: 25). In preparation for the fiction of world-annihilation, Husserl proposes a set of terms for this interruptive dis-position of the "thesis" of the world: "reduction [*Reduktion*]," "putting out of action [*außer Aktion setzen*]," "abstention [*Enthalten*]," "bracketing" or "parenthesizing" [*Einklammerung*]," and, most famously, *epochē*, a word that Husserl draws from the lexicon of ancient skeptics, who sought to "refrain" from both assenting to and dissenting from propositions.[32] By the detour of world-annihilation, which radicalizes the Cohenian method of annihilation by revealing its "content," consciousness is entirely removed from the causal schemata through which the world as a whole has been held together. In the terms Benjamin uses in "The Program for the Coming Philosophy" and "On Perception," phenomenology transforms the concept of knowledge, and by so doing it makes possible a transformation of the concept of experience. "Absolute consciousness"—or, as Benjamin writes, "pure epistemological (transcendental) consciousness"—is the sole "residuum" of world-annihilation: what appears in absolute consciousness in the course of the *epochē* is without relation to anything other than the "in" that it is. This "in-ness" is the ground of immediacy. Its structures, for Husserl, are those of intentionality: the correlation of *cogito* and *cogitatum*, whose richly nuanced modalities are the subject matter of concrete phenomenological investigation.[33] What appears in, and as, absolute consciousness "after" the fantasy of world-annihilation could be called nonsensuous "sense," or *noema*, as Husserl puts it in *Ideas* (HGW, 3: 219; I, 214).

As a technical term formed from Greek, *noema* could be retranslated into German, however inadequately, as "the thought" (*das Gedachtete*), in contrast to *noesis* as the act of thinking, on the one hand, and the actual psychic state, on the other.[34] Benjamin, who experiments with eidetic reduction in response to Paul Linke's essay in *Kant-Studien*, "The Right of Phenomenology,"[35] never explicitly analyzes *das Gedachtete* or the noema; but he develops a corresponding concept, *das Gedichtete* (the poetized), which contrasts with both the poetic task and the actual poem itself. Like *noema*, Benjamin's term, which would reappear in Heidegger,[36] registers a general dissatisfaction with the form-content distinction: the noema and the poeticized are form and content at the same time, and yet identifiable with neither. And both the noema and the poeticized are at once "product and object [*Erzeugnis und Gegenstand*]" (GS, 2: 105; W, 1: 18) of pure— which is to say, nonpsychological and nonpsychologizing—disciplines: in the case of the noema, it is object and outcome of "pure phenomenology," in the case of the poeticized, "pure aesthetics" (GS, 2: 105; W, 1: 18).

The methodological innovation of Benjamin's complex inquiry into the difference between two versions of a poem by Hölderlin—the earlier "Dichtermut" (The courage of the poet) and the later "Blödigkeit" (Diffidence)—finds expression in a technical term modeled after Husserl's neologism: instead of investigating *das Gedachtete*, he seeks out *das Gedichtete*. The two texts are versions of the same poem insofar as they share the same intention, which in this case is nothing other than the primary fiction of pure phenomenology: "an annihilation of the world of things," an annihilation that brings to light the world of *relation* among those reduced things. To enter into the sphere of this annihilation requires courage—the courage of the transcendental "fictioner" or poet. For, as Benjamin writes, courage "conceals a paradox, from whose perspective the structure of the poeticized of both versions [of the poem] is fully comprehensible: the danger exists for the courageous person, yet he does not heed it" (GS, 1: 123; W, 1: 33). Which is to say: those who are courageous remain "untouched" but are nevertheless transformed. The two versions of Hölderlin's poem relate to each other as empty versus full intention. The earlier version *designates* the intention— *Dichtermut*, "courage of the poet"—but does not carry it out. The failure to carry out this intention results from a lack of courage, more exactly, a diffident understanding of the "intuition" that fulfills the word *courage*. According to Benjamin, the earlier version of the poem "knows courage only as a property" (GS, 2: 123; W, 1: 33); it belongs to a heroic subject whose heroism consists in holding onto *himself* in the course of reducing the world of things. For this reason, he is *only* heroic. The later version of the poem, by contrast, understands the meaning of the word *courage* so well that it erases the word from the title—along with the word *poet*. No longer merely designated, courage is fully experienced as "a relation [*Beziehung*] of the human being to the world and the world to the human being" (GS, 2: 123; W, 1: 33); in other words, as the correlation of *cogito* and *cogitatum* to the point of absolute identity. Being untouched is the criterion of spirit; spirit gains dominion only under the condition that relationality alone— not self-subsistent substances or subjects—survives. This survival is the sole form of life left in "Diffidence":

> In it [the world of "Diffidence"] a spiritual principle [*ein geistiges Prinzip*] has become completely dominant: the heroic poet becomes one with the world. The poet does not have to fear death; he is a hero because he lives the middle of all relations [*er die Mitte aller Beziehungen lebt*]. The principle of the poeticized as such is the sole dominance of relation [*Alleinherrschaft der Beziehung*]. In this particular poem, formed as courage: as the innermost identity of the poet with the world, whose effluences are all the identities of the intuitive and the spiritual [*alle Identitäten des Anschaulichen und Geistigen*] in this poetic performance. (GS, 2: 124; W, 1: 34)

According to the first of Husserl's *Logical Investigations*, which constitutes the starting point of the phenomenological program as a whole, truth consists in the fulfillment of a signifying intention. Only an intuition—the fundamental trait of which is immediacy—can fulfill a signifying act: the phenomenon designated is itself accessible in its specific mode of givenness.[37] *Logical Investigations* takes this idea to ever deeper and ever wider levels of signification—from signs and expressions in the first investigation to assertions and categorial intuition in the sixth. Benjamin takes the same thought one step further—from assertion to poem. By doing so, he gives direction and drama to his analysis of Hölderlin's poem. The first version merely intends what is meant by *courage*; the second not only fulfills the intention of its predecessor but also, accordingly, fulfills "the poetized as such" in its own unique manner. Since the poetized as such is formed into a poem, this poem is a poem of poetry as such. Friedrich Schlegel calls for a "transcendental poetry" in a famous fragment Benjamin analyzes in his dissertation (GS, 1: 95; W, 1: 170). *Blödigkeit* can be understood as a response to this call, for it poetizes the poetic as such— which is to say that the poem is *true*: "In this sphere [of the poetized] the peculiar domain that contains the truth of the poem shall be disclosed. This 'truth,' which the most serious artists so insistently claim for their creations, shall be understood as the objectivity of their production, as the fulfillment of the artistic task in each case [*die Erfüllung des jeweiligen künst-lerischen Aufgabe*]" (GS, 2: 105; W, 1: 18–19).

As he extends Husserl's "logical investigations" from assertion to poem, Benjamin alters its direction as well. The intuition in which an assertion can fulfill its signifying intention and become true is a "categorial" one. The intuition in which a poem can fulfill its signifying intention and be-come true should therefore be a poetic intuition. Only there are none. And there *can* be no poetic intuitions insofar as the poetic task is fulfilled, and the poet *is* life living "the middle of relations"—not "in" the middle of re-lations, which would give evidence of a certain lack of courage, a reticence to annihilate the "thingly" character of the self in the same movement that annihilates the thingly character of everything else. Such is "diffidence," the overcoming of which erases the signifying intention—without signing it-self in terms of this erasure. The concept of the poetized develops in re-sponse to the impossibility of attaining a poetic intuition that would cor-respond to categorial intuition: "The mediation [*Ermitteling*] of the pure poetized, the absolute task, must remain, after all that was said, a purely methodological, ideal goal. The pure poetized would otherwise cease to be a limit-concept: it would be life or poem" (GS, 2: 108; W, 1: 20–21)—but not *poet*, still less audience or reader. The "fantastic" or "poetic" annihila-tion of the world of things is not an experience of anyone: it is closer to an experience of experience or experience of the concept of experience as it is transformed by the experience of experiencing the world "parenthesized" and thus deposed from the "thesis" through which diffident souls secure a place "in" the world for themselves. In any case, this much is clear: the in-tuition of the truth of intuition, which is the intention of Hölderlin's poem insofar as it is the poetizing of the poetic as such, cannot itself be intuited as if it were one intuition among others. For there is no one "there" to in-tuit—not even "absolute consciousness."

Benjamin does not follow the students of *Logical Investigation* at the

University of Munich, where he matriculated during the time in which "Two Poems of Friedrich Hölderlin" was written, in rejecting the "subjectivist" turn of *Ideas*, for, from the awkward perspective of Hölderlin's "Diffidence," *Logical Investigations* is already vitiated by a diffident subjectivism: a refusal to extend its critique of psychologism to the point where it criticizes the idea of intention. A radical phenomenology demands a foundation "beyond" or "before" that of consciousness, however it may be represented.[38] Just as the fulfillment of the intention designated by "the courage of the poet" demands the erasure of both terms by which this intention is designated, so, too, the intention to the phenomenological reduction must erase its own signifying act. No one, in other words, can intend to carry out the reduction without immediately disavowing this intention: the one who intends remains irreducible. An entirely different kind of reduction is required for the intention to be carried out—a reduction that erases its reductive intention and does not designate itself as such.

Benjamin marks out a sphere in which to explore such a reduction: that of childhood. "Colors Considered from the Perspective of the Child" (GS, 6: 110–12; W, 1: 50–51) is an exercise in phenomenological reduction in the literal sense of the term: it "leads back" to the pure—isolated, separated—vision of the child. This vision "goes entirely after [*geht ganz auf*] the spiritual essence of things, not after substance" (GS, 6: 118). The aim of the phenomenological reduction, for Husserl, is to suspend the "naive" or "natural" attitude in which the world is posited over against consciousness and is somehow supposed to act on it. This attitude is, however, for Benjamin, neither "natural" nor "naive." It is not natural insofar as it is learned; more exactly, it is a philosophico-historical legacy of the Enlightenment, no different in principle from any other mythological conception, including, as he notes in "The Program for the Coming Philosophy," the conception of causal interaction that underlies the practices of preanimism (GS, 2: 162; W, 1: 103). And this attitude is especially not "naive." Benjamin, who would have been far more sensitive to the Schillerian and Hölderlinian resonance of this term than Husserl, knows that a naif is at one with nature, not affected by it. Affection, by contrast, is the surest sign of sentimentality. The ancient Greeks and Goethe are naive, according to Schiller, who in his last critical endeavor seeks to define the term (NA, 20: 417–19). Hölderlin develops Schiller's schema of naive and sentimental poetry to a point where the latter is divided and the former is correspondingly radicalized. Instead of attributing naiveté either to the Greeks or to

Goethe, he ascribes it to the child. The opening chapter of *Hyperion* is, from this perspective, an exercise in the "naive" reduction that does not designate itself as such because it cannot be intended but only at best *remembered*. All of Benjamin's inquiries into the appearance of colors and color as a form of appearance in its own right are undertaken in and under the direction of this "naive" reduction, the aim of which is the delineation of a possible "sphere of total neutrality."

Like the disciples of Husserl in Munich who rebel against the master's "transcendental" turn, Benjamin dispenses with methodological prolegomena concerning the nature and validity of a phenomenological reduction. Like Heidegger, who does the same, Benjamin does not dispense with these methodological musings because he rejects the reduction as such. On the contrary, he breaks with the "sentimental" attitude from the start—so much so that there is no room left in the world for "consciousness," regardless of whether it is qualified as empirical, pure, transcendental, epistemological, or absolute. Because of this break, the *epochē* is freed from its methodological function of securing an indubitable foundation for the sciences, the first of which would be pure phenomenology, the second phenomenological psychology, and so on until the last of them—perhaps the *Geisteswissenschaften*—would be firmly grounded. But the *epochē* can be freed from its methodological function without falling back into the "natural" attitude according to which subjects are affected by objects only under the condition that a sphere be disclosed where this "attitude" does not *at first* prevail. For Heidegger, who follows a similar trajectory, this sphere is defined as "being in the world."[39] For Benjamin, it diversifies itself into a variety of spheres, two of which are particularly inviting: the landscape of color and the world of language; more exactly, the landscape of color as seen by a child and the world of language as experienced by an Adam. In both cases—and others besides—access to this sphere depends upon a paradisal *epochē* in which the epoch of paradise does not so much appear as take place. Benjamin himself does not carry out such an *epochē*, nor could anyone else; rather, he only outlines the structures of the spheres in which subjects remain unaffected by things and are, for this reason, not—or not yet—subjects, properly speaking. Since, however, the world of language can be outlined in greater detail and with greater precision than the landscape of color, it enjoys a certain methodological priority. What Benjamin calls "his little treatise" (GB, 1: 343; C, 81), "On Language as Such and on Human Language" (1916), constitutes his most sustained attempt to outline a "sphere of total neutrality"—an attempt to which he would regularly return and which would, in turn, give direction to almost all of his subsequent endeavors.

Being in Language

However bold Benjamin may appear in "On Language As Such and On Human Language," he still begins his "little treatise" on these topics with a note of caution. The word *language* can be said in many ways—and not all of these uses occur in the context of communicating thoughts with words. The meaningfulness of every human practice means that each one can be attributed a language of its own, which is to say, its own rationality or "logic," the description of which would be the task of something like a phenomenological anthropology. Replacing the Husserlian lexicon of "eidos" and "noema" with his own vocabulary of "spiritual content" and "spiritual essence," Benjamin opens his treatise by indicating that his "method" consists in a conceptualization of practices in a linguistic way:

> Every expression of the spiritual life of human beings [*Jede Äußerung menschlichen Geisteslebens*] can be conceived as a kind of language, and this conception [*Auffassung*], in the manner of a true method, discloses new questions to pose. One can speak of a language of music and of the plastic arts, a language of justice that has nothing immediately to do with the language in which German or English legal speech is formulated; one can speak of a language of technology that is not the disciplinary language of the technician. "Language" means in such contexts the principle directed toward the communication of spiritual content [*geistiger Inhalt*] in the subjects concerned: in technology, art, law, or religion. With a word [*Mit einem Wort*]: every communication of spiritual content is a language, whereby the communication through words is only a particular case, that of human language and that of those underlying or those founded on it (law, poetry). (GS, 2: 140; W, 1: 62)

"With one word," the language of words is not the only one. Benjamin's summation of his starting point is not entirely unambiguous, since some of the other languages—those without words—are "founded" on language with words. Such is the case with law and poetry. The aim of Benjamin's methodological preamble is not, however, to determine the relation of such languages to those, like music and plastic arts, which do without words; it is, rather, to demonstrate the applicability of the word *language* to contexts other than those in which "spiritual content" expresses itself in verbal form. Music is capable of communicating "spiritual content" without words, and so, too, the plastic arts and technology. Having demonstrated the legitimacy of applying the word *language* beyond the domain of verbal languages—in such contexts, Kant would use the word "deduction" (A, 84; B, 116)—Benjamin prepares the way for a bolder step, which bases itself neither on an object nor on a subject, neither on something about which is spoken nor on speakers who express themselves in speech. Taking this step is tricky, however, for Benjamin cuts himself off from the traditional source of legitimation for those who have undertaken similar adventures in the modern epoch: the "I," the colorless unity of which is transcategorial and thus "transcendental." None of Husserl's methodological protocols in *Ideas* are from this perspective of any use: regardless of his reservations about the "pure I,"[40] he has none about "absolute consciousness," for it alone—or perhaps in company with the "pure I"—is the "residuum after the annihilation of the world" (HGW, 3: 114; I, 109).

The step Benjamin takes in this treatise, as the title itself indicates, consists in applying the term *language* to every region of being—not only those that owe their meaningfulness to human intentionality. The advantages of scholastic inquiries into the phenomenon of intentionality are from this perspective obvious, since these pre-Cartesian meditations do not take their point of departure from the methodological priority of self-consciousness. Until Benjamin reconsidered the far from obvious achievement of Heidegger's inquiry into Thomas of Erfurt's speculative grammar (which was misattributed to Duns Scotus), he made efforts in this direction.[41] But Benjamin can nevertheless draw on the resources of at least one, and perhaps only one, modern philosophical project for guidance in this treacherous terrain: Kantian critique; in particular, the Transcendental Aesthetic, which precedes the Transcendental Analytic in both senses of the term, since it is earlier than, and takes priority over what follows. Before Kant concerns himself with the "I think," he lays out—or, as he writes, *erörtet* (discusses, more literally, "places")—the character of space and time. Benjamin's methodological "conception" (*Auffassung*) fastens onto Kant's mode of argumentation, for it already contains in a concentrated form all of the guidelines for the outlining of the "sphere of total neutrality" so far delineated: Husserl's, Cohen's, and of course Kant's own.

In order to justify his application of the term *language* beyond the regions circumscribed by human intentionality, Benjamin adopts and adapts

Kant's argument for the nonconceptual, noncategorial, and therefore non-
"I"-like character of these medial forms: that *in* which things appear and
thus announce or "communicate" themselves. Benjamin's treatise can even
be understood as a prolegomenon to the Transcendental Aesthetic in the
double sense of the term, which matches the double sense of the term "aes-
thetic" Kant himself notes (A, 21; B, 35–36): a "legomenon" in favor of "lo-
gos," and a "legomonenon" in which the priority of the logos—in its du-
plicity, as "word" and "reason"—is itself expressed. Those who argue that
Benjamin does not make arguments and cannot, for this reason, be con-
sidered a philosopher pay no attention to this argument,[42] which in a sense
is the only one he need formulate, for all others would only be reiterations.
Benjamin seeks to secure the nonmetaphorical character of his use of the
term *language* for at least one obvious reason: his remarks are supposed to
be *on* "language as such." If, however, this term is a metaphor, the remarks
will have been "on" something else—or perhaps "on" nothing at all. First,
Kant's argument with respect to the nonconceptual character of space;
then, Benjamin's argument for the nonmetaphorical character of his use of
the word *language*:

> *Kant*: Space is a necessary representation, a priori, which is the ground of
> all outer intuitions. One can never represent that there is no space, although
> one can very well think that there are no objects to be encountered in it [*Man
> kann sich niemals eine Vorstellung davon machen, daß kein Raum sei, ob man
> sich gleich ganz wohl denken kann, daß keine Gegenstände darin angetroffen wer-
> den*]. It is therefore to be regarded as the condition of the possibility of ap-
> pearances, not as a determination dependent on them, and is an a priori rep-
> resentation that necessarily grounds outer appearances. (A, 24; B, 39)[43]

> *Benjamin*: The existence of language, however, is coextensive not only with
> all the areas of human spiritual expression in which language is always in one
> sense or another inherent, but with absolutely everything. There is no event or
> thing in either animate or inanimate nature that does not in some sense par-
> take of language, for it is essential to everything that it communicate its spiri-
> tual contents. But this use of the word "language" is by no means metaphori-
> cal. For the following thought yields a full, content-filled knowledge [*eine volle
> inhaltliche Erkenntnis*]: we cannot represent to ourselves the spiritual essence
> of anything not communicating in expression [*wir uns nichts vorstellen können,
> das sein geistiges Wesen nicht im Ausdruck mitteilt*]; the greater or lesser degree
> of consciousness apparently (or really) bound to such communication cannot
> alter the fact that we cannot represent to ourselves a total absence of language
> in anything [*wir uns völlige Abwesenheit der Sprache in nichts vorstellen können*].

Something in existence [*Ein Dasein*] entirely without relationship to language is an Idea; but this Idea cannot bear fruit even within the realm of Ideas, the circumference of which designates the Idea of God [*diese Idee läßt sich auch im Bezirk der Ideen, deren Umkreis diejenige Gottes bezeichnet, nicht fruchtbar machen*]. (GS, 2: 140–41; W, 1: 62)

Benjamin's argument for the applicability of the term *language* beyond the regions circumscribed by human intentionality is modeled on Kant's argument for the space as the "ground" of all "outer appearances." Both arguments can be described, in phenomenological terms, as demonstrations of the paradoxical primacy of fantasy for the securing of *content* for philosophical knowledge. In both cases, moreover, the primacy of fantasy reveals itself in a "fiction": the annihilation of the thingly world. We cannot represent a complete absence of space, according to Kant, although we can think the abyssal thought that space has suddenly become completely devoid of objects—and he does in an early work.[44] According to Benjamin, we cannot represent to ourselves the total absence of language, although we can think the barren Idea of languagelessness. By a method of fantastic annihilation Kant arrives at a "full, content-filled knowledge": not knowledge of something, to be sure; rather, knowledge that anything we know "outside" of ourselves is still "internal" to our manner of knowing. By replacing space with language, Benjamin similarly arrives at "full, content-filled knowledge."[45] In recognition of the primacy of world-annihilating fantasy, Benjamin models his argument for the universal applicability of the term *language* on Kant's metaphysical exposition of space rather than on the parallel exposition of time for at least two reasons: both of these expositions or "placements" (*Erörterung*) are so thoroughly indebted to spatial language that the very criterion by which they are distinguished—the difference between an "outer" form of intuition (space) and an "inner" one (time)[46]—is itself drawn from the "amphibolous" logic of this language; and space, although less universal than time, is correspondingly released from any intimate connection to selfhood, self-consciousness, and the constitution of subjectivity in general. Because the model for Benjamin's argument for applicability of the transcategorial term "language" beyond the regions of human intentionality and consciousness resembles Kant's argument for the purely intuitive character of space, language cannot fail to appear *like* space in the course of its transcendental exposition.

Language, however, cannot really be like space for at least one reason: the former founds the latter; language is prior even to the a priori forms in which things appear, for it is the "space" of sense, which is to say, the "space" in which "spiritual essence" is communicable. Talk of the "space" of sense is doubtless metaphorical, and it may even be misleading, since it suggests that language, for Benjamin, is a "logical space," which determines the structure of an intentional act, especially that of judgment. Whereas logic is consigned to discursivity, the immediacy of language makes it not only prejudgmental but also in general prelogical and therefore—to use Benjamin's more colorful word—"magical." Magic consists in immediacy, which is to say, nondiscursivity and noncausality. As the first sentence of the "Transcendental Aesthetic" attests, the defining character of intuition, for Kant, is the immediacy of its relation to objects: the "pure intuition" of space is likewise immediate and, to this extent, magical.[47] In the context of Benjamin's prolegomenon, language thus appears as the prespatial "space" of prelogical sense, which, by virtue of its priority, cannot *itself* be signified or even designated—and therefore can be called "sense" only in quotation marks.[48]

Benjamin's treatise on language began as a letter to Scholem on the distinction between mathematics and language. Instead of entering into this "infinitely difficult theme," however, he concerns himself only with "the essence of language" (GB, 1: 343; C, 81).[49] In some of the notes for the continuation of the treatise he gives some indications of how he would elaborate the distinction between language as such and the symbols constructed in mathematics for the accomplishment of its tasks: "mathematics speaks in signs [*in Zeichen*]" (GS, 7: 788). "Designation" (*Bezeichnung*) distinguishes mathematics from language "proper." In Benjamin's argument for the literality of his use of the term *language*, this criterion plays a critical role. Language appears like space because it is the residuum of world-annihilating fantasy: we cannot imagine the complete absence (*Abwesenheit*) of language, and in any case, regardless of our powers of representation, the Idea of such absence can claim no function, for it does not belong to the order of "Ideas, the circumference of which designates [*bezeichnet*] the Idea of God" (GS, 2: 141; W, 1: 62).

At this point—and this point alone—Benjamin gingerly touches on the "infinitely difficult theme" to which he otherwise only alludes. Ideas function as mathematical symbols by "designating" a higher-order Idea—that of God. The unimaginable Idea of a complete absence, however, cannot claim even this function, for it "says" nothing; it is, therefore, entirely "fruitless" and can be henceforth disregarded. The same is not true of the other Ideas, none of which are ever named. Benjamin thus seems to do precisely this: disregard them, as he proceeds to delineate the structure of language, having secured the nonmetaphorical character of his own discourse. Nevertheless, the structure of the world of Ideas gives shape to the account of language developed in the "little treatise": just as lower-order mathematical terms, in conjunction with one another, designate higher-order ones, so, too, do lower-order Ideas. And the same can be said, *mutatis mutandis*, of language: lower-order languages do not designate but, rather, say higher-order languages. The task of the treatise lies in disclosing the nature of this saying. "On Language as Such and on Human Language," the very title of which emphasizes the relation of higher to lower, takes its point of departure, in sum, from this interrupted, abbreviated reflection on the "infinitely difficult theme."

Cantor, Continuity, and Density

Space, for Kant, is a "pure intuition." As an intuition, it belongs to the faculty of receptivity; by virtue of its purity, it does not receive anything but is, rather, the medium in which "outer" objects are represented in the first place. As an intuition, it is immediately related to its object; by virtue of its purity, there is no object to which it is related, which would determine and thus limit it. It can therefore only be represented as an infinite given whole. The medial character of space lies in its immediacy, and its immediacy is the ground of its infinitude. The same can be said—word for word—of language, once the word *language* is no longer restricted to languages finitely divisible into verbal units:

> Whatever is communicable *of* a spiritual essence, *in* this it communicates itself; that is to say, all language communicates itself. Or more precisely: every language communicates itself *in* itself; it is in the purest sense the "medium" of the communication. The medial [*Das Mediale*], which is the *immed*iacy [Unmittel*barkeit*] of all spiritual communication, is the fundamental problem of linguistic theory, and if one wishes to call this immediacy "magical," then the primary problem of language is its magic. At the same time, the notion of the magic of language points to something else: its infinitude. It is conditioned by its immediacy. For precisely because nothing is communicated *through* language, what is communicated *in* language cannot be externally limited or measured, and therefore every language contains its own incommensurable, uniquely-articulated infinity [*inkommensurable, einziggeartete*

Unendlichkeit]. Its linguistic essence, not its verbal content, designates its limit. (GS, 2: 142–43; W, 1: 64)

The infinitude of language does not derive from an iterative operation of synthesis but, rather, lies in its immediacy; it is therefore an incommensurable infinitude—like space understood as a pure intuition in which objects appear and not as a concept under which they fall. As the first "Antinomy of Pure Reason" shows, there can be no answer to the question whether the world, composed of homogeneous parts, is finite or infinite, for it makes no sense to speak of "the" world as a whole. There is no question, however, that space as such is an immediately given, infinite whole. The infinitude of space cannot therefore be likened to the infinitude of any collection of objects. The implicit analogy between language and space, understood as a form of intuition, allows Benjamin to explicate the immediately medial and incommensurably infinite character of language *as such*. Yet this analogy fails in another critical respect; it leaves no room for *different* languages, for, as Kant notes, "if one speaks of many spaces, one understands thereby only parts of one and the same unique space" (A, 25; B, 39). If one wants to speak of more than one language, Kant cannot help.

Cantor, however, can, for Cantorian mathematics delineates different kinds of infinity, and this delineation allows for an account of different orders of linguistic infinitude—and therefore an exposition of different languages. "Different languages" does not mean different human languages, the units of which would be finitely divisible into recognizable words; rather, it means different infinite languages, more exactly, different orders of linguistic infinitude, each of which is infinitely divisible in its own "differential" manner. Without Cantor's discovery—or invention—of a "Transfinitum ordinatum" (GA, 400), Benjamin's delineation of different orders of linguistic infinitude would be unthinkable. And Benjamin, of course, knew of Cantor's discovery. In the opening paragraphs of his contemporaneous "Theses on the Problem of Identity," Benjamin tentatively reflects on the structure of infinitude by starting an investigation into the relation between identity judgments and what Kant calls "infinite judgments" (A, 72; B, 97). Benjamin interrupts his reflections on the difference between the "potentially nonidentical infinite" (designated by *a*) and the "actually nonidentical infinite" (designated by *b*) with a directive for future research: "Investigation must be conducted into which modes of the mathematical infinite [*Arten des mathematischen Unendlichen*] belong to (*a*) or (*b*)" (GS, 6:

27; W, 75). What needs no further investigation, however, is the "fact"—unknown to Kant and of little concern to Cohen—that there *are* different "modes of the mathematical infinite," even if the status of this "fact" was by no means clear even among mathematicians who accepted his discoveries and sought to develop his work. Particularly prominent among the proponents of Cantorian mathematicians is Arthur Schoenflies, Benjamin's maternal great uncle, with whom he always maintained cordial and sometimes close relations.[50] His familiarity with Cantorian mathematics reached beyond his familial relations, moreover. Scholem was studying mathematics in Jena with Frege, among others. And Benjamin would have gained insight into Cantorian mathematics in the course of devising solutions—linguistic and metaphysical rather than logical or mathematical—to Russell's paradox of predicates not predicable of themselves.[51] Whatever else Benjamin may have garnered from these, and other, sources, he would have at least known that the problem of continuity is intimately related to the disputed status of the mathematical infinite and that, regardless of its centrality to Cohen's reformulation of Kantian critique, the exposition of this concept in the *Logic of Pure Knowledge* is far from adequate.[52] In order to resolve the problem of the multiplicity of languages, each of which is infinite in its own manner, Benjamin has no choice but to enter into the Leibnizian "labyrinth of the continuum."[53]

According to Kant, this labyrinth is generated only under the condition that forms of intuition are considered properties of things in themselves, and so the discovery of pure intuitions in the Transcendental Aesthetic is the true thread of Ariadne. Yet Kant does not give a precise definition of continuity, nor does Cohen, who nevertheless makes it into the original law of thought. Cantor, by contrast, is concerned with nothing else: the power—in the popular as well as the technical sense—of the continuum. By distinguishing between two orders of infinitude, he is able to make sense of a peculiar feature of the linear continuum that has been known since the Pythagorean discovery of "incommensurables": the apparently self-evident definition of continuity—between any two points lies a third—is inadequate, since it is possible to establish a set of points that conforms to this definition but nevertheless contains an infinite number of "gaps." The set of points that correspond to the order of rational numbers is such: between any two rational numbers there is another one, and yet a line composed of all the rational numbers would be missing the square root of two—to cite the example discovered by the Pythagoreans and stated in its canonical form in the tenth book of Euclid's *Elements*.[54] The discovery of different kinds of mathematical infinity allows Cantor to propose a definition of the continuum that takes account of the distinction between a series that conforms to the classical definition of continuity and one that is more precise, for it "fills" all the "gaps" that the other one leaves open. The first such series is called "dense" (*dicht*), whereas the second alone is continuous (Cantor, GA, 140). For a series to be continuous, it must be both "perfect" (*perfekt*) and "cohesive" (*zusammenhängend*): "here 'perfect' and 'cohesive' are not mere words but . . . entirely general predicates of the *continuum*" (GA, 194).[55] The distinction between density and continuity not only makes it possible to define the continuum without prior reference to spatial intuition—this is already true of Cohen's definition and the basis of its rejection of the Transcendental Aesthetic—but it also makes room for different orders of infinite "point sets," which is to say, different kinds of "spatial" infinitude.

The relation among mathematical terms is expressed by an equation (*Gleichsetzen*); the relation among linguistic ones is expressed by translation (*Übersetzen*). In the word *translation* or *Übersetzen* the spatial character of language is captured by an image: that which is communicated is transposed from one place to another. According to Benjamin, however, *nothing* is communicated in language. This is the paradoxical starting point of his "little treatise" on language. It is a paradoxical *starting* point because it gives no indication of how to proceed, and the investigation therefore can go no further—or can only fall into the "abyss" of linguistic mysticism. Instead of beginning at this point, then, Benjamin opens the treatise by discussing "spiritual content" and "spiritual essence." But language communicates neither of these—nor anything else. The denial that language communicates anything other than itself gives rise to his conclusion: language "communicates the particular linguistic essence [*sprachliches Wesen*] of things but their spiritual essence only insofar as this is immediately included in their linguistic essence, insofar as it is *capable* of being communicated"—which is to say, as Benjamin immediately concludes: "language communicates the linguistic essence of things" (GS, 2: 142; W, 1: 63). Once this principle is established, Benjamin erases the "insofar" through which the strict "equation" (*Gleichsetzung*) of spiritual essence with linguistic essence has been forestalled long enough for him to outline three orders of linguistic infinitude: the language of things, human language, and the language of God. By erasing the "insofar," Benjamin can fully empty language of its putative content and thus propose the central "thesis" of the "little treatise." On the basis of this linguistic kenosis he can then determine the fundamental operation of *Übersetzen*:

> If spiritual essence is identical with linguistic essence, then a thing, by virtue of its spiritual essence, is a medium of communication, and what is communicated in it is—in accordance with its medial relation—precisely this medium (language) itself. Language is thus the spiritual essence of things. Spiritual being is therefore posited [*gesetzt*] at the outset as communicable; or rather, it is posited *in* communicability, and the thesis [*Thesis*] that the linguistic being of things is identical with the spiritual, insofar as the latter is communicable, becomes in its "insofar" a tautology. *There is no such thing as a content* [Inhalt] *of language; as communication, language communicates a spiritual essence—a communicability pure and simple* [eine Mitteilbarkeit schlechthin]. The differences between languages are those of media that are distinguished, as it were, by their density [*gleichsam nach ihrer Dichte*], therefore gradually; and this with regard to the density both of the communicating (naming) and of the communicable (name) in the communication. (GS, 2: 145–46; W, 66)

The use of the term *density* in Benjamin's theory of language is doubtless metaphorical—but no more metaphorical than the use of the term in Cantor's mathematical theory. Cantor, of course, has an advantage over Benjamin, in that he can precisely define what the term *dense* means and thereby construct a new term, the use of which is no longer metaphorical. Yet Benjamin can do something a mathematician cannot: the metaphor of density enacts what it expresses—the transference (*meta-phorein, translatio*, or *Über-setzen*) of one language into another; in this case, the transference of mathematical language into the metalanguage of the "little treatise." The metaphor of density is therefore redoubled. Cantor had already transferred the term from physics to mathematics and, by so doing, taken it away from the register of mass and material substance. And Benjamin follows suit: the metaphor of density moves from point-set theory to language theory on the basis of the "thesis" that language as such is entirely without content and cannot therefore be conceived in substantial terms at all. In contrast to material media, therefore, nothing passes through linguistic media—neither thoughts nor "spiritual content." The only "passage" in language is that of translation, and translation, in turn, is an operation in which a lower order of linguistic infinity is transformed into a higher one. In one of Schoenflies's reports on the development of Cantorian mathematics, he proves the following theorem: "The derivation of an in-itself dense, imperfect set is perfect."[56] As if in response to this theorem, Benjamin proposes—without proof—the fundamental theory of translation. Instead of using the mathematical term "derivative" (*Ableitung*, leading away), however, he uses its linguistic counterpart: "transrivative" (*Überführung*, leading over):

> By the fact that, mentioned earlier, languages relate to one another as media of varying density, the translatability of languages into one another is given. Translation is the conveying of one language into another through a continuum of transformations [*Übersetzung ist die Überführung der einen Sprache in die andere durch ein Kontinuum von Verwandlungen*].
>
> The translation of the language of things into human language is not only a translation of the mute into the sonic; it is also the translation of the nameless into the name. It is therefore the translation of an imperfect language into a more perfect one, and cannot but add something to it, namely knowledge. (GS, 2: 151; W, 1: 70)

Even if Benjamin's exposition of translation as "transrivative" cannot be understood as the linguistic-theoretical version of any particular set-theoretical theorem, the direction of this almost untranslatable *Überführung* of *Übersetzen* (conveying of translation) is nevertheless clear: the theory of translation shows the "perfection" of lower orders of linguistic infinitude into higher ones. That there are different kinds of mathematical infinity is Cantor's principal discovery: such infinity may remain "bad," in Hegel's term,[57] but it is no longer conceivable in terms of an undifferentiated idea of bigger-than-any-given-magnitude. Benjamin's corresponding exposition of different orders of linguistic infinity would be unthinkable without this discovery. According to Cantor, the lowest order of mathematical infinity is equivalent to the "cardinality" or "power" (*Mächtigkeit*) of the natural numbers; its designation is $\aleph_0$. Sets of this power are "countable" or "denumerable" (*abzählbar*). In "The Task of the Translator," as an explication of the unfamiliar term "translatability" (*Übersetzbarkeit*), Benjamin makes the following claim: "certain relational concepts retain a good sense and perhaps even attain their best sense when they are not from the outset exclusively referred to human beings" (GS, 4: 10; W, 1: 254). No one is more aware of this than Cantor, for human beings cannot, of course, count $\aleph_0$, and yet it is nevertheless "countable." All of Benjamin's "able" terms—communicability, solubility, knowability, translatability, criticizability, and reproducibility—are constructed in line with Cantor's formulation of the "power" of infinite sets.[58] And in the "Epistemo-Critical Preface" to the *Origin of the German Mourning Play*, which, as Benjamin tells Scholem, is "a second stage of my early work on language" (GB, 3: 14; C, 261), he explicitly adopts and transforms the Cantorian term in accordance with the difference between mathematical point sets and philosophical configurations, the elements of which are the "points" called "Ideas" (GS, 1: 215; O, 34): "Their denominated plurality is numerable [*Deren benannte Vielheit ist zählbar*]. For discontinuity is predicable of the 'essentialities [*Wesenheiten*] . . . that lead a life *toto coelo* different from objects and their internal constitutions'" (GS, 1: 218; O, 37).[59]

Because the plurality of Idea-points can be counted, even if not by human beings, its power is lower than that of the linear continuum. Or more exactly, and more in line with Benjamin's calculation, the discontinuity of this plurality implies that it is "countable." The "little treatise" on language is both less explicit and more fully developed than the "Epistemo-Critical Preface": less explicit, since it avoids the Cantorian term *countable*; more developed, since it delineates the orders of linguistic infinitude: "every language contains its own incommensurable, uniquely-articulated [*einzig-geartete*] infinity" (GS, 2: 142–43; W, 1: 64). Although the number of languages is itself infinite (GS, 7: 789), they can be assigned to three orders, with a supplementary disorder: the language of things, the original language of human beings, the language of God, and, in addition, after the disintegration of the second order of linguistic infinite, the many languages of human beings. Every language is a unique function of infinite divisibility: in German, *Teilbarkeit*.[60] By virtue of its infinite divisibility, it is sheer communicability; in German, *Mitteilbarkeit*. And as long as language is infinitely divisible, which is to say, as long as language is itself, there can be no "parts of speech," which are generated by the fundamental functions of judgment (*Urteil*), separation and synthesis. Whenever a language is subordinated to *Urteil*, its divisibility is finitized and its communicability limited. Not only does the infinite divisibility of language preclude the possibility of "parts of speech," it also makes it impossible for there to be any linguistic *units* other than *languages themselves*—regardless of whether a language has been subordinated to the finite power of judgment. All languages, in short, are dense in the Cantorian sense, some more than others, and one—the highest—so dense that the term is no longer applicable.

Cantor was convinced that his discoveries were more than simply contributions to pure mathematics. Transfinite numbers were, for him, objectively valid and, as a consequence, could help solve otherwise intractable problems in contemporary physics. According to one of Cantor's more audacious hypotheses, the number of "corporeal monads" is equal to the power of the natural numbers, whereas the number of "aetherial monads" is equal to the power of the linear continuum (GA, 275–76). Benjamin's "little treatise" on the infinitude of language can be understood as a corollary and perhaps even as a self-conscious corrective to this Leibniz-inspired hypothesis. Instead of concerning itself with the physical correlates of the two fundamental transfinite powers, Benjamin's treatise implicitly identifies linguistic ones. The infinite language of natural things corresponds to the power of the natural numbers, which, for its part, is equivalent to the cardinality of dense but discontinuous domains like that of the rational numbers. The power of the linear continuum is higher: precisely how much higher is a question with which Cantor struggled throughout his life but which, for good reason, he could not properly answer. According to a much more famous conjecture that Cantor proposed, which was soon dubbed the "continuum hypothesis," the continuum is of the *second* power, which is to say that it *immediately* follows the first power, or smallest transfinite number.[61] Regardless of the undecidable status of this conjecture, however, the linear continuum can be shown to be infinitely "denser" than any merely dense point set. By virtue of its greater density, it is more "perfect," and by virtue of its greater perfection, it corresponds to human language, which, according to Benjamin, is purely sonorous (GS, 2: 147; W, 1: 67) or, in other words, "aetherial." And it consists in giving the nameless its name. Benjamin's terms for the infinitude of the name are closer to those of Kant than those of Cantor, but its correlation to the continuum is nevertheless unambiguous: "in name culminates both the intensive totality of language, as the absolutely communicable spiritual essence, and the extensive totality of language, as the universally communicating (naming) essence. . . . *The human being alone has the perfect language in its universality and its intensity*" (GS, 2: 145; W, 1: 65–66).

An intensive magnitude, for Kant, is a "quantum continuum" that cannot be represented by the synthesis of parts but must, instead, be represented as "a flowing sum" or, in Newtonian terms, as a fluxion (A, 170; B, 212). A flow cannot allow for any "gaps" and therefore generates the linear continuum. Since all segments of the continuum have the same power as the whole, every name in the original language of the human being is a "culmination." None is a unit in its own right; rather, all names are the names of particular languages of things and therefore wholes. Since the continuum contains every dense domain, it is "universal," and so, too, is the language of names. Since, finally, the power of the linear continuum is higher than that of $\aleph_0$—whatever power it may be—the original speaker of names has dominion over things: "he is the lord of nature and can give names to things" (GS, 2: 144; W, 1: 65).

Leopold Kronecker, who was Cantor's great antagonist in the debate over the legitimacy of transfinite mathematics, expressed his objection in theological terms: "God made the integers, and all the rest is the work of human beings."[62] Benjamin's exegesis of Genesis in his treatise on language functions as a nonmathematical response to this objection: in creating natural things, God, who, like Cantor, prefers Hebrew letters for expressions of infinite powers, first creates those things whose power corresponds to that of the natural numbers, namely $\aleph_0$. Thereafter, he creates the one "thing"—the human being—whose power is higher. The original task of the human language then consists in solving transfinite, "translative" tasks: imperfect languages are led "through a continuum of transformations" (GS, 2: 151; W, 1: 70) into line with the more perfect language of names. Names are therefore neither arbitrary nor grounded in extralinguistic reasons; rather, the names of things complete them, filling in their constitutive gaps. The interlinguistic relations established by this act of perfection, moreover, are the sole subject matter of knowledge, which means at the very least that knowledge has absolutely nothing to do with affection. Nothing transcends the sphere of language: neither things, nor consciousness, nor even—or especially—God. And therefore nothing "affects" an Adamic translator: "The translation of the language of things into that of the human being . . . is the translation of an imperfect language into a more perfect one, and cannot but add something to it, namely knowledge [*Erkenntnis*]" (GS, 1: 151; W, 1: 70).

"But," Benjamin immediately adds, "the objectivity of this translation is vouchsafed by God" (GS, 2: 151; W, 1: 70). The relation between different orders of infinity is itself grounded in an even more perfect language than the one Benjamin calls the sole language "perfect in its universality and its intensity" (GS, 2: 145; W, 1: 66). The power of infinity that corresponds to that of divine language must therefore be even higher than that of the linear continuum: "The infinity of human language always remains limited and analytic in nature, in comparison to the absolutely unlimited and creative infinity of the divine word" (GS, 2: 149; W, 1: 68). An unlim-

ited unlimitedness, in short: such is the divine word. In a letter to Dede-
kind, Cantor speaks of "an inconsistent, absolutely infinite plurality" (GA,
445), the designation of which is the last of the Hebrew letters, namely ת.[63]
Any formulation of absolute infinity gives rise to formal paradoxes, one of
which—Russell's—Benjamin seeks to solve in the course of developing a
theory of language. The power of divine language corresponds to an enig-
matic power higher than that of the continuum: a trans-transfinite, in
short, which corresponds to the only language into which that of names
is translatable. Not only is this language—if it can still be called "one" lan-
guage—perfect, cohesive, without gaps, and therefore full; it is *overfull* or
overflowing—which is to say, creative. Instead of presenting creation in
the "emanationist" terms of a supersaturated, self-sustaining fountain,
however, Benjamin remains loyal to the biblical text and a strictly Kant-
ian typic: the original language of God is related to the derivative language
of the original human being as *intuitus originarius* is related to *intuitus de-
rivativus*. The former is "spontaneous creation" (GS, 2: 150; W, 1: 69),
whereas the latter is the unity of spontaneity and receptivity. The spon-
taneity of creation runs counter to the neo-Platonic idea of emanation
into which "The Rainbow" issues in the process of liberating fantasy from
any association with the synthesis of the imagination. And this return to
Kant and Torah—without neo-Platonism—is fully justified here: emana-
tion is always continuous, like the overflowing of a fountain; absolute in-
finity is "inconsistent" and cannot, therefore, be presented either in terms
of continuity or through images of the continuum.

Any presentation of a language whose power is infinitely greater than
that of the linear continuum must respect its constitutive inconsistency.
Because this language alone can be called "true," the presentation of truth
cannot fail to be inconsistent, in turn. In the opening sections of his
"Epistemo-Critical Preface" to the *Origin of the German Mourning Play*
Benjamin makes three points concerning the nature of truth; the first dis-
tinguishes philosophy from mathematics, the second gives an historical
index of this difference, and the third determines the "postulates" of
"philosophical style." Unlike mathematics, philosophy must come to
terms with the problem of presentation—not because mathematics can do
without the presentation of its symbols, but (on the contrary) because
mathematics can dismiss any "inconsistent, absolutely infinite plurality"
as strictly irrelevant to the development of its doctrine. Philosophy, by
contrast, cannot; for this reason, it must remain true to the constitutive

inconsistency of what it seeks to present. The dream of a philosophical system, which flourished in the nineteenth century, models itself on Euclid's *Elements*. Before philosophy sought to present itself in terms of a system, and catch truth in the process, it knew how to distinguish itself from mathematical modes of demonstration. The philosophical form of the tractate, which Benjamin resumes, makes this knowledge its own: "presentation as detour [*Darstellung als Umweg*]—that is the methodological character of the tractate" (GS, 1: 208; O, 28). And fidelity to the constitutive inconsistency of truth expresses itself in the "postulates" of philosophical style: "The concept of philosophical style is free of paradox. It has its postulates," the first of which is "the art of interruption [*Absetzen*] in contrast to the chain of deduction" (GS, 1: 212; O, 32). Philosophical style is free of paradox because it is the style in which the order of infinitude whose power is infinitely higher than that of the continuum can alone be presented—but presented, of course, only in a roundabout, inconsistent manner.

Antonomasia, or, the Fate of the Proper Name

For Leibniz, proper names are problematic: there is no reason to give any particular thing one name rather than another. Leibniz therefore begins his most concentrated inquiry into the nature of historical languages with the following axiom: "*all the names that we call 'proper' were once appellatives*; otherwise they would not conform to reason."[64] In proposing this axiom, Leibniz is relying on an unspoken assumption: "reason" will be understood as "human reason." An infinite reason would have every reason in the world to give things their own names: the unreadable numbers engraved into the foreheads of those who occupy the doubly infinite pyramid of possible worlds with which Leibniz concludes the *Theodicy* (G, 6: 363; T, 371) are all proper. What "we" call "proper" names were once all appellatives because of the finite language in which "we" do this calling. Because of the finitude of human language, proper names must be generated by way of antonomasia. The original impropriety of proper names is thus a function of the difference between the finite language of human beings and the infinite language of divine calculation.

At the center of his treatise "On Language as Such," Benjamin makes a similar claim: "The theory of proper names is the theory of the limit [*Grenze*] of finite in relation to infinite language" (GS, 2: 149; W, 1: 60).

Yet Benjamin, unlike Leibniz, cannot simply subsume human language under the category of finitude and present divine language as the only infinite one, for language as such—human, divine, thingly—is infinite; more exactly, "every language contains its own incommensurable, uniquely-articulated infinity" (GS, 2: 143; W, 1: 64). Proper names, in this sense, seem to violate the very nature of language. And they violate this law even in the original language of human beings:

> Of all beings, the human being is the only one who names his own kind, as he is therefore the only one whom God did not name. It is perhaps bold, but scarcely impossible, to name the second part of Genesis 2:20 in this context: that the human being [*der Mensch*] named all beings, "*but* for man there was not found a helper fit for him." Accordingly Adam names his wife as soon as he receives her (woman [*Männin*] in the second chapter, Eve in the third). By giving names, parents dedicate their children to God; the names they give do not correspond—in a metaphysical rather than etymological sense—to any knowledge, for they name newborn children. In a strict sense, no name ought (in its etymological meaning) to correspond to anyone, for the proper name is the word of God in human sounds. By it every human being is vouchsafed his creation by God, and in this sense he is himself creative, as expressed by mythological wisdom in the intuition (which doubtless not infrequently comes true) that one's name is one's fate. The proper name is the communion of the human being with the *creative* word of God. (GS, 2: 149–50; W, 1: 69)[65]

Only in this passage does Benjamin name Adam by name, outside of quotation marks. This name, however, violates the law he himself lays down: "no name ought [*es sollte kein Name*] (in its etymological meaning) correspond to anyone." For, as he would have known—and Scholem, the original addressee of the letter from which the "little treatise" develops, would have known even better—God names in the proscribed manner: "the LORD God formed man [*'adam*] from the earth [*'adamah*]" (Gen. 2:7). Even more to the point, Benjamin silently recognizes the violation of his "thou shalt not" in the case of Eve: "this one," Adam says, "shall be called Woman [*'ishshah*], for from man [*'ish*] was she taken" (Gen. 2:23). Or, alternatively: "The man named his wife Eve [*hawwah*], because she was the mother of all the living [*hay*]" (Gen. 3:20). The rest of Genesis, after the expulsion from Eden, tells the same story: proper names are formed by way of antonomasia, which is to say, according to their etymological meanings. Eve names Cain by way of "gain" (*qanithi*), for the first such instance (Gen. 4:1). Leibniz's axiom is perhaps never more faithfully respected than in the Hebrew Bible, even if he generally refrains from its exegesis. Benjamin proposes an imperative that neither God, nor Adam, nor Eve respect—there shall be no names by way of antonomasia—for the same reason he runs counter to his own exposition of language as infinite: the finitude of human language resides in the limit to its *creative*—as opposed to its cognitive—dimension. It is creative only in the case of proper names, which, therefore, *ought* not have any cognitive character. And language can be creative in the case of proper names as long as no reason can be rendered for the decision to give someone this name rather than another. If there is any such reason, there is no decision; instead of de-cision or *Ent-scheidung*, there is—as Leibniz continuously argues—continuity. Naming, however, is sovereign power, the image of which—and Benjamin uses the term "image" (*Abbild*) in this context (GS, 2: 149: W, 1: 60)—is *creatio ex nihilo*. For the proper name to be proper and therefore to be what it says, it must come from nothing: not from *earth*, as in the case of Adam; not from *man* or *life*, as in the case of Eve; and not even—one might suppose—from the tautology "I will be what I will be," as in the case of God (Exod. 3:14).

The nothing from which every properly proper name derives must, moreover, manifest itself. It does so, as Benjamin writes, in "mythological intuition": names are seen as fates. Not at the *beginning* of life does one know why one name was chosen over another but only at its end. In death the reason for the decision makes itself known. Proper names therefore *demand* death—another name for "nothing"—as the price and proof of their propriety. Which is to say that from the beginning finitude enters into the infinitude of language under the insignia of the proper name. It is the "point" (GS, 2: 149; W, 1: 69) at which the infinitude of language fleetingly touches on the finite. That the proper name demands death is, moreover, felt, if not known, from the beginning: "To be named—even when the namer is godlike and blissful—perhaps always remains an intimation of mourning" (GS, 2: 155; W, 1: 73). The same is true, one might suppose, even when the namer is God, who alone possess the *proper* names of things. The pyramid with which Leibniz concludes his *Theodicy* is a remarkable monument to this intimation of mourning. And even if this infinite crypt grows out of a "mythological intuition"—signaled by the names of its gods—it nevertheless captures the limit-character of proper names, just as the "mythological intuition" concerning proper names often proves to be true: "Things have no proper names except in God. For in his creative word, God called them into being, obviously by their proper names. In the language of human beings, however, they are overnamed" (GS, 2: 155; W, 1: 73). And even when things are not over-named, the things named—especially things of the *same kind*, the same species—must die in order for their names to manifest their difference from all other possible names: as their own.

The expulsion from paradise is not, then, the source of mourning, as Paul claimed in a passage to which Benjamin alludes (Rom. 8:18–25): proper names are.[66] Finitude inhabits language regardless of its constitutive infinitude the moment a name is supposed to demonstrate its propriety—which is to say, its creation from *nothing*, its origin in sovereign power, its discontinuity. The expulsion from paradise does not change anything in this regard: more names are doubtless invented, but one name is not only sufficient to elicit the feeling of mourning; having only one name—and having to show that this name is one's own—is reason enough for the presentiment of this feeling, the "intimation of mourning." Having more names might even be a relief, and so, too, would knowledge of whence the name comes, as in the case of Adam, Eve, and even God.

The disastrous moment in which the language of names falls into the languages of communicative words is already prepared in the proper name. The collapse of the names derived from translation into the "human word" (GS, 2: 153; W, 1: 71) does not spell the end of either linguistic infinitude or linguistic immediacy, however; rather, they both take refuge in the dimension of language in which its wholeness disintegrates into "parts of speech" and these parts are recombined into abstract units—the dimension, namely, of judgment (*Urteil*). Even before anyone is judged, the proper name, as an independent part of speech, makes room for this disintegration and reintegration. The subsumption of the proper name under an evaluatory predicate is the primary "unit" of language after the collapse of the sole concrete linguistic unity: each infinite language itself. The infinity of judgment resides in its ability to determine guilt, for as soon as anyone is subject to judgment, there is no end to guilt. Its immediacy is similarly structured, for the judgment "you are guilty" immediately makes "you" guilty—and gives "you" a legally valid and therefore "proper" name. What cannot be known are the criteria of such judgments, for the fundamental terms through which they are carried out—good and evil—are themselves abstract parts of speech, mere predicates, not something God created and Adam in turn named. Because the criteria of judgment cannot be known, everything in the vicinity of judgment turns into hearsay, regardless of how much "evidence" may be marshaled for the purpose of condemnation. Explanations for judgment are hearsay, and so, too, are the terms of punishment: in Genesis, "death," which would be incomprehensible to Adam and Eve, or to anyone else. The end of knowledge is always the beginning of hearsay. Benjamin does not use the word "hearsay," but, instead, emphasizes its Kierkegaardian equivalent—"chatter": "The knowledge of things resides in the name, whereas that of good and evil is, in the profound sense in which Kierkegaard uses the word, 'chatter [*Geschwätz*],' and knows only one purification and elevation, to which the chattering one, the sinner, was therefore submitted: judgment" (GS, 2: 153; W, 1: 71).[67]

Geschwätz and *Gesetz*, chatter and law, belong together. The law "excites" chatterers into chattering about the very law that finds them guilty of chattering about what they cannot know—the law under which they will be condemned: "This judging word expels the first human beings from paradise; they themselves have excited [*exzitiert*] it in accordance with the eternal law by which this judging word punishes—and expects —its own awakening as the sole, the deepest guilt" (GS, 2: 153; W, 1: 71). The temporality of judgment lies in the condition of eternal expectation: whoever arouses judgment is condemned. There can be no innocence, therefore—only, at best, an eternal postponement of the inevitable condemnation. And all argument for innocence does nothing more than compound the guilt, since no argument can get at the core of the matter: knowledge of the criteria by which a judgment is decided. However calm and coherent it may appear, argument is always excited chatter. Something other than argument must be discovered to counteract the "judging word" and the legal order through which it rigorously maintains its integrity. One such discovery is prophetic speech, another tragic silence, and still another—neither prophetic nor tragic—is translation. For translation among languages of the same density is as vain and empty as chatter "in the profound sense in which Kierkegaard uses the word"—or more so. Nevertheless, at its best, it does not go outside of language and seek fulfillment in meaning.

Stop, Abstain (*Halt, Enthalten*)

Benjamin identifies the reason for the plurality of human languages in the structure of language as such: "Since the unspoken word in the existence of things falls infinitely short of the naming word in human knowledge, and since the latter in turn must fall short of the creative word of God, there is reason [*Grund*] for the plurality of human languages" (GS, 2: 152; W, 1: 70). This plurality is thus justified in the order of linguistic infinitude. It might be too bold to say that the *absence* of this plurality in the single language of paradise is unjustified—or even unjust. In some of the notes for the revision of his treatise into a *Habilitationsschrift*, Benjamin tends in this direction:

> The plurality of language is . . . a plurality of essences [*Wesensvielheit*]. The doctrine of the mystics concerning the decay [*Verfall*] of the true language cannot, therefore, in accordance with truth [*wahrheitsgemäß*], issue into a doctrine of dissolution into a plurality that would somehow contradict the original and God-willed unity, for the plurality of languages is not the product of decay any more than is the plurality of peoples and is indeed so far removed from any such decay that precisely this plurality alone expresses their essential character. (GS, 6: 24; W, 1: 273)

The original Adamic language, for Benjamin, is not true language: only God's can be so called. From the beginning, human language is infinitely removed from the infinitude of true language, which, for its part, is fundamentally inconsistent: it, too, is not "one" language among others, for it cannot be counted as *one*. The highest number is "subtracted from the order of number" (Irigaray, EDS, 107; ESD, 110)—or at least from the sphere of mathematical competence. Insofar as the power of divine language corresponds to that of "an inconsistent, absolutely infinite plurality" (Cantor, GA, 445), being true to true language means being inconsistent. In term of presentation, this fidelity postulates discontinuity; in terms of languages, plurality. By virtue of the power (*Mächtigkeit*) to which it corresponds—that of the continuum—the original human language is in itself disastrous. Adamic language is in this sense more fallen than fallen languages, for it cannot present a higher one.

Fallen languages, by contrast, can do so. Showing how they can present a higher language is the task Benjamin assigns himself in the essay he wrote as a preface to his translation of Baudelaire's *Tableaux parisiens*, "The Task of the Translator." According to Cantor's hypothesis, every infinite set of points has either the power of the natural numbers or that of the linear continuum. Not all infinite point-sets that have the same power as the linear continuum are continuous, however: the set of "incommensurable" or "irrational" numbers has the same power as that of the real numbers but is nevertheless "missing" the infinite set of points that correspond to the rational numbers. "On Language as Such" fails to examine languages that correspond to such sets—not so "The Task of the Translator." The fall into "the abyss of chatter" (GS, 2: 154; W, 1: 72) does not make human languages finite, nor does human language dissolve into languages of things. Rather, human language decays into a plurality of languages while nevertheless retaining in effect the same order of infinitude. Benjamin discovers an image of this retention outside of Genesis, more exactly, in the Lurianic Kabbalah. He thus likens the work of translator to the restitution of the shattered "vessel" from its "shards" (GS, 4: 18; W, 1: 260). Postlapsarian language is in shards; yet shards of the continuum are of equivalent power. The task of the translator, in turn, is different from the task of the original human being: not the translation of less dense languages into a denser one, but the translation of equally dense, discontinuous languages into one other. The purpose of this effort does not consist in filling up the gaps—which is impossible in any case—but, rather, in *concentrating* them so that the "missingness" of the gaps can be manifest. The concentration of gaps takes shape in the mismatch between content and language: "Whereas content and language form a certain unity in the original, like a fruit and its skin, the language of the translation wraps its content like a royal robe with ample folds" (GS, 4: 15; W, 1: 258). Concentrated looseness has a curious advantage over even the most concentrated linguistic "condensation" or "poetry" (*Dichtung*): by virtue of its irreversibility—a translation is itself untranslatable[68]—it "points [*hindeutet*]" (GS, 4: 15; W, 1: 257) toward that which "every language as whole" (*im ganzen*) in its complementary (*ergänzende*) relation to every other language "means" or "wishes to say": "pure language" (GS, 4: 13; W, 1: 257).[69] Pointing away (*Hindeutung*) from the sphere of human language is the very point of translating from one equally dense language into another, and this pointing alone—not the "point" of translation, its purpose or significance (*Bedeutung*)—determines the differential character of every translation:

> Just as a tangent touches [*berührt*] a circle fleetingly and at only one point; and just as this touch, not the point, prescribes the law according to which it is to continue on its straight path to infinity, a translation touches the original lightly and only at the infinitely small point of sense [*dem unendlich kleinen Punkte des Sinnes*] in order to pursue its own course according to the law of fidelity in the freedom of linguistic movement. (GS, 4: 19–20; W, 1: 261)

In the case of the greatest translations—Hölderlin's translations of Sopho-
cles are the "prototype"—the concentration of gaps is so great that there
is simply no room for anything else: "meaning plunges from abyss to abyss"
(GS, 4: 21; W, 1: 262).

"But," Benjamin immediately adds, "there is a stop [*ein Halten*]. No
text vouchsafes for it other than the holy one, in which meaning has
ceased to be the watershed for the flow of language and the flow of reve-
lation" (GS, 4: 21; W, 1: 262). Benjamin's fluxions of translation—which,
like Hölderlin's fluxions of tonal modulation, is concerned with the "cal-
culable law" (SW, 5: 265) of flowing sums and effluent rivers—comes
down to this ironic reversal: only a language that flows unencumbered,
without regard to the stopping points called "meaning," can stop the in-
herent tendency of translation to plunge into "the abyss of meaning" (GS,
4: 21; W, 1: 262), which is to say, in terms of Benjamin's treatise on lan-
guage, into "chatter" in the "profound sense in which Kierkegaard uses the
word." Meaning cannot be lost if it was never there in the first place. And
this condition—the absence of meaning in the first place—is what a holy
text "vouchsafes." Pure language, like every other language, is a medium.
Unlike the language of human beings, however, its mediality is constitu-
tively incapable of carrying meaning. For this reason, it is pure: it cannot
be made into a means for the transference of information, thoughts, or
even "spiritual content." And for the same reason, its motion is unen-
cumbered: *it* flows freely without carrying anything along the way. The
fluxion of this flow, in turn, cannot be measured by any tangent line, for
all tangents "touch" the point of meaning, even if only "fleetingly." Only
an absolutely free flow, the fluxion of which would be incalculable, arrests
the "enormous and original danger" to which all translators open them-
selves: losing themselves in the "bottomless depth of language" and thus
falling "silent" (GS, 4: 21; W, 1: 262).

The "stop" (*Halten*) to this fall into silence is not an infusion of speech,
much less a hope for divine afflatus, which could somehow give transla-
tors the courage to overcome the dangers they run when they open "the
gates" (GS, 4: 21; W, 1: 262) of language so widely that they can no longer
rest assured in the conviction that their language is *a* language, which is to
say, *one* solid language rather than two or more—or less than one. "The
Task of the Translator" is an essay on the courage of the translator, and
this courage, like that of the poet, does not consist in inspiration or en-
thusiasm. Rather, the courage consists in halting, that is, in abstaining

(*Enthalten*): abstaining from positing oneself in a positive world in the first case; abstaining from presenting the residue of the abstention in terms of "spiritual content" or meaning in the second. The *Halt* of translation is thus an *Enthalten* to the second power.

The mistake of all interpretation lies in representing the residue of the poetic reduction as meaning; the same mistake is repeated in the phenomenological *epochē* as practiced and promoted by Husserl. Courageous translators, by contrast, do not make this mistake. Such translators arrest the transference of meaning to the point of silence: there is nothing to say, no point to speaking. But the arresting of language is done for the sake of its free flow. Only holy texts can testify to the fact of this free flow and thereby arrest the fall of those who are drawn toward free-flowing, original, and therefore "Rhein"—*rein*, "pure"—language. Arresting the fall into linguistic flux by virtue of its pure flux is the sole "power [*Vermögen*] of translation" (GS, 4: 19; W, 1: 261). This arrest is not accomplished by a subject of any kind: neither transcendental nor transcendent. And it does nothing more than sustain the abstention—or *epochē*—to which translators commit themselves whenever they, as translators, completely enclose themselves within the sphere of language.

The Paradisal *Epochē*

Immediately before Benjamin introduces the term *density*, he emphasizes the "thesis" under which this metaphor drawn from Cantorian mathematics operates. The "little treatise" revolves around this thesis: "spiritual essence = linguistic essence." This "equation" (*Gleichsetzung*) enjoys the same status in Benjamin's treatise as "*A* is *A*" in Leibnizian metaphysics and "I = I" in German idealism. On its basis a theory of knowledge can be developed that has absolutely nothing to do with affection of any kind. Benjamin's first philosophy has no other guiding goal: the concept of experience is to be freed from every trace of affection—without thereby making the concept of knowledge into a matter of spontaneous self-positing, intellectual intuition, or conceptual self-development of the self. Things are knowable in their names; since everything knowable is always already linguistic, knower and known inhabit the same sphere—that of "totality neutrality" (GS, 2: 162–63; W, 1: 105). Things, in other words, do not in any sense "transcend" those who can know them. Instead of transcendence, there is translation, which not only operates *between* languages but also takes place *entirely* within the sphere of language. Or it does so as long as the "equation" is valid and "spiritual essence" is identical with "linguistic essence," which is to say that no language carries anything other than itself, and therefore every one "contains its own singularly-articulated infinity." In contrast to knowledge stands—or falls—*judgment* and the "just order of time" (Leibniz, FS, 297). For the predicates "good" and "evil" are precisely that: predicates, not names. They are applicable to things only under the condition that things be represented as subjects of judgment. The end of judgment is punishment. The "expectation" of punishment generates "excitement" (GS, 2: 153; W, 1: 71), and conversely, excitement generates subjects whose existence consists in constant expectation of eventual condemnation.

The condition of complete nonexcitement has already been named: it is "paradise." Children inhabit a paradise of colors, according to Benjamin's *Farbenlehre*, for colors do not excite them in any way: their senses are unaffected, since color is a form of appearance in its own right; and their soul is undisturbed, since colors do not stir their passions. Instead of being affected by color, children color themselves into the scenes they see. By virtue of a "naive" reduction, the parameters of a paradisal condition can be shown. And by virtue of an even more reductive *epochē*, the paradisal epoch can be exactly drawn. The three "transcendencies" identified by Husserl in the opening sections of *Ideas*—positive things, the pure I, and a transcendent deity—are all reduced: things are knowable in their names; there is no "I," still less a "pure" one, before the act of judgment; and God, too, participates in the paradisal condition from its inception. The *epochē* even reduces the "residuum" of the phenomenological reduction—"absolute consciousness"—which means, however, that the paradisal *epochē* cannot be an *accomplishment of consciousness*. No one, in short, can accomplish this *epochē*—not even "epistemological (transcendental) consciousness." And Benjamin therefore goes in search of this "no one."

The search for the "no one" who can accomplish the paradisal *epochē* gives direction to Benjamin's works from "The Rainbow" onward. The name of this "no one" varies, and sometimes, as in "The Rainbow," it is entirely anonymous: whatever "in" Margarethe's mind allows her to go outside of herself, forget herself, and color herself into the landscape of pure color is unknown—and not even known as the other side of consciousness. One of the names for "no one" does, however, silently traverse the conversation between Margarethe and Georg: youth. Only insofar as youth enacts a "naive" reduction does it generate its own youthfulness. In Benjamin's essay "Toward the Critique of Violence" (1921), he identifies another "no one": workers—but only workers who stop working. The "revolutionary general strike" (GS, 2: 184; W, 1: 239) not only brings work to a halt but also abstains from positing a new legal order under which it will be resumed. Under the name "youth" or "worker," however, this much is certain about the "no one" who accomplishes the paradisal *epochē*: it is never *one*—neither an identifiable individual, nor a specifiable kind, still less a self-consistent class, genre, or gender. Nor, however, is it any other number. Rather, this "no one" transforms itself into a constitutively *inconsistent plurality*. Its "number" is ℵ, which is to say, the "end" of number. Nothing in the world can be equal to the last number. Nevertheless, the plurality—Benjamin prefers the word "collective"—that undertakes the paradisal *epochē* becomes, for this very reason, *like* the numeric *eschaton*. Such likeness cannot be seen or otherwise sensed, of course, but it alone gives shape to a constitutively inconsistent "collective." Recognizing the shape of the collective, its likeness to the last number, is unlike the innumerable acts of recognition that consist in subsuming objects under concepts on the basis of the transcendental unity of colorless self-consciousness. And the recognition of the collective's shape cannot, in turn, be done at any time. Only at those times that correspond to this shape—the last times, eschatological time—is it recognizable.

No one—least of all an individual philosopher—can undertake the *epochē*, for the very intention to do so thwarts its accomplishment. Or, to cite one of the sentences from the "Epistemo-Critical Preface" to the *Origin of the German Mourning Play* that succinctly expresses Benjamin's revision of the phenomenological program: "Truth is the death of intention" (GS, 1: 216; O, 36). Truth, which would reveal itself by way of abstention, cannot reveal itself as long as the abstention has an *end*, which is to say, is finite and intended. Techniques other than "mental" exercises of phenomenological researchers must therefore be discovered and invented, but only nonmental and therefore, in a certain sense, "historical materialist" techniques can generate the "no one" who undertakes the paradisal *epochē*. One of these techniques—which Benjamin develops in the body of the *Origin* and elaborates most fully in the *Arcades Project*—is a parody of the phenomenological reduction: instead of "bracketing" the world, Benjamin brackets *words*, taking citations out of their "natural" contexts and thus making them legible for the first time. Other techniques operate on the "subject" and make "oneself" into configurations of inconsistency. Surrealism is an inventory of such techniques, and so, too, are epic theater, *In Search of Lost Time*, psychoanalysis, photography, film, and urban architecture—to say nothing of drugs, graphology, and even certain forms of violence.

All of these techniques are recognizable as techniques for the configuration of the "no one" who can carry out the paradisal *epochē*, however, only under the condition that the structure of paradise be precisely *outlined*—neither vaguely imagined, nor mystically revealed. Because paradise cannot be intuited in the fullness of self-evidence, Benjamin must rely on a few guides for its outlining; at least three of them are canonical enough to be of some assistance: Kantian critique, Cantorian mathematics, and the Bible. The outlining of paradise is not done for the sake of replicating it, much less to lament what has been lost. Rather, the outlining of the irreducible fault lines of paradise gives a formal indication of the "no one" who can carry out the *epochē*. The differential between the outline of paradise and the outcome of the paradisal *epochē* is incalculable—and messianic. Benjamin largely accomplishes the task of outlining the fractured structure of paradise with his dialogue on "The Rainbow," his treatise "On Language as Such," and its supplement, "The Task of the Translator." The other task—that of discovering, inventing, and cataloguing the cunning techniques of the collective "no one" who can carry out the paradisal *epochē*—occupies the rest of his life.[70] The latter task is far more difficult than the former, and the chance of its success is infinitesimal. The plurality of techniques is without any ordering rule—except perhaps one: shock. For whoever is in shock ceases to be "one" and turns, instead, into an inconsistent plurality. And the "no one" in shock is no longer affected by anything—at least for the enormously concentrated time of its distraction. This monadic time—which corresponds to "windowless" space (GS, 5: 661; AP, 532)—is the interruption of the "just order of time" (Leibniz, FS, 297) and the opening of the gates for a "multicolored, diverse self" (Kant, B, 134) through whom the Messiah might pass.

§ 7 Tragedy and Prophecy in Benjamin's *Origin of the German Mourning Play*

> Homer and the tragedians are the Moses and prophets for the Greeks.
> —Wilamowitz[1]

I. Benjamin Bound

The end of tragedy unfolds from its beginning. And so, too, the end of tragic theory. For example, in the case of Benjamin: "This work," he writes to Scholem, "is for me a conclusion—under no circumstances a beginning" (GB, 15; C, 261). With these words Benjamin leaves undecided the theory of tragedy he had proposed in "this work," *The Origin of the German Mourning Play*. He will not dispute Gottfried Salomon-Delatour's contention that the conception of the tragic hero that Franz Rosenzweig advances in the *Star of Redemption* and that Benjamin reworks is indebted to Hegel—and for good reason: he has only skimmed over the relevant Hegelian texts.[2] (He also admits that he had not read Rosenzweig very thoroughly either.)[3] Benjamin's theory of tragedy, like tragedy according to this theory, ends in a *non liquet*:[4] the decision—about the tragic hero, about the treatise in which his theory of tragic heroism is advanced—is final, to be sure, but the case itself is not.

Yet Benjamin's theory of tragedy bears an even closer resemblance to tragedy as it is defined by this theory, for the failure of tragic heroes, their defiant silence, corresponds to Benjamin's own failure. Benjamin's language is in this way "metaethical,"[5] as this term is understood by Rosenzweig: although incomprehensible to those who first condemned it, especially the academic judges at the University of Frankfurt, it nevertheless, like an "echo"—this is Benjamin's word—communicates to coming generations. A new community first "learns to speak"—once again Benjamin's words—from the depths of this defiant refusal to engage in the language of the then-constituted Greek or academic community: "the farther the tragic word remains behind the situation . . . the more the hero escapes the old statutes to which, when they finally overtake him, he throws the dumb shadow of his being, his self, as a sacrifice, while his soul is saved into [*hinübergerettet*] the word of a distant community" (GS, 1: 287–88; O, 109). Whereas Benjamin cannot speak to the University of Frankfurt in 1926, his language, especially that of the "Epistemo-Critical Preface" to the *Trauerspiel* book, which is often described in terms applied to Aeschylus— obscure, incomprehensible, forbidding, and for this reason magnificent— becomes, according to the logic of reversal for which tragedy has always been famous, the language of this very same university in, say, 1962. His soul is "saved over into" the word of this distant academic community. "Der Benjamin," the last-born, becomes Benjamin the first-born, and once again, this corresponds to Benjamin's own words: "in respect of its victim, the hero, the tragic sacrifice differs from any other kind, being at once a first and last" (GS, 1: 285; O, 107). But the relation between Benjamin and the tragic hero whom he describes is more intimate still, for the infantilism of the hero and the Aeschylean sternness of Benjamin's language share a common root: tragic heroes, according to Benjamin, know that they are better than the gods, even those of Olympus, and for this reason they are struck dumb (GS, 1: 288–89; O, 109–10)—and so, too, Benjamin. Better than those who condemn him to academic oblivion, better than the gods of German academia, unwittingly sacrificed in preparation for a new academic community that will learn to speak his as yet incomprehensible language—a language for which he himself is equally unprepared: "I have lost every measuring rod for this work" (GB, 3: 14; C, 261)—Benjamin is struck dumb, condemned to this, a magnificently defiant silence.

There is perhaps no more popular image of Benjamin. In countless portraits, he emerges as a heroic victim from whom new communities—and especially new academic communities—learn to speak. And at the heart of this tragedy is the failure of his theory of tragedy to secure an academic appointment. A recent version of "Walter Hero" presents this image in particularly concise terms: "In the tragedy that Benjamin's life is generally taken to have been, the incomprehension of the Frankfurt jury charged with evaluating his doctoral thesis [it was, in fact, a *Habilitationsschrift*] ranks second only to the rise of Nazism as a node of embitterment."[6] The collapse of Benjamin's academic career, the rise of Nazism—thus Jeffrey Mehlman, who in a book called *Benjamin for Children* apparently need not distinguish between a dissertation and a *Habilitationsschrift*, for what, after all, do children care about these matters? Yet, even if we disregard this way of characterizing "the tragedy that Benjamin's life is generally taken to have been," there is something wrong with this whole way of proceeding: Benjamin cannot be a tragic hero, and his life cannot be a tragedy, if the indispensable element of the theory of tragedy developed in the *Origin of the German Mourning Play* is in any way valid. To speak of the "tragedy" of Benjamin's life in the context of his *Habilitationsschrift* is to ignore Benjamin's first and in a sense final word about tragedy: it is a one-time, epoch-making dramatic form, never to be repeated, least of all revived in whatever describes itself in terms of "the tragic." Tragedy is not only not "tragic," it runs counter to sadness, sorrow, mourning—and "embitterment." The term *tragedy* belongs to fifth-century Athens, not twentieth-century Germany. And one reason for Benjamin's rigorous delimitation of the historico-geographic horizon of tragedy is apparent from the very first paragraph where it is discussed. "Cultural arrogance" (GS, 1: 280; O, 101) gives rise to talk of "the tragic," and this arrogance consists for the most part in a pernicious sentiment according to which "our culture" is equal to that of the Greeks, which generally means, better than yours. At perhaps no other time was talk of the "return of tragedy" or "the return of the tragic age" more pervasive than in the Germany in the early part of the twentieth century, and Benjamin's response to this talk is the only sober one: no, Attic tragedy was unique; there are no tragedies outside the theater of Dionysus.

But, as Benjamin also emphasizes, tragedy nevertheless claims an unsurpassable "topicality" (*Aktualität*). These two traits—uniqueness, topicality—define the difficulty, or better yet, the density of tragedy as a *geschichtsphilosophishe* (historico-philosophical) category. Tragedy does not return; but it—or something that claims it as its heritage—comes back again and again. Something in tragedy or something of tragedy comes back without tragedy itself ever returning, and this "something" distinguishes tragedy from itself, that is, distinguishes tragedy from what comes to be known under the rubric of "tragic" or, to cite the English translation of the title of Benjamin's book, "tragic drama." As his attention is drawn toward a dramatic form whose stages wander from place to place—toward the *Trauerspiel*, in short—Benjamin tracks down this self-divisive "something" and calls it "prophecy."[7] Tragedy is not only distinguished from *Trauerspiel* by virtue of its prophetic character, but is even distinguished from *itself*, for tragedy is, according to an enigmatic phrase of Benjamin, only the "preliminary stage of prophecy": *die Vorstufe der Prophetie* (GS, 1: 297; O, 118). Because it never goes beyond this "stage," however, it is forever distinguished from that which defines it: the prophetic as such. Tragedy opens onto a prophetic "step" or "stage" but is not itself prophecy. Beyond the distinction between tragedy and *Trauerspiel* lies the "internal" distinction between tragedy and prophecy, and this latter distinction not only demands a rigorous distinction between tragedy and *Trauerspiel* but also guarantees that tragedy—which is distinguished from prophecy by virtue of its preliminariness—will return as something other than itself: as *Trauerspiel*. Of prophecy *itself*, Benjamin has almost nothing to say in the *Origin of the German Mourning Play*, and it is in this near silence—and perhaps only here—that Benjamin's book touches on the tragic.

II. Nietzsche's Prometheus

Tragedy does not return. On this point Benjamin distinguishes himself from the crowd of contemporaneous writers for whom the "decline of the West" prepares the way for a return to "the tragic age." Benjamin opens his discussion of tragedy in the second section of the *Trauerspiel* book with a polemic against those, like Johannes Volkelt, who make "the tragic" into a universal psychological experience of causal determinacy.[8] But this polemic is only a preparation for an altercation with a much more challenging antagonist: the young Nietzsche. *The Birth of Tragedy*, according to Benjamin, "lays the foundation" (GS, 1: 280; O, 102) for the more recent lines of inquiry into the nature of tragedy that are pursued by Lukács and Rosenzweig; but it soon becomes apparent that Nietzsche lays a foundation by painting a dark background from which one can perceive the lucidity of a Lukács, a Rosenzweig, and, strangely enough, a Wilamowitz. What Benjamin describes as Nietzsche's original insights into the distinctive character of tragedy—"the connection of tragedy to legend [*Sage*]"—belongs to his great opponent in the world of classical philology, and it is by connecting tragedy to legend that Wilamowitz hopes to undo the damaging effect of Nietzsche's "philology of the future" once and for all.[9] This is only the beginning of the complications of quotation and attestation in which Benjamin's theory of tragedy is enmeshed, and all these complications circle around the name of "Nietzsche." Just as the allegorist exalts and at the same time devalues "the profane world" (GS, 1: 351; O, 175), Benjamin exalts and repudiates Nietzsche—exalts his repudiation of all moralizing interpretations of tragedy and devalues his replacement of moralism with an aestheticism in whose train a new and now Germanic tragic-artwork is supposed to appear. Nietzsche does not, of course, subject tragedy to the protocols of empirical psychology in the manner of a Volkelt, but according to Benjamin he does something equally errant: he dissolves everything specific to the "state of affairs" (*Sachverhalt*) of Attic tragedy into the "abyss of aestheticism" (GS, 1: 281; O, 103). This dissolution of tragedy into the "eternal" play of appearance and disappearance—regardless of whether this play is affirmed or denied—doubtless disentangles tragedy from its entrapment in moralizing frameworks; but it also leaves the specificity of Attic tragedy undetermined. Tragedy can thereafter become something general, something "tragic," a matter for "Dionysiac man." And like Dionysus himself, Dionysiac man can wander beyond the theater of Dionysus and migrate to other and, in particular, more northern climates.

The Birth of Tragedy may not have given rise to the rebirth of tragedy, but it did give rise to incessant calls for its Germanic rebirth. And these calls are sanctioned throughout the book, most conspicuously in the sections devoted to Wagnerian opera but also in its decisive, early sections. Tragedy, according to Nietzsche, not only can return; it already has done so—and with a clarity unknown to the Greeks. Thus Nietzsche writes in the ninth section of *The Birth of Tragedy*: "what the thinker Aeschylus has to say to us here [in *Prometheus Bound*], what, however, as a poet he only lets us intimate [*ahnen*] through this parable-like image [*gleichnissartiges Bild*], this is something that the young Goethe knew how to unveil to us in the bold words of his Prometheus."[10] This sentence summarizes one of the less trenchant tendencies of Nietzsche's early theory of tragedy; according to the young Nietzsche, a young German (Goethe) is incomparably more mature than an elderly Greek (Aeschylus, whose *Prometheus Bound* is often presented as a work of old age). Goethe lets "us," the Germans, know what Aeschylus surely thought but was unable to reveal to the Greeks, or even to himself. From this inability to bring thought into poetry arises the "parable-like image" of a still muffled, still uncreative Prometheus. An image of this Titan accordingly graces the book's cover. When the Greeks came to know what they said, it was under the tutelage of the twin inventors of rationality and dramatic realism, Socrates and Euripides, whose confidence in the saving power of knowledge sentences tragedy to death. The stony silence of the first tragedian, and indeed the only tragedian who, like Wagner, was reputed to be a musician, can now be understood for what it is: Aeschylus was waiting for Goethe to reveal what he wanted to say.

No wonder a later Nietzsche will smell something unpleasantly "Hegelisch" in his first book.[11] For the touchstone of a certain Hegelianism is this very thesis: Germania knows what Hellas merely intimated. And the proof of this statement lies close at hand: the *theory* of tragedy—the only theory of tragedy that has the courage to break with the late-born Aristotle—has blossomed on German soil. One might say that the Germans own a piece of Prometheus's rock. For, according to the ninth section of *The Birth of Tragedy*, the legend of the fire bearer is nothing less than a "primordial property of the entire Aryan congregation of peoples and a document of their gift for the meditative-tragic [*Tiefsinnig-Tragischen*]; indeed, it may not even be improbable that the same significance inhabits this myth for the Aryan that the myth of the Fall has for the Semitic."[12] The theory of tragedy has its roots in a talent for *Tiefsinn*, and this talent not only makes possible a revival of tragedy or a "tragic age," but may already be a revitalizing sign. That Benjamin concludes the *Origin of the German Mourning Play* by bringing the talent for *Tiefsinn* into connection not with the tragic but, on the contrary, with the fall of Satan—and thus with the "Semitic" myth—indicates at the very least a pointed repudiation of Nietzsche's conception of tragedy, but it also indicates in a subtle manner what has been at stake in the figure of Prometheus from the very beginning: the relation between Greekness, Germanness, and Jewishness.

Nietzsche also repudiates his own call for a rebirth of tragedy under the auspices of German music, but others—and especially those who only took Nietzsche's fate as a "sign" and had little inclination to read his writings—went even further in this direction. One of these new "prophets" of tragedy plays a small but not insignificant role in the *Origin of the German Mourning Play*. When Benjamin first takes Nietzsche to task for his "aestheticization" of tragedy, he takes over a critique of *The Birth of Tragedy* launched by Leopold Ziegler, a student of Eduard von Hartmann and author of the 1902 book entitled *Toward the Metaphysics of the Tragic*. Just as Benjamin asserts that only "historico-philosophical or religious-philosophical concepts [*geschichts- oder religionsphilosophischen Begriffen*]" (GS, 1: 283; O, 104), not aesthetic ones, grant access to tragedy, Ziegler had maintained some twenty years earlier that "the tragic is closely connected with the *religious problem*,"[13] and this problem is world-historical. More precisely, the problem is one of "cosmic" time:

Just as there are religions that snuff out a self-radiating tragic, so there are religions that are nothing but the tragicification [*Tragifizierung*] of the existence-process. In this sense it is no accident that *German* philosophy brings to completion theoretically the principal solution of the tragic problem, while the original mythology of the German race may be called the religion of the tragic.[14]

German theory of tragedy can solve the "tragic problem" because the Germans know that existence itself is problematic. "For they," Ziegler writes of the Germans, "already knew in the existence of the gods a mysterious, tragic primordial guilt [*geheimnisvolle tragische Urschuld*], and they believed that man is called upon to bring to completion the expiation of this guilt through the tragic end of the twilight of the gods."[15] And the Germans likewise know the solution to the problem of existence: "the mission of man" consists in the "redemption of God [*Erlösung Gottes*]": "by negating his will, man renounces the actuality of the divine will; by liberating himself from the burdensome curse of being an existence [*Dasein*] at the cost of God's being [*Sein*], he also frees God from this curse, this being-enclosed-in-itself."[16] From the knowledge that Nietzsche attributes to the young Goethe and that Ziegler, who was then a champion of Houston Stewart Chamberlain, attributes to the Germans as a "race," there arises the theory of tragedy, which, in turn, gives rise to a new tragic age. The tragic returns, according to Ziegler, as the catastrophic redemption of the cosmos in "a unique tragedy of totality [*einer einzigen Tragödie der All-heit*]."[17] Once redeemed, the tragedy of totality begins anew—without end. On the basis of an inner knowledge of the endlessness and purposelessness of the cosmos, Jewish-Christian religiosity can be overcome, and the Germans, as a result, can finally carry out the mission of man: to redeem the gods of their own tragic individuality without falsifying existence as a whole by positing a creator God beyond the world.

III. Distinguishing Tragedy from *Trauerspiel* and Jewish Silence from German Speech

Ziegler is not alone in proposing a German propensity toward "the tragic." The ghost of tragedy haunts post-Nietzschean Germany, a ghost that makes itself known in farcical repetitions of the great Nietzschean announcement: *incipit tragoedie*. But the ghostliness of tragedy, its status as a revenant, means, for Benjamin, that tragedy has not returned but *Trauerspiel* has.

Benjamin thus places his work in this context, the return of the Baroque mourning play to Germany. Benjamin is quite explicit about this: instead of viewing Franz Werfel's *Troerinnen* (Trojan women) as evidence of a return of Euripides, for example, he presents it in the penultimate section of the preface as a return of seventeenth-century *Trauerspiel* (GS, 1: 235; O, 54). Thus does the mourning play return, and the theory of the mourning play shows these plays to be nothing but the ostentatious display of "returnees." The gods return, antiquity returns, spirits return; indeed *everything* returns in the play of mourning, for this is the law of mourning: everything must come back again and again. The law of mourning expresses itself in Nietzsche's doctrine of the eternal return of the same, which, in the hands of a Ziegler, constitutes nothing less than the knowledge that "tragifies" existence. For Benjamin, by contrast, it is only in the mood of mourning that everything returns. The schema of return defines thinghood for the mourner in the first and last place—and defines it as ghostly, haunted by its own enigmatic phenomenality from apparent beginning to apparent end. Things return to the mourner in this way because mourning consists in the experience of holding onto the play of disappearing appearances; under this melancholic but by no means unpleasant condition it is impossible for anything, least of all the dead, to depart *for good*: all appearances—and there are, for the mourner, nothing but appearances—are absorbed into an endless play of devaluation and disappearance.

Everything, therefore, returns in the play of mourning—*except tragedy*. Or, when tragedy returns, as it must, it does so as a "slave" to the mourning play, not on its own (GS, 1: 278; O, 100). And this is, to use Ziegler's imprecise terminology, the "religious problem" of tragedy: it does not return because it has nothing to do with mourning. If tragedy has nothing to do with mourning, then with what does it have to do? Messianism (to use another imprecise term). Mourning and messianism have absolutely nothing do with each other; *absolutely* nothing, because messianism—or to us a more precise term, messianicity[18]—absolves itself of everything mournful: instead of appearances returning as they once were, everything is fulfilled as it never was. Just as history, according to Benjamin, disappears in the setting of the mourning play, and this setting freezes the "impure" history of "natural history" (*Naturgeschichte*), the destructive gesture of divine justice disappears from the scene of mourning only to be replaced by the endless play of unstable orders, each of which justifies itself on the basis of a "state of exception" whose violence, however brutal, never destroys the setting as such and is therefore never exceptional enough, which is to say, never exceptionally exceptional but only exceptional according to the rule.

Benjamin is drawn toward the German mourning play for precisely this reason: in it, more than in its English or Spanish versions, messianic time is absorbed into "natural history" without remainder—especially without the remainder to which Hamlet attests in his final words, "the rest is silence" (GS, 1: 335; O, 158). As Benjamin emphasizes from the title of the book onward, it is in the specifically *German* Baroque mourning play that eschatology altogether vanishes and, in turn, the world appears altogether "empty."[19] In view of this emptiness Benjamin presents the Idea of the *Trauerspiel*, for eschatology is the name for the gathering together of last things, and the presentation of an Idea, according to the methodological protocols of the "Epistemo-Critical Preface," depends upon the analysis of phenomena into their elements, which, as extremes, are no longer susceptible to the scientific labor of conceptualization for the precise reason that they mark out the limits of the concepts—and therefore the transcendental consciousness—under which they are subsumed. In the case of the Baroque *Trauerspiel*, the list of last things is a litany of woes: extremities of the State, "states of exception"; extremities of passion, martyrdom and tyranny; extremities of self-estimation, injured honor and self-glorification; extremities of loyalty and disloyalty, intriguer as both; extremities of kinship relations, incest; extremities of geographic space, the borderlands of Christendom; and finally the edge of the cosmos, Saturn, the most distant and slowest planet. But no extreme of time: in Greek, no *eschaton*. Instead of eschatological time, there is only time as limit. Thus does the *Trauerspiel* revolve around certain liminal moments and especially around the hour of midnight, the "very witching hour of night" (*Hamlet*, quoted in the Schlegel-Tieck translation at GS, 1: 314; O, 135), the time in which not only the day but also counterparts to daylight—dreams, ghosts, specters—return. Midnight is not only *not* eschatological, not an extremity, still less a last time; it is not even properly historical but is, instead, only "natural historical," for, as Benjamin writes, "the spirit world is without history [*geschichtslos*]" (GS, 1: 314; O, 135). The *Trauerspiel* is defined by this, the absence of nonnatural—but not, for this reason "spiritual"—history, which is to say, its absolute nonrelation to, or absolution from, messianic time. And so the theory of tragedy not only becomes the place in which the historical can be articulated without reference to "nature" or "natural history," it also bears responsibility for presenting the one element whose absence grants access to the Idea of the *Trauerspiel*: the element for which there is absolutely no analysis because there are absolutely no concepts under which it can be grasped, the extremity par excellence, the eschaton *kat exochen*, or messianic time.

In view of this criterion, then, Benjamin makes a rigorous distinction between tragedy and *Trauerspiel*: tragedy is related—in an as yet unspecified manner—to messianic time, whereas the *Trauerspiel*, especially its German version, belongs to the temporality of eternal return and thus to "natural history." Benjamin's earliest attempt to distinguish tragedy from *Trauerspiel* is clear on at least this point: "This Idea of fulfilled time," he writes in "*Trauerspiel* and Tragedy" some eight years earlier,

> is called in the Bible as its dominant historical Idea: messianic time. In any case, however, the Idea of fulfilled historical time is not to be thought as the Idea of an individual time. This determination, which of course entirely transforms the meaning of fulfillment, is what distinguishes tragic time from messianic time. Tragic time is related to the latter as individually to divinely fulfilled time. (GS, 2: 134; W, 1: 55–56)

Tragedy is defined by the same terms as messianicity—"fulfilled time"—and only because it is so defined can Benjamin undertake the critical work of distinguishing the time, temperament, and language of tragedy from those of the *Trauerspiel*. Tragedy has something to do with messianic time, not so the *Trauerspiel*. Benjamin understands this "something" as "fulfillment," but in the *Origin of the German Mourning Play* he imposes on himself a stern rule: he will not conduct what he calls a "frontal assault"[20] on his subject matter. Instead of speaking of "fulfillment," he only speaks of its negation: an "empty world" (GS, 1: 317; O, 139), the contours and cataracts of which were explored by the Lutheran dramatists of the seventeenth century. And instead of speaking of "tragic time" in relation to "messianic time," Benjamin introduces a new term: a third term, as it were, which implies in its own way *both* the individuality of "individually fulfilled time" and the totality of "divinely fulfilled time," namely "the prophetic." Once tragedy is brought into relation with prophecy—which is at the very least a term for a certain experience of language and history—it silently refers to the messianic, and it is in this silence that Benjamin finds the decisive trait of everything "tragic."

After Benjamin had decided to draw on his early efforts to distinguish tragedy from *Trauerspiel* for his *Habilitationsschrift*, he asks Florens Christian Rang to help him clarify the relation between tragedy and prophecy: "I recall that we are very much in accord on this matter [the theory of tragedy], but unfortunately with regard to the details (like the relation of tragedy to prophecy and so forth) not with sufficient clarity" (GB, 2: 371; C, 217). Benjamin makes this request to Rang, who knew little Greek and less Hebrew, at the end of a long letter devoted to an apparently different topic: the relation of *Deutschtum* to *Judentum*. All of these polar terms— tragedy and prophecy, Germanness and Jewishness, tragedy and *Trauerspiel*—form a shifting kaleidoscope through which at least two images of "moral speechlessness" (GS, 1: 289; O, 110) are uneasily brought to light: the silence of the tragic hero, on the one hand, and contemporary Jewish silence, on the other. "In the most terrible moments of a people," Benjamin writes in the same letter to Rang, "only those are called upon to speak who belong to this people—even more to the point, those who belong to it in the most eminent sense, who not only can say *mea res agitur* but also *meam propriam ago*. The Jew should certainly not speak" (GB, 2: 368; C, 215). At issue in this injunction to silence is the question of guilt for the war and reparations for its victims, to which Rang responds in his pamphlet *Deutsche Bauhütte*.[21] Although only Rang would understand— and even Rang, the "authentic reader" (GB, 3: 16; C, 262) of *The Origin of the German Mourning Play*, would perhaps have understood only up to a point—Benjamin has worked himself into a position where he no longer needs to pose the question of the silent hero as one of German foreknowledge but can pose it in terms of a certain Jewish propheticism: the silence of the hero echoes the silence of those who "should not speak" during the "most terrible moments of a people": those who have nothing to say and could not be heard in any case because they "do not belong," and they do not belong and in any case have nothing to say—tautologically or perhaps tautosigetically—because they *cannot* speak.

The silence of the tragic hero in the crisis of the Greek world corresponds to the silence of the Jews in the crisis of contemporary Germany—and, to add one more element to this constellation, the silence of the youth at its own congregation.[22] Language is arrested at these critical moments, and arrested language is paradoxically prophetic—paradoxically, of course, because the prophet, as the word itself indicates, is the one who speaks *before* everyone else and speaks *for* a divine figure who otherwise remains silent. And if it seems not only paradoxical but downright implausible that Jewish, or youthful, silence should be prophetic insofar as genuine prophets, unlike false ones, bear the burden of denouncing the wrongs of their *own* people, it is equally implausible that tragic heroes, as Benjamin presents them, should be associated with prophetism, even if only as a preliminary stage. For prophets—at least those of the Hebrew Bible, according to innumerable authorities, including the imposing one of Hermann Cohen[23] —speak out against nothing so much as the institution of sacrifice, which, for Benjamin, constitutes the very framework of tragic existence: "he throws the dumb shadow of his being, his self, as a sacrifice, while his soul is saved into the word of a distant community" (GS, 1: 287–88; O, 109). The sacrifice of the tragic hero does not, however, belong to a continuous sacrificial tradition; on the contrary: "the tragic sacrifice differs from any other kind, being at once a first and last" (GS, 1: 285; O, 106).

The end of sacrifice would be announced if only the "dumb shadow" of the tragic hero could speak: no longer dumb, the shadow would instead be something like the angel with which, according to a Jewish tradition that Benjamin invokes in private,[24] every soul is born and which, when revealed, marks the commencement of the messianic era. Individually fulfilled time of tragedy would thus become the divinely fulfilled time in which what never was—call it the realm of shadows—is first and finally saved. The silence of Greek heroes and that of contemporary German Jews are by no means equivalent, but in their respective enactments of a certain silence they prepare a stage for prophecy—or its renewal. For silence makes possible an entirely different practice of speech than those in which words are enmeshed in the juridical categories through which guilt, including guilt for the start of the war, is not so much judiciously determined as unjustly iterated. Evidence of the relation of the tragic to the Judaic, finally, would be the blossoming of tragic theory after Nietzsche in the works of a Lukács, a Rosenzweig, and of course, a Benjamin. *Trauerspiel*, by contrast, will be aligned with Germanness—or, more properly, with its return to Germany—and the link of Germany to the *Trauerspiel* will be forged finally by the latter's total exclusion of the tragic, which is to say, of the prophetic and so, silently, of the Judaic. As evidence for these unlikely alignments, one observation perhaps suffices: with the exception of the concluding section of the *Origin*, which reworks the final paragraphs of his treatise "On Language as Such and on Human Language," Benjamin nowhere else in his *Habilitationsschrift* cites a passage directly from the Hebrew Bible as preparation for an interpretation—or midrash—of his own:

"'You shall not make for you any engraved image'—this serves not only as a defense against idolatry. With incomparable emphasis the prohibition on the presentation of the body guards against the illusion that the sphere in which the moral essence of the human being is perceptible can be made into an image [*abzubilden*]" (GS, 1: 284; O, 105; Exod. 20:4).[25] Never, however, does Benjamin cite a single passage from an ancient Greek playwright—not even when he seeks to distinguish Greek tragedy from German *Trauerspiel.*

IV. Silence, Echo

But the interaction between Benjamin and Rang, which both of them understood as something like a dialogue between *Judentum* and *Deutschtum*, cannot be so easily reconstructed, for Benjamin never articulates his understanding of the relation between tragic silence, prophecy, and his admonition that German-Jews remain silent. What Benjamin emphasizes in *The Origin of the German Mourning Play* is something else: the singularity of tragedy, its uniqueness from a historico-philosophical perspective. In earlier drafts of his theory of tragedy, especially in "Fate and Character," Benjamin not only fails to emphasize the singularity of tragedy; he even makes tragedy into a drama of "fate," which, along with guilt or debt (*Schuld*), plots the ensnaring circle in which everything appears to return. Little of this survives into the *Trauerspiel* book, even though Benjamin finds occasion to quote "Fate and Character."[26] Tragedy, as Benjamin makes clear in the opening paragraph of his discussion (GS, 1: 279; O, 101), is no longer defined in terms of fate, guilt, and expiation, because any definition of this sort, any definition that would rely on the traditional notions of *moira* and *ananke*, to say nothing of "tragic guilt" or "tragic fault," would immediately implicate tragedy in the temporality of eternal return and thus undo the rigorous distinction between tragedy and *Trauerspiel.* Benjamin may be following a venerable philological tradition when he declares that Attic tragedy should not be compared with other supposed "tragedies" composed in other "tragic ages," but his declaration of tragedy's never-to-be-repeated status resembles nothing so much as the rabbinical doctrine that the time of prophecy is over—until, paradoxically, the messianic era comes and prophets, one or many, can then prophesize the coming of the messianic era.[27]

Benjamin enlists the theory of tragedy in two tasks: to disassociate Attic tragedy from all forms of "fate drama," regardless of how these dramas conceive of their provenance, and to associate tragedy with prophecy. To accomplish the first of these tasks, Benjamin reworks Wilamowitz's philological studies and, more problematically, Rang's speculations concerning the conversion of the *thymelē* from sacrificial altar into theatrical stage. Each of the elements of Benjamin's analysis of tragedy takes its point of departure from certain "pragmatisms" of Athenian public life, and especially its juridical forms and forums: the Aristotelian unities, in particular, are presented in terms of the space and time of the Attic courts and are therefore anything but rules for the production of plays outside of Athens. By presenting the "metaphysics of the tragic," to use Ziegler's title, in terms of the "pragmatics" of Athenian jurisprudence, Benjamin comes close to formulating in a very precise and concise manner the methodological—or contramethodological—principle that gives direction to many of his later inquiries, including his massive study of the "primordial history" of the nineteenth century: "as everywhere else, so here the most fruitful layer of metaphysical interpretation lies at the level of the pragmatic itself" (GS, 1: 296; O, 117). The presentation of the pragmatic, in other words, *is* metaphysics, and metaphysics, in its turn, must be an interpretative—rather than deductive or intuitive—enterprise. Beyond interpreting the Aristotelian unities in terms of Athenian juridical procedures, however, Benjamin does not follow through on his own suggestion. Despite its great merits in developing an account of Attic tragedy—and the work of Vernant and Vidal-Naquet has gone in precisely the direction of Benjamin's analysis[28]—this emphasis on the affinity between legal forums and tragic spectacle comes to serve two specific functions within the economy of the work as a whole: on the one hand, it allows Benjamin to avoid both the "abyss of aestheticism" toward which *The Birth of Tragedy* was said to be drawn, and the converse of this aestheticism, that is, the moralizing interpretations of tragic figures and fates against which Nietzsche rebelled; and on the other hand, it makes Attic tragedy into the paradoxical representative of singularity as such. These two perspectives meet at a single point: universal singularity is what no mythic, legal, or conceptual order can grasp. It takes up residence in the paradoxes of tragedy, and its home—if it can be said to have one—would be among the Ideas, each of which, according to the "Epistemo-Critical Preface," is singular and total at the same time. The arrested language of the tragic hero is the paradoxical voice of singularity within the context of the *Origin of the German Mourning Play*, for what the hero does without saying—and such "doing without saying" is another name for heroic passivity—is to condemn the mythic-legal order: the general order of law that accommodates itself to, and draws its strength from, demonic retribution.

In the space of the tragic contest, Athens thus opens up an arena in which the justice of its own legal order *would have been* condemned but *could not* for lack of words—or because the only words for judgment and the space of its jurisdiction were themselves defined by the prevailing legal norms. The opening up of the arena of contestation is therefore incomplete, and the contest is a *non liquet* (GS, I: 296; O, 116). For Rang, whose tendentious exposition of the tragic agon gives direction to the initial moments of Benjamin's analysis, tragedy is nothing less than a cosmic process in which the astrological circle is partially opened up and turned into the semicircle of the stage. The struggle, *das Ringen*, concerns, for Rang, the ring, *der Ring*.[29] And so, too, for Benjamin, up to a point: whereas Rang understands the Athenian stage according to the same schema through which he sought to understand the Roman carnival—as a semicircle or semicircus in which astrological cycles are gradually perforated[30]—Benjamin makes the opening up of the circle into the defining character of the specifically Athenian legal order. Nowhere is *The Origin of the German Mourning Play* both closer to and farther from *The Birth of Tragedy* than in its account of this opening:

> For the Athenian legal order the most important and characteristic feature is the Dionysian puncture [*der dionysische Durchschlag*]—that the drunken, ecstatic word was allowed to break through [*durchbrechen*] the regular circling of the agon; that a higher justice develop from the persuasive power of living speech rather than from the trial of conflicting tribes by weapons or prescribed verbal forms. The logos breaks through the ordeal into freedom. This is at its deepest the affinity between the trial and tragedy in Athens. (GS, I: 295; O, 116)

Dionysus carries out the juridical—and *not* aesthetic—function of freeing the word from fixed, Apollonian formulas. Because of its affinity with the Athenian order of right, tragedy can then be defined as "agonal prophecy" (GS, I: 286; O, 107). The agon is for, as it were, free speech.[31] The prophecy, by contrast—and one can only understand this term "by contrast"— consists in a liberation of language from this "higher justice" for an even higher justice, which, by virtue of its height, would destroy the perspectives of retribution and distribution alike. Without words for justice of this order, tragedy can only remain an incomplete opening of the circle, a thwarted breakthrough in which, as Benjamin writes, "the old legal order of the Olympians is disempowered" (GS, 1: 285; O, 107)—without, however, being destroyed.

By virtue of the "metaethical" character of the tragic hero—where the "metaethical" names the defiant experience of becoming a self—tragedy functions as a paradoxical representative of self-enclosed singularity. Unlike death in the *Trauerspiel*, which is "communal fate," death in tragedy (and indeed the death of tragedy) is singular, *Einzelgeschick* (GS, 1: 314; O, 136). The life of tragic heroes, according to Benjamin, is nothing but the framework of their death: so fitting is this framework that they have no life outside of it, which is to say, no oscillation of feeling and therefore no life at all. Without naming his source Benjamin then quotes—and quotes incorrectly—an aphorism from Nietzsche's *Beyond Good and Evil*: "'Not the strength but rather the duration of high feeling makes the high human being'" (GS, 1: 294; O, 115).[32] To which Benjamin adds, as if it goes without saying that the "higher human being" for Nietzsche is the tragic one: "This monotonous duration of heroic feeling is only guaranteed in the pregiven framework of his life" (GS, 1: 294; O, 115). With this idea of the "'force of the framework'"—again a phrase Benjamin cites without giving the source of his citation—he can remove tragedy from its association with fate. And he can do something more: he can suggest the direction from which tragedy comes to an end, not as an incomplete *non liquet* but in a complete liquidation: "Necessity, as it appears built into the framework, is neither casual nor magic. At the slightest breath of the word it would melt like snow before the south wind. But only of an unknown word. Heroic defiance, closed in itself, contains this unknown" (GS, 1: 294; O, 115). The breath of the word—what is this but *ruah hakodesh*, the holy breath with which and sometimes of which the prophets speak? Ezekiel, for example: "And he said to me, Prophesy to the breath [*hinave' el-haruah*], prophesy, son of man, and say to the breath, Thus says the Lord God: Come from the four winds, O breath, and breathe upon these slain, that they may live" (Ezek. 37:9).

Such speech is, of course, entirely out of place in Greek tragedy—not least because the "crisis of death [*Todeskrisis*]" (GS, 1: 286; O, 107) it stages devolves into a sacrifice of its heroes instead of resolving itself in the resurrection of the unjustly slain. Tragedy is nevertheless "epochal" (GS, 1: 314; O, 135), in a literal sense, since it suspends the fatal continuity of mythic consciousness in the same way that the phenomenological *epochē* suspends natural attitudes. Instead of mythic continuity in both senses of the term, the arrested language of tragedy constitutes an unprecedented discontinuity, and according to Benjamin, the discontinuing of this discontinuity begins with Socrates, who interrupts the tragic interruption. Platonic dialogue saves the Idea of justice at the cost of its historicity, which is to say, in terms of Benjamin's work, its counterrhythmic "originariness." Universal singularity takes refuge in a world beyond, and justice becomes an Idea in the Platonic sense. From the perspective of this Idea *everything* historical is debased and condemned. By converting justice into an eternal Idea, Plato does not transcend, complete, or even negate tragedy; on the contrary— and in contrast to Nietzsche—Benjamin claims that Platonic dialogue constitutes a *return* to an historical stage against which tragedy had silently and, therefore, indecisively protested. According to one of Benjamin's more audacious proposals, Platonic dialogue constitutes a restoration, a *Wiederherstellung*, of the *mysterium*; but it is precisely this—the *mysterium* and the mystery cults—that both tragedy and comedy had been in the process of "secularizing" (*Verweltlichung*), that is, making worldly. Thus the strange and wholly undecidable sentence in which Benjamin speaks about the decision for *and* against tragedy: "Den Kampf aber, den dessen Rationalismus der tragischen Kunst angesagt hatte, entscheidet Platons Werk mit einer Überlegenheit, die zuletzt den Herausforderer entscheidenender traf als die Geforderte, gegen die Tragödie [But Plato's work decides the struggle that its rationalism announces against tragic art with a superiority that in the end strikes the one who challenges more decisively than the one challenged —against tragedy]" (GS, 1: 297; O, 118).[33]

Plato's work—and philosophy in turn—is the decisive victor, but the very decisiveness of its victory makes this work more decisively stamped by the struggle with tragedy than tragedy itself, which in a sense *escapes* the struggle because the decision against it—"against tragedy," against its propheticism perhaps—is in the nature of tragedy itself. It is not, for Benjamin, the "rationalistic spirit" of Plato's dialogues that grants them "superiority" over tragedy, but their dramatic, or "purely dramatic" (*reindramatisch*), form: dialogue does tragedy one better by doing away with everything impurely dramatic, everything nondramatic, everything in tragedy that disrupts the performance. Which is to say: it does away with the inaction—or better yet, counteraction—of those heroes who contain the unknown word that would liquidate them. By contrast, nothing ever disturbs Socrates' dialogues, least of all the prospect of his death. Benjamin, who perhaps stands under the influence of the penultimate stanza of Hölderlin's "Der Rhein," does not refer to Socrates's statement in the *Apology* concerning his desire to engage in dialogue in the afterworld, but to the conclusion of the *Symposium*, in which Socrates, having outlasted the tragedian and the comedian, returns to speak in the agora: "The purely dramatic restores the *mysterium*, which in the forms of Greek drama had gradually been made worldly [*verweltlicht*]; its language is that of the new drama and also that of the *Trauerspiel*" (GS, 1: 297; O, 118).

Instead of offering a place for a defiant and disruptive silence, dialogue gives voice to a restored *mysterium* in whose aura an unjust death sentence can be accepted, if not as a sacrifice, then at least as the way of this, the debased because "lower" world. Whereas the tragic agon belongs to *this* world—to death, to prophecy, and implicitly to the messianic—the latter belongs to another world, access to which is found in academies. The arrested language of the tragic is epochal in both senses of the term. As Benjamin emphasizes in his essay on Goethe's *Elective Affinities*, "tragic silence" (*Verstummen*) can be understood in Hölderlin's terms as the "caesura, the pure word, the counterrhythmic interruption" (GS, 1: 181; W, 1, 340; Hölderlin, SW, 5: 196). The continuum of dramatic language, by contrast, recognizes no caesura, no interruption, and no "pure word," and for this reason is purely *dramatic*. Its silence bespeaks self-conscious irony. Not only has Socrates, the "hero" of this new dramatic form, already learned to speak an uninterruptible language; he has already taught it to his "flock of youths, his young speakers" (GS, 1: 297; O, 117). This, in short, is Benjamin's response to Nietzsche's famous account of the death of tragedy at the hands of Socratic rationalism: the death of tragedy is, to be sure, the work of Socrates, yet tragedy does not die because of its "rational spirit" but because of its "rational mysticism" (GS, 1: 310; O, 131), to use a phrase of Lukács cited by Benjamin: the "worlding" in which tragedy and comedy alike are in the process of performing falls silent when the *mysterium* is restored. Mystery versus silence: this is the heart of the conflict. The *mysterium* guards its secrets and teaches the youth how to speak—and especially how *not* to speak, which is to say, how to be ironic. Instead of keeping or revealing the silence, a "popular community," Benjamin emphasizes from the beginning of his account of Attic tragedy, speaks "out of it." But what does it mean to speak out of a silence? This question corresponds to a long-postponed one: *who* learns to speak from the arrested language of tragedy? Which *Volksgemeinschaft*?[34]

All the difficulties of Benjamin's theory of tragedy—and of his attempt to wrest tragedy away from those who proclaim its return—revolve around the question, the details of which, as he admits to Rang, are still unclear to him: how does tragedy relate to prophecy? And this question comes down to a determination of those to whom tragic silence speaks after all. The "content" of this both agonistic and agonizing speech is incontestable: it speaks of a redemption from the fateful cycle of retribution—an incomplete, postponed redemption, to be sure, and as such a redemption far removed from the one about which prophets, properly speaking, would perhaps be able to speak. As the "preliminary stage of prophecy," however, tragedy is scarcely in a position to say anything about the latter. All Benjamin can say is that the preprophetic corresponds to the pretemporal: "tragic is the word and is the silence of the pretime [*die Vorzeit*] in which the prophetic voice tries itself out [*sich versucht*], suffering and death where they redeem this voice" (GS, 1: 297; O, 118). If the time of the tragic is *die Vorzeit*, then the time of which its language speaks would have to be *die Zeit*: "the" time, which is to say "our time, and "time itself," and that means, to use an expression Benjamin avoids throughout his *Habilitations-schrift*, although it is implied in its first words—"Sketched 1916"—*erfüllte Zeit* (GS, 2: 134; W, 1: 55). "Fulfilled time" gives tragedy an irreducible duplicity: it is at once altogether *topical* (as topical as a newspaper called *Die Zeit*) and completely foreign to "the times," that is, to unfulfilled historical time, including the time of *Trauerspiel*, dramatic and nondramatic alike. In its topicality it always remains the condemnation of these times as unfulfilled precisely because the voice of the tragic remains preprophetic. Tragedy is for—and against *because* it is for—"the times."

The place where "suffering and death redeem the prophetic voice" is likewise doubled: it is the place of tragic performance, Athens, to be sure, and yet again not *this* place: "In view of the suffering hero the community learns awesome thanks for the word with which his death endowed it—a word that, with every turn the poet wins from the legend, lights up another place as a renewed gift" (GS, 1: 287–88; O, 109). The "distant community" is, on the one hand, the community itself, and the temporal structure of the tragic performance is like that of Virgil's *Aeneid*: a "prophecy" of the very regime under which this "prophecy" is spoken. The time and place of "redemption" is the time and place of the tragic performance. But, on the other hand, the community to which the word and the silence of the tragedy speak remain *distant*, in another place. Every new "turn"

(*Wendung*) the poet extracts from the legend lights up the word "at an-other place" (*an anderer Stelle*)—that which escapes the community, its laws, its gods, and its language. Benjamin's single reference to Hölderlin in the *Trauerspiel* book clarifies the law of this "lighting up": tragedy turns from a judgment against the hero to a trial against the Olympians "at which the former gives testimony and, against the will of the gods, an-nounces 'the honor of the half-god'" (GS, 1: 288; O, 109)[35]—an honor that would be his *own* honor, the honor of the hero, if the "half-god" were indeed the hero and not, to use another term of Hölderlin, "an Other," other than a human being and other than a god, other than itself insofar as it, the half-god, is precisely *halved*.[36] Or, in terms of the messianic po-etics and politics of "Patmos," destructive of the *ground* of distinction to the point where nothing appears to appear any longer:

> . . . wenn die Ehre
> Des Halbgotts und der Seinen
> Verweht und selber sein Angesicht
> Der Höchste wendet
> Darob, daß nirgends ein
> Unsterbliches mehr am Himmel zu sehn ist oder
> Auf grüner Erde, was ist diß? (SW, 2: 169)[37]

> . . . when the honor
> Of the half-god and of his [disciples]
> Blows away and his own face
> The highest turns
> Away, so that nowhere is an
> Immortal to be seen any longer in the sky or
> On the green earth, what is this?

Whatever "this" may be—and "Patmos" is concerned with nothing so much as this question—the announcement of the "honor of the half-god" is nontriumphal: like the honor itself, it is blown away by a devastating wind. And this wind does not have the power to melt away the frozen frameworks within which tragic heroes live out their deaths. The word "saved over into the distant community" cannot fail to be a distancing and divisive word: less a word—or *the* word—than a fickle sign of immeasur-able distance and endless divisibility. Benjamin no longer needs to pose the question Nietzsche touched upon when he spoke of "the deep Aeschy-lean trait toward justice"—a phrase of Nietzsche Benjamin cites but unjustly attributes to Max Wundt[38]—the question, that is, of the tragedians only intimating what later generations come to know. What is said in tragic silence does not belong to the order of knowledge, and even when the poet "wins" something of the tragic word for the "popular community," the people cannot claim this "word" as its own. Ownership of this "word" makes "the" people into "dumb shadows." And yet, according to the direction of Benjamin's argument, only by owning such a "word" can there be anything like *a* people in the first place.

Far from being a mystery around which "a popular community" gathers, tragic silence distances and divides the *Volksgemeinschaft* from itself: the *Volk* departs from the *Gemeinschaft*, which, for its part, cannot be anything other than the commonality of silent selves. Its counterpart is the loquacious group of speakers around Socrates. The *Gemeinschaft* must part ways with the *Volk* insofar as the silence from which the "distant community" (*fernen Gemeinschaft*) learns to speak is not a source but is already an *echo*—an echo without source, a reverberation of emptiness.[39] The self of the hero—but this is, for Benjamin, drawing on Rosenzweig, the self as such—comes to light and comes to speech only by virtue of something unheard-of. Tragedy is the spectacle of the appearance of selves *e contrario*; but the origin of tragedy does not lie in the "sin" of individuation, according to a line of thought common to Schopenhauer, the young Nietzsche, and especially Ziegler. For the unheard-of is not the totality from which the individual departs to its peril; it is, rather, the very echo that the self repeats as the insignificant—because always inarticulate—sign of its selfhood. Tragic heroes say nothing because they have nothing to say, and they have nothing to say because they are dead from the start: "His life unfolds from his death, which is not its end but its form. . . . This has been expressed in many different ways. Perhaps nowhere better than in a casual reference to tragic death as 'merely . . . the outward sign that the soul has died'" (GS, 1: 293; O, 114). Benjamin takes—or rescues—this last quotation from Ziegler's *Toward the Metaphysics of the Tragic*, and draws the following conclusion: "Yes, the tragic hero is, if one wishes, soulless. Out of the enormous emptiness [*ungeheuere Leere*] his interior resounds [*widertönt*] with the distant, new commands of the gods [*Göttergeheiße*], and from this echo coming generations learn their language" (GS, 1: 293; O, 114).[40] Coming generations do not simply learn to speak from an echo, but from an echo as "uncanny" or "enormous emptiness," an echo, therefore, that makes every word equally—or doubly—enormous, uncanny, and hollow. And the mark of this uncanniness can be found in Benjamin's own description: the commands that resound from the "soulless" hero are *multiple*, commands *of the gods*, not, as the English translator writes, "divine commands" (O, 114). Whatever *Göttergeheiße* means (*heißt*), the gods who speak—whatever they may be called (*heißen*)—are many. If, as Benjamin writes when the question of tragic silence first arises, the tragic hero is offered "to the unknown god [*unbekannten Gott*], as the first fruits of a new harvest of humanity" (GS, 1: 285–86; O, 107), then this one god has multiplied by the time it or they speak(s). One unknown god, the commands of a multitude: this is less a double bind than the mythic expression of "the" *Volksgemeinschaft* to whom tragic silence "speaks." No one, strictly speaking, is receptive to the arrested language of the tragic hero. Wherever there is tragedy, whenever there is tragedy, there is always something other than "one"—or any other recognizable number: the dead soul of the living hero, the many gods who reverberate in the "enormous emptiness" of the "self," and an endlessly divisible "popular community."

But this is the singularity of tragedy: it may never have come even once. Tragic silence, true to its word, cannot be heard—not even by members of the *Volksgemeinschaft* who are supposed to learn to speak from its emptiness. And yet, only those who do learn to speak in this manner have a right to say anything about it: the rest—and the name for this "rest" in Benjamin's letter to Rang is "the Jews"—should remain silent. Benjamin, who, perhaps as a memorial to Rang, cites without quotation marks the last words of Hamlet at the conclusion to the section of the *Origin of the German Mourning Play*, entitled "*Trauerspiel* and Tragedy," keeps to the promise of these words—"the rest is silence" (GS, 1: 335; O, 158)—by not giving the rest any form or figure. That the remnant, the *Rest*, is silent may be the one prophetic saying that tragedy or its theory prepares. The arrested language of tragedy gives way at last to the arresting silence of a messianic—or, to use Rang's term, "christic"[41]—"rest."

§ 8 "Subtracted from the Order of Number": Toward a Politics of Pure Means in Benjamin and Irigaray

At the heart of the legal orders that arose in conjunction with the modern idea of law as rules of conduct universally applicable to all those who belong to a properly instituted political body lies a formula for the justification of the violence on which the law depends in order for it to be an actual, effective, and therefore "living" force—and not merely an idea: violence is justified insofar as it is a means for the control of violent acts that are not themselves means for the control of immediate threats of violence. As Walter Benjamin indicates in the opening paragraphs of his most explicit exposition of legal and political theory, "Toward the Critique of Violence," the justification of violence as a means is the point of contention around which arguments over the origin, nature, and purpose of the modern state endlessly circle. Justified violence is supposed to be of a different order than unjustified violence, and in the context of legal reasoning it is therefore no longer called "violence" but "coercion" or "punishment." Yet, as the formula for the justification of violence indicates, the violence of the legal order is not sanctioned for the purpose of subduing immediate threats to one's own life—this is the justification for the extralegal violence of "private persons"—but for the purpose of preserving the law itself: the law is inviolable. As long as the legal order makes the law effective and thus gives it life, it, too, is inviolable, and all violence other than its own can be interpreted as an immediate threat not to life itself—however this may be understood—but to that of the legal order. The end of legally sanctioned violence, its purpose and function, is not to put an end to violence as such but, instead, to thwart all threats to the law in the name of which violence can be sanctioned. Everything that enters into the space

over which the legal order imposes its sentence is implicated in this dis-
quieting—or, as Benjamin says, "rotten" (GS, 2: 188; W, 1: 242)—ambi-
guity of legal violence: the legal order can justify its violence only insofar
as it functions as a means to an end, but the end it serves can never be sep-
arated from itself as means, for the law, by virtue of its generality, is at bot-
tom unconcerned with the lives of those who happen to fall under its ju-
risdiction. The violence of the legal order is concerned solely with itself,
with its own majesty—without, however, ceasing to present itself as a
means and reverting to what, according to Benjamin, all legal violence
once was: immediate manifestation.

Nothing that enters into the space of the legal order can therefore escape
the ambiguity of the violence through which the law comes to life. Or at
least nothing can escape this ambiguity as long as the space on which the le-
gal order founds itself does not accord with the strict universality of the law
as such: a universally accessible and infinitely divisible space that is capable
of endlessly supple diversification, coordination, and individuation—so
much so that it cannot be represented as *one* space of which all others are
delimited parts. In place of this space, the legal orders that arose in Europe
over the course of the last five centuries laid out its parody: generally inac-
cessible and finitely divided domains, the borders of which are mementos
of the extralegal violence to which every legal order owes its origin. At least
one species of being has always been seen to move outside of legal orders—
a species whose specificity and spatiality are matters of interminable analy-
sis: the angels. The space that angels traverse—and, in particular, those that
enter into Luce Irigaray's writings—does not suffer division into homoge-
neous domains but does not therefore amount to an undifferentiated ex-
panse, a yawning abyss, or a formless chaos; rather, the limits, borders, and
horizons of this space are newly opened at the very moment they are tra-
versed. It is therefore a space whose regions cannot be represented in terms
of finite divisions and whose demarcations cannot be contained in figures
of envelopment: "The angel is the one that ceaselessly *traverses the envelope,*
envelopes, going from one side to the other" (EDS, 22; ESD, 15).

Exposing a space that has not been brought entirely into line with the
domain of the modern legal order and recovering the forgotten space of
angelic mediation are in this sense complementary projects. If in these pre-
liminary remarks the exposition of the space of the modern legal order is
associated with Benjamin and the recovery of the place of angelic media-
tion with Irigaray, it would be equally possible to reverse this association

and speak of Benjamin's angels in relation to Irigaray's critique of violence. But in any case the further task would be the same: discover spaces beyond—or in between—the legal order from which to launch a critique of its violence. If the discovery of such spaces runs counter to the means and mechanisms by which space has otherwise been "discovered"—which is to say, made homogeneous with that of specific legal orders and thus "globalized"—then so much the worse for these means and mechanisms. Another kind of exploration is in this case, and not only in this case, necessary. In keeping with these opening remarks, this chapter will first concentrate on Benjamin's critique of violence and then turn toward Irigaray's exposition of angelic movement.

I.

In the middle of "Toward the Critique of Violence," Benjamin begins to outline a space outside that of the contemporary legal order, but he just as quickly interrupts his line of thought because it "leads too far." About the place toward which it leads Benjamin remains silent, but he does indicate its direction: it is a higher place or, more exactly, the domain of unnamed "higher orders." Since the discovery of a space outside that of the legal order motivates the thought that Benjamin pursues in "Toward the Critique of Violence," this brief gesture toward "higher orders" in the middle of the essay cannot be easily ignored, even if it has attracted little attention:

> To motivate human beings to the peaceful resolution of their interests beyond all legal orders, there is, in the end, regardless of all virtues, one effective motive that often enough puts into the hands of even the most recalcitrant will pure instead of violent means: it is the fear of mutual disadvantages that threaten to arise from violent confrontations, whatever the outcome might be. Such motives are clearly visible in countless cases of conflict of interest between private persons. It is different when classes and nations are in conflict, since the higher orders that threaten to overwhelm equally victor and vanquished are hidden from the feelings of most and from the insight of almost all. Here the seeking out of such higher orders and the common interests corresponding to them, which constitute the most enduring motive for a politics of pure means, would lead too far. (GS, 2: 193; W, 1: 245)

Benjamin limits himself to two manifestations of pure means in politics that are "analogues to those that govern peaceful intercourse between private persons [*friedlichen Umgang zwischen Privatpersonen*]" (GS, 2: 193; W,

1: 245): the strike as a means for the resolution of conflicts between classes, and diplomacy as a means for the resolution of conflicts among nations. Of the latter Benjamin has little to say: the diplomatic method of resolution, unlike those of judges, belongs to a higher sphere, for it lies "beyond the entire order of the law and therefore violence" (GS, 2: 195; W, 1: 247). Of the former, by contrast, Benjamin has much more to say: one version of the strike—"the proletarian general strike"—corresponds to diplomacy insofar as it circumvents the legal order and therefore does without violence:

> Whereas the first form of interruption of work is violent, since it causes only an external modification of labor conditions, the second, as pure means, is without violence [*gewaltlos*]. For it takes place not in readiness to resume work following external concessions and this or that modification to working conditions, but in the determination to resume only a wholly transformed work, no longer enforced by the State, an overthrow that this kind of strike not so much occasions as carries out (GS, 2: 194; W, 1: 246)

When Benjamin turns away from drawing the outlines of politics of pure means in order to pursue a distinction within violence itself, this paradoxical politics—paradoxical because the "proletarian" general strike distinguishes itself from its limited and therefore "political" counterpart—is not entirely forgotten, for the conclusion of the essay, if not its very motivation, rests on an uncertain identification: the politics of pure means is the enactment of a pure violence; more specifically, the proletarian general strike carries out the law-destroying violence of God. This identification cannot be ascertained because, as Benjamin writes at the end of the essay, divine violence "cannot be recognized with certainty" (GS, 2: 203; W, 1: 252). But the force of the essay, perhaps even its own critical violence, consists in this outlandish suggestion: the politics of pure means makes room for *infinite* division. Infinite division destroys without leaving a finite trace of the thing divided; least of all is there a recognizable limit or border. Purified of all finite ends, the "proletarian general strike" can thus be understood to execute the sole and infinite end that purifies itself of all means: justice.

Benjamin may refrain from seeking out those "higher orders" on the basis of which a politics of pure means can be motivated apart from all virtues, but he cannot avoid making reference to these orders and their corresponding "interests" once he has introduced this strange term: "pure means [*reine Mittel*]." No wonder the politics of pure means carries with it something of a paradox, for the very idea of pure means is paradoxical.[1]

Benjamin leaves two marks of its paradoxical character in his description of the strike: the exercise of the right to strike can become violent without ceasing to be a "right," and the "proletarian general strike" is not "political." Means can be defined as such only if they are means to certain ends, and means are even more dependent on the ends that they serve than ends are on the means through which they are accomplished. For pure ends—or to use Kant's term, ends-in-themselves—are those that do without means and are therefore, in their own way, unmediated or immediate. The categorical imperative may, according to Benjamin, set out a "minimal program" for the critique of the legal order when it determines "the humanity in your person and in the person of every other" (GS, 2: 187; W, 1: 241) as ends-in-themselves, but this program can go no further, for every legal order—and especially a militaristic one—can present itself as a means to preserve "your person" as its end. The idea of a pure means, by contrast, cannot issue into that of a "means in itself," for something can be declared to be "in itself" only on the condition that it is, in the Aristotelian sense, "perfect," which is to say, at its end. One can speak of a pure means only if the end in view of which means are defined as means is not so much nullified or emptied of content as indefinitely delayed, extended, distended, or enfolded on—rather than "in"—itself. Means cannot be purely severed from the ends they serve; but they can be purified of these ends on the condition that the finite end, final purpose, or *Endzwecke* in which ends cease to function as further means be suspended for a time or withdraw into its own space. Perhaps for this reason Benjamin concludes his investigation into the "true" politics that would run counter to the "objective mendacity" of contemporary regimes with a section entitled "Teleology Without Final Purpose [*Endzwecke*],"[2] but in any case this much is clear: only by exposing the space and time in which final purposes are suspended can one disclose a dimension of pure means. Benjamin has a name for the space and time in which final purposes are not only *not* suspended but extended in ever more invasive and homogenizing ways—without, however, ever being able to be intensive or universal. He calls it the "legal order [*das Recht*]": "the legal order maintains itself only apparently for the sake of justice, in truth for the sake of its own life" (GS, 6: 106; W, 1: 232). Pure means can therefore operate only in those spaces and times in which the law has no say or where the saying of the legal order, its imposition of a final sentence for the sake of its own life—and not the life of those over whom it disposes—is indefinitely delayed and distended.

Of the spaces and times over which no legal order can preside, Benjamin has little to say except that they are spaces and time of *language*—understood not so much as the means for coming to agreement but as this "coming to agreement" itself: "there is a sphere of human agreement that is non-violent to the extent that it is wholly inaccessible to violence: the proper sphere of 'coming to an understanding,' language [*die eigentliche Sphäre der 'Verständigung', die Sprache*]" (GS, 2: 192; W, 1: 245). Drawing on a vocabulary that is clearly inadequate to the exposition of this sphere, since it is a sphere of sheer in-betweenness, Benjamin outlines the "subjective" premises for, and the "objective" appearance of, the politics of pure means:

> Courtliness of the heart [*Herzenshöflichkeit*], inclination, love of peace, trust, and whatever else might be named here are its subjective presuppositions. But the law (whose mighty extent cannot be discussed here) determines its objective appearance by saying that pure means are never immediate but always mediate solutions. They therefore never apply immediately to the settlement of conflicts between human being and human being [*Mensch und Mensch*] but only by way of things. The domain of pure means opens itself in the most concrete relation of human conflicts concerning goods. For this reason, technique [*Technik*] in the broadest sense of the word is its most proper region. Its profoundest example is perhaps conversation [*Unterredung*], considered as a technique of civil agreement. (GS, 2: 191; W, 1: 244)

The politics of pure means, which distances itself from every order of the law, cannot escape its jurisdiction, for the law demands that pure means appear only in one "objective" form: as means to a legally sanctioned end, namely, the ownership of goods. "Human agreement" can be reached on this point. Of the *real* character of pure means, however, which would show itself only in the relation "between human being and human being" and which may not show itself at all as long as showing is understood solely in terms of legal evidence, Benjamin remains silent, for it, too, perhaps leads "too far."

Benjamin does not therefore explore the specific spatiality in which the politics of pure means could take place, even though every paragraph after the one in which he first describes its subjective presuppositions and its objective appearance implies a space other than the one posited by the law in order to preserve itself—the space, namely, of enforced and finite division:

> The positing of limits [*Grenzsetzung*: establishing of borders], the task of "peace" after all the wars of the mythic age, is the primordial phenomenon of

law-positing violence in general. Here we see most clearly that power, more than the most extravagant gain in property, is what is guaranteed by all law-positing violence. Where limits are firmly posited [*festgesetzt*], the adversary is not simply annihilated; on the contrary, he is accorded rights even when the victor's superiority in power is complete. And indeed in a demonically ambiguous way, "equal" rights; for both parties to the treaty, it is the same line that may not be crossed. Here appears, in fearsome originality, the mythic ambiguity to which Anatole France refers satirically when he says, "Poor and rich are equally forbidden to spend the night under the bridge." (GS, 2: 198; W, 1: 249)

Pure means are implicated in a space other than that of finite division not only because, as Benjamin writes, they allow for "non-violent settlement [*gewaltlose Einigung*]" (GS, 2: 191; W, 1: 244) but, more importantly, because the idea of pure means implies a space of the middle (*Mitte*) rather than that of the limit, border, or frontier. A pure middle would be one whose middleness is no longer defined with respect to determinable end points; rather, it would have to be an infinite and infinitely divisible space. Nothing can withstand this space *intact*: infinite divisibility is the "law" of this space, which, however, cannot itself be posited *as* a law, since this division is never governed by an identifiable rule. The "law" of this space, as the rule by which its infinite divisibility is articulated, must likewise be infinitely codivisible: in German, *mit-teilbar*, which is to say, "communicable." Instead of being a space in which one could build a bridge under which rich and poor alike were forbidden to spend the night, the space of pure means would be the movement in-between: a flux—of language— over which bridges are built for the purpose of finite and definite communication. Moreover, a pure middle would have to be an *unmediated* or *immediate* middle: not a middle determined by an act of measurement but a middle that immediately mediated itself. Such a middle would be less a "means" than a medium, and this, too, is implied in Benjamin's strange term *reine Mittel*.[3] A pure medium would be one through which no content would be communicated but in which its own "law" of infinite codivisibility would destroy all "bridges"—including those "between human being and human being." In terms of Benjamin's treatise "On Language as Such and on Human Language," the medium would not be a means to an end—the communication of content—but an infinite language in its own right. Or in terms of "Toward the Critique of Violence," the medium would be the sole mode of language removed from the jurisdiction of the legal order: "conversation [*Unterredung*]" as the means for the peaceful resolution of conflicts among "private persons."

But this last "or" is undeserved, for, as Benjamin makes clear, the law determines the "objective appearance" of those conflicts that are resolved by pure rather than violent means and thus resolved through "conversation": pure means can never be immediately applied to conflicts between "human being and human being" but must always be assigned some *object* over which the conflict is supposed to solidify. This object serves as the point of discussion, and in this way it, too, is brought into the sphere of means. But not completely: "conversation" cannot be understood as a pure medium or constitute a pure middle because it must be guided by the *appearance* of an end—the ownership of the object. Even if the terms of ownership are not determined by contractual obligation or "perfect duties," they are nevertheless finite and therefore recognizable by the legal order. At this point Benjamin's remarkably daring essay gives out: he does not grant himself the space to speak of "conflict between human being and human being" outside of the legal requirement that this conflict appear as a dispute over an object that one of the "equal" parties in the dispute can possess. If, by contrast, Benjamin were to speak of other appearances of pure means—or speak of pure means themselves, regardless of their appearance—he would have to break his own injunction on speaking of "higher orders" and thus lead his essay, if not "too far," then beyond its hitherto respected confines. And this he does, but only by way of suggestion. For the proletarian general strike, as the purest means to settle conflict between classes, carries out the higher-order violence of God. The conflict out of which the strike arises may appear from the perspective of the law to be about the ownership of the means of production, but it is in truth about nothing other than the purification of these means of the ends they serve—especially the "cultic" end of producing more means of production for the sake of maintaining control over them. Insofar as a work stoppage arrests the means-ends schema through which the production of means of production gives rise to more and more "debt" or greater and greater "guilt,"[4] it accomplishes something like divine work. Means are given over to human beings; ends are left to God alone.

Having disclosed the future possibility of a pure means that stands in conflict with the order of law itself—the proletarian general strike—and having made mention of the now moribund version of pure means that once took place under the rubric of diplomacy, Benjamin does not want to proceed any further. In other contexts he is less circumspect, and in certain circumstances he seems as though he were under a compulsion to speak of the "higher orders" on the basis of which a politics of pure means might be motivated. These "orders" do not consist of interclass or international agencies that somehow make visible the threat of mutual destruction to classes and nations alike; rather, they are the orders of angels. For angels are means of communication that undertake their mission, not for the sake of the message communicated, but in the name of the one whose message they communicate. And insofar as angels are *pure* means of communication—which is to say, not means to an end but sheer media—they are as useless for the purposes of communicating a message as they are for anything else. Being an angel does not therefore mean working without a reward, selfless service, "being an angel" in the colloquial sense of the term, for "being an angel" in this sense means selflessly subordinating oneself to those who are unable to accomplish arduous tasks on their own. The trait of the angelic order of which Benjamin writes is, by contrast, their out-of-workness: for all their incessant movement, they are nevertheless permanently on strike. At the conclusion to the editorial announcement for the journal *Angelus Novus* (1922), the purpose of which is to "regain force [*Gewalt*] for the critical word" (GS, 2: 242; W, 1: 293), Benjamin first mentions the legend through which he characterizes the angelic order: "according to a legend in the Talmud, the angels—who are born anew every moment in countless throngs [*unzähligen Scharen*]—are created in order to cease and vanish into nothingness, once they have sung their hymn before God" (GS, 2: 246; W, 1: 296). In the passage of the Talmud to which he refers, the source of these "countless throngs" of disappearing angels is an infinite flux—or, more colorfully, a "fiery stream": "Samuel said to R. Hiyya b. Rab: 'O son of a great man, come, I will tell thee something from those excellent things which thy father has said. Every day ministering angels are created from the fiery stream, and utter song, and cease to be, for it is said: They are new every morning.'"[5] The most far-reaching consequence of Benjamin's exposition of the politics of pure means is the one about which he has nothing to say in "Toward the Critique of Violence": the purer a means, the closer it resembles the angels created from an infinite flux, and the closer it resembles one of these angels, the less independent it is as a means. The angel is the image of a pure means that cannot become a means for the production of more means of production. For this reason, angels—or at least the ones of this Talmudic legend—are always *new*: appearing only to disappear. And for the same reason they appear actively useless: teleological without end.

By confining himself to the sphere in which the law says that pure means can be used only to settle conflicts about goods, Benjamin breaks off his line of thought. But he may have interrupted this line, not wanting to "lead" his search for a motivation for a politics of pure means "too far," for another reason: he points toward, but refrains from investigating, the sphere in which the politics of pure means is irreplaceable inasmuch as the solutions to conflict cannot assimilate themselves to the legal form of judgments about the rightful ownership of goods. This sphere is the one in which "conflict between human being and human being" cannot be decided by reference to a specific object or a determinable borderline. If this conflict appears to be over some*thing*—either an object or the space of its containment—it does so only from the "mighty" yet still limited perspective of the law: the conflict appears to be over an object of desire about which a decision can be made as to its owner, a finite division can thus be enforced, and a border firmly established. A conflict "between human being and human being" as such, by contrast, would not be *about* anything; it would be the conflict of human beings or "in" being human that is *de jure* incapable of being decided by legal means, insofar as the legal order requires everything about which it makes a decision to appear *as one.* Around some-one-thing legal persons can stand in conflict with one another. One name for a conflict that *appears to appear* as a conflict over something from the mendaciously objective perspective of the law is "sexual difference." Benjamin, who concerns himself with the conflict between classes and nations, does not address this difference in "Toward the Critique of Violence."[6]

When, however, Benjamin does speak of sexual difference in a legal-critical manner, he is drawn once again to the same Talmudic legend. More precisely, in his essay on Karl Kraus, which, unlike "Toward the Critique of Violence," places the question of *sexus* at its center, he constructs a new image of the *angelus novus*, an image in which the angel marks the force of this question. For the angel is on neither side of this difference—nor is it on both sides, ambiguous, or neutral. Nor is it "beyond" or "before" this difference. Rather, the new angel to whom Benjamin refers is one who overcomes ambiguity, equivocation, and duplicity without thereby turning into an identifiable kind, genre, or gender—or becoming two-of-a-kind either. Angels are "subtracted from the order of number" (EDS, 107; ESD, 110), to borrow a paradoxical phrase of Luce Irigaray. If the "throngs" to which the "new angels" belong are "countless," then they themselves are even more so, and the order of angels as a whole cannot be considered *one*—or any other number, including zero. Of all the terms on which Benjamin draws to sketch the image of the angel, none captures its character better than the one to which his earliest writings are in large part dedicated: youth,[7] in the case of which, as in that of the angel, it is possible to speak of teleology without final purpose—or sexuation without sex. Benjamin's name for ambiguity, equivocation, and duplicity is "demonic." The angel overcomes both the duplicity of the demon *and* the univocity of the "all human" (*Allmensch*), which mutually reinforce each other, especially in the domain of law, where the difference between "mine and thine" represents and reproduces duplicity and univocity at once:

> Neither purity nor sacrifice mastered the demon; but where origin and destruction come together, its mastery is over. Like a creature sprung from the child and the cannibal, its conqueror stands before it: not a new human being; a nonhuman being [*Unmensch*], a new angel. Perhaps one of those who, according to the Talmud, are at each moment created anew in countless throngs [*unzähligen Scharen*], and who, once they have raised their voices before God, cease and vanish into nothingness. (GS, 2: 367; W, 2: 447)

By presenting the image of the angel as an *Unmensch* (nonhuman, monster) that overcomes demonic ambiguity without the restoration of primordial purity or the execution of final sacrifice, Benjamin confirms the suspicion that his discussion of the politics of pure means in "Toward the Critique of Violence" does not simply break off for lack of space but leaves a lacuna. It fails to investigate the "conflict between *Mensch* and *Mensch*" that cannot be represented as a dispute mediated by an object or a borderline. At the threshold of the resolution of any unmediated conflict is the *Unmensch*: the "one" who, as subject of an "infinite judgment," cannot be represented as a member of a kind, genre, gender but cannot therefore be turned into the representative of an ambiguous kind, duplicitous genre, or equivocal gender. The conflict can thus be said to be that of sexual difference: it does not simply supplement the other two conflicts Benjamin analyzes in "Toward the Critique of Violence"—between classes and nations. Still less can it be assigned without further ado to the sphere of "private persons," and yet this difference, as Benjamin indicates in certain contemporaneous remarks, gives rise to conflicts—so much so that it is the deci-

sive one in this place (Europe) and during "this time": "This time partici-
pates in the consummation of one of the mightiest revolutions [*gewaltig-
sten Revolutionen*] ever to take place in the relation between the sexes" (GS,
6: 72; W, 1: 229). That Benjamin does not include the "battle of the sexes
[*Kampf der Geschlechter*]" (GS, 6: 72; W, 1: 229) among the revolutionary
"conflicts [*Konflikte*]" he addresses in "Toward the Critique of Violence" is
all the more surprising, since the inability of men—and especially "Euro-
pean man"—to recognize this difference, according to the same remarks,
makes it "flare up" into a conflict in the first place.[8] The source of the con-
flict, according to Benjamin, lies in the incapacity of "man" to recognize a
unity that transcends that of natural numbers: "the unity [*Einheit*] of eroti-
cism and sexuality in woman" (GS, 6: 73; W, 1: 229). Instead of recogniz-
ing such unity, contemporary "European man" retreats in "horror": "where
they do not see it [this unity] as supernatural [*übernatürlich*], they blindly
feel it as natural and must flee. And precisely under this blindness of man,
the supernatural life of woman atrophies into natural and, as such, into un-
natural life. For this alone corresponds to the strange disintegration [*selt-
samen Zersetzung*] that today, proceeding from the primordial drives
[*Urtreiben*] of man, allows the feminine to be conceived only under the si-
multaneous images of prostitute and untouchable beloved" (GS, 6: 73; W,
1: 229). Although these enigmatic remarks "On Love and Related Matters
(a European Problem)" remain silent about the solution to this "strange
disintegration," which appears in the form of two radically opposing im-
ages, they nevertheless indicate its provenance: the *Zersetzung* (disintegra-
tion) will not be repaired by an act of *Setzung* (positing), least of all the
positing of a new, more equitable legal order; rather, the disintegration it-
self disintegrates—along with its images—whenever the unity in question
can be recognized as "supernatural." The consummation of the violent rev-
olution in which this time participates may, in turn, consist in the creation
of those conditions—beyond the modern legal order—in which "super-
natural" unity is once again, or for the first time, recognizable.

None of these reflections on "a European Problem" makes its way into
"Toward the Critique of Violence." Nevertheless, the essay does not re-
main entirely unconcerned with sexual difference. On the contrary, it sub-
tly guides Benjamin's puzzling discussion of the violence from which the
legal order owes its origin: the mythic fatality of the gods. Niobe turned
into a boundary stone is the very image of this limited and delimiting vi-
olence. Although in tears over the "bloody death" of her children, Niobe

herself does not die, and her metamorphosis grants Benjamin the chance to do something he otherwise disavows—to determine a visible, even visceral, criterion for the distinction between the mythic violence to which the legal order owes its origin and the divine violence in which this order comes to an end: "if the former is bloody, the latter is lethal without spilling blood. The legend of Niobe may be confronted, as an example of this violence, with God's judgment on the company of Korah. . . . [A] deep connection between the lack of bloodshed and the expiatory character of this violence is unmistakable. For blood is the symbol of mere life" (GS, 2: 199; W, 1: 249–50). Infinite division, in other words, leaves no definite traces; finite division leaves at least two—territorial limits and flowing blood. As Benjamin notes at the inception of his discussion of this "outstanding example," mythic violence does not simply attack the one who, by challenging fate, brings to light the law of finite division; it attacks in a finitely differential manner—mothers first.[9] The metamorphosis of the mother into a legally sanctioned limit constitutes the creation of political space: "It could certainly seem as though the action of Apollo and Artemis is only a punishment. But their violence sets up a law much more than punishes an already established one" (GS, 2: 197; W, 1: 248). Even if the law applies equally—out of children flows blood, out of their mother water—the agents of mythic violence and, accordingly, the mechanisms of the law are different: Apollo strikes the sons, Artemis the daughters.

II.

In light of these agents and mechanisms the opening sentence of Irigaray's *An Ethics of Sexual Difference* can be understood as an appeal not so much to make up for the lacuna in Benjamin's analysis as to direct it toward an exposition of the reasons for Niobe's petrifaction: "Sexual difference is one of the major philosophical issues, if not the issue, of our epoch" (EDS, 13; ESD, 6). For what Irigaray proceeds to do, as perhaps no one else has done, including those who loyally follow Benjamin's itinerary, is to explore the dimension of *reine Mittel*: pure means, unmediated middleness, and immediate mediacy. And like Benjamin, her exploration heads toward the motility of certain bodily elements—not only blood and water but also mucous. Of this latter fluid Benjamin has nothing to say, and yet it is as worthy of attention as blood in any critique of violence, for its dimensions curiously correspond to those of *reine Mittel*:

Never merely something available, never merely a material ready for some hand or some tool to use to construct a piece of work. And equally something that cannot possibly be denied. . . . Impossible to suppress or forget entirely, without trace, it is only in an act that the mucous perceives without thesis, without position outside itself. The potency achieves "its" act which is never set in a finished piece of work. But which is always *half open* [*Toujours* entrouvert(e)]. (EDS, 108; ESD, 111)

Irigaray also shows the danger to which mucous is exposed—being turned into impure means, which is to say, means in service of finite, teleological, and "entelecheial" ends:

The mucous has no permanence, even though it is the "tissue" for the development of duration. The condition for the possibility for the extension of time? But only insofar as it is made available to and for a masculine subject that erects itself out of the mucous. And which believes it is based on substances, on something solid. All of which requires the mucous to blur in its potency and its act (in its potentially autonomous *hypokeimenon*?) and to serve merely as means for the elaboration of the substantial, the essential. (EDS, 107; ESD, 109–10)

If the dimensions of mucous correspond with those of *reine Mittel*, there is nevertheless one feature of the former that distinguishes it from the means of which Benjamin speaks—and perhaps indicates the reason why he failed to speak of it in the context of his critique of violence: as a means, mucous cannot be applied to the resolution of conflicts, for it does not appear to belong to the "proper domain" of pure means: *Technik* (technology, technique). Indeed, it seems to belong to the very opposite, if not of "technique," then at least of technology. But the apparent neutrality of the "one" who disposes over means in view of ends is in question wherever the idea of *pure* means is proposed, and this question becomes particularly acute when Benjamin names "language" as the sphere from which the legal order is in principle excluded. Only with reference to the no longer valid right to lie does Benjamin lend credence to the thesis implied in this invocation of language, for lying can take place only after language has been transformed into a means for specific, although sometimes inarticulate or unconscious, ends. The purer the means, by contrast, the more it is estranged from the viewpoint of ends, the further it is from arbitrary disposability. Benjamin's decision to name "technique" as the "domain" of pure means and "conversation" its "most proper region" may be an indication that he, too, remains entangled in the equivocations of the legal order and does not therefore seek out those means that cannot appear as the means for the resolution of conflicts over goods. If these means are "natural" ones, then this means that both the idea of "natural ends" (*Naturzwecke*) and that of the "final purpose of nature" must be rethought—and this project, too, is implied in the enigmatic formula with which Benjamin wished to conclude his investigation into true politics, "teleology without final purpose." But even in the absence of a renewed *Naturphilosophie*, this much is clear: pure means cannot *appear* to be pure, especially if "pure" is understood as the nonsensuous. Such is the case with mucous: it cannot be seen to apply mediately to conflicts "between human being and human being" but, instead, applies itself immediately to differences—in and in between living beings. The differences to which mucous immediately applies itself are not "differences of opinion" and cannot therefore be resolved in the course of "conversation" but are, rather, material differences, even if these differences always appear from the perspective of the law—whose "mighty extent" cannot be overestimated—as conflicts over objects, goods, or borders.

The critique of violence cannot, in short, do without a thought of mucous as *reine Mittel*, and the politics of *reine Mittel* cannot be motivated unless it is brought into connection not only with blood but with mucous. If, as Benjamin writes, blood is the "symbol of mere life,"[10] mucous is the symbol of a "higher" one: just living. The image of Niobe transformed into a weeping boundary stone is something like a photographic negative of just living, for it presents violent liquidation as sheer solidification: no space is left in the still living Niobe for mucous—or air. Speaking of a life higher than that of "mere" or "naked" life demands that one speak, in turn, of certain higher orders in which life is wrapped, clothed, or veiled. A certain secrecy, rather than "privacy," stamps the character of the "person" who remains outside the purview of the legal order. And it is in reference to higher orders, their corresponding envelopes, and the secret of this correspondence that Benjamin's and Irigaray's lines of thought tend to converge. For Irigaray, the thought of mucous would point in the direction of such heights if mucous were itself subtracted from the order in which subtraction operates—the order of number: "the subtraction [*soustraction*] of mucous from the order of number might indicate the place of its threshold, its limit, its relation to the divine, which up until now is unthought" (EDS; 107; ESD, 110). This paradoxical subtraction gives rise to a limit—but an *infinite* limit or a limit "between" that which is limited and that which definitely is not. Such a limit cannot be one among others; least of all can this limit be calculated in accordance with a calculus of homogenous segments. The only way in which the limit can be "indicated" is by the aporetic way of infinite codivisibility in which both "sides" are "equally"—and completely—divided. Such infinite codivisibility appears as infinite diversification: membership in "countless throngs." Subtraction from the order of number does not amount to zero, nothingness, or a yawning abyss. Rather, the "unity" of the subtracted "thing" cannot be counted—or expected. An old name for unity other than that of numerical oneness is "transcendental unity." Like the transcendentals of scholastic thought—*unum, verum, bonum*—mucous transcends the basic categories through which subjects are "accused" in the competitive space of the *agora*. Unlike the old transcendentals, however, mucous does not transcend these categories by virtue of its immunity from alteration; it cannot therefore be understood to go beyond the senses as it transcends categoriality, and it does not, accordingly, determine the order higher than that of "mere life" to be a supersensible one. As a transcendental unity whose unity does not depend upon the idea of a supersensible point of identity, mucous does not so much serve as the passage from the transcendent to the sensible as stand in the way of every mode of transcendence other than that in which sensibility itself is brought to its threshold.

Yet there is another, even older name for a unity other than that of numerical oneness: the angel. The transcendence of angels, like that of mucous, does not consist in their immutability but, rather, in their unity without numerical oneness. For this reason, they are uncountable members of "countless throngs." If, as Heidegger writes, "there is never, strictly speaking, *an* equipment [ein *Zeug*],"[11] this is all the more true of angels, these "higher" instruments. Subtracted from the order of number, mucous enters into a relation with the order of angels. Or, as Irigaray writes in the first essay of *An Ethics of Sexual Difference*, "mucous doubtless figures itself on the side of the angel [*se figure sans doute du côté de l'ange*]; the inertia of the body deprived of its relation to the mucous and its gesture, on the side of the fallen body or corpse" (EDS, 23; ESD, 17).[12] Mucous makes itself into a figure and thus shows itself *as* something in connection with those beings whose spatiality consists in endless codivisibility. For tough-minded empiricists, who hate to see time wasted on such matters, the famous question debated by scholastic philosophers—how many angels can dance on the head of a pin?[13]—is a privileged example of pointless chatter; but the pointlessness of this conversation may nevertheless point somewhere: toward the most capacious possible space and therefore toward a politics of pure means.

Irigaray does not, however, introduce angels into the introductory essay of *An Ethics of Sexual Difference* solely on account of their much debated spatiality; rather, they enter into her discussion, above all, because of their even more elusive temporality. Angels are not only said to traverse the middle, coming from horizons they themselves open in passing, but they come as means, media, and mediators in the middle of time—which is to say, *in the mean-time*. The mean-time is the time of pure means. Angels, for Irigaray, do not so much serve as means for the execution of arbitrary tasks as announce in every one of their actions that one act remains unaccomplished—"the sexual act" (EDS, 22; ESD, 15):

> There remain the aftermaths [*séquelles*] of the nonaccomplishment of the sexual act. Many aftermaths. To consider only the most beautiful and to display it once again from the perspective of time and space, there are *angels*. These messengers who never remain enclosed in a place, nor are they ever immobile. Between God, who would be the perfectly immobile act, man, who is surrounded and enclosed by the world of his work, and woman, whose task would be to take care of nature and procreation, *angels* would circulate as mediators of that which is not yet due, of what is still going to happen, of what announces itself. Ceaselessly reopening the enclosures of the universe, of universes, identities, the unfolding of actions, of history. (EDS, 22; ESD, 15)

The nonaccomplishment of the sexual act is the flux—or "fiery stream" —out of which the angels arise. Whatever else may be said of this act, which the angels then announce, it brings an end to the ends-mean schema. For this reason, if for no other, it is cause for joy. And angels are the paradoxical means by which the means-end schema itself comes to an end "for the time being"—to cite the title of W. H. Auden's great poem of angelic mediation in the midst of political programs dedicated to the eternalization of imperial conditions.[14] Appearing in the meantime, angels not only announce the end of the time in which they appear but also destroy whatever would make the mean-time into the *only* time. Like the "new angel" about whom Benjamin speaks, Irigaray's angels thus appear only to disappear. In order to disappear, they, like Benjamin's *Unmensch*, must conquer those things—demons, ghosts, or monsters—that make it impossible for anything to disappear *for good*: "Angels destroy the monstrous, that which hampers the possibility of a new epoch" (EDS, 22; ESD, 15).

Irigaray's angels are therefore not without a violence of their own. Drawing on the famous opening lines of Rilke's *Duineser Elegien*, she insists in "Belief Itself" that every angel is "terrible, terrifying" (CM, 45; SG, 39).[15] They destroy the apparent unity of time. This unity is founded on the belief in the eternal or eternalizing return of the same. Indeed, this belief is, for Irigaray, "belief itself": *la croyance même* as the *croyance* in the return of *la même*.[16] And there is perhaps no more appropriate place to look for the scene of its origination than in the serious game of *fort-da* Freud witnesses in *Beyond the Pleasure Principle*: the same mother, the little boy believes, will return as *la même même*.[17] Upon this belief the little boy constructs the space in which he will henceforth play out his life: "horizontal and vertical, strings and veils, which exist only because she is faraway and because he believes that, when he sent her far off like this, she will return the same, whereas she returns to the other in the same. This difference undermines the truth of his language: a credulity is introduced in the power of the subject that thereby constitutes itself" (CM, 35; SG, 34-35). Whereas "returning the same" has no place for a destination, returning "in the same" always has one: "the other." Without such a destination—which abrogates fate, necessity, and destiny—no encounter is possible. This difference is ever so slight, but it is the difference upon which the politics of pure means stands or falls. And as pure means, mediators, and media, angels are the remnants and reminders of a difference between a return of the same thing to the same one whose final guarantor is the violence of the legal order and a return of the other *in* the same which the law can at most—and this characterizes the best—accept.

Angels are therefore not matters of belief, certainly not "religious belief," but are, on the contrary, those who come to unsettle and devastate "belief itself": the belief in the return of the same itself, the belief upon which all credit, debt, and guilt—along with the endless variety of programs for their eventual cancellation—are founded. Angels cannot therefore return as the same ones, regardless of their apparent permanence: each one is new. Or if they do return as the same, they are no longer angels but, rather, their doubles. One name for the double of angels would be "ghosts," but Irigaray chooses an even more alarming term: "devils." Unlike the angels, devils are never new. They do not "imperceptibly assure mediation between" (CM, 46; SG, 39) but, instead, make mediation into a means for the attainment of a perceptible end: the ownership of an object or the establishment of a border. If there were no devils, it would be possible to perceive that certain "things" and "events" remain outstanding whenever the same returns again and again—the other, the encounter, and the sexual act—but as long as these doubles last; as long as any news of the other, the encounter, and the act is intercepted, imitated, or simply represented, the circuit and site of exchange is closed, complete, and eternalized: every return must be the return of the same to the same, the giving back of what is due, the rendering of what is owed, the restitution of things to their rightful order—in accordance with, or under the protection of, the rule of law.

Under a diabolic reign there is no encounter but only an approach of doubles to doubles: "approaches where no announcement of the future remains. Everything would be assimilated-disassimilated. Nothing remains but to pursue this seriography. Unless, perhaps, in the coming to term [*échéance*] of an essential difference" (CM, 49; SG, 41). The meaning of angelic mean-ness is to be found here: in the *chance* of an *échéance*. Angels do not so much destroy the diabolic reign in which "the future endlessly recycles the past" (CM, 49; GS, 41) as bring to light the possibility of its end. This is the defining character of angelic orders. They bring such a possibility to light by means of their specific mode of mediation: "keeping space open and marking the trail from the most ancient to most futurial" (CM, 48; GS, 40). Under diabolic reigns there is no encounter, no immediate middleness, and thus no sexual act but only—at best—a space and time kept open for a nonviolent resolution of conflict between "private persons." At worst, "the whole thing bursts instantaneously into flames" (CM, 49; GS, 41). Regardless of belief, then, and even "regardless of all virtues" (GS, 2: 192; W, 1: 245), certain "higher orders" can motivate a politics of pure means: those orders that make it possible for "victor and vanquished alike" to feel that they will be overwhelmed—if not by flames, then at least by the very belief in which they recognize themselves as victors and vanquished alike. Whether or not these orders are called angelic is of little importance, but whatever imperceptibly makes perceptible the threat of the same returning only as and to the same—in ever greater numbers, with ever greater rapidity, and in ever greater quantities—is in its own way angelic: a means without a final end in view and therefore a means for opening up not only enclosures and divisions but also judgments and verdicts.

∿

Angels open up a dimension other than those created and maintained by the positing of a specific legal order. For this reason at least they belong to the sphere—or atmosphere—of pure means. The appearance of angelic images could, accordingly, serve as an indication that the homogeneous and finitely divisible spaces and times through which legal orders violently define themselves have begun to wither, fray, or even unravel. Wherever angels appear, there is no place and no time for the modern state, and wherever the modern state continues to hold sway, there is no space or time in which angels can appear to appear. And today no image appears with more regularity: angels show up again and again, day after day, week after week, in almost every media of communication, old and new—and around the globe. If, twenty years ago, Irigaray could confidently claim that "angels have been as misunderstood, forgotten, as the nature of that first veil, except in the poet and in religious iconography" (CM, 37; GS, 35), the contrary could be said today—at least with respect to "forgetting."[18] And this may say something about the space and time of the modern state: they have withered, begun to fray, or even come to the point of unraveling. Anecdotes of the angelic are perhaps a sign and instrument of this unwinding. But just as the images of angels through which the global media "touch" its audience cannot be confused with the angel itself—for there is no angel itself—the eruption of spaces outside that of the legal order cannot be considered the "good news" angels have been said to announce. Nothing is less anecdotal in the original sense of this term than such tightly controlled and corporately authored images. If, however, these images belong solely to the transnational agents of mobile capital to which they are registered, so, too, does any extralegal space of which they are a potential index and agent. They are incorporated into a global space—which is precisely not the wider, more open, more capacious, more diversified, infinitely divisible spaces that angels are said to traverse. By virtue of its finite unboundedness the globe is a particularly powerful and pernicious parody of a universe. Between these two spaces—the global one of transnational capital and the universal one of the angels—there lies the mean-time. And there lie the "monsters" that the angels, according to Irigaray, "destroy."

Reference Matter

Notes

Introduction: "From an Awkward Perspective"

1. A translation of the "Remarks on *Antigone*" and "Remarks on *Oedipus*" can be found in Hölderlin, *Essays and Letters on Theory*, which includes the pagination of the Beißner edition (SW) in the margin.

2. For an authoritative exposition of Hölderlin's theory of the alteration of tones and "lawful calculus," see Ryan, *Hölderlins Lehre vom Wechsel der Töne*; for a succinct description, see Fenves, "Hölderlin."

3. A translation of "The Earthquake in Chile" can be found in Kleist, *The Marquise von O——*, 51–67.

4. As Benjamin writes in his essay on Goethe's *Elective Affinities*, the passage on the caesura in the "Remarks on *Oedipus*" is of "fundamental significance for the theory of art in general, beyond serving as the basis for a theory of tragedy," and he further notes that this significance "seems not yet to have been recognized" (GS, 1: 181; W, 1, 340).

5. Søren Kierkegaard is another figure who could be appended to this list. Having completed his pseudonymous "authorship," he presents his voice in terms of an unauthorized command to halt: "The movement is *Back!* And although it is done without 'authority,' there is, nevertheless, something in the tone that recalls a policeman when he faces a riot, and says Back!" (*Point of View of My Work as an Author*, 75; see Fenves, "*Chatter*," 243–49).

6. For a discussion of the idea of the microcosmos, see the extensive survey of Conger, *Theories of Macrocosms and Microcosms*.

7. The term "aesthetics" stems from Alexander Baumgarten, who first developed it in his treatise of 1735, *Meditationes philosophicae de nonnullis ad poema pertinentibus* (Philosophical meditations on some matters pertaining to poetry); reprinted with a German translation in Baumgarten, *Philosophische Betrachtungen*; an English edition can be found in *Reflections on Poetry*. For an analysis of the origin of the "science" of aesthetics, see Baeumler, *Irrationalitätsproblem*. It

would be worth analyzing Baeumler's treatise (which was supposed to have been the introduction to a never completed exposition of Kant's *Critique of Judgment*) in relation to his later works on Nietzsche and his active engagement with the Nazi party, pedagogy, and "aestheticization of the political" (Benjamin, GS, 1: 508; *Illuminations*, 242).

8. See in particular § 441 of Baumgarten's *Aesthetica* (1750/58), partially reprinted and translated in *Theoretische Ästhetik*, 70–71.

9. Benjamin is probably alluding to a famous statement Leibniz makes to Nicolas Remond: "I have found that most of the sects are right in a good part of what they assert, but not so right in what they deny" (G, 3: 607; L, 655). The term "postulate" is itself mathematical, more exactly, Euclidean. The *Elements* begins with five "axioms" or "common notions" (*ennoia*) and five "demands," "requests," or "postulates" (*aitēma*), the last of which—and the only one that makes reference to infinity—is the famous "parallel postulate" (*Elements*, 1: 154–55). Kant borrows this term for his exposition of the principles of experience that correspond to modal categories (A, 217–35; B, 265–87), and he thereafter develops the three famous "postulates of pure practical reason," namely God, freedom, and immortality (Ak, 5: 122–34).

10. The privileged place accorded to Leibniz's work in Benjamin's exposition of philosophical style is not only unmistakable; it is unsurprising. For Benjamin's *Origin of the German Mourning Play* as a whole concentrates after all on the Lutheran Baroque world in which Leibniz lived. For an examination of the relation between Leibniz's work and the world of the Baroque, see Schmalenbach, *Leibniz*, esp. 11–18; Deleuze, *Le Pli*, esp. 164–89.

11. No adequate exposition of the relation between Leibniz and Benjamin can ignore the astoundingly diverse character of both thinkers. Summarizing a few aspects is scarcely sufficient. The danger of doing so can perhaps be illustrated by a recent essay of Hans Heinz Holz entitled "Idee." While seeking to demonstrate the Kabbalistic character of Benjamin's thought, Holz indicates several points in which it comes into contact with that of Leibniz, but then quickly explains the "unbridgeable distance" (474) between the two and summarizes his findings: "Benjamin's use of the metaphysical cipher *Idea* is embedded in a theological conception whose kernel forms an understanding of Kabbalistics stamped by romanticism" (475). But it could be well argued that Leibniz's thought is more forcefully stamped by the Kabbalah than Benjamin's. At least this much is clear: Leibniz is the only one of the two who wrote—more accurately, ghost-wrote— a Kabbalistic text. Under François-Mercure van Helmont's name he published *Quaedam praemeditatae et consideratae cognitationes super quatuor priora capita libri Moysis, Genesis nominati* (Some premediate and considerate thoughts upon the first four chapters of the first book of Moses called Genesis); see Anne Becco, "Aux sources de la monade," which first revealed Leibniz's "ghost-writing." And

see Coudert, *Leibniz and the Kabbalah*, for an extensive discussion of this complex topic; see also Edel, *Die individuelle Substanz bei Böhme und Leibniz*, esp. 163–205. Benjamin's attraction to the idea of the monad is due in no small measure to its Kabbalistic provenance.

12. With his friend Florens Christian Rang, the "authentic reader" (GB, 3: 16; C, 262) of the *Origin of the German Mourning Play*, Benjamin is even more explicit: "The entire vision of Leibniz, whose thought of the monad I am adopting for the determination of Ideas and whom you invoked for the equation of Ideas and numbers—because, for Leibniz, the discontinuity of whole numbers was a decisive phenomenon for his doctrine of monads—appears to me as though it embraces the summa of a theory of Ideas" (GB, 2, 393; C, 224–25). Rang is not a particularly reliable exponent of number theory—nor of Leibniz. And Benjamin makes a philological error in his remarks on Leibniz in the "Epistemo-Critical Preface": he attributes the idea of the monad to the "Discourse on Metaphysics" (1686); but Leibniz did not begin to use the term *monad* until a decade or so later. One possible reason for this confusion can be found in Benjamin's use of the term *virtuality*, which plays a role in the "Discourse" (A, 6, 4: 1540; L, 307) but not in the "Monadology." Benjamin may have drawn much of his knowledge of Leibniz' work from his dissertation advisor, Richard Herbertz, one of whose works—and the only one recently reprinted—concerns Leibniz's thought, specifically his conception of *petites perceptions*, which is to say, those perceptions that are too "small" to enter into consciousness as themselves, like the immense number of sounds that make up the sound of the sea; see Herbertz, *Die Lehre vom Unbewußten im System des Leibniz*. For a discussion of Benjamin, Leibniz, and Herbertz, see McLaughlin, "The Coming of Paper," esp. 987–98.

13. Although Ideas, for Benjamin, are intimately related to the problem of the task, they are not—as they are for Kant—given only as a task (*Aufgabe*). According to Kant, Ideas can be given only as tasks, for each one is a concept of reason that transcends all possible experience, "for, as the concept of a maximum, nothing congruent to it can ever be given *in concreto*" (A, 327; B, 384); nevertheless, they are not empty, since they give direction to the systematization of knowledge. For Benjamin's reflections on the "infinite task" in Kant, see GS, 6: 51–52.

14. Leibniz's famous metaphor of windowlessness can be found in the seventh paragraph of the so-called "Monadology": "Monads have absolutely no windows through which anything could enter or leave" (G, 6: 606; L, 643). Benjamin's presentation of the Idea as a sun appears in the section of the "Epistemo-Critical Preface" entitled "The Word as Idea": "Every Idea is a sun and is related to others of its kind just as suns are related to each other" (GS, 1: 218; O, 37). In the *Arcades Project* Benjamin returns to the Leibnizian metaphor, but it no longer functions as a mere metaphor; on the contrary, the idea of windowlessness—as the idea of the Idea itself—opens onto the architecture and the archi-structure of

truth: "The interest in panoramas is in seeing the true city—the city indoors [*im Hause*]. What obtains in the windowless house is the true. And the arcade, too, is a windowless house. The windows that look down on it are like loges from which one gazes inside, but one cannot look out from them. (The true has no windows [*Das Wahre has keine Fenster*]; nowhere does the true look out to the universe)" (GS, 5: 661, AP, 532; Q 2 a, 7).

15. Of particular importance for Leibniz's idea of harmony is the doctrine of "panharmony" proposed by John Bisterfeld; see Mugnai, "Der Begriff der Harmonie."

16. The term "Faustian mothers" refers to a scene in the first act of *Faust*, part 2, in which Mephistopheles reveals "the mothers" to Faust: "goddesses, unknown to you mortals, by us not happily named" (*Goethes Werke*, 15: 70; ll. 6216–27).

Chapter 1: Antonomasia

1. Wilhelm Gottfried Leibniz, "Dissertatio praeliminaris: De alienorum operum editione, de Scopo operis, de Philosophica dictione, de lapsibus Nizolii," in Marius Nizolio, *De veris principiis et vera ratione philosophandi contra pseudophilosophos*, ed. G. W. Leibniz (Frankfurt am Main, 1670). For a slightly more complete translation of the "Preliminary Dissertation" than Loemker's, see Leibniz, *Schöpferische Vernunft*, 1–29. For a translation of Nizolio's treatise, see *Vier Bücher über die wahren Prinzipien und die wahre philosophische Methode, gegen die Pseudophilosophen*. An easily accessible source of information about Nizolio's work and its relation to Leibniz can be found in Breen's introduction to his edition of *De veris principiis*, esp. 1: lxiii–lxxiv. Other than the unfocused analysis of Tillmann at the beginning of the last century (*Leibniz' Verhältnis zur Renaissance*), there are few extensive examinations of Leibniz' relation to the late Renaissance humanist; see, however, the collection edited by Albert Heinekamp, *Leibniz et la Renaissance*, especially the essay of Mathieu, "Leibniz, Nizolius et l'histoire de la philosophie." For an appreciation of Nizolio's work, especially his conception of truth, see Wesseler, *Die Einheit von Wort und Sache*; see also Rossi, "Il *De principiis* di Mario Nizolio." On Nizolio's relation to Renaissance rhetoric in general and his relation to Valla in particular, see Monfassani, "Humanism and Rhetoric," esp. 209–11; and Barilli, *Rhetoric*, 61–62. Published in 1670, Leibniz's dissertation on "philosophical style" corresponds and even perhaps contributes to the major "crisis" in his thought that Robinet astutely captures in his *G. W. Leibniz*, 41–77.

2. Spinoza, *Opera*, 3: 34; *A Theologico-Political Treatise*, 31. For an analysis of Spinoza's conception of style—and the problem of philosophical style in general—see Lang, *The Anatomy of Philosophical Style*, 217–42. The prominence of style in both Leibniz's "Preliminary Dissertation" and Spinoza's *Treatise* is very likely a response to Descartes's liberal use of the term (see Lang, 45–85), on the

one hand, and Robert Boyle's *Some Considerations Touching the Style of the H. Scriptures*, on the other. (Boyle's treatise was translated into Latin as early as 1665.)

3. Leibniz undertook the task of editing Nizolio's treatise at the behest of his benefactor during those years, Baron Johann Christian von Boineburg, to whom he dedicates his edition; see Aiton, *Leibniz*, 30–32. At the opening of his "Preliminary Dissertation" Leibniz defends the general practice of editing and cites significant precedents of this practice among now famous philosophers; see A, 6, 2: 401–5. According to Breen, Leibniz also corrects Nizolio's Latin (as well as his Greek); see *De veris principiis*, 1: lxiii–lxiv.

4. Leibniz, *Dissertatio de arte combinatoria* (1666), reprinted in A, 6, 1: 165–230.

5. For Leibniz's use of the phrases "exact language," "philosophical language," "alphabet of human knowledge"—all of which are associated with the voice of Adam—see the notes reprinted in G, 7: 198–99. For his use of "universal language," see A, 2, 1: 384; and A, 6, 4, 65–68; for "rational language" and "rational writing," see A, 2, 1: 380; and A, 6, 4, 116–18, 643–44. A particularly insightful exploration of the relation between Leibniz's program for an "art of combination" and his inquiries into the history of historical languages can be found in Heinekamp, "Ars characteristica und natürliche Sprache bei Leibniz." See also Mugnai, *Astrazione e realtà*, 99–112. For a wide-ranging analysis Leibniz's inquiries into language from the perspective of contemporary linguistics, see Dascal, *Leibniz, Language, Signs, and Thought*. And a concise exposition of Leibniz's complex reflections on language from his earliest to his latest writings can be found in Rutherford, "Philosophy and Language in Leibniz."

6. Nietzsche, "Über Wahrheit und Lüge in aussermoralischen Sinn," *Werke*, 3: 314.

7. Bartholomew Westhemerus was a sixteenth-century author and printer who published, among other texts, Guillaume Philandrier's "corrections" of Quintilian's *Institutiones oratoriae* (1536). For Leibniz's other considerations of rhetoric as trope in the *New Method*, see A, 6, 1: 291, and especially A, 6, 1: 338–39. A brief account of Leibniz's analysis of tropes in *A New Method* can be found in Piro, "Are the 'Canals of Tropes' Navigable? Rhetoric Concepts in Leibniz' Philosophy of Language," 139; Piro's essay is a consistently insightful exploration of Leibniz's discussion of tropes from the *New Method* onward. See also Gensini, "Leibniz, Linguist and Philosopher of Language: Between 'Primitive and 'Natural,'" esp. 125–26.

8. See Wittgenstein, *Philosophical Investigations*, § 41: "the meaning of a word is its use in language" (20).

9. Kraus, *Worte in Versen*, 1: 69 ("Der sterbende Mensch"): "Ursprung ist das Ziel."

10. See in particular Leibniz's two famous essays, neither of which was published during his lifetime, "Ermahnung an die Teutsche ihren Verstand und

Sprache besser zu üben" (generally dated in the early 1680s) and "Unvorgreifliche Gedancken, betreffend die Ausübung und Verbesserung der Teutschen Sprache" (after 1697); a readily available version of the edition published by Paul Pietsch (with modernized spelling) can be found in Leibniz, *Unvorgreifliche Gedanken*. See especially § 11 of "Unvorgreifliche Gedancken" where Leibniz asserts that "we Germans have an extraordinary touchstone that is unknown to others" (*Unvorgreifliche Gedanken*, 9). In § 64 of *A New Method*, Leibniz also recommends German for the purposes of legal reasoning (see A, 6, 1: 337). For an indispensable guide to Leibniz's proposals for and investigations into the German language—as well as to Leibniz's other linguistic researches—see Sigrid von Schulenburg, *Leibniz als Sprachforscher*; an equally indispensable assessment of Leibniz's place in the history of etymological research is Aarsleff, "The Study and Use of Etymology in Leibniz," reprinted in *From Locke to Saussure*, 85–100.

11. See Bohl, *Disputatio prima-duodecima pro formali significationis eruendo primum in explicatione Scripturae Sacrae*. Elsewhere, including in the *New Essays*, Leibniz commends Bohl's idea of "formal meaning" (see, for example, A, 6, 6: 330–31). For an attempt to reconstruct what Leibniz might have meant by the Bohlian term "formal meaning," see Piro, "Are the 'Canals of Tropes' Navigable?" 142–44.

12. For an extensive exploration of Leibniz's thought in terms of the interplay between envelopment and development, see Deleuze, *Le Pli*. Unfortunately, Deleuze nowhere analyzes the twists, turns, and folds in language, although reflection on its "development" may very well have given direction to Leibniz's effort to unravel the thematics of the fold from his first to his last project.

13. Just as Leibniz ignores the Parcae in his exposition of the etymology of *fatum*, he leaves aside the astrological provenance of *influere*, which doubtless had some "influence" on Suarèz. By contrast, in the preface to the *Theodicy*, he speaks of the "principles of astrology" in relation to the "flux and reflux of fortune" (G, 6: 32; T, 56).

14. For a detailed exploration of the idea of a "natural language" in Leibniz, see Gensini, *Il naturale e il simbolico: Saggio su Leibniz*, esp. 61–102; see also, Gensini, "Leibniz, Linguist and Philosopher of Language: Between 'Primitive and 'Natural.'"

15. These remarks open Leibniz's notes to Martin Fogel's *Lexicon philosophicum* (1689); A, 6, 4: 1307–37: "Origo Homonymiarum est, quod infinita sunt nominanda, nomina autem pauca." Leibniz then proposes his most extensive explication of the term *trope*: "TROPUS est vocis affectio vel externa denominatio, secundum quam propria vocis significatio in alienam mutatur, cognatam tamen propriae, ob mutuam aliquam generalem *relationem*" (A, 6, 4: 1307).

16. Leibniz first articulates this famous proposition as the twenty-fourth—and last—axiom of the "Fundamenta praedemonstrabilia" for his treatise of 1671,

Theoria motus abstracti seu Rationes Motuum universales, a sensu et Phaenomenis independentes (G, 4: 228–32). For a brief discussion of the function of this proposition in the *Theoria motus abstracti*, see Heidegger, *Der Satz vom Grund*, 63–64.

17. From the beginning of his work to its end Leibniz was interested in the problem of the divine name and, in particular, the name that the God of the Hebrew Bible pronounces in the presence of Moses: "Ehyeh Asher Ehyeh" (Exod., 3: 14). In a lecture that Leibniz delivers in Vienna on his sixty-eighth birthday (July 1, 1714), he translates these famous Hebrew words from which the tetragrammaton is drawn with the rather flat "Sum qui Sum [I am who I am]" (*Political Writings*, 239). In the *New Essays*, by contrast, he proposes a stronger and doubtless more accurate translation: "je seray ce que je seray [I will be what I will be]" (A, 6, 6: 361). In this explication of the name in which the God of the Hebrew Bible reveals himself, Leibniz may very well have also heard *fatum*: "it is said," which, by the mere fact of having been said, will be. And the "I," as a *pronominative* or (in Greek) *antonomasia*, is what will be by virtue of its saying "I will be." For an analysis of Leibniz's reflections on the tetragrammaton, see Wöhrmann, "Je seray ce que je seray."

18. In a contemporaneous dictionary of Latin etymologies Gerard Jan Voss (Gerardus Johannes Vossius) offers the following explanation for the transformation of *fari* into *fatum*: "FATUM à fando. Nam ita dicitur *Dei fatum*, hoc est, *dictum, jussum, decretum, volantas Dei*" (*Etymologicon linguae latinae*, 207). Leibniz does not follow Voss in pointing out the distinction between the Roman conception of fate, which is tied to the Parcae, and Christian conceptions of *dictum Dei*: "Quà haec de Parcis, eà aspernantur Christiani; non item *fatum* ejúsque etumon" (207).

19. See especially the first major philosophical essay Leibniz chose to publish, namely "Meditationes de Cognitione, Veritate, et Ideis": "distinct knowledge is either inadequate or *adequate*, and also either symbolic or *intuitive*. The most perfect knowledge is that which is both adequate and intuitive" (G, 4: 422; L, 291).

20. For a discussion of the relationship between Voss's attempt in his *Institutiones oratoriae* to classify all tropes under the categories of metaphor, metonymy, and synecdoche, see Battistini, "Tradizione e innovazione nella tassonomia tropologica vichiana." As Battistini notes, Vico undertakes a similar operation, and both the attempts of Voss and Vico to reduce tropes to these three—along with irony—owe a debt to Omar Talon's *Rhetorica* (1548) and, more generally, to Peter Ramus's repudiation of Aristotelian logic. (Vico mentions Voss several times in the *Scienza nuova*, including §§ 428, 641, and 858.) In the *New Essays* Leibniz reproduces this threefold schema and, like Vico, adds irony as something like a trope of reversal (A, 6, 6: 260). For similar passages (without the addition of irony), see § 16 of the "Epistolica de historia etymologica dissertatio" (Gensini, *Il naturale e il simbolico*, 217), and the passage from the notes to the revision of *A*

New Method quoted above; for brief discussions, see Mugnai, *Astrazione e realtà*, 59, and Piro, "Are the 'Canals of Tropes' Navigable?" 148.

21. See, for example, Leibniz's remarks in "De casibus perplexis" (A, 6, 1: 241) and many years later in his "Epistolica de historia etymologica dissertatio," § 16 (Gensini, *Il naturale e il simbolico*, 217).

22. Quintilian, *Institutiones oratoriae*, 3: 316 (bk. 8, sec. 6, par. 29); further reflections on antonomasia can be found at 3: 325 (8, 6, 43) and 3: 351 (9, 1, 6). These later remarks both concern the relation of antonomasia to epithet: only insofar as an epithet functions as an antonomasia can it be considered a trope; otherwise, it is "natural" discourse. Martin Opitz faults German poets for the failure to enrich the lexicon of epithets; see *Buch von der Deutschen Poeterey*, 29–33.

23. Quintilian, *Institutiones oratoriae*, 3: 317 (8, 6, 29). The text of the *Institutiones oratoriae* proceeds to delineate a third version of antonomasia—"acts clearly indicating the individual" (3: 319)—but as Butler notes, this addition violates Quintilian's "twofold division . . . and may therefore be spurious" (3: 318). Or perhaps it gives a further indication of the tendency of antonomasia to slip away from classificatory schemata. For another such indication, see the remarks of the renowned rhetorician Pierre Fontanier, who presents antonomasia as a "true metaphor" (*Commentaire raisonné*, 2: 133–34). Henri Morier, by contrast, presents antonomasia as a species of metonymy in his *Dictionnaire de poétique et de rhétorique*, 116. For a brief exposition of the history of antonomasia, see the entry under this name in Ueding's edition of *Historisches Wörterbuch der Rhetorik*, 1: 754.

24. In the "Preliminary Dissertation" Leibniz mentions Voss's *De vitiis sermonis, et glossematis latino-barbaris* (A, 6, 2: 423), a work that can be understood as a companion piece to Nizolio's *De veris principii* (an alternative title of which is *Anti-barbarus philosophicus*), since both treatises describe and catalogue the "barbaric" neologism of medieval Latin; a few pages earlier (A, 6, 2: 416) Leibniz also mentions Voss's *De quatuor artibus popularibus*. In *A New Method* Leibniz specifically refers to Voss's *Commentariorum rhetoricum* (A, 6, 1: 326).

25. Voss, *Elementa rhetorica*, 21. What Voss calls the "first mode" of antonomasia came to be known as "Vossian antonomasia" or—by an antonomasia of antonomasia—a "Voss." For an account of the transformations undergone by the term *antonomasia*, see the two magisterial works of Lausberg, *Handbuch der literarischen Rhetorik*, 300–302 (§§ 580–81); and *Elemente der literarischen Rhetorik*, 71–73 (§§ 202–7). For an illuminating examination of Voss's transformation of antonomasia in relation to Vico's *Scienza nuova*, see Battistini, "Antonomasia e universale fantastico." An interesting point of transition between Quintilian and Voss can be found in Geoffrey of Vinsauf's *Poetria nova*, a medieval rhetorical treatise in verse (c. 1208–14) that lists among its many modes of "translatio" a trope in which a proper name is "applied metaphorically to the subject for purposes of praise or blame, like a cognomen" (Gallo, *The "Poetria Nova" and Its*

Sources in Early Rhetorical Doctrine, 63). Gallo classifies this trope as "antonomasia" or "pronominatio" on the authority of Puttenheim (203); but neither term appears in the text itself—for good reason: Voss was the first to "unify" two diametrically opposed modes in a systematic manner.

Nowhere does the trope of antonomasia find a more eloquent defense than in a curious passage of *Don Quixote* where Señora Trifaldi recounts the fabulous fate of "la niña Antonomasia"; see Miguel de Cervantes, *El ingenioso hidalgo Don Quijote de la Mancha*, 2: 332; *Don Quixote*, 636–38 (bk. 2, chap. 38; see the epigraph to this chapter). By virtue of antonomasia the name of the generic heroine of romance is thus turned into Princess Antonomasia. At the conclusion of a short chapter on "Grammatical and Rhetorical Technical Terms as Metaphors," Curtius interprets the appearance of Princess Antonomasia as a "protest against contemporary Mannerism" (*European Literature and the Latin Middle Ages*, 416).

26. Piro, who notes Leibniz's indebtedness to Voss, suggests that Leibniz first sought to reduce the number of tropes in the 1690s, but he also notes that the "Preliminary Dissertation" cannot be completely integrated into the account of Leibniz's development that he proposes (see "Are the 'Canals of Tropes' Navigable?" 148–52).

27. See especially the fourth chapter of Nizolio, *De veris principiis*, 1: 41–53: "De nomibus propriis et appellativis tam collectivis quam simplicibus et non collectibivis, ac de eorum proprietatibus et differentiis: contra philosophastros."

28. According to Voss's argument in his *Commentariorum rhetoricum*, synecdoche and metonymy are symmetrical operations, and the same should be true of antonomasia: "nam quemadmodum non tantum *metanomia* est, cum causa pro effectu aut subiectum pro adiuncto ponitur, verum etiam fit contrarium; neque tantum *sunechdoche* est, cum totum pro parte accipitur, sed et cum pars usurpatur pro toto; itidem neque *antonomasia* solum erit, cum commune sumitur pro proprio, quod Fabius et Isodorus existimarunt, verum etiam *cum proprio utimor pro communi*" (Voss, *Commentariorum rhetoricum*, 2: 170; quoted in Lausberg, *Handbuch der literarischen Rhetorik*, 301, § 581.) The success of Voss's efforts to broaden the application of the term *antonomasia* to include its opposite can be measured by a brief glance at Johann Christian Gottlieb Ernesti's compendium, *Lexicon technologiae Graecorum rhetoricae*, 32. See also Nietzsche's brief discussion of antonomasia in his early lectures on rhetoric: "Antonomasia est dictio per accidens proprium significans. Statt eines Eigennamens ein ihn kennzeichnendes Epitheton" (Nietzsche, *Friedrich Nietzsche on Rhetoric and Language*, 58). The brevity of this discussion is surprising, since Nietzsche has just outlined one of the fundamental traits of language in his analysis of synecdoche: "Die Sprache drückt niemals etwas vollständig aus, sondern hebt überall nur das am meisten hervorstechende Merkmal hervor" (56).

29. According to Group µ, both synecdoche and antonomasia correspond to

"the first category of metasemenes" (a neologism introduced as a replacement for the traditional term "trope"), and as long as one is content with a "primitive taxonomy" of things, antonomasia can be treated "as a simple variety of synecdoche," for, as they proceed to explain, "Cicero, when compared with the whole group of orators, is like a species compared with the genus" (*A General Rhetoric,* 102). But in a footnote they qualify this remark to the point of reversing it: "Rigorously, of course, Cicero as an individual is not a species. . . . But we do not understand 'species' here in the meaning of the School" (240).

30. In conjunction with the late-nineteenth- and early-twentieth-century revival of Leibniz as one of the founders of modern logic (in Russell and Couturat), the problem treated under the rhetorical term *antonomasia* gained renewed importance. Instead of discussing "epithets," Russell and others speak of "definite descriptions." And Frege, for his part, quotes one version of the *salva veritate* principle in his essay "Über Sinn und Bedeutung" (On sense and meaning) and discusses its significance in his review of Husserl's *Philosophie der Arithmetik*: "Since any definition is an identification, identity itself cannot be defined. Leibniz's explanation could be called a principle that brings out the nature of the relation of identity, and as such it is of fundamental importance" (*Collected Papers,* 200). Without naming the trope as such, Ruth Marcus discusses the symmetrical character of antonomasia in historical languages; see "Modalities and Intensional Languages," 261–63.

31. For Leibniz's speculations on the fall of Lucifer, which he attributes to an anonymous "man of spirit," see his *Theodicy,* G, 6: 112; T, 55. For a brief account of Leibniz's alchemical experimentations in relation to Heinrich Brand's discovery, see Aiton, *Leibniz,* 78–79. According to Fontenelle's famous eulogy, Leibniz skillfully employs a wide range of poetic technique in the epicedium he wrote on the death of John Frederick of Brunswick; but this poem is particularly resourceful in its account of the discovery of phosphorus: "A remarkable part of this poem is the one in which he speaks of phosphorus invented by Brand," whom Leibniz calls "a new Vulcan"—and thereby makes use of antonomasia; see Bernard le Bouyer de Fontenelle, *Oeuvres complètes,* 1: 227. The poem to which Fontenelle refers can be found in *Gesammelte Werke,* 4: 33–42 (on Brand's discovery, 38).

32. "Théophile" is the name of the character who represents Leibniz in the dialogues he wrote on religion around 1678 (A, 6, 4: 2220–40; partially translated in L, 213–20). As Théophile argues at the very outset of these dialogues, "love of God"—once this phrase is properly understood—suffices as "religion": obedience to arbitrary authority is excluded from divine service properly speaking (A, 6, 4: 2220–21; L, 213–14).

33. See Aiton, *Leibniz,* 68.

34. For a study of Leibniz's (flawed) analysis of Locke's theory of language, see Aarsleff, "Leibniz on Locke on Language," reprinted in *From Locke to Saussure.*

35. Leibniz, "Brevis designatio meditationum de originibus gentium, ductis potissimum ex indicio linguarum," originally printed in *Miscellanea Berolinensia* (1710), reprinted in *Opera omnia*, ed. Dutens, 4, 2: 186: "Illud enim pro axiomate habeo, *omnia nomina quae vocamus propria, aliquando appellativa fuisse*, alioqui ratione nulla constarent" (Leibniz's emphasis). For an earlier formulation (perhaps the earliest), see "Characteristics verbalis," A, 6, 4: 335. For similar passages, see Schulenburg, *Leibniz als Sprachforscher*, 101–2.

36. After quoting the opening of the "Brevis," Aarsleff makes the astute comment: "This passage states the very important principle that proper names must at the outset be appellatives, for otherwise they would exist without any reason, and Leibniz could not allow that sort of inconsistency in his philosophy" (*From Locke to Saussure*, 48). Aarsleff also indicates in the notes the provenance of Leibniz's "axiom" in Johann Georg Schottel's investigations into German names, which are themselves indebted to a brief text entitled "Aliquot nomina propria germanorum ad priscam etymologiam restituta" (1554), which was attributed to Luther (*From Locke to Saussure*, 73); see also Schulenburg, *Leibniz als Sprachforscher*, 133–37.

37. Leibniz, "Epistolica de historia etymologica dissertatio," § 17 (Gensini, *Il naturale e il simbolico*, 219). In the *New Essays* Leibniz discusses a similar series of sounds, including *qu* (as in *quickly* and *erquicken*), *r* (as in *rheo* and *rauschen*), and *l* (as in *leben* and *lauf*); see A, 6, 6: 282–86.

38. For a summary account of Leibniz's directives for linguistic research, none is better than the words with which Schulenburg introduces her magisterial study: "This connection [between sign and signified] is neither necessary nor arbitrary. But it is grounded, and indeed by the nature of the speakers, their physical and mental dispositions, and by the nature of the things toward which their thoughts are directed" (Schulenburg, *Leibniz als Sprachforscher*, 1).

39. In addition to Schulenburg's exposition of Leibniz's changing theories on the origin of language and the original language (*Leibniz als Sprachforscher*, 68–114), see also *Leibniz and Ludolf on Things Linguistic*, along with the few comments Leibniz included in the *New Essays* itself (A, 6, 6: 280–82).

40. Quintilian calls onomatopoeia a trope; indeed, his analysis of the trope follows his account of antonomasia. Leibniz does not list onomatopoeia among the list of four primary tropes in the *New Essays* (A, 6, 6: 260) or anywhere else, as far as I know.

41. See, for example, Leibniz's "Reflections on the Doctrine of a Single Universal Spirit" (1702): "We have an infinity of little perceptions which we are incapable of distinguishing" (G, 6: 534; L, 557); see also A, 6, 6: 53–55.

42. See Piro, "Are the 'Canals of Tropes' Navigable?" 152–57.

43. Quintilian associates onomatopoeia with antonomasia insofar as he considers the latter immediately after the former. The reason for this association may lie

in the close association between the Latin terms for the two tropes, *nominatio* and *pronominatio* respectively; see Quintilian, *Institutiones oratoriae*, 3: 319; 8, 6, 31–32.

44. See, for example, the notes dated around 1677: "*Everything possible demands that it should exist*, and hence will exist unless something else prevents it, which also demands that it should exist and is incompatible with the former" (G, 7: 194; trans. Russell, *A Critical Exposition of the Philosophy of Leibniz*, 296); see also "The Radical Origination of Things" (1697; G, 7: 302–8; L, 486–91) and § 10 of the "Principles of Nature and Grace" (G, 6: 603; L, 639). Russell's most detailed account of Leibniz's contention that essences or possibilities demand existence in accordance with their degree of reality can be found in "Recent Work on the Philosophy of Leibniz," 376–78; for an informative discussion of current debates about the status of Leibniz's "metaphysical mechanics" grounded in the idea of *essentiae exigentia*, see Catherine Wilson, *Leibniz's Metaphysics*, 275–81.

45. Quintilian, *Institutio oratio*, ed. Butler, 3: 317; 8, 6, 29; Virgil, *Aeneid*, trans. H. Rushton Fairclough, 244 (bk. 1, l. 65): "father of the gods and king of men."

46. See Voss, *Elementa rhetorica*, 21.

47. These two terms—*kat exochen* and *perfectissimo*—are the ones through which Leibniz explicates his use of "antonomasia" in the "Preliminary Dissertation": the first in relation to *fari* and the second in relation to the distinction between popular and technical uses of the word *square* (in Latin, *quadrat*): "If even greater rigor is demanded, the words *line, bounding, intersection,* and *quality* must be further resolved, for their popular use does not exactly fit the concepts of geometry, as in, for example, the word *square*, which, according to both its origin and its common use, can be attributed to every quadrilateral, whereas geometricians attribute it only to an equilateral rectangle by way of antonomasia, as if it were a perfection [*per antonomasiam . . . tanquam perfectissimo*]" (A, 6, 2: 412; partially translated at L, 123). Leibniz's use of *tanquam* (namely, *tamquam*) indicates that his use of *antonomasia* is itself figural insofar as it concerns the replacement of the general term ("quadrilateral") by a more specific one ("equilateral rectangle")—instead of a noun by a name. For the purposes of geometry, terms like "equilateral rectangle" can be understood as something like "proper" ones.

48. Leibniz's remarks on the derivation of proper names is, of course, far from unprecedented. One point of departure for the traditions that issue into these remarks in the *New Essays* can be found in Quintilian's complicated reflections on the idea of properness or propriety in speech: "the salient characteristic of an individual comes to be attached to him as a proper name: thus Fabius was called 'Cunctator,' the Delayer, on account of the most remarkable of his many military virtues" (*Institutio oratio*, 3: 203; 8, 2, 11).

49. Réne Descartes, *Meditationes de prima philosophia* (1641), reprinted in *Oeuvres de Descartes*, 7: 27. See also Descartes's use of *moy* in the fourth section of the *Discours sur la méthode*, in *Oeuvres*, 6: 33.

50. According to Leibniz's extensive notes on Voss's *Aristarchus sive de arte grammatica libri septem,* "Pronomen quod primario nomen respicit, secundario rem" (A, 6, 4: 611); one of the major functions of pronouns is to express something (*res, chose, ding*) whose proper name is unknown (A, 6, 4: 611).

51. The quotation is drawn from Leibniz's "Lettre touchant ce qui est indépendent des Sens et de la Matiére" (1702), addressed to Queen Charlotte. For a brief analysis of this letter, which, however, does not take into consideration the function of the pronoun, see Heidegger, "Aus der letzten Marburger Vorlesung," in *Wegmarken,* 87–88. For similar uses of the "personal pronoun" in Leibniz, see esp. § 11 of "A New System of the Nature and Communication of Substances" (G, 4: 472; L, 456); § 5 of the "Principle of Nature and Grace" (G, 6: 601; L, 638), a treatise addressed to Prince Eugene of Savoy; and the so-called "Monadology," § 30 (G, 6: 612; L, 646).

52. According to Leibniz, "*haecceitas* does not have the usual analogy; *hoccitas* (or *hoccimonia*) would be better. . . . The definition of *hoccitas* can be formed from its root and the analogy" (A, 6, 2: 411; L, 123).

53. The popular, although inaccurate, derivation of the name "Caesar" is the phrase *a caeso matris utere* ("from the incised womb of his mother").

54. See the introductory remarks of Brunschwig to his edition of *Essais de Théodicée,* 10–11. In a letter to the French officer Hugony, Leibniz made clear that he did not want his name attached to the treatise (see G, 6: 11).

55. In conjunction with a discussion of the Book of Job, Hobbes accuses those who would bring an omnipotent being to court of thereby indicting themselves: "Power irresistible justifieth all actions and properly, in whomsoever it be found. Less power does not. And because such power is in God only, he must needs be just in all his actions. And we, that not comprehending his counsels, call him to the bar commit injustice in it" (Hobbes, *Liberty, Necessity, and Chance,* reprinted in *English Works,* 116).

56. See Luther's famous sermon, *Von der Freiheit eines Christenmenschen.*

57. See Bayle, *Dictionaire historique et critique,* 3: 2599–612. Like Leibniz, Bayle "applies" the system of preestablished harmony "to the person of Caesar" (2: 2611).

58. Virgil, *Aeneid,* 244 (bk. 1, l. 65); Quintilian, *Institutio oratio,* 3: 317; 8, 6, 29.

59. Virgil, *Aeneid,* 244 (bk. 1, l. 39).

60. See the entry on *arrest* in the first edition of the *Dictionnaire de l'Académie française* (1694):

> Arrest (ARRESTER): Arrest. s. m. Jugement d'une Cour, d'une Justice superieure, par lequel une question de fait ou de droit est arrestée. . . . Il signifie aussi, Saisie, soit en la personne, soit aux biens. . . . Arrest, Se dit aussi de l'action du cheval quand il s'arreste. . . . Il se dit aussi de l'action du chien couchant qui arreste le gibier. . . . Arrest, Se dit aussi de la piece du harnois où un gendarme appuye & arreste sa lance, pour

rompre en lice ou autrement. . . . Il se dit aussi en fait d'armes à ressort d'une petite pièce de fer qui arreste le ressort & l'empesche de se debander. . . . On dit fig. qu'Un esprit n'a point d'arrest, qu'il est sans arrest, pour dire, qu'Il est irresolu ou égaré.

The English translator of the *Theodicy* renders *l'arrest de sa sagesse,* strangely enough, by "award of his wisdom" (T, 269).

61. As Robinet has shown, "Leibniz inverted the order of paragraphs 405–17 and paragraphs 377–404" ("Leibniz: La Renaissance et l'age classique," 26). Originally, Leibniz had written "FIN" after the words, "To complain of not having such power [to will without rhyme or reason] would be to argue like Pliny, who finds fault with the power of God because God cannot destroy himself" (G, 6: 357; T, 365). The concluding fiction is, as a whole, a replacement for the word "END."

62. See Plato, *Republic,* 297–303 (614b–21d); Cicero, *De republica,* 260–83 (6, 9–26). Only the conclusion to Cicero's treatise, generally known as "Somnium Scipionis" (Scipio's dream), was known to Leibniz; a longer, still incomplete manuscript of *De republica* was not discovered until 1820.

63. This term—"the mythology of reason" (*Mythologie der Vernunft*)—first appears in the much disputed so-called "Oldest System-Program of German Idealism," a version of which can be found in Hegel, *"Der Geist des Christentums,"* 342.

64. For an insightful analysis of Leibniz's relation to Valla, see Struever, *Theory as Practice,* 131–33.

65. "With all wisdom and insight he has made known to us the mystery of his will, according to his good pleasure that he set forth in Christ, as a plan for the fullness of time, to gather up [*anakephalaiosasthai*] all things in him, things in heaven and on earth" (Eph. 1:10).

66. In an exposition of the problem of contingency Giorgio Agamben discusses certain aspects of the concluding paragraphs of the *Theodicy* and, in particular, indicates that, against Leibniz's intention, the Jupiter who "recapitulates" the moment of his choice must be understood as a Gnostic demiurge: "It is difficult to imagine something more pharisaic than this demiurge, who contemplates all uncreated possible worlds to take delight in his single choice" (Agamben, "Bartleby, or, On Contingency," in *Potentialities,* 266). Leibniz may not have been as deaf to the Gnostic implications of his "little fable" as Agamben indicates, nor would he so casually refer to the Pharisees.

67. "O the depth [*bathos*] of the riches and wisdom and knowledge of God! How unsearchable are his judgments and how inscrutable his ways" (Rom. 11: 33). As Riley notes, "it is fideists [like Pascal or Bayle] who usually appeal to Pauline *O altitudo* and have their reasons for doubting reason" (*Leibniz' Universal Jurisprudence,* 137).

68. In his *Lectures on the History of Philosophy,* Hegel says that Leibniz's thought appears to be a "metaphysical novel" (*metaphysischer Roman*) until one recognizes what he sought to avoid; see *Werke,* 20: 238.

69. Some of Leibniz's late reflections on eschatological themes and millenarian movements have been collected and analyzed by Antognazza and Hotson, *Alsted and Leibniz on God, the Magistrate, and the Millennium*; see also Leibniz, *De l'Horizon de la doctrine humaine*.

70. See Schestag, "Komische Authentizität," on the resonance of *theocide* in *theodicy*.

71. Riley emphasizes that Leibniz's response to Pliny recapitulates his argument against those, like Hobbes, who emphasize power over other divine attributes; see Riley, *Leibniz' Universal Jurisprudence*, 137–38.

72. As Idel notes, "the Golem appears to its creators with the inscription *'emet*, truth, on his forehead" (*Golem*, 306). When those who produce golems wish to "kill" them, they erase the aleph, leaving *meth* (death). Like all Hebrew words, אמת (*'emet*, "truth") is also a number. Scholem translates an extraordinary passage from an early Kabbalist text entitled *The Secret of the Name of 42 Letters*:

> The prophet Jeremiah busied himself alone with the *Book Yetsirah*. Then a heavenly voice went forth and said: Take a companion. He went to his son Sira, and they studied the book for three years. Afterward they set about combining the letters in accordance with the Kabbalistic principles of combination, grouping, and word formation, and a man was created to them, on whose forehead stood the letters *YHWH* Elohim Emeth [the Lord God is truth]. But this newly created man had a knife in his hand, with which he erased the aleph from the *emeth*; there remained: *meth*. Then Jeremiah rent his garment [because of the blasphemous message: God is dead]. (*On the Kabbalah*, 180)

For the identification of the manuscript, see Idel, *Golem*, 67.

Theocide is thus inscribed into these "creatures" of a second creation. Like the Jeremiah of this story, Leibniz studied the *Sefer Yetzirah* (Book of Creation), although, of course, he did so only in Christian-Kabbalistic versions of this great treatise on aleph-numerical combination. As Coudert notes in her impressive study, Leibniz read François-Mercure van Helmont's *Kurtzer Entwurff des eigentlichen Naturalphabets der heiligen Sprache* in 1667 (see *Leibniz and the Kabbalah*, 144). Although the provenance of Leibniz's proposal for an *ars combinatoria* is often said to be Raymond Lull, it should also be sought in the *Sefer Yetzirah*: "The similarity between Lull's art and the description in the *Sefer Yetzirah* of the twenty-two Hebrew letters revolving with each other on spheres (more probably circles) presents a very Lullist picture (or vice versa!). Pico [della Mirandola] was the first to draw a parallel between the two practices" (Coudert, *Leibniz and the Kabbalah*, 148–49). Leibniz himself notes the similarity between Kabbalistic theories of language and his own *ars combinatoria*: "Atque ea vera foret sive Cabbala vocabulorum mysticorum, sive Arithmetica numerorum Pythagoricum, sive Characteristica Magorum hoc est Sapientum" (G, 4: 199). Leibniz would have known how golems were supposed to be produced, since the requisite conditions and formulas can be found in the second volume of Knorr von Rosenroth's *Kabbala denu-*

data; but Knorr von Rosenroth did not know the term *golem* and instead used *moles* or *corpus* (see Rosenfeld, *Die Golemsage*, 37–38). And Leibniz may also have known about the function of *'emet* in the creation and destruction of golems, since it was reproduced in Reuchlin and later in Johann Wagenseil. Robinet notes the resemblance between golems and the apparitions that Athena calls into existence; see "Leibniz: La Renaissance et l'age classique," 30. (Robinet's note on this matter is strangely missing, and his account of the process by which golems are produced seems to be based on a misunderstanding).

73. In the *New Essays* Leibniz entertains a corresponding fantasy: "Suppose for instance that the imaginary 'Australians' came to inundate our country, it is likely that some way would have to be found of distinguishing them from us; but if not, and if God had forbidden the mingling of races, and Jesus Christ had redeemed only our race, then we should have to try to introduce artificial marks to distinguish the races from one another. No doubt there would an inner difference, but since we should be unable to detect it we should have to rely solely on the extrinsic denomination of birth, and try to associate it with an indelible artificial mark that would provide an intrinsic denomination and a permanent means of telling our race apart from theirs" (A, 6, 6: 400–401). Leibniz proceeds to reiterate the fictional character of this violent fantasy: "This is all fiction: since we [the children of Adam] are the only rational animals on the globe, we have no need to resort to this kind of differentiation. Still, such fictions help us to know the nature of the ideas of substances, and of general truths about them" (A, 6, 6: 400–401). For an insightful analysis of a similar, more startling, and far less innocent fantasy of making extrinsic "racial" distinctions intrinsic, see Dascal, "One Adam and Many Cultures," esp. 390–94.

74. For a detailed analysis of Leibniz's conception of the infinite (especially the infinitely small), see Ishiguro, who emphasizes the difference between ideal entities (*entia rationis*) and fictional ones (*entia fictitum*); *Leibniz's Philosophy of Logic and Language*, 79–100. See also Russell, *A Critical Exposition of the Philosophy of Leibniz*, 109–10.

75. For Cantor's definition of "aleph-null" ($\aleph_0$), see § 6, "Beiträge zur Begründung der transfiniten Mengenlehre" (GA, 292–93). For his definition of ה, see his letter to Dedekind of July 28, 1899: "*The system of* μ *of all numbers is an inconsistent, absolutely infinite plurality* [Vielheit]. . . . I call 'alephs' the cardinal numbers that belong to the transfinite numbers of the system μ, and the *system of all alephs* is called ה (*tav*, the last letter of the Hebrew alphabets)" (GA, 445). Cantor was particularly attracted to Leibniz, whose reflections on the "actual infinite" are analyzed in his "Grundlagen einer allgemeinen Mannigfaltigkeitslehre" (GA, 175–77, 179–81). Leibnizian monadology, moreover, provided Cantor with the opportunity to respond to Gösta Mittag-Leffler's challenge and show the manner in which transfinite numbers could be understood to be objectively valid: "On this

point there arises a question, to which neither Leibniz nor his successors gave any thought: which powers [*Mächtigkeiten*] accrue to those two forms of matter with regard to their element, insofar as they are considered sets of corporeal or aetherial monads? Responding to this question, I formulated a number of years ago the hypothesis that the power of corporeal matter is what I call in my investigations the first power and that, by contrast, the power of aetherial material is the second" (GA, 275–76; see Schoenflies, "Die Krisis," 22; Dauben, *Georg Cantor*, 292–94). According to Dauben, whose work on Cantor remains indispensable, "Leibniz was the source of [his] greatest inspiration" (Dauben, 292), even if, as Sophie Kowalevski indicates in a letter to Mittag-Leffler, he was unable to communicate this enthusiasm:

> [Cantor] began during the previous semester [1884] to lecture on Leibnitz's [*sic*] philosophy. In the beginning he had 25 students but then little by little, they melted together first to 4, then to 3, then to 2, finally to a single one. Cantor held out nevertheless and continued to lecture. But, alas! One fine day came the last of the Mohicans, somewhat troubled, and thanked the professor very much but explained that he had so many other things to do that he could not manage to follow the professor's lectures. Then Cantor, to his wife's unspeakable joy, gave a solemn promise never to lecture on philosophy again!

Dauben, 313; Dauben's translation from the Swedish.

76. See Cantor's remarkable reflections in his "Mitteilungen zur Lehre von Transfiniten" (1887): "The transfinite numbers are in a certain sense *new irrationalities*. . . . [Transfinite and irrational numbers] are like each other in their innermost being" (GA, 395).

77. Leibniz also associates an ancient Arminius (much more ancient than the one who fought against the Romans) with Hermes: "Who knows but he may have penetrated even into Egypt, like the Scythians who in pursuit of Sesostris came nearly so far" (G, 6: 193; T, 211–12). Leibniz is also the author of the famous *Consilium Aegyptiacum* (1671), a plan he devised to end the aggression of Louis XIV against Holland by turning his martial ambitions in the direction of Egypt, thus becoming another Alexander the Great. For an account of this strange work, which has been (inaccurately) said to have inspired Napoleon's Egyptian venture, see Riley, *Leibniz' Universal Jurisprudence*, 246–50.

78. This definition of joy (*Freude*) follows on a description of happiness (*Glückseeligkeit*):

> Happiness is a state of constant joy [*beständigen Freude*]. Whoever is happy does not, to be sure, feel joy every moment, for he sometimes rests from his contemplation [*nachdenken*] and usually also turns his thoughts to practical affairs. But it is enough that he is in a state to feel joy [*in stand ist, die freude zu empfinden*] whenever he wishes to think of it. (G, 7: 86; L, 425)

One can therefore be "in" the state of joy without feeling any joy: it is the fundamental character of this feeling. In the margins to a section of manuscript of

1681 entitled "Definitiones" Leibniz offers the following clarification of the Latin definition of *laetitia*: "Freude ist, wenn das gemüth mit eigner lust gedancken eingenommen" (G, 7: 75). It is worth noting that Leibniz's first response to Bayle concerns the nature of a dog's joy (see G, 4: 517–18; L, 492–93).

79. See LH, 108–11. This text, like the conclusion to the *Theodicy*, can be understood as a combination of two *Republics*: Plato's and Cicero's. With respect to Cicero, the fragmentary fiction once again resembles "Scipio's Dream" (see note 62 above); with respect to Plato, it rewrites, of course, the famous "allegory of the cave" that begins the seventh book of the *Politeia*. For an appreciation of the centrality of this fragment to Leibniz's overall philosophical vision, see Rutherford, *Leibniz and the Rational Order of Nature*, 289–90.

80. Franz Kafka, "Ein Bericht für eine Akademie," in *Gesammelte Werke*, 1: 243. For a more extensive presentation of the relation between Leibniz's "little fable" and Kafka's stories, see my "Continuing the Fiction."

81. One descendent of Theodore would be the eponymous protagonist of Novalis's novel *Heinrich von Ofterdingen*, who sees his *Ebenbild* (image) in a book housed in a subterranean library and learns that it is a "novel of the marvelous fate of a poet in which the art of poetry is presented and praised in its manifold relations" (Novalis, *Werke*, 205). The conclusion to the manuscript, which hails from Jerusalem, is lost. Only in this way does it distinguish itself from the books of fate that Athena, the perfect librarian, preserves.

82. Bayle devotes a lengthy article to the papess Joan, and like Leibniz, disputes the "fable"; see his *Dictionaire historique et critique*, 1: 610–11 (article on David Blondel); 2: 1258, and 2: 1269–70 (quoting Martin Franc, "Vers touchant sur la Papesse Jeanne"). The text of Friedrich Spanheim to which Leibniz refers is *De papa foemina inter Leonem IV. et Benedictum III., disquisitio historica* (published in 1691 and translated into French as early as 1694 and into German in 1737). Spanheim was a Protestant professor of philosophy at the University of Leyden; he collected over five hundred references to Joan and argued for her existence. In the wide-ranging literature on the papess, three recent works are of particular note: D'Onofrio, *La Papessa Giovanna*, Boureau, *La Papesse Jeanne*, and especially Gössmann, *Mulier papa*, which devotes a section to Leibniz (256–72). Long before and long after Leibniz recommended the story of the papess to poets, the papess had been the subject matter of literary works. For accounts of these works, which range from misogynist plays and antipapal operas to romantic novellas and feminist romances, see Boureau, *La Papesse Jeanne*, 277–320; Gössmann, *Mulier papa*, 337–94. Commemoration of Joan can also be found in tarot cards, the second of which is called "the papess" or, more indirectly, "high priestess." See the cover of this volume for an example of her image.

83. Gössmann's remarkable work presents the fable of the papess as an exemplary chapter in the history of Western misogyny. Gössmann emphasizes that

the novelty of Leibniz's work does not lie in its arguments against the historicity of the papess but in its (silent) renunciation of the misogyny that animated debates about her existence; see *Mulier papa*, esp. 271–72.

84. On Aventinus, otherwise known as Johannes Thurmair, and his attribution of the "little fable" of the papess to Theodora in his *Annalium boiorum* (1519–21), see Gössmann, *Mulier papa*, 103–9.

85. When, at the beginning of his treatise, Leibniz indicates that the story of the papess deserves a better poet than he—one who could make something of this "Heroine and lover [*Heroinam & amentum*]" (FS, 297)—he is perhaps alluding to the story of Theodora; but the emphasis nevertheless falls on the first word: *Heroinam*.

86. Christian Ludwig Scheidt, "Vorbericht" to *Bibliotheca historica Goettingensis*, liii. Scheidt does not cite Aventinus but, rather, Christoph August Heumann's *Dissertatio de origine vera traditionis falsae de Ioanna papissa* (1739). Like Aventinus, however, Scheidt speaks of the "whore-government" of Theodora (FS, liii). Edward Gibbon, who drew on Leibniz's history of the House of Brunswick (L, 8), offers a similar explanation for the origin of the story of the papess, namely "the two sister prostitutes, Marozia and Theodora," who manage to place their lover on the papal throne (*Decline and Fall of the Roman Empire*, 5: 317–18).

87. One of the very few commentaries on Leibniz's treatise on the papess emphasizes its ecumenical intention; see Herse, "Leibniz und die Päpstin Johanna."

88. Leibniz, "Theodicaea," in *Textes inédits*, 1: 370.

89. Leibniz, who takes no position on this rumor, reproduces three sketches of the seat upon which popes-to-be are rumored to be examined at the time of the election; all of these sketches bear resemblance to birthing stools, as if the confirmation of the pope-to-be's gender were at the same time a repetition of the event that calls for the examination in the first place. See Leibniz's reproduction of the sketches provided by one of the many anti-Catholic pamphlets of Gilbert Burnet (FS, unnumbered page between 334 and 335); for a discussion of this rumor and corresponding ritual, including the announcement "Habet duos testiculos et bene pendentes," see Boureau, *La Papesse Jeanne*, 15–51. Des Bosses may have shown no interest in having Leibniz's treatise on the papess published (even as he was translating the *Theodicy* into Latin) because he did not approve of its reproduction of the rumor about the secret ceremony to certify the masculinity of the new pope.

90. See, for example, article 14 of Leibniz's "Critical Thoughts on the General Part of the Principles of Descartes," G, 4: 358–59; L, 386.

91. Leibniz was a major proponent of the theory of preformation and believed that Leeuwenhoek's experiments confirmed this theory; see, for example, the sixth paragraph of the "Principles of Nature and Grace" (G, 6: 601–2; L, 638) and paragraph 403 of the *Theodicy*, which immediately precedes Leibniz's recounting of Valla's "little fable" (G, 6: 356–57; T, 364). Yet it should also be re-

membered that the *Theodicy*, like many of Leibniz's more extensive writings (in French), are directed toward the edification of princesses. When Leibniz offers des Bosses's publisher the choice between the *Essays of Theodicy* and *Flores sparsi*, he presents in effect the choice between a book against Bayle dedicated to a recently deceased princess (Sophie Charlotte) and a book in agreement with Bayle and against the existence of a perhaps impossible papess.

92. The title of Leibniz's book may owe something to the work of Philippe Labbé, *Cenotaphium Ioannae papissae* (1660); see Boureau, *La Papesse Jeanne*, 276.

Chapter 2: Language on a Holy Day

1. The "best friend" to whom Mendelssohn refers in this note is unnamed but hardly unknown: he obviously alludes to Lessing, whose apparent confession of Spinozism to Jacobi launched the bitter *Pantheismusstreit* that would in a sense claim Mendelssohn's life within a few years. For the major texts of this controversy, see Scholz's edition of *Die Hauptschriften zum Pantheismusstreit zwischen Jacobi und Mendelssohn*; translations of some of these works can be found in Jacobi, *The Spinoza Conversations Between Lessing and Jacobi*. For a readily available account in English, which does not always do justice to Mendelssohn's writings, see Beiser, *The Fate of Reason*, 44–126; a useful review of the controversy, including a critique of Beiser's analysis of Mendelssohn, can be found in Arkush, *Mendelssohn and the Enlightenment*, 69–97.

2. On Lessing's idea of friendship, see Arendt, "On Humanity in Dark Times: Thoughts About Lessing," in *Men in Dark Times*, 3–31; for an exposition of Mendelssohn's concept and practice of friendship, see Berghahn, "On Friendship: The Beginnings of a Christian-Jewish Dialogue in the 18th Century."

3. For a review of Mendelssohn's contributions to contemporaneous debates about the nature, function, and origin of language, see Engel, "Die Freiheit der Untersuchung." Various attempts have been made to analyze Mendelssohn's theories of language from the perspective of Lessing and Herder; yet no one, to my knowledge, has undertaken a thorough analysis of Mendelssohn's linguistic philosophy that takes into consideration the full range of his work, especially his treatises in Hebrew along with his theory and practice of translation. For some important guidelines of the latter pursuits, see two works by Sorkin, "The Internal Dialogue: Judaism and Enlightenment in Moses Mendelssohn's Thought," and especially *Moses Mendelssohn and the Religious Enlightenment*, esp. 64–74; see also the careful analysis of Mendelssohn's relation to the development of modern historiographic philology in Breuer, *The Limits of Enlightenment*.

4. For an intricate exposition of Leibniz's thematics of folding and unfolding, explication and implication, see Deleuze, *Le Pli*.

5. The "Eternal" (*der Ewige*) is Mendelssohn's translation of the tetragramma-

ton by way of synecdoche: a part is taken for the whole. As Mendelssohn explains in his Hebrew commentary on Exodus 33:23, German has no single term that encompasses all three attributes of the divine substance: "there is no word that better unites the meaning of omnitemporality, necessity of existence, and providence than does this holy name: 'the eternal, necessary, providential being' [in German]. So we have translated 'the Eternal,' or 'the Eternal Being'" (JubA, 16: 26; see Sorkin, *Moses Mendelssohn and the Religious Enlightenment*, 64–65, who, however, misidentifies the trope under consideration). Mendelssohn thus takes one of the three attributes and makes it into the name of the substance itself. As Franz Rosenzweig argues, Mendelssohn's decision to translate the tetragrammaton as "the Eternal" (or even "the Eternal being"), although not without precedent (Calvin led the way), was a bold gesture of great consequence—all of which, according to Rosenzweig, was for the worst; see Rosenzweig, "'Der Ewige': Mendelssohn und der Gottesname," in *Zweistromland*, 801–15; "'The Eternal': Mendelssohn and the Name of God," in Buber and Rosenzweig, *Scripture and Translation*, 99–113.

6. See the magisterial study of Prodi, *Il sacramento del potere*. For another informative discussion of swearing (which draws heavily from Prodi's work), see Holenstein, "Seelenheil und Untertanenpflicht." Prodi argues (and Holenstein concurs) that the practices of swearing and oath-taking, as "sacraments of power," declined as the state successfully arrogated to itself the "monopoly of violence." As Carl Schmitt writes (with his usual pithiness), "the oath is a characteristic sign of an existential entrance with the entire person. It must therefore vanish from an order of society founded on a free contract" (*Verfassungslehre*, 67–68; see also the work of a Schmitt student, Friesenhahn, *Der politische Eid*, esp. 11–12). Mendelssohn, who seeks to demonstrate in the first section of *Jerusalem* that the state alone should have coercive powers and that a religious institution cannot even exercise the right of expelling members with whom it disagrees, is drawn to the critique of oath-taking. As Prodi notes in the conclusion to his massive study, it was in Nazi Germany that swearing (in the form of the oath of fidelity to the Führer) once again assumed a decisive role in a modern state; *Il sacramento del potere*, 493–506.

7. For an insightful account of Mendelssohn's legal theory, see Thomas Mautner, "Mendelssohn and the Right of Toleration," in *Moses Mendelssohn und die Kreise seiner Wirksamkeit*, esp. 205–7.

8. Among Christian sects, the Anabaptists took the lead in opposing swearing in general and oath-taking in particular; see Prodi, *Il sacramento del potere*, 339–86; Holenstein, "Seelenheil und Untertanenpflicht," 41–58. Of far greater importance to Mendelssohn than radical Christian attacks on the practice of swearing, oath-taking, and the interpretation of the Third Commandment are Talmudic and rabbinical teachings concerning these matters. Of equal importance are the slanderous misrepresentations of these Talmudic and rabbinical teachings. Mendels-

sohn's discussion of oath-taking resulted in a controversy that was more conse-
quential to European Jewry than the far more famous *Pantheismusstreit* in which
Mendelssohn was concurrently engaged. Johann David Michaelis, who consid-
ered himself the Christian expert on all things Jewish, attacked Mendelssohn for
his discussion of oath-taking because, according to Michaelis, the Jew slandered
the English clergy when he asserted that some of them might entertain doubts in
the course of their lives about the thirty-nine articles of faith to which they must
swear (or, as Michaelis writes, seeking to correct Mendelssohn, "subscribe"). Mi-
chaelis then changes the subject and asserts that Jews cannot be trusted when they
take oaths and therefore should not be "emancipated." See the appendixes to the
volume of Mendelssohn's *Gesammelte Schriften* that includes *Jerusalem*, especially
Mendelssohn's "Ueber die 39 Artikel der englischen Kirche und deren Besch-
wören" (JubA, 8: 207–24). For a detailed presentation and analysis of Michaelis's
relationship to Mendelssohn, see Löwenbrück, *Judenfeindschaft im Zeitalter der
Aufklärung*; see also Barbara Fischer, "Residues of Otherness: On Jewish Eman-
cipation During the Age of German Enlightenment."

9. For an analysis of seriousness in "speech act theory"—which is itself neither
serious nor nonserious—see Derrida, *Limited, Inc.* Derrida does not consider the
relation of seriousness to solemnity in this or, to my knowledge, any other text;
he does, however, direct his attention to the question of swearing and conjura-
tion throughout *Specters of Marx*.

10. Wittgenstein, *Philosophische Untersuchungen*, § 38, reprinted in *Werkaus-
gabe*, 1: 260; *Philosophical Investigations*, 19.

11. Mendelssohn briefly considers the Leibnizian program for a universal
characteristics in his prize essay "On Evidence" (JubA, 2: 290–91; *Philosophical
Writings*, 264–65), and although he works for linguistic reform—as for example,
in his translation of the Hebrew Bible and his proposal for the revival of biblical
Hebrew—he never expects metaphysical problems to be solved with the swift-
ness and sureness of the famous imperative with which Leibniz hopes to end all
controversies: "let us calculate!" In the margins to a brief dialogue on the Hobbes-
ian contention that names are arbitrary, Leibniz jots down a now famous propo-
sition: "When God calculates and thinks, the world is made" (A, 6, 4: 22; L, 185).
For a fuller discussion, see section five, "Lucifer," of the previous chapter.

12. At the heart of the other major work Mendelssohn writes late in his life,
Morgenstunden (Morning hours), he describes a similar temporal mismatch—
between "sound understanding [*gesunde Menschenverstand*]" and "rational knowl-
edge [*Vernunfterkenntnis*]"; see JubA, 3, 2: 33–34. Arkush accurately captures
Mendelssohn's exposition of the temporal relation between these two cognitive
faculties: "The only difference between them is the speed with which they go to
work. Whereas reason investigates the path before it very cautiously and pro-
ceeds fearfully, watching every step, sound understanding, operating without

self-consciousness, moves ahead swiftly and fearlessly" (*Mendelssohn and the Enlightenment*, 76).

13. In his extensive commentary on *Jerusalem*, Altmann presents Mendelssohn's decision to speak of "ceremony"—which has no good synonym in Hebrew and no equivalent in Talmudic or rabbinical commentary—as a response to Spinoza (see JubA, 8: 349); he does not mention the central importance of the phrase "ceremonies of practice" for the exposition of Leibniz's project of "theodicy" (G, 4: 25; T, 49). Nor does Altmann make anything of Mörschel's use of this term in close proximity to the sole reference to Jerusalem in *Jerusalem*. (Mendelssohn uses the term *ceremony* before his encounter with Mörschel, but his decision to deploy it in so conspicuous a place as the second section of *Jerusalem* indicates a desire to transform a term of abuse into one of approbation.) On the back page of a copy of his polemical response to Mendelssohn's book, which is enigmatically entitled *Golgatha und Scheblimini! Von einem Prediger in der Wüsten* (1784), Hamann suggests that, for all his enlightenment, Mendelssohn remains in the dark about his decision to name his treatise after the city: "Why he named his writing after a *destroyed city* no critic has yet bothered to ask, and perhaps the author himself does not know" (*Schriften*, 8: 353). But there is no mystery here, even if the title, like ceremonial script itself, is so "full of meaning" that it stands outside the horizon of fixed signification: Mörschel challenges Mendelssohn to show why "true divine service" should be linked to Samaria or Jerusalem, and Mendelssohn does precisely that. Another title that would serve the same function would be *Not Samaria*.

14. Mendelssohn's conception of Jewish law as a "mode of writing" has been the point of discussion for a wide range of commentators, from Hegel onward; see his attack on Mendelssohn in "The Spirit of Christianity and Its Fate" (*Hegels theologische Jugendschriften*, 253–54). For a discussion of the relation of *Jerusalem* to Hegel's early writings, see Derrida, *Glas*, 51–57; and Hamacher, *pleroma*, in Hegel, "*Der Geist des Christentums*," 32–35. For an analysis of Mendelssohn's exposition of Jewish law, see Eisen, "Divine Legislation as 'Ceremonial Script.'" For a judicious evaluation of Eisen's essay and the tradition of commentary to which it responds, see Arkush, *Mendelssohn and the Enlightenment*, 212–18.

15. Most commentary on this section of *Jerusalem* has been concerned with Mendelssohn's "supposition" that idolatry originates in the misrecognition of hieroglyphs: the written sign for a specific quality was taken for the quality itself and then transformed into an idol. The provenance of Mendelssohn's theory of hieroglyphs is the massive work of Bishop William Warburton, *The Divine Legation of Moses*; see especially 2: 437. Altmann says of Mendelssohn's "supposition" that it is "the least substantiated of all theories he ever advanced" (*Moses Mendelssohn*, 546). For a recent analysis of Warburton's conjectures, which unfortunately does not consider Mendelssohn's adaptation of them, see J. Assmann,

Moses the Egyptian, 110–12. It should also be emphasized, however, that, for Mendelssohn, alphabetic script—and therefore presumably the script of the biblical text—is as dangerous as hieroglyphic signs, even if the danger runs in the opposite direction. Alphabetic writing does not invite idolatry, to be sure, but it does give rise to something almost as disabling: isolation. Ceremonial practices, by contrast, "have the advantage over alphabetic signs of not isolating the human being, of not making him to be a solitary creature, brooding over writings and books [*über Schriften und Bücher brütenden Geschöpfe*]" (JubA, 8: 184; J, 119). The image of "brooding over writings and books" is not only one of the most pervasive images of the Jew in Christian society, it is also image of the secular scholar. Where the two are combined, there is Moses Mendelssohn. Although for obvious reasons most commentary on this section of *Jerusalem* is drawn toward Mendelssohn's tenuous theory about the origin of idolatry, it is possible to understand this theory as a ruse that allows him to introduce a counterimage of the Jewish man: no longer the one "brooding over writings and books," as if he were a chicken brooding over her eggs; rather, the one who is fully open to, and actively engaged in, a public world—even if this world is, ironically enough, that of publication. For an insightful review of eighteenth-century images of the bookish Jew that closes with a consideration of Mendelssohn's attempt to combat the image of the "brooding Jew" in his preface to Israel ben Manasseh's *Rettung der Juden*, see Kassouf, "The Shared Pain of the Golden Vein."

16. "Very little"—not none—because, as Altmann remarks in his commentary, Mendelssohn conceals a messianic reference in the course of *Jerusalem* when he writes the year 2240 apparently at random; in the Jewish calendar, 2240 C.E. is 6000, which, according to Talmudic tradition, marks the end of the world (JubA, 8: 318–19).

17. For a variety of reasons and with regard to a wide range of passages, commentators on *Jerusalem* are drawn to the word "paradox" in describing Mendelssohn's endeavor. See, for example, Altmann's introduction to his edition of the *Jerusalem* in the complete works (JubA, 8: lix); see also his introductory remarks to the English translation (J, 17). Similar remarks can be found by Jospe, ed. and trans., *Moses Mendelssohn*, 34 and 37; Rotenstreich, *Jews and German Philosophy*, 57; Liebeschutz, "Mendelssohn und Lessing in ihrer Stellung zur Geschichte," 172; and Hinske, "Mendelssohns Beantwortung der Frage."

18. Sorkin strenuously argues that Mendelssohn's work as a whole belongs to the "Andalusian" tradition of Jewish thought; see *Moses Mendelssohn and the Religious Enlightenment*, 13 and *passim*. But the opposition between these positions cannot capture the subtlety and almost perverse complexity of *Jerusalem*, for the specific practice (or "good deed") Mendelssohn promotes is the ever renewable act of conversing about theoretical matters. Speculation in joyous conversation—as opposed to contemplation in blissful isolation—is a good deed in its own right.

19. For an exposition of the Kabbalistic thesis that the letters of the Torah precede the created world, see Scholem, *On the Kabbalah and Its Symbolism*, 32–86; see also A. Assmann, "Prädisposition und Vorgeschichte."

20. Ten sentences later Mendelssohn generalizes Luria's dictum: "But laws cannot be abridged. In them everything is fundamental; and in this regard we might rightly say: to us, all words of Scripture, all of God's commandments and prohibitions are fundamental" (JubA, 8: 168; J, 101).

21. This epithet owes its origin to Mendelssohn's translation, adaptation, and rewriting of Plato's *Phaedo* in 1767; see Altmann, *Moses Mendelssohn*, 140–78.

22. Near the end of the dialogue Socrates asks Phaedrus: "is there another sort of discourse that is a brother to the written speech, but of unquestioned legitimacy? Can we see how it originates, and how much better and more effective it is than the other? . . . [It is] the sort that goes together with knowledge, and is written in the soul of the learner [*graphetai en tē tou manthanontos psuchē*]" (276a; *Collected Dialogues*, 521).

23. For a detailed account of the context with which Mendelssohn rejects Lessing's proposals concerning the "Education of the Human Race," see Breuer, "Of Miracles and Events Past," esp. 40–45.

24. Although Rosenzweig criticizes Mendelssohn for having chosen to translate the tetragrammaton by *der Ewige* (see note 5, above), his own efforts in *The Star of Redemption* are not so different in principle from the procedures Mendelssohn adopts in *Jerusalem*, even if the two endeavors have vastly different conceptions of both time and language.

25. The absence of any legacy among Mendelssohn's followers among the Maskilim has been decisively demonstrated by Sorkin, *The Transformation of German Jewry*, 79–104.

26. Arkush persuasively argues for such a view in *Moses Mendelssohn and the Enlightenment*, 133–239.

27. See Hamann, *Golgatha und Scheblimini!* reprinted in *Hauptschriften erklärt*, 7: 128.

28. It would far exceed the bounds of a note even to outline Kant's curious and complicated response to Mendelssohn's writings. Suffice it to say that Kant waits until Mendelssohn dies before he decisively and explicitly refutes the proofs of immortality proffered in his *Phaidon*. Only in the second edition of the *Critique of Pure Reason*, which was published a year after Mendelssohn's death, does Kant find space for this refutation—as if he waited for the Jewish philosopher to die in order to prove that he is dead after all, destroyed (so to speak) by the "all-destroying Kant." And Kant was by no means sanguine about *Jerusalem*: he returns to this treatise in order to refute it again—or from another perspective. Something clearly bothered Kant about *Jerusalem*, and it is not difficult to identify one source of his irritation: by presenting *the law* as a revelation and thus giv-

ing primacy to "holy" practice, *Jerusalem* anticipates the breakthrough that Kant believes he achieves two years later in his *Groundwork for the Metaphysics of Morals* (1785): holiness is found in a revealed law, and nowhere else. In a text first published in 1959 (entitled the "Krakauerfragment"), Kant indicates that he is even more troubled by Mendelssohn's denial of historical progress than he elsewhere acknowledges ("On the Common Saying," one subtitle of which is "Against Moses Mendelssohn," Ak, 8: 307–9; "Ein Reinschriftsfragment zu Kants *Streit der Fakultäten*"). When Kant published the text for which the "Krakauerfragment" serves as a draft, he replaced Mendelssohn's view of history with that of the Hebrew prophets whose voices are lost in the wilderness; in this way, Kant links Mendelssohn with his great antagonist, Hamann, whose *Golgatha und Scheblimini!* is subtitled *From a Preacher in the Desert.*

Chapter 3: "The Scale of Enthusiasm"

1. See Plato, *Ion* in *Opera*, 539b; *Two Comic Dialogues*, 21. The statement that the *Ion* contains Plato's first use of the term *entheos* is not without controversy, of course; see Moore, "The Dating of Plato's *Ion*."

2. Socrates' speech thus speaks of itself: it is not grounded in a recognizable *technē*, and to the extent that it does speak of itself, it could belong only to a *technē* of *technē*, which would not itself be a *technē*, but would have to be philosophy— or poetry. After Socrates explains for a second time that poetry consists in being "enthused," Ion is less excited, and makes the following remark: "You speak well, Socrates, but I would be amazed [*thaumazoimi*] if you could speak well enough to convince me that I am possessed and maniacal [*mainomenos*] when I praise Homer" (536d). *Thauma* is the other "explanation" (*aition*) for the scandal of singularity; but *thaumazein* explains *philosophical* speech: how someone can come to ask about *physis* as such. That Ion is not "amazed" means that he is "enthused."

3. In the *Cratylus*, Socrates explains the iota of *ion* (infinitive, *ienai*) as an expression of "subtle elements that pass through all things. This is why he [the one who has mastered the *technē* of speaking] uses the letter iota to mimic motion, *ienai, iesthai*" (426d). Ion (whom no one has yet been able to identify with any historical figure) passes through all *poleis*. From Socrates' perspective, he is less a subtle element than an unsettling one: an excited ion, in short, in the contemporary sense of the term. Not surprisingly, he is associated with a magnet.

4. The terms "representative" and "spokesman" are used to translate the Greek word *hermeneus*, but it almost goes without saying that both terms are inadequate. For an attempt to translate the "hermeneutic" character of Plato's *hermeneus*, see Nancy, *Le Partage des voix*. For an explication of the "kind" of community in which one-of-a-kinds (singularities) take part, see Agamben, *The Coming Community*.

5. Lessing, "Über eine zeitige Aufgabe: Wird durch die Bemühung kaltblutiger Philosophen und Lucianischer Geister gegen das, was sie Enthusiasmus und Schwärmerei nennen, mehr Böses als Gutes gestiftet. Und in welchen Schranken müssen die Antiplatoniker halten um nützlich zu sein?" (On a timely task: Is more evil than good established by the effort of cold-blooded philosophers and Lucianian minds against that which they call enthusiasm and *Schwärmerei*? And within which limits must the anti-Platonist stop so as to be useful?), reprinted in *Sämtliche Werke*, 16: 297. Less incisive definitions of the term *Schwärmerei* can be found in the *Deutsches Wörterbuch* begun by the Grimm brothers, 9: 2290–93. Luther's attacks on radical sectarians gave direction to the widespread use of this term; see Steck, *Luther und die Schwärmer* and Gritsch, "Luther und die Schwärmer." *Schwärmer* are the ones who cannot belong to any stable society because they want something more than society. They therefore play a particularly important function in a large number of eighteenth-century literary texts in which the limits of civil society were, so to speak, tested for the first time; for an introductory examination of these issues, see Lange, "Zur Gestalt des Schwärmers im deutschen Roman des 18. Jahrhunderts." For a fuller discussion, see La Vopa, "The Philosopher and the *Schwärmer*."

6. The previous quotation comes from a letter that Maternus Renus sent Kant in 1796: "I cannot describe to you how enthusiastically [*enthusiastisch*] people have taken up your principles, even those who otherwise are against them, and even now our ladies have taken them up since we read in a number of newspapers that you have been called to France to act as lawgiver and patron of peace" (Ak, 12: 69). According to Conrad Stang, men rejected Kantian thought, whereas women could be counted on for its dispersion:

> But if the men are struggling so vigorously against critical philosophy, its fortunes are better among the women. You cannot believe how enthusiastically [*enthusiastisch*] young ladies and women are taken with your system and how eager they all are to learn about it. There are many women's groups here in Würzburg, where each one is eager to outdo the others in showing knowledge of your system: it is the favorite topic of conversation. (Ak, 12: 100)

The formation of these reading societies deserves attention in the context of any discussion of "Kant and enthusiasm," for the solitary activity of reading, according to Kant, contributes to the spread of *Schwärmerei*. One of Kant's earliest attempts to connect certain mental aberrations, especially "melancholic vapor," with too much reading can be found in the "Essay on the Sicknesses of the Head" (Ak, 2: 266). One of his last attempts in this direction can be found in the concluding chapter of *The Conflict of the Faculties*, "On the Power of the Mind to Master Its Morbid Feelings by Intention Alone." Of particular importance is Kant's open letter to Ernst Borowski, which was later printed as an appendix to his book on Cagliostro (1790): "As I see it, the universally disseminated *mania for reading* [Lesesucht] not only is the guiding instrument (vehicle) in the spread of this disease but also is the poison (miasma) that engenders it" (Ak, 11: 107).

7. Kant's earliest use of the term "enthusiasm" draws it into an even closer relation to freedom or, more precisely, the "love of freedom": "*Enthusiasmus* inspired [*begeistert*] ancient peoples toward great things," and this enthusiasm may be connected to the warming of the earth's surface; see "The Question Whether the Earth Aged, Considered Physically" (1754), Ak, 1: 212. For a brief description of Kant's use of the term *Enthusiasmus* and his attempt to distinguish it from *Schwärmerei*, see my *Peculiar Fate*, 241–43.

8. See Kant, *Critique of Practical Reason*, Ak, 5: 47; for a standard commentary on, and a useful guide to the difficulties of this peculiar phrase, see Beck, *A Commentary on Kant's 'Critique of Practical Reason'*, 166–70. Kant sometimes speaks of the "sole fact [*Faktum*] of pure reason" (e.g. Ak, 5: 31), sometimes of the "fact, as it were, of pure reason" (e.g., Ak, 5: 47), sometimes of "practical data of reason" (e.g., B, xxii and xviii).

9. See the useful concordance assembled by Hinske, "Zur Verwendung der Wörter 'schwärmen,' 'Schwärmer,' 'Schwärmerei,'" 73–81; see also Hinske's introductory essay to *Die Aufklärung und die Schwärmer*. Within the context of the anthropological writings, *Schwärmerei* generally includes a moment of unbound imagination: "The originality (not imitated production) of imagination [*Einbildungskraft*], if it harmonizes with concepts, is called 'genius'; if it does not harmonize, *Schwärmerei*" (Ak, 7: 172). It is not only in the anthropological writings, however, that Kant refrains from explicating *Schwärmerei* in terms of principles. In the second edition of the *Critique of Pure Reason* Kant accuses Locke of having "opened the door" to *Schwärmerei*, by "sensualizing" concepts (see B, 127–28).

10. Kant, *Critique of Practical Reason*, 88.

11. But Schlosser is only one example—and by no means the most interesting or important one. He is, however, the only one to whom Kant makes an explicit and well-articulated response. It is a common project among a wide variety of Kant's critics in the 1790s to insist, not so much that his moral doctrine be made to fit the limits of humanity, as that it be revised from the perspective of those demands that cannot be formulated according to a categorical command precisely because they do not admit of formally defined limits—demands like "grace" (Schiller), "love" (Hölderlin), or "life" (Hegel).

12. See Johann Georg Schlosser, "Plato's Briefe über die Syrakusianische Staats-Revolution aus dem griechischen übersetzt" (Plato's letters on the revolution in Syracuse, translated from the Greek). Schlosser's translation and commentary was first published in a journal in 1793, then republished as a book in 1795. For a description of the struggle between Schlosser and Kant, see my *Raising the Tone of Philosophy*, esp. 72–76; see also Bubner, *Antike Themen und ihre moderne Verwandlung*, 80–93.

13. Count Friedrich Leopold zu Stolberg, *Auserlesene Gespräche des Platon*; for a brief discussion of Stolberg's concept and practice of enthusiasm, see note 38 below.

14. See Kant, *Logic,* Ak, 9: 25.

15. For a striking example of Kant's use of the word "holy" (*heilig*) to describe the moral law, see the *Critique of Practical Reason,* Ak, 5: 77; for his use of the term "divine" (*göttlich*) in connection with the law, see the *Religion Within the Limits of Reason Alone,* Ak, 6: 113.

16. The first of these novels is Wilhelm Karol von Wobester's *Elisa, oder, das Weib, wie es seyn sollte* (Elisa, or, how a woman should be). This novel was reprinted at least seven times before the turn of the century, and it was translated into French, English, Dutch, and Danish. It gave rise to a swarm of imitators, including a series of counterparts to Elisa's story of "how a woman should be," the first of which was *Robert, oder, der Mann, wie er seyn sollte* (Robert, or, how a man should be). A novel depicting how an officer "should be" soon followed, and so did a parody of the newly invented genre in which a family is shown how it "ought to be." Elisa is closer to a Stoic than to the one who acts according to Kantian moral doctrine, and indeed she conforms to the image of moral *Schwärmerei* that Kant rejects in the *Critique of Practical Reason.* These novels deserve more attention than they have received, since they point toward how Kant's work was interpreted as it first appeared throughout Europe. For a brief description of *Elisa* and a list of the novels to which it gave rise, see Adickes, *German Kantian Bibliography,* 234–36.

17. For an analysis of Kant's discourse of sleeping, dreaming, and awakening, see Fenves, *Peculiar Fate,* 69–80.

18. For an especially rich example, see Kant's exposition of the moral law in terms of a "veiled goddess" in "On a Newly Arisen Superior Tone in Philosophy" (Ak, 8: 405).

19. For the texts of this controversy and accounts of its progress, see the first note to the previous chapter.

20. See Friedrich Jacobi, *Werke,* 3: 44.

21. Kant made notes for an essay on "Philosophical *Schwärmerei*" in which he would trace the development of this disorder from Plato to Spinoza: see *Reflexionen* 6050, Ak. 17: 434–37. "Spinozism is the true conclusion to dogmatic metaphysics. Critique of propositions has no success here. For the difference between the subjective and the objective with respect to their validity cannot be recalled, because the subjective propositions that are at the same time objective have not been previously distinguished" (Ak, 17: 436). Kant's conception of both Plato and Spinoza is, of course, firmly rooted in eighteenth-century commonplaces about these philosophers. Kant's anti-Platonism, which he owes in large part to the historian of philosophy whom he generally relies on (J. J. Brucker; see the

Critique of Pure Reason, A, 316; B, 372), never goes as far as his anti-Spinozism, for Plato—or at least Plato "the academic" (Ak, 8: 62)—poses a genuine philosophical problem, whereas Spinozism, according to Kant, derives from a failure to distinguish subjective and objective propositions. There is one philosopher whom Kant calls an enthusiast whose enthusiasm never gives rise to philosophical *Schwärmerei*; namely, Rousseau. As early as "On the Sicknesses of the Head," Kant calls Rousseau a *Phantast* (Ak, 2: 267), but because Kant presents Rousseau's *Schwärmerei* in terms of moral, not theoretical, positions, he never enters into Kant's accounts of the genesis of contemporary philosophical enthusiasm. For analyses of the early Kant's ambivalent relation to Rousseau, see Velkley, *Freedom and the End of Reason*, 32–44; Shell, *Embodiment of Reason*, 81–87.

22. All references are to the first series of volumes of HKA. Fritz Marti's idiosyncratic translation of *Philosophical Letters* can be found in Schelling, *The Unconditional in Human Knowledge*.

23. In this sense Schelling's *Philosophical Letters* belongs to at least two specific genres: epistolary philosophy, of which Schiller's *Letters on Aesthetic Education* is the most famous example, and the anti-*Schwärmerei* novel. Novels that belong to the later genre set out to describe a cycle of *Schwärmerei*; once the *Schwärmer* has passed through the entire cycle, the novel comes to an end: the hero is "cured" of his "sickness of the head." Wieland's *Geschichte des Agathon* (History of Agathon) is perhaps the best known example of this genre, but it could also be seen to include, with certain important modifications, Hölderlin's *Hyperion*; see Erhart, "'In guten Zeiten giebt es selten Schwärmer.'"

24. *Little* doubt, not *no* doubt. For in the note Schelling added to the *Letters* when he republished them in 1809 he emphasizes something else entirely: the ninth letter contains the "clearest germs of later and more positive views" (HKA, 3: 49). The possibility that the *Letters* were not entirely devoted toward the explication of "criticism" did not escape Fichte, whose "First Introduction" (to the *Wissenschaftslehre*, 1797) consists of a tacit evaluation and refutation of Schelling's exposition of the difference between dogmatism and criticism. A translation of this text, along with a useful guide to the philosophical controversies in which it plays an important role, can be found in Fichte, *Introductions to the Wissenschaftslehre and Other Writings*.

25. "If the *Critique of Pure Reason* spoke against dogmatism, it spoke against dogmaticism, that is, a system of dogmatism that is erected blindly, and without a preceding investigation of the faculty of knowledge" (HKA, 3: 69). Kant had several definitions of "dogmatic," but as Breazeale points out (*Introductions to the Wissenschaftslehre*, xxiii–xxiv), Schelling and Fichte take over the succinct definition of Solomon Maimon: according to Maimon's *Philosophisches Wörterbuch* (1790), dogmatism is the belief that one possesses cognition of things-in-themselves.

26. The Kabbalistic motif of "withdrawal" becomes ever more important in

Schelling's subsequent writings, especially those that are no longer attempts to "elucidate" Fichte's *Wissenschaftslehre*. Of particular interest is his use of the term *Kontraktion* in the so-called *Stuttgarter Privatvorlesung* (1810), in *Sämmtliche Werke*, 7: 429 and *passim*. The "contraction" of which he speaks in these lectures is not, of course, the withdrawal of the I into itself but the withdrawal of God into himself. As Christoph Schulte accurately observes at the beginning of his thorough analysis of this motif, "Schelling never once uses the word *zimzum* [withdrawal] in his works and letters. Nevertheless, *zimzum* is the decisive, dominant, and fundamental conception in some of his most important and influential writings" ("Zimzum bei Schelling," 97).

27. Much has been written about "intellectual intuition" in Kant, Fichte, Schelling, and Hölderlin. For an assessment of what is at stake in this variously spelled term, see Neubauer, "Intellektuelle, intellektuale, und ästhetische Anschauung "; Frank, "'Intellektuale Anschauung.'"

28. And is also perhaps Hölderlin, who, as a young man, wrote a poem entitled "Schwärmerei" (1788), which begins with the apostrophe: "Freunde! Freunde!" It has been suggested that Hölderlin is the addressee of the *Philosophical Letters*; see the introduction to the Bavarian academy edition by Pieper (HKA, 3: 29–34) and the monograph of Wegenast, *Hölderlins Spinoza-Rezeption*, 106–23. Pieper rejects the suggestion, whereas Wegenast argues strenuously for it.

29. In the *Philosophical Letters* Schelling does not draw on the distinction between absolute and transcendental freedom that he had developed in the final sections of *On the I as the Principle of Philosophy*. This distinction may allow him to reformulate the idea of a "*Schwärmerei* of criticism," but Schelling has good reason to avoid it in the last sections of the *Philosophical Letters*. Transcendental freedom *is* absolute in the *active* sense of the term "absolute": to be free in a transcendental sense is to absolve oneself of all relations other than one's own self-relation. Any talk of absolute freedom in contrast to transcendental freedom runs the risk of making the absolute into an inert substance and therefore falling into what Schelling calls "dogmatism."

30. See, for example, the compilation of eighteenth-century examples of *Fittich* in the Grimm brothers' *Deutsches Wörterbuch*, 3: 1693–94. For an example of its contemporaneous use, see the striking lines of the first stanza of Hölderlin's "Patmos," lines that defy translation of sense (*Sinn*) because they are precisely about the translation (and return) of "the most faithful sense": "O Fittige gib uns, treuesten Sinns / Hinüberzugehen und wiederzukehren" (ll. 14–15).

31. Schelling, like Hölderlin, inspired comparison with bees. August von Platen concludes one of his odes to Schelling ("An Schelling, Bei demselben Anlasse") in the following way: "Du aber [in contrast to Platen, who compares himself to a butterfly] taucht die heil'ge Bienenschwinge / Herab vom Saum des Weltenblumenrandes / In das geheimnißvolle Wie der Dinge" (*Gesammelte*

Werke, 2: 95). I thank Arndt Wedemeyer for drawing my attention to von Platen's poem.

32. The degree to which Schelling understood Kant's polemical attack against Schlosser and Stolberg as an attack on every use of the term "intellectual intuition," including his own, can be gauged by his review of the controversy in the *Allgemeine Literatur-Zeitung*, the official organ, as it were, of Kantian thought; see HKA, 4: 283–87.

33. A more thorough investigation into Schelling's disclosure of a "secret, marvelous capacity"—which confirms Nietzsche's suspicion that the young men in the Tübingen Theological Seminary (Hegel, Schelling, and Hölderlin) sought to discover new "capacities" after having read Kant's *Critiques* (*Beyond Good and Evil*, § 11)—would have to consider in detail the theory of modality Schelling proposes in the recently published *Vom Ich als Prinzip der Philosophie* (On the I as the principle of philosophy; 1795). According to Schelling, modal judgments (possibility, actuality, necessity) are not, as Kant argues in the "Principles of Empirical Thought," synthetic but rather "sylleptic" (a term he invents): they do not add anything to the judgments of quality, quantity, and relation; they "take up" (syllepsis) what has already been "posited together" (synthesis). Modal terms cannot therefore be applied to the absolute I, understood as an absolute act of positing; but these terms can then, in turn, serve to describe the *structure* of the I or the unconditioned. (To show how this is done, how the modal terms turn into the "powers" of Schelling's later thought, would be impossible within the confines of this chapter.) The "secret, marvelous capacity" of the I to intuit itself must therefore be understood not as a property of the I but as a moment of its structure: in Schelling's later thought, the unconditioned to the first power (where the term *Potenz*, "power," replaces the Kantian word *Vermögen*, "faculty" or "capacity").

34. This is a reference to Fichte's "Second Introduction" (to the *Foundations of the Entire Wissenschaftslehre*). But this reference points in another direction as well—toward the last widely contested battle among philosophers over the sense and direction of *Schwärmerei*. For it is Fichte who accuses Schelling of *Schwärmerei* after the latter abandons his efforts to "elucidate the idealism of the *Wissenschaftslehre*" and begins to articulate his own philosophy of identity coupled with "natural philosophy" (*Naturphilosophie*): "Contemporary *Schwärmerei*," Fichte writes in 1806, consists in a "reaction" to the formalism and emptiness of current concepts of experience and knowledge. This reaction finds its expression in the speculative *Naturphilosophie* of Schelling and his associates (Ritter, von Baader): *Schwärmerei* "is and will necessarily be *Naturphilosophie*" ("Basic Features of the Present Age" reprinted in Johann Gottlieb Fichte, *Sämmtliche Werke*, 7: 118). Schelling responds almost immediately to this accusation: *Schwärmerei*, he asserts, is rooted in the fundamental insufficiency of the I as the principle of philosophy. "Luther and his contemporaries" invented the term in view of the in-

ability of the isolated subject to ground its activities: "The *Schwärmer* needs someone else in order to confirm his belief; everyone who does not clearly know what he wants swarms. . . . If an inflexible striving to drive home his subjectivity through his own subjectivity and to make it universal, to exterminate all nature wherever possible . . . is called *Schwärmen*, who in these times has in a proper sense 'swarmed' more spitefully and more loudly than Herr Fichte?" ("Laying Out the True Relation of *Naturphilosophie* to the Improved Fichtean Doctrine" [1806], in *Werke*, 7: 45 and 47).

35. He makes good on this promise in the concluding section of the *System of Transcendental Idealism*, but the paradoxes to which the phrase "philosophical spirit" bears witness are not resolved in this section where the "postulate" of intellectual intuition is supposed to find its conclusive demonstration: it should cease to be a sheer demand made on the philosopher to actualize his potential for self-intuition and become, instead, a self-evident axiom or—to use the Aristotelian-Euclidean vocabulary to which the term "postulate" alludes—a "common notion." Artworks are therefore the organon of philosophy; but *the* artwork of which all other ones are merely parts—the artwork of artwork—is and perhaps always will be absent. The absence of this artwork is no small failure: as Schelling indicates in the first footnote to the section on "aesthetics as the organon of philosophy," artworks are by definition something present (*eine Gegenwart*), and only insofar as they are "a present" can they convert the demand for self-intuition into an axiom on which philosophy can henceforth rely; see *Werke*, 3: 614. In the final pages of the *System*, which proudly displays 1800 as the date of its birth, Schelling displaces these paradoxes concerning philosophical spirit onto another epoch. This epoch will find—and be founded on—a "new mythology," which is itself the solution.

36. A translation of Hölderlin's "Reflections" can be found in *Essays and Letters on Theory*, which includes references to Beißner's edition of *Sämtliche Werke*.

37. For analysis of this reception, see Vöhler, "Hölderlins Longin-Rezeption."

38. The first sentence in this quotation is introduced by a *deswegen* (for this reason), which refers to an incomplete sentence concerned with "love." Within the context of the *Phaedrus* and the *Symposium*—the two dialogues to which Hölderlin is particularly drawn—the subject of love cannot be detached from that of "enthusiasm." But any discussion of these texts in relation to Hölderlin would go far beyond the boundaries of this chapter. One representative of late-eighteenth-century Platonism, whose work serves as a point of intersection for the thought of Kant, Goethe, and Hölderlin, is Count Friedrich Leopold zu Stolberg. Like Kant, Goethe rejects his version of Platonism and especially his interpretation of the *Ion* (see *Raising the Tone of Philosophy*, 74–75). Hölderlin never explicitly attacks Stolberg, and there is good reason to think that he learned something about lyric form from his verse; nevertheless, the opening

aphorisms of "Reflections" can be read as an implicit critique of Stolberg's essay "Über die Begeisterung" (1782), which is a direct assault on the Berlin *Aufklärung* (the essay has been reprinted in Stolberg, *Über die Fülle des Herzens*, 32–42). Stolberg translates Plato's *enthousiazein* by *Begeisterung* (34–35); but this translation, he concludes, cannot define the nature of *Begeisterung* itself, for "Enthousiasme ist noch nicht Begeisterung. Inspiration (Eingebung) ist etwas ganz verschiedenes. Der Begeisterte elektisiert, der von Enthusiasmus Erfüllte wird elektrisiert" (*Über die Fülle des Herzens*, 42; for an account of Hölderlin's debt to Stolberg, see Gaier, *Hölderlin*, esp. 414–16).

39. Throughout his theoretical writings Hölderlin uses the term *Erkenntnis* for philosophical knowledge; see especially the proposition he poses in the so-called "Verfahrungsweise des poetischen Geistes" (a proposition that can be read as a direct response to the section of Schelling's *System of Transcendental Idealism* on "art as the organon of philosophy"): "Just as the knowledge [i.e., philosophy] intimates the language [i.e., poetry], thus does the language remember the knowledge" (SW, 4: 261). One of Hölderlin's most often cited versions of the same thought can be found in the final chapter of the first book of *Hyperion*: "Poetry, I [Hyperion] said, certain of my matter at hand, is the beginning and end of this [philosophical] science" (SW, 3: 81). The letter in which Hyperion relates his certainty with regard to the beginning and end of philosophy is addressed to a certain Bellarmin, which is to say, "The Beautiful German" (Bell-Arminius). Schelling was known as a young man to be quite beautiful, and for this reason (among others) it is possible to read the addressee of this remark as Schelling.

40. Evidence for this dissatisfaction can be found in many quarters. Of particular interest is a novel by Johann Jung-Stilling, *Theobald, oder, die Schwärmer, eine wahre Geschichte*. The editors of the *Deutsches Wörterbuch* note a "transformation of the strict meaning into a milder one during the last quarter of the eighteenth century" (*Deutsches Wörterbuch*, 15: 2292), and they cite some lines from Goethe to demonstrate this tendency. In one of his *Venetianische Epigramme*, however, Goethe demonstrates that he could use this term with the same degree of invective fury as Luther himself—but with the opposite intention: "Jeglichen Schwärmer schlagt mir an's Kreuz im dreißigsten Jahre; / Kennt er nur einmal die Welt, wird der Betrogne der Schelm" [Let me have every *Schwärmer* nailed to the cross in his thirtieth year; if he ever gets familiar with the world, the deceived becomes a deceiver] (*Werke*, 1: 179). In other words, Jesus, the arch-*Schwärmer*, should have been crucified *before* he took up his "enthusiastic" mission. Goethe's poem plays an important role in Hölderlin's "An den klugen Ratgeber" (To the clever advisor), for it allows him to respond to Schiller's "clever advice" that he limit his enthusiasm and seek out concrete objects for his poetry (see his letter of November 24, 1796).

41. Novalis writes his "Apologie der Schwärmerei" (sometime between 1788

and 1790) in order to attack "apostles of enlightenment and preachers of reason" (*Schriften*, 2: 20–22); Novalis's youthful note is primarily directed against Wieland's essay "Enthusiasmus und Schwärmerei," in *Teutscher Merkur*, 1775.

42. Hölderlin almost repeats the point on which Kant first distinguishes enthusiasm from *Schwärmerei*: "nothing great in the world has been done without it" (Ak, 2: 267).

43. "Objectivity as such" cannot mean the counterpart of subjectivity. Since "pure, great objects" are defined in relation to "something true and real," and since this "something" is a singularity of which both truth and reality are its predicates, these "pure, great objects" cannot simply be objects *for* a subject; they must be objects as such, objects before the distinction between subject and object. The term Hölderlin uses for this "before"—as absolutely original a priori— is "being" (*Seyn*). See the much-discussed fragment that often goes under the misleading title "Urteil und Sein" (SW, 4: 216–17).

44. The following would be easy to say: the "pure, great objects" and the "other kinds of being" about which Hölderlin here speaks are "the gods"; knowing the relation between gods and human beings is the basis of everything "poetic"; poetry, as a result, is "mythological," and mythology is from its inception poetic (the last terms are taken from a fragment of a philosophical treatise in epistolary form which Hölderlin probably wrote around 1797 and which has been called "On Religion," esp. SW, 4: 280–81). All of this is, as far as it goes, correct; but since each of the words in quotation marks means something very specific to Hölderlin, and all of them deviate from their colloquial usage, saying something like this would be more misleading than informative. The same can be said of another correct statement: the *Schwärmer* is the term Hölderlin uses in "Reflections" to designate what he elsewhere calls "the half-gods" (*Halbgötter*). The complicated relation between the *Schwärmer* and the *Halbgott* is directly presented at the end of the central stanza of "Der Rhein." In these lines, Hölderlin indicates that Herakles is condemned to destroy his own house because he is the one who "sein will und nicht / Ungleiches dulden, der Schwärmer" (wants to be and will not bear inequality, the *Schwärmer*) (SW, 2: 145). There is no more incisive "definition" of *Schwärmerei* than the following: *Schwärmerei* are those who do not simply want to be equal to absolutely pure beings—or equivalent to being, pure and simple— but want also *to be* without accepting the condition for the *demonstrability of being*, namely "inequality," or to use a term Hölderlin elsewhere favors, "difference."

45. "In the philosophical letters I want to find the principle that explains to me the divisions in which we think and exist, yet which is also capable of dispelling the conflict between subject and object, between our self and the world, even between reason and revelation—theoretically, in intellectual intuition, without our practical reason having to come to our aid. We need aesthetic sense for this, and I will call my philosophical letters 'New Letters on the Aesthetic Edu-

cation of Man'" (SW, 6: 202–3). In this same letter Hölderlin indicates in very subtle terms that he finds Schelling's *Philosophical Letters* unacceptable (presumably because it seeks a ground for philosophical knowledge in practical reason).

46. Since Hölderlin was "rediscovered" in the early part of this century, scholars have staged elaborate arguments about the function and significance of the term *Geist* (spirit) in his work—whether it should be understood in light of Hegel's *Phenomenology of Spirit* or as another name for "the coming God" ("Brot und Wein"). For an analysis of "Reflections" in relation to the theological themes in which Hölderlin was educated, see Dierauer, *Hölderlin und der spekulative Pietismus Württembergs*, esp. 34–44.

47. For an incisive analysis of intensive magnitudes, see Anneliese Maier, *Das Problem der intensiven Grösse in der Scholastik.* (I thank Daniel Heller-Roazen for alerting me to this work.)

Chapter 4: On a Seeming Right to Semblance

1. See Kant, *Opus postumum*, in Ak, 22: 320–26; 22: 357–59; English ed., 107–10, 115–17. In the first set of reflections the appearance of appearance is understood in terms of concept formation; in the second, in terms of the subject, whose body allows for a transition from the metaphysics of natural science.

2. Nietzsche, "How 'the True World' Finally Became a Fable," in *Twilight of the Idols*, in *Sämtliche Werke*, 6: 81.

3. See the four-volume collection, François Gayot de Pitaval, *Merkwürdige Rechtsfälle als ein Beitrag zur Geschichte der Menschheit* (Remarkable legal cases as a contribution to the history of humanity), edited by Schiller; the "French work of Pitaval" is his popular twenty-six-volume *Causes celebres et interessantes, avec les jugements qui les ont decidées.* Schiller also wrote an introduction for a volume by his fellow Swabian, Immanuel Niethammer, who, as a friend of Schelling, Hegel, and Hölderlin, and as editor of the *Philosophisches Journal* played an important role in the transformation of Kantian critique. Schiller also edited one volume of a planned four-volume *Geschichte der merkwürdigsten Rebellionen und Verschwörungen aus den mittlern und neueren Zeiten* (History of remarkable rebellions and conspiracies from the medieval ages and modern times). For an insightful analysis of Schiller's attraction to the "sensational," see Bloch, "The Art of Speaking Schiller," in *Literary Essays*, 83–86. As Rainer Kawa indicates, making Schiller's story into the beginning of German "criminal literature" is a dubious enterprise; see Kawa, *Friedrich Schiller*, 25–26; nevertheless, as the German editor of Pitaval's collection, Schiller did play a significant role in promoting "crime stories" during the early 1790s.

4. See Schiller, "Was heißt und zu welchem Ende studiert man Universalgeschichte" (NA, 17: 359–76). For a lucid exposition of Schiller's early attraction

to Kant's philosophy of history, which predates his interest in his *Critiques*, see Reed, *Schiller*, 51–61.

5. A characteristically precise exposition of the distinction between legal and moral philosophy can be found at the opening of Kant's *Metaphysic of Morals* (1797–98): "Duties in accordance with rightful [*rechtlich*] lawgiving can only be external duties, since this lawgiving does not require that the idea of this duty, which is internal, itself be the determining ground of the agent's choice; and since it still needs an incentive suited to the law, it can connect only external incentives with it" (Ak, 6: 227). But Kant, of course, was hardly alone in devising systems of laws. The same is true of Fichte, Schelling, and Hegel—to name only the most famous philosophers immersed in reflection on the relation of legality to morality and "first philosophy." In the letter to von Augustenburg in which Schiller announces his intentions, he refers to the fervent study of the foundations of jurisprudence (NA, 26: 184; 9 February 1793). The years in which Schiller worked out the *Aesthetic Letters* coincide with the years during which the decision was made about the implementation of the first great code of laws since Justinian's Digesta: Prussia's *Allgemeines Landrecht* of 1794.

6. See the remarks of Wilkinson and Willoughby in their edition of *On the Aesthetic Education of Man*, 300.

7. On the reflexive use of *herschreiben*, see the Grimms' *Deutsches Wörterbuch*, 10: 1164.

8. For a lucid discussion of the disputes about the nature of property and property rights, see Ryan, *Property and Political Theory*.

9. Schiller is hardly a stranger to such *coups de théâtre*, since *Der Geisterseher*, to say nothing of his early dramatic work, is built out of them. Furthermore, Schiller would have been familiar, of course, with Goethe's attempt in *Der Groß-Cophta* (1791) to understand the Revolution as something like a *coup de théâtre*.

10. In preliminary notes on "method" for the *Aesthetic Letters*, Schiller indicates the direction he would take a study of natural law: "Aus dieser seiner Natur [mächtig, gewaltsam, listig, geistreich] und nicht aus seiner vernünfitgen müßte das Naturrecht und die Politik deduciert werden" (NA, 21: 90). Needless to say, Kant took a very different position, to which Schiller seems to respond in *Wallenstein*; see Guthke, *Schillers Dramen*, 204. The test case for Schiller's conception of natural right is, of course, *Wilhelm Tell*. For some inquiries into the immense field of questions raised by the issue of natural versus positive law and the codification of the latter, see Gierke, *Natural Law and the Theory of Society*; Koselleck, *Preußen zwischen Reform und Revolution*; Hans Hattenhauer, *Europäische Rechtsgeschichte*; Ziolkowski, *The Mirror of Justice*, 187–214; Schneewind, *The Invention of Autonomy*, 17–166. An informative guide to juridical discourse (and practice) in Germany can be found in Hattenhauer, *Die geistesgeschichtlichen Grundlagen des deutschen Rechts*.

11. For a recent description of the Schlegel brothers' evenings in which they would lampoon Schiller's poetry, see Boyle, *Goethe,* 2: 646. See de Man, "Kant and Schiller," in *Aesthetic Ideology,* 129–62. For an analysis of the vicissitudes of Schiller's reception, with particular emphasis on those who find Schiller ridiculous, see the introductory chapter of Guthke, *Schillers Dramen,* 11–30.

12. On the general trope of personification (understood as *fictio personae*) in relation to the specific tropes of prosopopoeia and eidolopoeia, see Lausberg, *Handbuch der literarischen Rhetorik,* 1: 411–13. As Lausberg notes, the French *personnifaction* is an eighteenth-century invention (2: 932), and the same seems to be true of both the corresponding English and German words (*personification* and *Personifikation*). The German term also, or primarily, means "impersonation." For an analysis of the function of prosopopoeia, see de Man, "Autobiography as De-Facement," in *Rhetoric of Romanticism.* For a complementary exposition of the poetico-legal character of prosopopoeia, apostrophe, and personification, see Johnson, "Double Mourning and the Public Sphere," in *The Wake of Deconstruction.* In the latter, Johnson reflects on the function of de Man's own tendency toward prosopopoeia, and she quotes one use of the trope that, strangely enough, echoes Schiller's *Schein*: "allegory designates primarily a distance in relation to its own origin, and, *renouncing the nostalgia and the desire to coincide,* it establishes its language in the void of this temporal difference" (33; Johnson's emphasis).

13. On the transition from the *Curfürstlich badische gnädigst priviligierte Landkalender für die badische Markgrafschaft lutherischen Anteils* to the almanac edited by Hebel, see Friedrich Voit, *Vom "Landkalendar" zum "Rheinländischen Hausfreund" Johann Peter Hebels.*

14. See Heidegger, *Hebel—der Hausfreund,* 12.

15. Quoted in Kully, "Johann Peter Hebel als Theoretiker," 172.

16. An English translation of the stories discussed in this chapter can be found in Hebel, *The Treasure Chest.* The Zundel brothers appear in the following eight stories: "Die drey Diebe" (1809; H, 2: 153–56; "The Three Thieves," *Treasure Chest,* 57–60); "Wie der ZundelFrieder und sein Bruder dem rothen Dieter abermal einen Streich spielen" (1810; H, 203–5; "How Freddy Tinder and His Brother Played Another Trick on Carrot-Top Jack," 82–83); "Der Heiner und der Brassenheimer Müller" (1810; H, 217–20; "Harry and the Miller from Brassenheim," 95–97); "Wie der ZundelFrieder eines Tages aus dem Zuchthaus entwich und glücklich über die Gränzen kam" (1811; H, 254–55; "How One Day Freddy Tinder Escaped from Prison and Came Safely over the Border," 112–13); "Der Lehrjunge" (1812; H, 3: 336–37; "The Apprentice Boy," 128); "Die Tabaksdose" (1812; H, 3: 339–40; "The Snuffbox," 129–30); "Wie sich der Zundelfrieder hat beritten gemacht" (1813; H, 374–79; "How Freddy Tinder Got Himself a Horse to Ride," 130–34); "List gegen List" (1815; H, 3: 481–84; "Cunning Meets Its Match," 147–49).

17. Voss, "Die drei Diebe" (original published in *Musenalmanach für 1791*); in *Sämmtliche poetische Werke*, 5: 195–209.

18. See Wolf, *Vom Wesen des Rechts in deutscher Dichtung*, 181–221. The chapter on Hebel was originally given as a lecture in Freiburg in May 1941 and published in 1942. It is an understatement to say that Wolf's interpretations of German literature are Heideggerian; the section on Stifter is dedicated to Heidegger, and almost every pronouncement in the book parodies those Heideggerian *Erläuterungen* through which the *Wesen* of (German and Greek) *Dichtung* is supposed to resonate. But unlike Heidegger—or the Heidegger who speaks of Hebel—Wolf concerns himself with *Recht*, and in response to the implicit question "who is the friend of the *Zuchthaus?*" he does not hesitate to answer "Hebel":

> Es kann daher nicht verwundern, daß wir bei Hebel, unangefochten von Zeitströmungen, ein konservatives Festhalten an überlieferten Straf- und Justizreformen finden. Das Hängen für Diebstahl is selbstverständlich. . . . Auch wird sie öffentliche Strafe als ein mit dem Zuchthaus notwendig verbundener Erziehungsfaktor erwähnt.* (187–88)

The footnote then refers to the stories of the Zundel brothers (219). Wolf gives no indication how he arrived at the notion that the *Zuchthaus* functions as an *Erziehungsfaktor*, especially since the Zundel brothers learn nothing, least of all discipline (on the contrary). The point of these stories, for Wolf, lies not in the justification of the space of *Zuchthaus* but in the space he (and of course, he is not alone in this in 1941) calls *Lebensraum*: "*Auch das Unrecht*—erkennt er—*hat seinen Lebensraum*" (204; Wolf's emphasis). The chapter on Hebel then turns toward the justification of *Lebensraum* in which injustice reigns, until it issues into some concluding remarks whose very title is reminiscent of the Heideggerian origin of Wolf's legal project, "Die Grenzen des Im-Recht-seins." Interpreting "Heimliche Enthauptung" (a story in which a henchman is forced to execute a woman in secret, without knowing anything of the process that led her to be sentenced to death by anonymous judges, or tyrants), Wolf arrives at a formulation for the delimitation of the *Lebensraum* of injustice and calls it "history":

> Das "Gesetz", was sie [Macht] damit erfüllt, ist das Gesetz der Geschichte, die weder gut noch böse, aber notwendig ist. . . . Diese ursprüngliche Einsicht des abendländischen Geistes [Wolf has just quoted Heraclitus in a Heideggerian translation] hat Hebel geahnt und zugleich ein Sinnbild der unaufhebbaren Dialektik von Macht und Recht in der Geschichte der sündigen Menschen mit seiner Erzählung vor uns aufgerichtet. (213)

Wolf may say that the dialectic of might and right is *unaufhebbar*, but the recourse to the necessity of history belies this judgment: *history* justifies the secret beheading of a blindfolded woman by anonymous men. When Heidegger himself turns to Hebel, he seems to forget everything of Wolf's lecture, especially its disturbing appeal to Hebel as one who, as a self-conscious conservative and an unconscious spokesman of the oldest Western wisdom, justifies outrageous violence in the name of *Lebensraum*. But this is not because Heidegger has forgotten Wolf; on the contrary, in the controversy after the war about his role as rector, Heidegger appeals to Wolf as one who can vouchsafe for the uprightness of his character; see Ott, *Martin Heidegger*, 238. Wolf, author of *Richtiges Recht im nationalsozialistischen Staate*, was the one whose academic escapades forced Heidegger's resignation from the post of rector; see Ott, 236–49.

19. The integration of the story into a narrative of punitive practices is not so easily accomplished, for the term *Zuchthaus* no longer meant what it says: whereas *Zuchthaus* indicates some form of "correctional," disciplinary, or even educational institution—and its use during much of the eighteenth century tended in this direction—by the beginning of the nineteenth *Zuchthäuser* were generally considered worse, more punitive and less "correctional," than *Gefängnisse*; see the entry of Gustav Rosenhagen in the Grimm brother's *Deutsches Wörterbuch*, 16: 267: "allmählich aber wird es [Zuchthaus] die schärfere strafanstalt zur verbüszung von verbrechen, im gegensatz zum gefängnis, und gilt so seit anfang des 19. jh im amtlichen wie allgemeinen gebrauch. . . . zuchthaus ist die freiheitsstrafe, in neuerer zeit die der verschärften form." For an account of the character of *Zuchthaüser* in Baden during the nineteenth century, see Rudolf Quanter, *Das deutsche Zuchthaus- und Gefängniswesen von den ältesten Zeiten bis in die Gegenwart*, esp. 187. All of the German states, especially Prussia, according to Quanter, fell behind the English and Americans (particularly the Pennsylvania prison "reformation" undertaken by the Quakers). In contrast to Rosenhagen, however, Quanter emphasizes that *Zuchthaüser* of the early part of the century functioned as houses in which its inhabits were disciplined, if not educated: "denn es war in Wirklichkeit ein Haus, in dem arbeitsscheues Gesindel zu arbeitsamen Leuten erzogen werden sollte" (122). Quanter, who, as far as I know, is the last writer to develop a systematic account of the history of prisons in German-speaking countries, argues for the virtues of the modern prison reforms initiated in London by John Howard (1726–90). As a champion of the "reformation" and "systemization" of prisons during the nineteenth century, Quanter functions, so to speak, as the counterpole to the account of the French penal system that Foucault presents in *Surveiller et punir*.

20. Benjamin, "Johann Peter Hebel" (*Westdeutsche Allgemeine Zeitung*, 1926); reprinted in GS, 1: 278; W, 1: 429. Benjamin describes Zundelfrieder as a figure "from the rebellious, enlightened, minor bourgeoisie of the Rhenish states around the turn of the century" (GS, 2: 326). He also notes that Hebel comically identifies himself with the world of thievery when, in response to the report of a phrenologist, he asks "'The thief organ?'" (GS, 2: 278). A full analysis of Benjamin's relation to Hebel would require more space than a note; but its importance can be judged by his description of Hebel's humor as "applied justice" (GS, 2: 628).

21. In a letter to Friedrich Hitzig (presumably from February 1797), Hebel recounts his experience with Kant. It appears to be the opposite of Kleist's—but appearances are deceptive; see *Werke*, 2: 221. Hebel's early "protean" experiments constitute something like protection against the infection of philosophical reflection, but this protection only works as long as Hebel is able to accept the systematic results of Kantian philosophy, as it was debated in the *Atheismusstreit* of the late 1790s—that the I on which everything rests turns out to be either God or nothingness.

22. For a description of *Zuchthaüser* in Baden, which was in many ways one of the more "progressive" German regimes, see Quanter: "The prisoners are locked up together in a basementlike room. Nowhere is there the slightest trace of comfort" (*Das deutsche Zuchthaus- und Gefängniswesen*, 147–48). According to Quanter, the *Zuchthaüser* of the early part of the eighteenth century were not essentially different from the ones in operation at the end of the seventeenth century.

23. As Driehorst points out, the narrator replaces Zundelheiner with Zundelfrieder as the protagonist of the story "Der Heiner und der Brassenheimer Müller"; see Driehorst, "Hebels Diebesgeschichte," 23–24.

24. In the introduction to a talk he gave to the Theologische Gesellschaft in 1804 under the title "Über den Ausdruck der heiligen Schrift: *Dieb in der Nacht*" (On the expression of the Holy Scripture, "Thief in the night"), Hebel compares "exegetical eyes" to those of the cockroach: both are "wondrously bright, where everything is at its darkest"; see Hebel, *Sämtliche Werke*, 4: 318. But "exegetical eyes" are also like those of the Witch of Endor, which see "something where *nothing* is [*Etwas, wo* Nichts *ist*]." For the expression "thief in the night," see 1 Thess. 5:2: "For you yourselves know very well that the day of the Lord will come like a thief in the night." On the relation between this talk and the thieves in his stories, including those in his *Biblische Geschichten*, see Thomas Schestag, *Para*, esp. 223–58.

25. Hebel's vocabulary recalls that of Kafka, especially "Die Verwandlung" (Metamorphosis)—not only the reference to *Anwandlung des Wunsches* (impulse of a wish), but also, of course, the *Ungeziefer* (vermin, insects) with whom the Jews live. On this passage, see the remarks of Bloch, "Afterword to Hebel's *Schatzkästlein*," in *Literary Essays*, 154. A fuller evaluation of Hebel would require a detailed analysis of the Jewish figures in his calendar—from the upright Moses Mendelssohn (H, 151, whose name Hebel misspells) to the crafty thieves whom Zundelfrieder, in his last appearance, outwits (H, 3: 481–84). And it would similarly have to examine the function of the "Morgenland" (East, land of the morning) in Hebel's work, since the "thievery" of the Jews, including that of the apostle who speaks of the "thief in the night," is rooted, according to Hebel, in their "morning-land" character and origin; see H, 3: 609. That Hebel refers to the moon in the context of the Messiah indicates that he may be reflecting on the im-

plication of this verse from Deutero-Isaiah: "The sun shall be no more your light by day; nor for brightness shall the moon give light to you; but the Lord shall be to you an everlasting light, and your God your glory" (Isa. 60:19). This passage reworks an earlier one: "Moreover the light of the moon shall be as the light of the sun, and the light of the sun shall be sevenfold, as the light of seven days, on the day that the Lord binds up the breach of his people, and heals the stroke of their wound" (Isa. 30:26). Although Hebel would not have known it—or would he have?—the moon is one of the principal elements of the *Zohar*'s exposition of the divine countenance, for it is the symbol of the Shekinah in exile, and the moon is, for the pseudonymous author of the *Zohar*, also the first calendar maker; see *Zohar*, 1: 19a–20a (standard pagination); on the symbolism of the moon in the *Zohar*, see Scholem, *On the Kabbalah and Its Symbolism*, 107–8, 151–53. Whether Hebel might have heard of this often mentioned but little read mystical book is an open question.

26. Christian Wolf is associated with the sun, because his criminal pseudonym is *Sonnenwirt*, named after the inauspicious inn run by his family. The emphasis on "Ehre" (honor) in Hebel's story leaves little doubt that the character of the lighthearted Zundelfrieder is a parody—or perhaps even a travesty—of Schiller's story; see "Der Verbrecher aus verlorener Ehre: Eine wahre Geschichte" (NA, 16: 7–29). The famous last line of Schiller's story, "Ich bin der Sonnenwirt" (NA, 16: 29), is echoed in each of the last three stories of Zundelfrieder: "ich bin der Zundelfrieder sagte er" (H, 3: 336); "der bin ich selber" (H, 3: 378); and most conspicuously, "Ich bin der Zundelfrieder" (H, 3: 482) in the last of the stories, "List gegen List." Incidentally, *Die Räuber* includes at least two similar moments: an innocent man is tortured into saying "er sey der Spiegelberg" (NA, 3: 54), and most famously, near the end, Karl Moor says "dieses Opfer bin ich selbst" (NA, 3: 135).

27. See the Holzstich illustration of Zundelfrieder and the soldier in the *Kalender auf das Jahr 1813*. The illustration is probably the work of Hans Kaspar Hegi (the "talented Hegi in Straßburg" whom Hebel mentions in various letters from March 11, 1807, to April 19, 1812). According to Rohner, Hebel designated the exact place in the text where he wanted to place an illustration: "Hebel wollte vom Zeichner keine künstlerische Interpretation, sondern die Sache selbst" (*Kommentarband*, 40).

28. In an anecdote that immediately precedes "Wie sich der Zundelfrieder hat beritten gemacht," the narrator emphasizes, in reverse, the falsifying function of "big ears." See "Der Nachtwächter von Neuhausen," the last lines of which are: "Der geneigte Leser verstehts, was er [der Wächter] meinte mit den großen Ohren" (H, 3: 373). Large ears belong to a certain "Müller von Brassenheim," who is familiar to the *Hausfreund*'s readership because of his encounter with Zundel-Heiner in "Der Heiner und der Brassenheimer Müller" (H, 2: 217–20).

29. A translation of "The Earthquake in Chili" can be found in Kleist, *The Marquise of O—— and Other Stories*, 51–66. Kleist punctuates the story with theodicical reflections, some of which are far less nuanced: for example, the two lovers, Josephe and Jeronimo, "were very moved when they thought how much misery had to come over the world so that they would be happy" (SWB, 2: 150). As a whole, the story can be understood as a response to what Kant called "the failure of all philosophical attempts in theodicy." Kant published an essay with this title in 1791 (Ak, 8: 255–71); thirty-five years earlier, he had written three essays on the earthquake in Lisbon (Ak, 1: 417–72), one of which, as Helmut Sembdner points out, entrusts to "more capable hands" a story of the human dimensions of the earthquake that shook the European imagination like no other (see SWB, 2: 903; Kant, Ak, 1: 434; for an account of the effect of the earthquake on contemporaneous literature, see Weinrich, *Literatur für Leser*, 64–76). The theodicical character of Kleist's story reaches even deeper, however, for, as Hamacher notes, it is built from elements of an apparently anti-"optimistic" and decidedly anti-Leibnizian narrative: "important aspects of the thematic content of Kleist's story can already be found in a series of scenes from *Candide* and that these scenes are themselves travesties of clichés Voltaire had encountered in contemporary literary productions" (*Premises*, 265).

30. The story first appeared under the title "Jeronimo und Josephe. Eine Scene aus dem Erdbeben zu Chili, vom Jahr 1647" (*Morganblatt für gebildete Stände*, September 10–15, 1807). Kleist was in a French prison when he entrusted the manuscript of the story to his friend Rühle von Lilienstern. On the history of the story's publication, see Appelt and Grathoff, *Erläuterungen und Dokumente*, 80–91. Appelt and Grathoff reproduce an interesting nineteenth-century retelling, discovered by Sembdner, in which Jeronimo and Josephe do in fact come "happily over the border" (*Erläuterungen und Dokumente*, 109–11).

31. Investigations into the conception of law Kleist develops in his stories often concentrate, for obvious reasons, on "Michael Kohlhaas." Of the many interpretations of this story, two recent and starkly contrasting ones are instructive, for they both seek to bring "The Earthquake in Chile" into line with their analyses of "Michael Kohlhaas." (1) In the course of showing the exemplary status of the example in law and literature, J. Hillis Miller reduces the conclusion of "The Earthquake in Chile" to a familiar (and unsupportable) theme—the return of the law in all its forms: "In 'The Earthquake in Chili' a great earthquake briefly suspends, in an idyllic interlude, the implacable operation of social, civil, moral, and ecclesiastical law. All these laws return with a vengeance in the final scene" ("Laying Down the Law in Literature," 1495). Miller does not indicate how the operation of the moral law is suspended during the idyllic interlude, and it is similarly unclear how any form of *law*—as opposed to pre- or extralegal representation of supposedly divine vengeance—returns in the final scene. (2) In the

course of an extensive examination of Kleist's work in light of Prussia's *Allge-meines Landrecht*, Ziolkowski argues that Kleist "believed that he could find this social order in the *ALR* and, by analogy, in the codifications of any society that he was depicting in his works. Accordingly the existing positive law is almost always affirmed again at the end" (Ziolkowski, *The Mirror of Justice*, 211). In support of this view Ziolkowski makes the following claim:

> Over and over again at the end of these literary works the legal system that prevailed at the beginning is reinstated: that is, law and the sense of right wrenched apart through the plot come together in a renewed sense of justice and the social order. In "The Earthquake in Chili" Don Fernando and Donna Elvire remain in South America and continue to live with their adopted son under the same law that at the beginning plunged his parents, Jeronimo and Donna Josephe, into misfortune. (210)

This is a statement that, as a plot summary, may be correct (the identity of the "real" father of "their adopted son" is far from clear), but in any case it does not support the thesis that a "renewed sense of justice and social order" obtains at the end. Ziolkowski, moreover, reads the failed intervention of the marine officer as though he, who has no *civil* authority, were a representative of the legal order: "And at the end it is again a representative of the Church—this time, to be sure, a Dominican monk—who stirs up the people against the young couple, despite the attempts of civil law in the person of a military officer to restore order" (212). If only Don Alonzo had not hesitated and had indeed tried to restore order! But that would be another story than the one Kleist wrote. And it is in any case unclear how *civil* law can appear "in the person" of a *military* officer. Ziolkowski is, I believe, far closer to the heart of the matter in his earlier remarks on the story: "What is doubted or made ambiguous [in "The Earthquake in Chili" or "The Foundling"] is not the law but the spiritual meaning of the world, in which law alone provides a semblance of order" (*German Romanticism*, 120). I would only add: the *real* "semblance of order" appears in the semblance of law—and there alone.

32. On the nature of accident (*Zufall*), collapse, and contingency in Kleist's story, see Hamacher, *Premises*, esp. 263–72.

33. See Leibniz, *Flores sparsi in tumulum Papissae*, discussed in the final section of the first chapter.

34. On the nature of Chilean law during the seventeenth century, see Wohl-haupter, *Dichterjuristen*, 1: 521–23. According to Wohlhaupter, who consults the relevant paragraph of Spanish penal law (Partida I, Titl 18, "de los sacrilegios"), the penalty for the *sacriligium carnale* and *fornicatio* is not death but, rather, excommunication, and if it is supposed that the more drastic sentence was imposed by the Inquisition, there would have been "no room for the commuting of the death sentence into a milder form by the viceroy" (523). Wohlhaupter's three-volume work is an unequaled source of information on the legal careers of German writ-

ers and the legal character of their works; for a study of Wohlhaupter's own career, see Hattenhauer's *Rechtswissenschaft im NS-Staat.*

35. There is some reason to understand the genesis of Kleist's story as the intersection of two Kantian essays: "On the Failure of All Philosophical Attempts in Theodicy" (for "The Earthquake in Chili" is concerned with nothing but this failure) and the famous essay against Benjamin Constant, "On a Supposed Right to Lie Out of Love for Human Beings" (Über ein vermeintes Recht zu Lügen aus Menschenliebe) (Ak, 8: 425–30; this essay first appeared in a journal Kleist would have doubtless known, *Berliner Blätter* 10 [6 September 1797]: 301–14). The narrative that Constant (mistakingly) attributes to Kant closely resembles the mise-en-scene of Kleist's story:

> The moral principle 'it is a duty to tell the truth' would, if taken unconditionally and singly, make any society impossible. We have proof of this in the very direct consequences drawn from this principle by a German philosopher, who goes so far as to maintain that it would be a crime to lie to a murderer who asked us whether a friend of ours whom he is pursuing has taken refuge in our house. (Ak, 8: 425)

Don Fernando, who is otherwise the image of Kantian autonomy, lies out of "love for human beings [*Menschenliebe*]"; Don Alonzo, the "marine officer," *hesitates* to play his part in the play spontaneously Don Fernando invents, and the reason for this failure seems to lie in a voice that calls to his "conscience [*Gewissen*]."

36. By means of these "false pretenses" Don Fernando keeps his wife in the dark about the "full extent of the misfortune" (SWB, 2: 159). A large number of interpretations of "Das Erdbeben in Chili" gravitate toward the figure of Don Fernando, who could easily serve as a focal point for an analysis of the history of Kleist's reception. Don Fernando, who is described as "free" from the mob and who turns his back on the Church as he fights off the attack of the "satanic horde," seems to be something like an image of rational autonomy; see, for example, Wittkowski, "Skepsis, Noblesse, Ironie." But Don Fernando is a dubious character to undertake this emancipation, for he is, as Ellis notes, wholly self-centered (*Narration in the German Novelle*, 59–61). Don Fernando is also, as Helmut Schneider points out, strangely unfamiliar to the populace, even though his father is supposed to be the commandant of the city; see "Der Zusammensturz des Allgemeinen," 122. Although Schneider does not say so, it is possible that Don Fernando is not even "really" Don Fernando but an impostor, since, although both he and Josephe insist that everyone knows him, no one seems to be able to say who he is (SWB, 2: 156). Don Fernando's freedom from the mob, moreover, can also be understood as something other than ethical freedom; as an aristocrat, if he *is* an aristocrat and not an impostor, he is "naturally" free of the mob; see Kittler, "Ein Erdbeben in Chili und Preußen."

37. See Kant's famous description in the *Doctrine of Virtue* of conscience as a tribunal (Ak, 6: 437–41). In his epistolary instruction to Wilhelmine von Zenge,

Kleist gives another interpretation of the voice of conscience: "Let no one say that a secret voice tells us clearly what is right. The same voice that calls on the Christian to forgive his enemy calls on the South Sea Islander to roast his, and he piously eats him up. If conviction can justify such acts, should one trust any conviction?" (SWB, 2: 683).

38. See note 36 above. On the inconsistency of Constant and Kant's concomitant sequestering of his name—he, Kant, *is* constant—see my essay, "Politics of Friendship—Once Again."

39. As Werner Hamacher indicates in a footnote to his remarkable essay on Kleist's story, it appears as though *the voice*—not the father—kills Jeronimo; see *Premises*, 285. One may wonder in the context of this story if there is something like "the father himself" outside of a violent voice *claiming* fatherhood, for it is far from certain that even the most obvious of fathers, Jeronimo, is in fact the father of his supposed son.

Chapter 5: Anecdote and Authority

1. For a particularly lucid analysis of the concept of *auctoritas*, see the remarks of the great nineteenth-century scholar of Roman law, Theodor Mommsen, *Römisches Staatsrecht*, esp. 1034–39; for an amplification of Mommsen's insights, see Arendt, *Between Past and Future*, esp. 120–28.

2. See Procopius, *Opera omnia*, vol. 3; *The Secret History*. The title *Anekdota* apparently stems from the lexicographer Suidas.

3. Analyses of "gossip" often remark on the capacity of this amorphous form of discourse to maintain and strengthen a given structure of social relations; for a study of literary texts, see Spacks, *Gossip*; for a social-psychological study, see Thiele-Dohrmann, *Unter dem Siegel der Verschwiegenheit*; see also my "*Chatter*."

4. Palazzi, *Enciclopedia degli anedotti*. Palazzi's original collection of over eleven thousand anecdotes was soon supplemented by three thousand more. For a useful guide to the ambiguous "genre" of the anecdote, see Grothe, *Anekdote*.

5. In a remarkable fragment, or anecdote, entitled "Art of Anecdoting [*Kunst des Anektotisierens*]," Novalis proposes, "History is a great anecdote" (*Fragmente*, 615). Despite its informality, Joel Fineman's "History of the Anecdote" can be understood as a programmatic description of the principles of a "new" historicism: "The anecdote, let us provisionally remark, as the narration of a singular event, is the literary form or genre that uniquely refers to the real" ("History of the Anecdote," 56).

6. For Novalis's reflections on the anecdote, see the note above. For Issac D'Israeli's reflections, see *A Dissertation on Anecdotes* (1793). Perhaps no one has grasped the relation between anecdote and authority more succinctly—more authoritatively and more anecdotally—than Walter Benjamin, who distinguishes

the anecdote from the "constructions of history," on the one hand, and from "newspaper reading," on the other. In comparison to the former, which "commandeers the true life and confine it to barracks," the anecdote enacts a "street insurgence [*Straßenaufstand*]"; in opposition to the former, it leaves no room for "empathy" (GS, 5: 1014; AP, 846; I°, 2; quoted as an epigraph to this chapter). Benjamin's formulations make possible a precise delineation of the lines of conflict around which the anecdotes Kleist publishes in his newspaper form: between the guerrilla tactics of the anecdote, which destroys "larger contexts," and the conciliatory intention of the newspaper, which makes up for the impoverishment of tradition by means of "empathy." No wonder Kleist's anecdotes are attracted toward the fault lines of empathy, where it gives way to inexplicable antipathy and irrepressible horror.

7. The *Berliner Abendblätter* (Evening paper) is the first daily newspaper in German—"daily" except for Sunday. When a young man asks his father asks "why doesn't the *Evening Paper* also come out on Sundays?" the response of the paper provided by Friedrich Baron de la Motte-Fouqué is not so much an answer as a lament: "That in a Christian city, a Christian can ask something like that— I must ponder this and am very gloomy, my son" (BA, 1: 74). A generally reliable translation of Kleist's anecdotes, including "The Beggarwoman of Locarno," can be found in *An Abyss Deep Enough*, 258–92.

8. For an insightful reading of "The Stylus of God," see Jacobs, *Uncontainable Romanticism*, 171–96. Kleist was fond of the phrase "engraved in bronze," and in a sense it summarizes his attitude toward the anecdotes he recounts in his paper. As he writes to Eduard Prinz von Lichnowsky, he wishes one of his stories could be "engraved in bronze" (23 October 1810; SWB, 2: 840). The expression "wert in Erz gegraben zu werden" (worthy to be engraved in bronze) is the subtitle of the first anecdote published in the *Berliner Abendblätter*. The subject matter of this anecdote, "French Justice," also serves as the subject matter for one of the stories Hebel publishes under the anonym of the *Hausfreund*, "Bad Reward" (H, 2: 135). A comparison of Hebel's and Kleist's narrative techniques can be found in Sembdner, *In Sachen Kleist*, 102–8. Sembdner notes that Kleist is more concerned with the political, Hebel with the "universal-human," but he does not relate these concerns to the forms of publication in which their respective narrative techniques develop; see also the detailed reconstruction of Kleist's and Hebel's techniques in Weber, "Zu Heinrich von Kleists Kunst der Anekdote."

9. As Kleist writes in the letter to Eduard Prinz von Lichnowsky discussed in the previous note, the paper "should be a *people's paper* [*Volksblatt*], that is (because there is no center to the nation), a paper for all classes of the people" (SWB, 2: 840). The story to which Prince von Lichnowsky objects is "Anecdote from the Recent War." The previous anecdote, "The Brandy Guzzler and the Berlin Bells," speaks of a "soldier from the former Lichnowsky regiment" (BA, 1: 69). In his

posthumously published "Instruction Manual of French Journalism" Kleist emphasizes the "private" character of journalism: French journalism, he writes, "is the art of making the people believe what the regime considers good" (SWB, 2: 361). "Journalism in general," by contrast, "is the true-hearted and noncaptious [*unverfänglich*] art of instructing the people about what happens in the world. It is an entirely private affair, and all of the purposes of the regime, whatever they may be called, are alien to it" (SWB, 2: 361). For extensive presentations of Kleist's journalistic commitments, practices, and procedures, see Sembdner, *Die Berliner Abendblätter Heinrich von Kleists*, esp. 316–23; see also Aretz, *Heinrich von Kleist als Journalist*.

10. See Hegel, *Phänomenologie des Geistes*, in *Werke*, 3: 145–55; *Phenomenology of Spirit*, 111–19.

11. The magistrate's ability to escape the law that throws him into embarrassment contrasts with Judge Adam's inability to escape a similarly embarrassing law in Kleist's comedy *The Broken Jug*. The situation of "The Embarrassed Magistrates" also bears a close resemblance to the central conflict of *Prince Friedrich von Homburg*: "The law of war [*Kriegsrecht*] had to arrive at death; / Thus reads the law according to which it is judged" (SWB, 1: 670). "The Embarrassed Magistrate" plays out this (suspended) tragedy in miniature; it could even be understood as its anecdotal parody.

12. "The Embarrassed Magistrate" was published on October 4, 1810; "The Beggarwoman of Locarno" on October 11. There is, incidentally, good reason for "The Marquise von O . . . " to return to its earlier, anecdotal status, for the story published in *Tales* turns on the function of newspaper publication (see SWB, 2: 131).

13. Critics who have correctly placed "The Beggarwoman of Locarno" under the rubric of "anecdote" include Emil Staiger in a famous essay in his *Meisterwerke deutscher Sprache*, 103; Silz, *Heinrich von Kleist*, 29; and Dyer, *The Stories of Kleist*, 85. Some attention has been paid to the "triviality" of the story's content to the explosive, even revolutionary scene of the marquis's demise; see, in contrast, Horn, "Wie trivial ist die Gespenstergeschichte 'Das Bettelweib von Locarno'?" in *Heinrich von Kleists Erzählungen*, 148–67.

14. All quotations will be drawn from the version of the story published in the *Berliner Abendblätter* under the cryptogram "mz." The version published in the second volume of *Tales* can be found in SW 2: 196–98; a translation can be found in *The Marquise of O——*, 214–16 (unfortunately, the English translator "corrects" Kleist by regularizing the tense of the story).

15. Analyses of property relations in the anecdote can be found in Horn, "Wie trivial ist die Gespenstergeschichte 'Das Bettelweib von Locarno'?" and Fischer, *Ironische Metaphysik*, 84–90. It is peculiar that the one reading that pays the greatest attention to the acoustical features of "The Beggarwoman of Locarno"

fails to indicate the interplay between *Hören* and *Gehören*; see Kraft, *Erhörtes und Unerhörtes*, 94–108.

16. Nietzsche, *Die fröhliche Wissenschaft* (The gay science), in *Sämtliche Werke*, 3: 513. Nietzsche several times traveled through the St. Gotthard Pass; see Krell and Bates, *The Good European*, 79 and 138.

17. See the anecdotal version of "Saint Cecilia and the Power of Music," which appeared in the *Abendblätter* on November, 15–17, 1810; BA, 1: 155–57, 159, and 163–64. Signed by "yz," this story of acoustical disturbances is linked with both "The Embarrassed Magistrate" and "The Beggarwoman of Locarno."

18. So close is the connection between the "groaning" of the beggarwoman and the "force of music" that Kleist uses the word *Aechzen* to designate the musical voice of another kind of "beggarwoman" who, like the one from Locarno, causes men to lose their minds: "[A siren] did not learn to speak, her tones resembled the groaning of someone dying" ("Seamen and Sirens," BA, 2: 124).

19. Staiger, *Meisterwerke deutscher Sprache*, 109. A more accurate assessment of the relation of drama to narrative in "The Beggarwoman of Locarno" can be found in Max Kommerell's characterization of Kleist's novellas: "One shouldn't say that Kleist dramatizes the novella. The latter is related to his drama insofar as it renounces language at decisive, inner moments of crises [*Wendungen*]" (*Geist und Buchstabe in der Dichtung*, 303).

20. On the difference between "empty talk [*parole vide*]" and "full speech [*parole pleine*]," see the first section of Jacques Lacan's "Fonction et champ de la parole et du langage en psychanalyse," *Ecrits*, 1: 123–43; "The Function and Field of Speech and Language in Psychoanalysis," *Ecrits*, esp. 40–56. The classic case of the "primordial scene" is, of course, Freud's "Aus der Geschichte einer infantilen Neurose," generally known as "The Wolf Man," reprinted in *Freud-Studienausgabe*, 8: 129–232, esp. "Traum und Urszene," 149–65; *Three Case Histories*, 187–316, esp. 213–34.

21. For Kafka's appreciation of Kleist's anecdotes, see *Gesammelte Werke*, 5: 148.

22. Kleist's article "On the Marionette Theater" appeared in the *Berliner Abendblätter* from December 12 to 15, 1810. According to "Herr C——," the bear faced him, "eye to eye, as though he could read my soul therein" (SWB, 2: 345).

23. On this disarticulation, see Mehigan, *Text as Contract*, 191–97. Mehigan, who closely follows Staiger, goes similarly astray when he speaks of the marquis's sudden "memory" of the beggarwoman (195). No such memory is even suggested in the text; only neutral and masculine terms (*Mensch* and *man* and *ihm*) are used to describe the improbable phenomenon that drives the marquis crazy.

24. On the use of this term, see the discussion of Hebel's great story "How Zundelfrieder One Day Escaped From Prison and Happily Crossed Over the Border" in Chapter 4.

25. Rainer Maria Rilke, "Archaïscher Torso Apollos," in *Sämtliche Werke*, 1: 557.

Chapter 6: The Paradisal Epochē

1. "The Rainbow: Dialogue on Fantasy" (Der Regenbogen: Gespräch über die Phantasie), Benjamin's last dialogue, was feared lost by Benjamin's German editors but was discovered by Giorgio Agamben in Rome among the papers of Benjamin's childhood friend, Herbert Belmore-Blumenthal.

2. Hegel, *Phänomenologie des Geistes*, in *Werke*, 3: 22; *Phenomenology of Spirit*, 9.

3. Both of the "Transcendental Deductions of the Categories" in the *Critique of Pure Reason* are principally concerned with the transcendental synthesis of the imagination or, as Kant writes in the second edition, *synthesis speciosa* (B, 151).

4. See Fichte, *Grundlage der gesammten Wissenschaftslehre*, in *Werke*, 1: 213–17; *The Science of Knowledge*, 191–95; for an analysis of this passage in Fichte, see Hamacher, "Position Exposed," in *Premises*, 240–41.

5. In one of his earliest writings, Schelling calls Kant's faculty of the imagination "wondrous": "It is to be hoped that time . . . will . . . foster and eventually develop, unto the completion of the whole science, those seeds of great disclosure about this wondrous faculty that Kant has sown in his immortal work" (HKA, 1: 332; *The Unconditional in Human Knowledge*, 190). In *Faith and Knowledge*, Hegel is similarly hopeful: "the main point is that productive imagination is a truly speculative Idea, both in the form of sensuous intuition and in that of comprehending intuition or experience" (*Werke*, 2: 306; *Faith and Knowledge*, 71).

6. See Hegel, *Differenz des Fichteschen und Schellingschen System der Philosophie* (The difference between the Fichtean and Schellingian philosophy), in *Werke*, 2: 35. For an illuminating reflection on Hegel's metaphorics of the night in relation to Hölderlin's, see Andersen, *Poetik und Fragment*, 32–44.

7. This is not to say that Kant, Fichte, Schelling, and Hegel do not consider color; on the contrary, all four—along with many of their contemporaries—develop theories of color. A study of color in the course of German idealism has, so far as I know, never been carried out; see, however, Élie's *Lumière, couleurs, et nature*, which notes in the conclusion the close relation between the kind of color studies pursued by Goethe and those of Husserl (187–88). Without reference to any of the attempts during the "Goethezeit" to make sense of color—not even Goethe's—Caygill begins his study of Benjamin with an account of what he calls, misquoting Benjamin, "transcendental but speculative philosophy'" (*Walter Benjamin*, 4); for an analysis of this work, see my review in the *Review of Metaphysics*. Aware of the vastness of the topic under discussion, Benjamin compiles a list of investigations into the phenomenon of color that ranges from art-historical studies to research reports in experimental psychology, from Rudolf Steiner's exposition of Goethe's theory of color to psychoanalytic inquiries into the basis of blushing (*Erröten*); see the editors' account of Benjamin's list of twenty-five bibliographical entries concerning the phenomenon of color, GS, 6: 699–700.

8. The significance of Goethe's *Farbenlehre* for Benjamin can be measured by two indexes: it provides the epigraph for the "Epistemo-Critical Preface" to the *Origin of the German Mourning Play* (GS, 1: 207; O, 27); and after reading Georg Simmel's account of the Goethean *Urphänomenon* (primordial phenomenon), Benjamin notes that it is closely related to what he understands by origin; see GS, 5: 577; AP, 462 (N 2a, 4). This is one of the few places Benjamin designates his own thought as "Jewish" (in contrast to the "pagan" thought associated with Goethe).

9. Only one of Benjamin's sketches in any sense resembles Goethe's efforts to arrive at the relation among colors; see "Schein," GS, 6: 119. The diagram of green, blue, yellow, red, and shadow (the crux of Goethe's color theory) is flanked by terms Goethe would certainly not have used: "paradisal" and "elysian." Goethe's *Farbenlehre* can be found in the first five volumes of the second series of *Goethes Werke*. For an incisive analysis of Goethe's *Farbenlehre*, which could similarly give (negative) insight into the motivations of Benjamin's own, see Schöne, *Goethes Farbentheologie*.

10. For Schelling's early version of "intellectual intuition," see part three of Chapter 3.

11. Benjamin enrolled at the Albert-Ludwigs University in Freiburg in 1912, and he attended the lectures of Heinrich Rickert along with Heidegger; for a brief discussion, see Brodersen, *Spinne im eigenen Netz*, 47–48.

12. On Schopenhauer's preference for the "Transcendental Aesthetic" over the "Transcendental Logic," see, for example, his "Critique of Kantian Philosophy," in the first volume of *The World as Will and Representation*, in *Werke*, 1: 558: "The 'Transcendental Aesthetic' is a work of such merit that it alone would be sufficient to immortalize the name of Kant. Its proofs have such a complete power of conviction that I number its propositions among the incontestable truths" (*Werke*, 1: 558; *World as Will and Representation*, 1: 437). For Schopenhauer's theory of color, see *Über das Sehn und die Farben* (reprinted in *Werke*, 3: 632–728). For Heidegger's initial emphasis on receptivity over spontaneity, see *Kant und das Problem der Metaphysik*, 20–24.

13. Such is the doctrine of the "fact of reason" first developed in the *Critique of Practical Reason*, Ak, 5: 31; for the phrase "practical data of reason," see the second edition of the first *Critique*, B xxii and xviii. The "enthusiastic" character of this doctrine is examined in the second section of Chapter 3.

14. See Aristotle, *Metaphysics*, 1026a8–32.

15. Kant defines "canon" as "the sum total of the a priori principles of the correct use of certain cognitive faculties" (A, 796; B, 824). The Transcendental Analytic is thus the canon of the understanding, whereas the canon of pure reason lies in the laws that reason dictates to itself. In the first *Critique* Kant retains the idea that human beings cannot act on these laws alone but demand some "incentive"—namely *hope* (see A, 809; B, 837).

16. See Heidegger, *Kant und das Problem of Metaphysik*, 165–88.

17. For Benjamin's use of "typic" (*Typik*), see his "Program for a Coming Philosophy," GS, 2: 165; W, 1: 106. Kant denies that the "Typic of Practical Reason," which corresponds to the section on schematism in the first *Critique*, has anything to do with imagination; Ak, 5: 67–71.

18. In the first and second edition of the third *Critique* Kant writes: "If, following Euler, we assume that colors are vibrations (*pulsus*) of the aether in uniform temporal sequence, as in the case of sound tones are such vibrations of the air, and if assume—what is most important (and which I nevertheless doubt very much)—that the mind perceives not only, by sense, the effect that these vibrations have on the excitation of the organ but also, by reflection, the regular plays of impressions . . . , the color and tone would not be mere sensations but would already be the formal determination of the manifold in these, in which cases they could even by themselves be considered beautiful" (Ak, 5: 225). In the third edition, Kant reverses himself, and between the dashes writes: "what is most important (and which I do not doubt at all)." For a discussion of the alteration, see Pluhar's note to his translation of the *Critique of Judgment*, 70.

19. For a remarkable analysis of clouds in Benjamin's later reflections on childhood (his own in Berlin around 1900), see Hamacher, "The Word *Wolke*—If It Is One."

20. See "Socrates," GS, 2: 129–32; W, 1: 52–54.

21. In a long footnote to his dissertation, *The Concept of Art Critique in German Romanticism*, Benjamin is similarly reticent about this Hölderlinian term (GS, 1: 104–5; W, 1: 175–76).

22. By the opening of the "Transcendental Logic" Kant has (to use Benjamin's word) "sublimated" affection to a point where the object is "internal" to consciousness (A, 92; B, 125–26). For an insightful exposition of this passage in conjunction with Kant's earlier discussion of affection in his famous letter to Markus Hertz, see Longuenesse, *Kant and the Capacity to Judge*, 18–26.

23. Benjamin proceeds to criticize neo-Kantianism for the "extreme extension of the mechanical aspect of the relatively empty Enlightenment concept of experience" (GS, 2: 165; W, 105). For an extensive analysis of Benjamin's relation to Cohen, see Deuber-Mankowsky, *Der frühe Walter Benjamin*. Deuber-Mankowsky rightly emphasizes that Benjamin's attitude toward Cohen is very different from Scholem's (64–72), but she never investigates in detail the two Cohenian themes to which Benjamin responds: intensive magnitude and continuity.

24. For Cohen's critique of the "Anticipations of Perception" (A, 166–76; B, 207–18), see *Kants Theorie der Erfahrung*, esp. 553–54.

25. On intensive magnitude in Cohen and Benjamin, see Werner Hamacher, "Intensive Sprache." The direction I am taking in this chapter is due in large part to Hamacher's remarks on some previous essays.

26. This *Sprung* (leap, crack) corresponds to the one Benjamin seeks to rescue in the thought of *Ursprung* as "historical" (GS, 1: 226; 46). Benjamin also presents "presentation [*Darstellung*]" as a "detour [*Umweg*]" (GS, 1: 208; O, 28).

27. By the time Benjamin began his studies of color, Husserl's prolegomenon to *Logical Investigations* was already understood as a canonical refutation of psychologism; see "Prolegomenon zur reinen Logik" (HGW, 1: 19–258).

28. See, for example, Jacobi, *Werke*, 3: 15–16; Benjamin may have been familiar with the detailed historical treatment of the problem of affection in Vaihinger's *Commentar zu Kants Kritik der reinen Vernunft*, 2: 26–55. One of the monuments to this problem is a study of Adickes, *Kants Lehre von der doppelten Affektion*.

29. "Both of these philosophers [Kant and Plato] share a confidence that the knowledge of which we can give the purest account will also be the most profound. They have not dismissed the demand for depth in philosophy" (GS, 2: 157; W, 1: 100). For Husserl's dismissal of the demand for depth in philosophy, see the closing words of "Philosophy as a Rigorous Science" (HGW, 25: 59–60; PRS, 144–45), to which Benjamin implicitly replies. The pairing of Kant and Plato is one of the basic traits of Cohen's *Kants Theorie der Erfahrung*.

30. Benjamin notes that he is reading Moritz Geiger's *Beiträge zur Phänomenologie des ästhetischen Genusses* along with Husserl's *Ideas* "in order to gain access to his school" (GB, 1: 301–2).

31. See the still unsurpassed exposition of Levinas, *Théorie de l'intuition dans la phénoménologie de Husserl.*

32. Husserl first defines the *epochē* as the "abstaining [*Enthalten*]" from "any judgment concerning the doctrinal content of any previous philosophy and carrying out all of our demonstrations within the limits set by this abstention" (HGW, 3: 40–41; I, 34) and then proceeds to broaden this definition: "a certain refraining from judgment that is compatible with the unshaken conviction of truth, even with the unshakable conviction of evident truth. This positing is 'put out of action,' parenthesized, converted into the modification, 'parenthesized positing,' the judgment simpliciter is converted into the 'parenthesized judgment'" (HGW, 3: 66; I, 59–60).

33. Benjamin's effort to uncover the "ground of intentional immediacy" (GS, 6: 11–14; W, 1: 87–89) is one such investigation.

34. For Husserl's reservations concerning all the terms in the vicinity of "sense" (*Sinn*), "meaning" (*Meinen*), "intention" (*Vermeinung*), "signify" (*bedeuten*), and "signification" (*Bedeutung*), see HGW, 3: 237–39; I, 231–33.

35. Linke's "Das Recht der Phänomenologie" seeks to demonstrate the manner in which Husserl undertakes his own "Copernican turn." By associating Husserl's work with Kantian critique, Linke strongly attacks some of the critiques that confuse phenomenology with Humean empiricism. As Benjamin himself notes in a letter to Scholem, Linke "does not seem to be particularly well esteemed in

phenomenological circles," yet he also indicates that "Das Recht der Phänome-
nologie" is the source of his knowledge of "the essence of phenomenology" (GB,
1: 380; C, 92). Other than Linke and Frege, Scholem held none of his other pro-
fessors at Jena in particularly high regard (see *Walter Benjamin*, 48–49). Ben-
jamin's notes on Linke's essay, "Eidos and Concept" begin with an exercise in ei-
detic reduction (GS, 6: 29–30). By means of this reduction, Benjamin hopes to
discover the criterion by which concept is distinguished from essence. At the
same time, the reduction grants insight into what Husserl calls the eternal *ape-
iron* of phenomenology, namely singularity (HGW, 25: 36; PRS, 116). The
"singular-factuality" of something—a piece of red blotting paper is Benjamin's
example—falls away with the reduction and can be recovered, if it *can* be recov-
ered outside of unreduced intuition, only in a concept. The problem then is to
develop a concept of concept formation that does justice to the singularity of the
"singular-factual" without being based on a theory of abstraction from sense data.
Benjamin's "Epistemo-Critical Prologue" to the *Origin of the German Mourning
Play* proceeds in this direction.

36. See Heidegger, *Erläuterungen zu Hölderlins Dichtung*, 15–16.

37. For the starting point of Husserl's exposition of truth as the intuitive ful-
fillment of an otherwise empty signifying intention (*leere Bedeutungsintention*),
see *Logical Investigations*, 1, § 9; HGW, 2: 43–45. As Tugendhat writes,

> The concept of meanings [*Bedeutungen*] as unfulfilled intentions and of intentions
> (viz., their correlates) as their fulfillments is the ground-laying step in Husserl's clarifi-
> cation of truth and truth-relation. This conception of the intuitive as a "fulfillment" of
> an objectively equivalent intention is new, although it is related to the Leibnizian dis-
> tinction between intuitive and blind = symbolic representations, which Husserl knew
> by way of Brentano. (*Wahrheitsbegriff*, 49)

For an analysis of Husserl's idea of truth as it develops from the first "logical in-
vestigation," see Derrida, *Speech and Phenomenon*. Scholem says that Benjamin
had "only an indistinct impression" of *Logical Investigations* "from his Munich
period" (*Walter Benjamin*, 48). This is an odd remark, since Munich was one of
the places (along with Göttingen) where the program articulated in *Logical In-
vestigations* took precedence among phenomenologists over the one proposed in
Ideas. Perhaps Scholem is mistaken, or perhaps Benjamin's "indistinct impres-
sion" granted him otherwise unclear insights into the nature of the problem.

38. In his dissertation *On the Concept of Art Critique in German Romanticism*
Benjamin analyzes the infinite character of "infinite reflection" in Novalis and
Schlegel as a continuation of his early reflections on the idea of the "infinite task"
in Kant; see GS, 6: 51–52.

39. For a lucid exposition of the manner in which Heidegger absorbs and
thereby dispenses with the phenomenological reduction, as he undertakes the "An-
alytic of *Dasein*" in *Sein und Zeit*, see Tugendhat, *Der Wahrheitsbegriff*, 262–64.

40. See § 57 of *Ideas*, "The Question of the Exclusion of the Pure I" (HGW, 3: 137–38; I, 132–33).

41. Having read Heidegger's *Habilitationsschrift* (1916), *Die Kategorien- und Bedeutungslehre des Duns Scotus* (*Frühe Schriften*, 133–353), on Scholem's recommendation, Benjamin first dismissed it as nothing more than "a good piece of translation work" (GB, 2: 108; C, 168). He then seems to have developed his notes on the Scotian theory of meaning (GS, 6: 22; W, 1: 228) from Heidegger's book, and he admits in a later letter to Scholem that "the text of Heidegger nevertheless perhaps renders the most essential aspect of the scholastic thinking for my problem—in an entirely indistinct manner" (GB, 2: 127; C, 172).

42. The nonphilosophical character of Benjamin's writings is a major theme of Witte's *Walter Benjamin*. Citing Witte's work, Gasché agrees: "The total disregard in Benjamin for any form of sustained conceptuality and argumentation, as well as the elitist, esoterical, if not idiosyncratic nature of at least Benjamin's early writings . . . runs counter to the philosophical requirement of transparency and systematic exposition of arguments" ("Saturnine Vision," 83–84). It is unclear where Gasché draws this "requirement," especially since philosophical texts from Parmenides and Heraclitus ("the obscure") onward have clearly violated the supposed requirement of transparency, and systematicity is a late-born desideratum of philosophical reflection, which, in any case, is borrowed from another field of discourse: mathematics in general and Euclidean geometry in particular.

43. The parallel argument with respect to time runs: "Time is a necessary representation that grounds all intuitions. In regard to appearances in general one cannot remove time, although one can every well take the appearances away from time. Time is therefore given a priori. In it alone is all actuality of appearances possible. The latter could all disappear, but time itself (as the universal condition of their possibility) cannot be removed" (A, 31; B, 46). In an earlier version of this essay, "The Genesis of Judgment," the difference between the "metaphysical exposition" of space and that of time led me in the wrong direction.

44. In a footnote to *Observations on the Feelings of the Beautiful and the Sublime*, Kant describes a dream of total spatial isolation, even from God, who is otherwise supposed to be everywhere: see Kant's depiction of "Carazan's dream," in which a man is brought to the edge of the world and finds himself absolutely and completely alone, bereft of objects (Ak, 2: 209–10). Kant's imaginary experiments with world-annihilation in his *Universal Natural History and Theory of the Heavens* point in the same direction (see Ak, 1: 306–22), as does his life-long fondness for Haller's poem "Unvollkommenes Gedicht über die Ewigkeit" (*Die Alpen*, 75–79); see my *Peculiar Fate*, 67–75.

45. In his "Program for the Coming Philosophy," Benjamin connects the idea of annihilation with that of fulfillment in the context of Kant's theory of experience (GS, 2: 161; W, 1: 102).

46. For Kant's discussion of the nonspatial use of *inner* and *outer*, see the "Amphiboly of Reflective Concepts" A, 265–66; B, 321–22.

47. See Kant, *The Critique of Pure Reason*, A, 19; B, 33. On the concept of magic in Benjamin's treatise, see Menninghaus, *Walter Benjamins Theorie der Sprachmagie*. Menninghaus's historical sources for Benjamin's reflections, strangely enough, do not extend to Kant, and phenomenology is ignored in favor of structuralism (with which Benjamin had no contact). For a brief analysis of Benjamin's early reflections on language and Kant, see Michael Bröcker, "Sprache." While trying to relate Benjamin's reflections on language to Wittgenstein's *Tractatus*—with which it has little in common—Wiesenthal mentions Husserl, who is accused of making the "thoroughly traditional" distinction between "'impure' phenomena and essential components" (*Zur Wissenschaftstheorie Walter Benjamins*, 18); a more misleading statement is difficult to imagine.

48. From this perspective Benjamin's exposition of language as such could be fruitfully analyzed in relation to what Giles Deleuze undertakes in his *Logique du sens* and what Jean-Luc Nancy similarly calls "sense" in contrast to "signification" (see, in particular, *Le Sense du monde*). The most powerful point of comparison would, however, be Heidegger's similarly motivated project during the 1920s (and afterwards) of arriving at the original "sense" (*Bedeutsamkeit*) from which all objectifying acts of signification derive and which these acts therefore constitutively miss—and thus fall into "chatter" (*Gerede*).

49. Scholem's initial reaction to Benjamin's treatise is largely negative, for he seems to have been unhappy that it does not in fact indicate how mathematical symbolism is to be distinguished from language; see *Tagebücher*, 467–68.

50. As Benjamin writes after his uncle's death, they "often saw each other and got along very well" (GB, 3: 382; C, 336). Schoenflies's prominence among German Cantorians can be judged by the series of reports he wrote for the Deutsche Mathematiker-Vereinigung, especially the eighth volume of the Vereinigung's yearly publication, *Die Entwicklung der Lehre von den Punkmannigfaltigkeiten* (1900; supplemented in 1908). Schoenflies also wrote the article "Set Theory" (*Mengenlehre*) for the *Encyklopädie der mathematischen Wissenschaften*, published by the academies of the sciences at Göttingen, Leipzig, Munich, and Vienna. In 1922 Schoenflies wrote the obituary for Cantor in the yearly publication of the Vereinigung as well, "Zur Erinnerung an Georg Cantor" (four years after his death). Of particular interest is Schoenflies's "Krisis in Cantors mathematischem Schaffen."

51. See the unpublished notes on "The Judgment of Designation [*Bezeichnung*]" (GS, 6: 9–11) and "Attempt at a Solution to Russell's Paradox" (GS, 6: 111), along with Benjamin's attempts to solve the corresponding paradox of the Cretan liar (GS, 6: 57–59; W, 1: 210–12). The fullest formulation of Russell's paradox can be found in PM, 101–7 (the chapter entitled "The Contradiction"); the liar's para-

dox is extensively treated in a book Benjamin mentions, Rüstow's *Der Lügner* (GS, 6: 59; W, 1: 212). Benjamin's efforts are attempts to show (in very rough terms) that predicates cannot be predicable of themselves because they cannot be independently designated. A full explication of Benjamin's efforts in this area would require much greater space, but suffice it to say here that he clearly recognizes that the paradox is closely connected to the problem of identity and—more importantly—to that of order in general, including the order of *law* in every sense. Benjamin had access to mathematical ideas from other avenues: his friendship with the man whom he called the "universal genius," Felix Noeggerath, whose dissertation includes an excursus on non-Euclidean geometry (see Scholem's account in *Walter Benjamin*, 98–99); his acquaintance with Hans Reichenbach, who sent him a copy of his dissertation on *The Concept of Probability for the Mathematical Presentation of Reality* (1915), apparently with confidence that he could understand it (GB, 1: 315); and his study of mathematical texts, including, for example, Ernst Barthel's *Die geometrische Grundbegriffe* (see GS, 7: 438).

52. Russell devotes a full chapter of his *Principles of Mathematics* to an attack on Cohen's *Prinzip der Infinitesimal-Methode* (PM, 338–45; this chapter repeats Russell's scathing review of Cohen's work along with that of his student, Ernst Cassirer; see "Recent Work on the Philosophy of Leibniz"). Frege, too, subjects Cohen's work to a devastating critique in 1885 (translated in *Collected Papers*, 108–11). It is not clear that either Frege or Russell adequately represents Cohen's general project, however. Frege closes his review by noting that they both reject the notion that psychology has anything to do with the theory of knowledge but nevertheless suggests that Cohen wants to ground mathematics in sensation— which is nonsensical for anyone committed to antipsychologism. And Russell, who opposes any trace of Kantianism in the philosophy of mathematics, is under the mistaken impression that Cohen relies on "pure intuition" as the basis of mathematical operations (PM, 339). Not only is this erroneous, it contradicts the explicit directive of Cohen's refashioning of Kant: transpose pure intuitions along with everything else associated with the Transcendental Aesthetic into a new transcendental logic or "logic of pure knowledge."

53. For an insightful inquiry into the origin of Leibniz's solution to the problem of continuity, see O. B. Bassler, "*Labyrinthus de compositione continui.*" I thank Professor Bassler for clarifying certain points about Cantorian mathematics; any errors in conceptualization are, of course, my own.

54. For an account of the Pythagorean discovery, see Boyer and Merzbach, *History of Mathematics*, 72–73.

55. In his dissertation *The Concept of Art Criticism in German Romanticism* Benjamin draws attention to a passage where Hölderlin, too, discovers the nature of the infinite in the precise structure of cohesion. Appropriately enough, the passage comes from the concluding lines of the "Pindar Commentary," entitled

"The Infinite": "Hölderlin, who . . . writes, in a passage where he wants to express an intense [*innig*], most thoroughgoing cohesion: 'cohering infinitely (precisely)' [*unendlich (genau) zusammenhängen*]" (GS, 1: 26; W, 1: 126). For a generally accessible explanation of the mathematical terms, see Russell, PM, 288–95. For an even more generally accessible exposition of Cantorian mathematics that places it in its intellectual-historical context, see A. W. Moore, *The Infinite*, 118–22. Cantor's own discussion of linear manifolds is prefaced by a lucid presentation of the idea of the continuum from Democritus to Kant. Cantor, like Russell, opposes Kant's concept of pure forms of intuition (GA, 191). In his edition of Cantor's writings, Zermelo seeks to correct the record and indicate the validity of the Kantian problematic, if not the exposition of space in the Transcendental Aesthetic: "in this doctrine of the 'antinomies' a deeper insight, a gaze into the 'dialectical' nature of human thought comes to expression. And it is a peculiar fate that precisely the 'antinomies of set theory,' whose at the very least *formal* analogy with the Kantian ones cannot be dismissed, have for an entire generation stood in the way of the development and recognition of Cantor's accomplishments" (GA, 377). For an interesting analysis of Kant's concept of space as a pure intuition from the perspective of later mathematical developments around the Cantorian conception of continuity and density (viz., denseness), see Friedman, *Kant and the Exact Sciences*, esp. 56–95. And for an insightful comparison between Kant and Cantor that notes how deeply the latter still thinks within the framework of the former, see Parsons, "Arithmetic and the Categories."

56. Schoenflies, *Die Entwicklung der Lehre von den Punktmannigfaltigkeiten* (1900), 63: "Die Ableitung einer in sich dichten, nicht perfecten Menge ist perfect." These terms, which are taken from Cantor, are defined by Russell in the following manner:

> We now proceed to the consideration of the fundamental series contained in any one-dimensional series *M*. . . . Any term of *M* which is the limit of some fundamental series in *M* is called a principal term of *M*. If all the terms of *M* are principal terms, *M* is called *condensed in itself* (insichdicht). If every fundamental series in *M* has a limit in *M*, *M* is called *closed* (abgeschlossen). If *M* is both closed and condensed in itself, it is *perfect.* (PM, 297)

These definitions allow for an ordinal definition of the continuum: *M* must be "perfect and contain within itself a denumerable series *S* of which there are terms between any terms of *M*" (PM, 297). Russell also gives a "popular" explanation of derivative: "the first derivative consists of all points in whose neighbourhoods an infinite number of terms of the collection are heaped up; and subsequent derivatives give, as it were, the different degrees of concentration in any neighbourhood. Thus it is easy to see why derivatives are relevant to continuity: to be continuous, a collection must be as concentrated as possible in every neighbourhood containing any term in the collection" (PM, 324).

57. See, for example, Hegel, *Enzyklopädie der philosophischen Wissenschaften*, § 251, in *Werke*, 9: 36–37. As Cantor writes, in connection with a critique of the Hegelian idea of the infinite,

> among all philosophers the principle of difference [*Prinzip des Unterschiedes*] in the transfinite is lacking, which leads to different transfinite numbers and different powers. Most even confuse the transfinite with *undifferentiated highest one*, with the absolute, the absolute maximum, which of course is inaccessible to determination and therefore to mathematics. (GA, 391)

On Benjamin's relation to "bad infinity," see García-Düttmann, "The Violence of Destruction."

58. For an astute analysis of Benjamin's construction of "able" terms, see Sam Weber, "Benjamin's Writing Style."

59. Benjamin draws the quotation from Jean Hering, "Bemerkungen über das Wesen, die Wesenheit und die Idee," which is an early contribution to Husserl's journal for phenomenological research. Benjamin continues this discontinuous thought of discontinuity in a later section of the preface: "For Ideas form an irreducible plurality [*Vielheit*]. As an enumerated [*gezählte*]—properly speaking, however, named [*benannte*]—plurality, the Ideas are given for contemplation" (GS, 1: 223; O, 43). The English translator misses the sense of Benjamin's remark by translating *zählbar* as "finite" (O, 37), instead of as "countable" or "denumerable." For Benjamin's further exposition of the plurality (*Vielheit*) as essences, see the notes on "language and logic," GS, 6: 24–25; W, 1: 273. At the opening of these notes, Benjamin insists that "truth is not dense [*Die Wahrheit ist nicht dicht*]. Much that we expect to find in it slips through the net" (GS, 6: 24; W, 1: 272). This thought is then rearticulated at the beginning of the "Epistemo-Critical Preface" in relation to the "system concept of the nineteenth century" (GS, 1: 207; O, 28)—not, in other words, in terms of density, which presumably is too closely associated with the mathematical term, where it functions as something other than a correlate to the concept of the comprehensive "system."

60. Benjamin's concern with division is not confined to his early work, of course. One of the decisive fragments of the convolute of the *Arcades Project* devoted to the theory of knowledge is a meditation on infinite divisibility: "thus the historical evidence polarizes into fore- and after-history always anew, never in the same way. And it does so at a distance from its existence, in the present instant—like a line that, divided according to the Apellian cut [*nach dem apoll(i)nischen Schnitt*], experiences its division [*Teilung*] from outside itself" (GS, 5: 588; AP, 470, N 7 a, 1). The reading of this obscure reference offered by the Italian edition, is the most plausible; see the note to the AP, 989–90. The mathematical correlate to the graphic term "Appelian cut" would be "Dedekind cut."

61. For a discussion of Cantor's monadological hypothesis, see note 75 of Chapter 1. In his article on set theory for the *Encyklopädie der mathematischen*

Wissenschaften, Schoenflies formulates Cantor's conviction in the following manner: "Cantor believed he should suppose that for all infinite point-sets of a space $R[n]$ there are only two different power classes, namely either the power of the countable series of numbers or the power of the continuum" ("Mengenlehre," 187; see also Schoenflies, *Entwicklung der Lehre*, 18–19). In Cantor's own words:

> If we clothe this problem in geometrical dress and understand by a *linear* manifold of real numbers any thinkable collection of infinitely many distinct real numbers, then one can ask *how many* and what classes the linear manifolds fall into, if manifolds of the same power are put into one and the same class and manifolds of different power into different classes. By an inductive process . . . we are led to the proposition that the number of classes which arise according to this principle of classification of linear manifolds is finite and indeed that it is equal to *two*. (GA, 132; Fauvel and Gray, *History of Mathematics*, 580–81, which unfortunately mistranslates the final sentence)

In his analysis of the "continuum hypothesis," Lavine offers a succinct exposition of Cantor's conjecture: "Cantor . . . stated that he could show that every infinite set of points could be placed into one-to-one correspondence with either the natural numbers or the real numbers—that there are no intermediate possibilities" (*Understanding the Infinite*, 43). An account of the origin of the "continuum hypothesis" can be found in G. Moore, *Zermelo's Axiom of Choice*, 39–51. The reason Cantor could not prove his conjecture was discovered in the course of the century: Kurt Gödel showed that, given the nine axioms of Zermelo-Frænkel set theory, it is impossible to show that the conjecture was false, after which Paul J. Cohen proved that it would be impossible (with the same axioms) to show that it is true. It is therefore in the exact sense of the term undecidable.

62. For an account of Kronecker's opposition to Cantor, see Schoenflies, "Die Krisis in Cantors mathematischem Schaffen," 1–23; for a brief analysis, see Boyer and Merzbach, *History of Mathematics*, 569–70. Benjamin may also have approved of David Hilbert's characterization of Cantor's achievement: "No one can expel us from the paradise which Cantor has created for us"—with an emendation that would have been amenable to Cantor: "rediscovered for us."

63. See his letter to Dedekind, July, 28, 1899: "*The system of* µ *of all numbers is an inconsistent, absolutely infinite plurality* [Vielheit]. . . . I call 'alephs' the cardinal numbers that belong to the transfinite numbers of the system µ, and the *system of all alephs* is called ת (*tav*, the last letter of the Hebrew alphabet)" (GA, 445); for Russell's exposition of the argument, see PM, 362–63. In a footnote to one of his papers on infinite point-manifolds Cantor writes, "The absolute can only be acknowledged [*anerkennt*], not known [*erkannt*], not even known by approximation" (GA, 205)—at which point he quotes precisely the same poem that fascinated Kant, Albrecht von Haller's "Unvollkommenes Gedicht über die Ewigkeit." As a gloss on this poem and on his own efforts, he writes: "The absolutely infinite series of numbers seems to me therefore in a certain sense as an appropriate sym-

bol of the absolute [*Symbol des Absoluten*]" (GA, 205). For an analysis of the difference between the transfinite and the absolute in Cantor, see Lavine, *Understanding the Infinite*, 51–57. How Haller's poem and its symbolization of the absolute relates to Cantor's other hypothesis—that Shakespeare was really Francis Bacon—would be the topic for another investigation; see his edition, *Die Rawleysche Sammlung*.

In a series of philosophical-mathematical reflections Cantor seeks to defend the "actual infinite." Transfinite numbers, he argues, "are delimited forms [*abgegrenzte Gestaltungen*] or modifications (*aphorismena*) of the actual infinite" (GA, 395–96). The term *aphorismenon* is drawn from Aristotle, who, as is well known, recognizes only potential infinity (*apeiron dunamei*) as opposed to *apeiron hōs aphorismenon* (*Physics*, 208a6; GA, 396): a "separated" infinity would be in some sense actual. For Cantor's exposition of the three "positions" from which the actual infinite can be considered, see especially his paper, "Über die verschiedenen Standpunkte in bezug auf das aktuelle Unendliche" (GA, 370–76). Cantor, like Benjamin, opposes emanationism—and perhaps for the same reason: "for me the absolute freedom of God is beyond question" (GA, 387). God is closely related to the mathematician, since, as Cantor—and Schoenflies quotes this as the epigraph for his report on Cantorian set theory—"The essence of mathematics lies precisely in its freedom" (*Entwicklung* [1900], 1; GA, 182). Although Cantor would doubtless object to the following characterization of his reflections on the actual infinite, it nevertheless indicates an ironic continuity with Benjamin: as "separated" infinities the transfinite numbers are pure "aphorisms"—not attributes—of the absolute. Or, as Sophie Kowalevski reports, "These powers, the Cantorian alephs, were, for Cantor, something sacred, in a certain sense the steps that lead up to the throne of infinity, to the throne of God" (quoted in Purkert and Ilgauds, *Georg Cantor*, 118). How this conception of the infinite is to be understood in relation to his attempt in the privately published *EX ORIENTE LUX* to prove that Joseph of Arimathea was the father of Jesus, based on material from the New Testament along with "equally valuable historical sources, among them the Talmud" (quoted in Purkert and Ilgauds, *Georg Cantor*, 120)—this, too, would demand a separate investigation; but at least this much can be said: the absolutely infinite remains "set apart."

64. Leibniz, "Brevis designatio meditationum de originibus gentium, ductis potissimum ex indicio linguarum," reprinted in *Opera omnia*, ed. Dutens, 4, 2: 186. See the sixth section of Chapter 1, above.

65. For an impressive reading of the emphatic "but" (*aber*) in Benjamin's "bold" suggestion, along with an analysis of the gender politics at work in the treatise as a whole, see Carol Jacobs, *In the Language of Walter Benjamin*, 107–12.

66. On Benjamin's allusion to Paul's Epistle to the Romans, see Taubes, *Die politische Theologie des Paulus*, 100–102; see also Giorgio Agamben, *Le Temps qui reste*. In a footnote to his essay on Benjamin's "Critique of Violence," Hamacher

formulates the law of irony according to which the paradisal language must always already be inhabited by its "parody" (GS, 2: 153; W, 1: 71; "Afformative, Strike," 136–38).

67. Benjamin does not cite the text of Kierkegaard to which he refers; but it is likely that he has in mind the sections of *En literair Anmeldelse* (A literary review) translated by Theodor Haecker for *Der Brenner* under the title "Kritik der Gegenwart" (Critique of the present); for an account of Haecker's influential translation, see Janik, "Haecker, Kierkegaard." A translation of the passages concerning "chatter" (*snak*) can be found in Kierkegaard, *Two Ages*, 97–99. Benjamin's reading of Genesis takes its direction—almost the opposite—from Kierkegaard's *The Concept of Anxiety*, especially the following words: "The imperfection in the narrative—how could it have occurred to anyone to say to Adam what he essentially could not understand—is eliminated if we bear in mind that the speaker is language, and also it is Adam himself who speaks" (47). Benjamin's treatise is "on" this Kierkegaardian "also." On Kierkegaard's concept of chatter, see Fenves, "*Chatter.*"

68. The word *Dichtung* (poetry) does not, of course, derive from *Dichte* (density) but from *dictare*; yet it suggests compactness nevertheless. In the eighth of his "Theses on the Problem of Identity," Benjamin makes the following claim: "The identity relation is not reversible [*nicht umkehrbar*]. This assertion remains to be proved. Nevertheless it can be made plausible, for example, by the linguistic distinction between 'I' and 'self'" (GS, 6: 28; W, 1: 76). Tautology, as identity judgment, cannot express irreversibility—which is one of the reasons for its inadequacy as a guide to the problem of identity. Translation, however, is different, even as it, like tautology, "says the same" (*to auto legein*). The difference in the absolute identity relation, which distinguishes "formal-logical" identity from "a further metaphysical identity" (GS, 6: 29; W, 1: 77), can be found in translation. Translation is irreversible—a "one-way street"—because a translation cannot be translated *back*.

69. This is the central thesis of "The Task of the Translator": every language as a whole (*im ganzen*) in complementary (*ergänzende*) relation to every other one "wishes to say" (*sagen will*) pure language. Such is the meaning (*Meinen*) or intention (*Intention*) of every language. Although the terms *Meinen* and *Intention* are closely associated with the theory of meaning that Husserl develops throughout his work, from the first of the *Logical Investigations* onward, Benjamin's line of argument in "The Task of the Translator" is an extrapolation of Frege's work (which he would have known from Scholem, who was studying in Jena, and from an extensive appendix to Russell's work, PM, 501–22). Benjamin's extrapolation operates in two coordinated directions—a radicalization of Frege's already radical antipsychologism and a deepening of its inherent wholism. With respect to antipsychologism: for Frege, "thoughts" are not psychological phenomena; for Benjamin, even a purified concept of thought is too closely associ-

ated with psychology, so he makes no reference to it. With respect to wholism: according to Frege, the *Bedeutung* (meaning, significance) of a "proper name" is the object designated by the term. In this respect, Frege and Benjamin say the same and even use the same terminology. When Frege turns to a larger linguistic, "the whole assertoric sentence," he invokes the term *thought*. The "objective content" of an assertoric sentence is a thought and its *Bedeutung* is a "truth value" (*Collected Papers*, 162; *Funktion, Begriff, Bedeutung*, 46): "Every assertoric sentence concerned with what it means"—unlike a poem like the *Odyssey*—"is therefore to be regarded as a proper name, and its meaning, if it has one, is either the true or the false [*das Wahre oder das Falsche*]" (*Collected Papers*, 163; *Funktion, Begriff, Bedeutung*, 48). For Benjamin, by contrast, the only "whole" is "every language as a whole" and the wholeness of every "whole" language is itself predicated on every other language in a "making-whole" relation to one another. This linguistic whole to the second power—the whole made whole—contains no *thought* whatsoever, and for this very reason, it *means* "pure language," which is to say, in Fregean terms, *the true*. Benjamin's commitment to antipsychologism is so complete that he replaces "connotation" by a purely nonpsychological category: "mode of meaning [*Art des Meinens*]" (GS, 4: 14; W, 1: 257). On Benjamin and Frege, see my "Unterlassung der Übersetzung."

70. In one of his *Lebenläufe* Benjamin emphasizes the continuity of his program of research with that of phenomenology (GS, 6: 218), a continuity, as he indicates in one of his later essays, that consists in a common fidelity to discontinuity: "Husserl replaces the idealistic system with discontinuous phenomenology" (GS, 4: 536). And the section of the *Origin of the German Mourning Play* devoted to an analysis of melancholia begins with a dense "phenomenology" of feeling; see GS, 1: 318–19; O, 139. For a consideration of Benjamin's attempt to develop a "phenomenology of discontinuity," see Ferris, "Aura, Resistance, and the Event of History." Benjamin occasionally returns to phenomenology in the course of working on the *Arcades Project*, prompted in large part by Adorno's work on his anti-Husserl manifesto, *Zur Metakritik der Erkenntnistheorie*; see GB, 5: 66. Benjamin's general attitude toward Husserl is at odds with Adorno, however, as he explains in one of his letters: "I'm eager some day to know more about your annihilation of 'the intuition of essence.' Wouldn't Husserl reconcile himself to such an annihilation, after he could take into account what purpose this instrument could serve in the hands of a Heidegger" (GB, 5: 110). The culmination of this reconsideration is the famous note on dialectical images in convolute N of the *Arcades Project*: "What distinguishes images from 'essentialities [*Wesenheiten*]' of phenomenology is their historical index" (GS, 5: 577; AP, 462, N 3, 1). This note corresponds to those in convolute M that seek to determine the "objective correlate" of *Erlebnis* (lived experience, Husserl's term for "mental processes in general"); see esp., GS, 5: 962; AP, 801; M 1 a, 5.

Chapter 7: *Benjamin's* Origin of the German Mourning Play

1. Wilamowitz-Moellendorff, *Einleitung in die griechische Tragödie*, 95. Wilamowitz was fond of comparing the tragedians to the prophets; see, for example, his edition of *Griechische Tragoedien*, 2: 47. It is worth noting that Wilamowitz's analogy seems to have had little influence on either biblical or classical studies. In an otherwise admirable collection of essays on the relation of Greek poetry to Hebrew prophecy, none of the Greek tragedians is even mentioned, much less discussed; see Kugel, ed., *Poetry and Prophecy*.

2. See GB, 3: 15; C, 261. In a previous letter to Salomon-Delatour Benjamin describes his theory of tragedy as "a crux"—one, however, that he will not be able to avoid entirely.

3. See GB, 2: 300; C, 205.

4. See Benjamin's remark to Florens Christian Rang, who, as Benjamin admits, is almost the coauthor of the theory of tragedy he proposes in the *Origin of the German Mourning Play*; GB, 2: 416; C, 231.

5. See Rosenzweig, *Der Stern der Erlösung*, 67–90.

6. Mehlman, *Walter Benjamin for Children*, 1–2.

7. Nowhere in the *Origin of the German Mourning Play* does Benjamin explain what he means by *Prophetie* ("prophecy," "prophetism," or "prophetic tradition"), and his correspondence does not give the impression that he undertook a comprehensive study of the concept of the prophet (*nabi*) as it develops in the Hebrew Bible. Nor does it appear that he had anything but a passing acquaintance with the kind of reflections that led a theologian like Leo Baeck—to mention only one instance of this trend—to present Judaism's prophetic tradition as "tragic" by virtue of its defiant "optimism": "Moral and tragic pathos here becomes one. The Bible is a world of this fortifying and optimistic tragedy, and by experiencing its truth Judaism grasped the meaning of the prophets and their successors" (Baeck, *The Essence of Judaism*, 86). Nor does Benjamin stake out a position with respect to various proposals for a "renewal of prophetic Judaism," including the young Martin Buber's famous call: "The self-affirmation of the Jew has its tragic aspects as well as its grandeur. . . . And to live as a Jew means to absorb this tragic aspect as well as the grandeur of self-affirmation" (*On Judaism*, 21). Even though his exposition of tragedy relies upon the formula "preliminary stage of prophecy," Benjamin shows little interest in such matters as the much debated question concerning the significance of the prophetic tradition in Judaism, the contentious problem of the historical end to this tradition (which gave anti-Semitic polemicists the opportunity to accuse postprophetic Jewry of having lost its former "creativity"), or the idiosyncratic suggestions that the prophetic tradition can somehow be renewed.

One of those who understood his work in part as a preparation for a renewed reception of the gift of prophecy did, however, attract Benjamin's attention during the time he wrote the *Trauerspiel* book, even as his presence physically repulsed him: Oskar Goldberg, who could not be further removed from Leo Baeck in the wide spectrum of early-twentieth-century Jewish thought (see, for example, Benjamin's comments in GB, 3: 111). Although Goldberg favored the prescriptive rites of the books of the Torah over the "moralizing tendency" of the prophetic books, he nevertheless expected to receive the *ruah hakodesh* (holy spirit or breath) once again. For an extensive inquiry into Goldberg, see Voigts, *Oskar Goldberg*; see also the brief but consequential remarks of Taubes, "From Cult to Culture"; for Benjamin's interest in the Goldberg circle, see the account of Scholem, *Walter Benjamin*, 95–98. Although it would have made sense to only a very few, if any, Benjamin's talk of a "preliminary stage of prophecy" may implicitly refer to the work of Goldberg, even as it seeks to determine the distinctive character of Attic tragedy.

8. Benjamin's critique of Volkelt's *Ästhetik des Tragischen* conforms with his general rejection of psychologism, and in the first draft of the preface to the *Origin* his critique explicitly has this function; see GS, 1: 940–41. By presenting "the tragic" as a matter of causality, Volkelt's treatise can be understood as psychologism to the second power: the mind is affected in a causal manner, and causality is the tragic disturbance of the mind.

9. Benjamin presents the work of Wilamowitz under the allegorical title of "philology" (perhaps because, as the case of Kurt Hildebrandt attests, Wilamowitz was still involved in university affairs; see GS, 2: 441–42). According to Wilamowitz, Attic tragedy is defined by its transformation of Homeric legend. This basic trait of tragedy "distinguishes it from all other dramatic poetry that has hitherto emerged and, most likely, will ever do so" (Wilamowitz, *Einleitung*, 119).

10. Nietzsche, *Die Geburt der Tragödie*, reprinted in *Sämtliche Werke*, 1: 67. Of the many peculiarities of this sentence, at least three should be mentioned: (1) the impossibility of deciding on the nature of a *gleichnissartiges Bild* as long as every *Bild* (image, picture) is understood to be *gleichnissartig* (in the nature of a likeness, parable-like); (2) the removal of quotation marks around the term *ahnen* (intimate). Only a few pages before, Nietzsche had ridiculed another, specifically political use of this latter term:

> With reference to the classical form of the chorus as we know it from Aeschylus and Sophocles, we would also consider it blasphemous to speak of an intimation of a "constitutional representation of the people" [*Ahnung einer "constitutionellen Volksvertretung"*], a blasphemy from which others have not shrunk. The ancient constitution of the state *in praxi* knew nothing about a constitutional representation of the people, and it is to hoped that they have not "intimated" [*geahnt*] it in their tragedy. (*Sämtliche Werke*, 1: 52–53)

At stake in this "intimated" is the question: who is the heir to tragedy? Who learns to speak its own language from its infantilism? And (3) the passage from

Goethe's "Prometheus" also figures prominently in Schopenhauer's *Welt als Wille und Vorstellung* (World as will and representation), but far from indicating anything about the intimate relation between Germans and Greeks, it designates a "standpoint" that can also be found in the *Bhagavad Gita*, Bruno, and Spinoza (Schopenhauer, *Die Welt als Wille und Vorstellung*, § 54; *Werke*, 1: 373). The passage where Schopenhauer discusses the "standpoint" designated by Goethe's "Prometheus" is of particular importance for an assessment of the relation of the young Nietzsche to Schopenhauer, for it is this passage in which he first articulates the "standpoint" of the "affirmation of the will to life," precisely the point, according to Nietzsche, on which Greek tragedy stands or falls. And, of course, Goethe's "Prometheus" also figures prominently in the so-called *Pantheismusstreit* of the 1780s in which the relation of *Judentum* (Jewishness), represented by both Spinoza (the heretic) and Moses Mendelssohn (the defender of the faith), to *Deutschtum* (Germanness), represented by Lessing (the heretic) and Jacobi (the defender of the faith), first enters into philosophical discourse.

11. See Nietzsche, *Ecco Homo*, in *Sämtliche Werke*, 6: 310.

12. Nietzsche continues: "and between these two myths there exists an affinity like that between brother and sister" (*Sämtliche Werke*, 1: 68–69), that is, between active and passive, public heroism and private cunning.

13. Ziegler, *Zur Metaphysik des Tragischen*, vii.

14. Ibid.

15. Ibid., viii.

16. Ibid., 81–82.

17. Ibid., 102.

18. This term stems from Jacques Derrida; see *Specters of Marx*, esp. 167–69. Although Benjamin never uses the word *messianicity*, he nevertheless employs a (Greek-Hebrew-German) equivalent, namely *Christlichkeit*—a word perhaps chosen in memory of Florens *Christian* Rang, who gave himself his middle name. On the significance of the odd term *Christlichkeit* in the *Origin of the German Mourning Play*, see my "Marx, Mourning, Messianicity." For an account of Rang's life and thought, see Jäger, *Messianische Kritik*.

19. In the first draft of the preface Benjamin considers the specifically German character of the mourning play and asks whether it is an "idea" (see GS, 1: 946–47). He notes that the "investigations" that make up his treatise are prolegomena to a "theory of the 'Origin of the Mourning Play'" (GS, 1: 947).

20. This is Benjamin's term for his earlier procedure. See his letter to Hugo von Hofmannsthal where he insists that he will no longer treat *Schicksal* (fate) in the same manner as he had done in his essay on Goethe's *Wahlverwandtschaften* and, presumably, in "Fate and Character" (GS, 2: 410; W, 201–6).

21. See Florens Christian Rang, *Deutsche Bauhütte*; in addition to Benjamin's short letter (reprinted in GS, 4: 791–92), Rang's book includes addenda from Martin Buber, Ernst Michel, and Karl Hildebrandt, among others.

22. See especially Benjamin's essay, "Die Jugend schweigt" (GS, 2: 66–67).

23. See Hermann Cohen, *Religion of Reason from the Sources of Judaism*, 165–77; chap. 10, "The Individual and the I." This chapter of Cohen's *Religion* corresponds to the section of Rosenzweig's *Star of Redemption* devoted to the "meta-ethical," and in both cases the "origin" of the self, or the individual, is understood in terms of Greek tragedy. This is hardly surprising. Even if neither Cohen nor Rosenzweig discusses in detail either Schopenhauer or Nietzsche, the basic scenario by which the latter philosophers recount the emergence of tragedy dovetails with the way the former two philosophers account for the birth of the self through individuation. For Schopenhauer, it is a "sin"; for Cohen, an advance beyond paganism to "religion"; for the young Nietzsche, an eternal game of disappearing appearances; and for Rosenzweig, a propaedeutic for any philosophy that seeks to come to terms with the distinction between and relation among world, human being, and God.

24. See the strange autobiographical text of Benjamin that Scholem famously analyzes in terms of its Kabbalistic intentions, "Agesilaus Santander," in Gershom Scholem, *Walter Benjamin*, 40–43; see also the remarks of Agamben, "Walter Benjamin and the Demonic: Happiness and Historical Redemption," in *Potentialities*, 138–59.

25. For Benjamin's notes in preparation for this midrash, see GS, 1: 923–94.

26. See, especially, GS, 1: 288–89; O, 109–10. Benjamin's discussion of tragedy in the *Trauerspiel* book is peculiar in at least one other respect: although "Fate and Character" was written before Benjamin could have had any familiarity with Rosenzweig's *Star of Redemption*, the two works are remarkably similar in their description of tragedy as a decisive stage of "pagan man." And although these two works are not interchangeable, Benjamin leaves the impression that the presentation of tragic "infantilism" in his own essay is largely the same as Rosenzweig's exposition of tragic silence. For an inquiry into the immensely complicated relation between Benjamin and Rosenzweig, see Mosès, *L'Ange de l'histoire*.

27. A canonical account of the end of the prophecy can be found in the Talmudic treatise *Sanhedrin*:

> Our Rabbis taught: Since the death of the last prophets, Haggai, Zechariah and Malachai, the Holy Spirit [of prophetic inspiration] departed from Israel; yet they were still able to avail themselves of the Bath-kol {daughter of the voice}. Once when the Rabbis were met in the upper chamber of Gurya's house at Jericho, a Bath-kol was heard from Heaven, saying: "There is one amongst you who is worthy that the Shechinah {the divine presence} should rest on him as it did on Moses, but his generation does not merit it." The Sages present set their eyes on Hillel the Elder. And when he died, they lamented and said: "Alas, the pious man, the humble man, the disciple of Ezra [is no more]" (*Talmud*, "Sanhedrin," 11a13–15; small brackets are included in the text of the English edition of the Talmud edited by Isaac Epstein; large brackets are my own; see also 1 Macc. 4:46 and 14:41.)

For a consistently insightful inquiry into the complicated question of the end of the prophetic tradition, see Sommer, "Did Prophecy Cease?" Sommer quotes a passage from *Tanhuma Beha'alotka* 6 concerning this matter: "when the temple was destroyed . . . five things were hidden away: the ark, the menorah, the fire, the holy spirit (*ruah hakodesh*), and the cherubim. And when the Holy One, blessed be He, rouses Himself in His mercy and rebuilds His temple, he will return them to their place" ("Did Prophecy Cease?" 36).

28. See, for example, the compilation of Vernant and Vidal-Naquet's writings published under the title, *Myth and Tragedy in Ancient Greece*, 49–84.

29. Rang's notes on tragedy are reprinted in Benjamin, GB, 2: 425–27; C, 231–32, 233–35.

30. See Rang, *Historische Psychologie des Karnevals*.

31. Both Rang and Benjamin draw heavily from Burckhardt, *Griechische Kulturgeschichte*, which, in turn, draws inspiration from Nietzsche's early interest in Greek agonistics.

32. Nietzsche writes: "Not the strength but rather the duration of high sensation [*hohen Empfindung*] makes the high human being" (*Sämtliche Werke*, 5: 86; *Beyond Good and Evil*, § 72).

33. In one of the most rewarding essays on the *Trauerspiel* book yet published, Samuel Weber has drawn attention to this strange sentence and proposed a reading of it; see "Genealogy of Modernity: History, Myth, Allegory in Benjamin's *Origin of the German Mourning Play*."

34. As Weber indicates in "Genealogy of Modernity," the term *Volksgemeinschaft* was one of the categories dear to Nazi ideology, and as Hannah Arendt explains with characteristic lucidity, the function of this category lies in its mendacious evocation of a future already at work in "the movement":

> To a certain extent, the *Volksgemeinschaft* was the Nazis' attempt to counter the Communist promise of a classless society. . . . The even greater advantage of the *Volksgemeinschaft* [over the idea of the classless society], however, was that its establishment did not have to wait for some future time and did not depend upon objective conditions: it could be realized immediately in the fictitious world of the movement (Arendt, *The Origins of Totalitarianism*, 361)

For an incisive analysis of the term *Volksgemeinschaft* in the Nazi regime, see Hattenhauer, *Die geistesgeschichtlichen Grundlagen des deutschen Rechts*, 307–10. For Benjamin's own evaluation of this term, see the following note in the *Arcades Project*: "The *Volksgemeinschaft* aims to root out from single individuals everything that stands in the way of their fusion into a mass of consumers without remainder [*restlosen*]" (GS, 5: 469; AP, 371; J 81 a, 1). Yet the word *Volksgemeinschaft* was also used in other contexts, one of which may have had a certain importance for Benjamin's deployment of the term in the *Origin of the German Mourning Play*. Whereas Benjamin explicitly contrasts his concept of origin from that of

Hermann Cohen (GS, 1: 226; O, 46), he implicitly associates the *Volksgemein-schaft* that learns to speak from the word and silence of the tragic hero with the *Volksgemeinschaft* to which Cohen sometimes refers as he seeks to define the "national" character of the people whose historical mission consists in advancing the idea of monotheism: "I hope to have demonstrated that the religious substance of Jewish monotheism is compatible with a historically conceived Christianity and is sufficient for a *Volksgemeinschaft*" (*Jüdische Schriften*, 78).

35. As he indicates in the notes, Benjamin is quoting from the first version of Hölderlin's "Patmos" (ll. 144–45), and this alone is enough to indicate the eschatological character of Benjamin's theory of tragedy. Needless to say, "Patmos" concerns "der Christ," which is to say, translating literally from the Greek, "the Messiah." And the stanza from which Benjamin draws his sole quotation of Hölderlin concerns the devastation of the disciples—precisely those who can under no condition become a *Volksgemeinschaft*.

At the end of the preliminary "Schemata" for his *Habilitationsschrift* Benjamin notes: "Hölderlin's tragedy translations, especially *Antigone* with respect to the *Trauerspiel*" (GS, 1: 917)—*not* with respect to tragedy. The very structure of the *Origin of the German Mourning Play* owes a debt to the poetological reflections of Hölderlin, which reach their pinnacle in the "Remarks to *Antigone*" (SW, 4: 265–72). The dynamic tension between *Grundstimmung* (basic mood) and *Kunstcharakter* (art character), according to Hölderlin's poetological program, sets a poem into motion, determines its subsequent *Wechsel der Töne* (alteration of tones), and thereby defines the character of its final resolution. Each of the three modes of poetic composition Hölderlin analyzes—lyric, epic, and tragic—corresponds to one of the basic moods: naive, heroic, and tragic, respectively; for a brief description, see Fenves, "Hölderlin." What cannot in principle enter into the system of tonal alterations are two even more basic moods: joy (*Freude*) and mourning (*Trauer*). Together, they may perhaps be called *Abgrundstimmungen*: abssyal (rather than basic) moods. Benjamin has the audacity—or, to use his own word, the "chutzpah" (GB, 3: 14)—to do what Hölderlin refrains from doing: determine the "art character" of the abyssal mood of mourning. Such is allegory, the art character of which is art-destructive. Both the abyssal mood of mourning and the art-destructive character of allegory, moreover, are subject to the law of alteration: having gone through all the stations of mourning, melancholia (in the figure of Hamlet) overcomes itself in the spirit of *Christlichkeit* (which is to say, messianicity: GS, 1: 335; O, 158), and having run through the "infinity of hopelessness," allegory, in turn, turns around in "*one* about-turn [einen *Umschwung*]" (GS, 1: 406; O, 232). The law under which they stand is, however, a law of rigorous infidelity, for, as Benjamin writes at the close of the penultimate section of the work, "the intention [of allegory] does not faithfully rest in the contemplation of bones but faithlessly [*treulos*] leaps over itself and into resurrection" (GS, 1: 406; O, 233). And once again, with this law of infidelity, Benjamin draws his resources from Hölderlin's late poetological writings, especially his "Remarks on *Antigone*"—which is concerned with nothing else. For this reason, the citation of "Patmos" is the "crux" of the matter: the "honor of the half-god," blown away, is the devastated region in which allegory reigns—until utter emptiness, too, is allegorized. No "lawful calculus" can determine this "until," but there is no "until" without a "lawful calculus" in which the incalculable can—to use Hölderlin's term—be "felt."

36. See the central stanza of "Der Rhein," in SW, 2: 145.

37. Hölderlin, "Patmos," first version, ll. 144–50; SW, 2: 169. Benjamin cites the edition initiated by Norbert von Hellingrath. The same stanza of "Patmos" serves as the epigraph to Benjamin's cycle of sonnets, which gives some indication of Friedrich Heinle's significance to Benjamin's life and work (GS, 7: 27): he is a "disciple" of one who dies after saying "all is good."

38. "Der tiefe aischyleische Zug nach Gerechtigkeit" (GS, 1: 288; O, 109)—this phrase appears in the ninth section of the *Birth of Tragedy* (*Sämtliche Werke*, 1: 71) at precisely the same point where Nietzsche presents Goethe's "Prometheus" as the fulfillment of Aeschylus's *Prometheus Bound*. It is worth comparing Nietzsche's remarks on "the deep Aeschylean trait [or pull] toward justice" with Hermann Cohen's positive assessment of the Aeschylean solution to tragic fate in his *Religion of Reason*: "Thus with Aeschylus too [as in both philosophical consciousness and among the Jewish prophets] ethics leads to religion" (*Religion of Reason*, 169).

39. On the uncanny character of Benjaminian echoes, see Nägele, *Echoes of Translation*.

40. As a counterpoint to his approbation of Ziegler's *Zur Metaphysik des Tragischen* at this point in the text, Benjamin harshly condemns the same work later in the same section for its presumptuous condemnation of *Hamlet* (see GS, 1: 315; O, 136). Benjamin may have borrowed the word *seellos* from Hölderlin, more specifically from the famous central lines of "Andenken": "Nicht ist es gut, / Seellos von sterblichen / Gedanken zu sein" (ll. 30–32). On this, the "crux" of the poem "on" or "in" remembrance, see Bahti, *Ends of the Lyric*, 143–45.

41. See, for example, Rang, *Shakespeare der Christ*, 14: "We are christic [*christisch*]—which is fundamentally different from Christian!"

Chapter 8: "Subtracted from the Order of Number"

1. For an analysis of "pure means" (*reine Mittel*), see Hamacher, "Afformative, Strike." The account of "Toward the Critique of Violence" developed here is indebted to Hamacher's remarkable essay. I am also grateful for the remarks of Pheng Cheah and Elizabeth Grosz on an earlier version of this chapter.

2. Benjamin entitled the work into which "Toward the Critique of Violence"

was supposed to be integrated *Die wahre Politik* (True politics), the first section of which would elucidate *Der wahre Politiker* (The true politician); see the editorial notes in GS, 2: 943–45. Benjamin's emphasis on "true politics," if not truth in politics, responds to what he calls the "objective mendacity [*objektive Verlogenheit*]" of the contemporary European political and legal orders (see the dense fragments published in GS, 6: 60–64). Benjamin's discussion of *Gewalt* ("violence," "might," "force," the "sway" in holding sway) sets out to unsettle two closely related legal-political doctrines: (1) that legally sanctioned coercion is removed from the violence in which the legal order first imposes itself, and (2) that parliamentary compromise is removed from the coercive mechanisms through which a legal order maintains itself. "Toward the Critique of Violence" takes its point of departure from two divergent but complimentary critiques of the parliamentarian practices of France and Germany in the early part of the century: Sorel's *Reflexions sur la violence* and Unger's *Politik und Metaphysik*. Benjamin draws extensively on Sorel's presentation of the general strike as an immediate remedy to the mendacity of parlimentarianism, but he uses Unger's now forgotten work only sparingly, citing his critique of the concept of compromise and referring in a footnote to his exposition of certain "higher orders" in view of which a politics of pure means can be motivated. Because Unger, who was a student of the Kabbalah and a disciple of Oskar Goldberg (see note 7, Chapter 7), points toward a "philosophical politics," his presentation of orders higher than those of the state may be of more importance for Benjamin's overall project than Sorel's pronouncements on the general strike.

3. The word *Mittel*, which is generally translated as "means," at first meant "middle" and then came to mean "medium" (see the dictionary begun by the Grimm brothers, *Deutsches Wörterbuch*, 6: 2381–93).

4. See Benjamin's contemporaneous sketch of the cultic character of capitalist accumulation, "Capitalism as Religion" (GS, 6: 100–103; W, 1: 288–91). For a discussion of this workstoppage in terms of the phenomenological *epochē*, see the last section of Chapter 6.

5. *Talmud, Chagigah*, 14a. The term "fiery stream" derives from a previous passage:

> It is taught: Rabbi said in the name of Abba Jose b. Dosai: "Thousand thousands ministered unto Him",—this is the number of one troop; but of His troops there is no number. But Jeremiah b. Aba said: "Thousand thousands ministered unto Him"— at the fiery stream, for it is said: A fiery stream issued and came forth from before Him; thousand thousands ministered unto Him and ten thousand times ten thousand stood before Him. Whence does it come forth?—From the sweat of the "living creatures", And whither does it pour forth? R. Zutra b. Tobiah said that Rab said: Upon the head of the wicked in Gehinnom, for it is said: Behold, a storm of the Lord is gone forth in fury, yea, a whirling storm; it shall whirl upon the head of the wicked. (*Chagigah*, 13b)

6. This does not mean, of course, that Benjamin has nothing to say about sexual difference in other writings. On the contrary, as some of the most incisive analyses and critiques of his work in recent years have shown, sexual difference constitutes one of the most persistent points of congruence for the interpretations of his ever changing "constellations." See, for example, the studies of Weigel, *Body- and Image-Space*, esp. 63–94; Buci-Glucksmann, *Walter Benjamin und die Utopie des Weiblichen*; and Geulen, "Toward a Genealogy of Gender in Walter Benjamin's Writing." Benjamin even interprets the idea of the general strike in terms of sexual difference as it enters into another constellation: "Male impotence—the key figure of solitude—under its sign the standstill of productive forces is completed—an abyss separates a human being [*Mensch*] from its kind" (GS, 1: 679).

7. Before Benjamin acquired Klee's *Angelus novus* and before he saw the capitulation of the German youth to nationalist warmongering, he placed the question this movement posed—especially as it concerned the relation of sexuality to language—at the center of his thought. Geulen points toward the significance of Benjamin's early writings on youth in the context of his reflections on sexuality, gender, and language; see "Toward a Genealogy of Gender in Walter Benjamin's Writing," 173–76. For a comparison of Benjamin's "Metaphysics of Youth" with Irigaray's theorization of sexual difference in language, see Weigel, *Body- and Image-Space*, 85.

8. Benjamin finds this difference in "the unity of the erotic and the sexual in woman," and it is "on the basis of the saddest act of veiling [*Verschleierung*]" that this unity "appears to be natural" (GS, 6: 72; W, 1: 231). Whatever else may be said of this fragment of 1920, "On Love and Related Matters (A *European* Problem)" (GS, 6: 72–74; W, 1: 229–30), at least one thing is clear: the "battle of the sexes" is not, according to Benjamin, an eternal struggle but a historico-geographical conflict.

9. Benjamin's decision to draw on the "outstanding example" of Niobe for the presentation of the mythic violence through which the fateful reign of the Olympian gods established itself may owe something to his long-standing interest in Bachofen's conjectures concerning "das Mutterrecht" (see esp. GS, 2: 219–33). That Benjamin did not allow Bachofen's thought to enter into the explicit discussion of mythic violence is a further indication that his investigation into the sphere of pure means outside of its legal appearance falls short of its immanent goal.

10. With reference to Irigaray's discussion of blood in *Speculum*, the following question cannot fail to be posed: is the blood about which Benjamin writes red or white? However urgent the question, however, no clear response can be expected, for a third term enters into the formula through which answers to this question are decided: Niobe's tears, the source of the image's pathos. This matter of redness, whiteness, and purity is further complicated, moreover, when Iri-

garay's angels are brought into discussion, for they are supposed to be not only white but also pure (see CM, 37; SG, 35). Irigaray qualifies this last characterization by indicating that the purity of the angels should be understood in terms of Rilkean "animals." But this reference serves only as a gesture toward the explication of a "purity" that would not depend on the Platonic and Kantian criterion of nonsensuousness, for Rilke's animals are as little able to leap out of the poems they inhabit as to escape from the cages in which some of them are kept.

11. Heidegger, *Sein und Zeit*, 68.

12. Helpful analyses of Irigaray's tendency to touch on angels can be found in Grosz, *Sexual Subversions*, 161–62; Whitford, *Luce Irigaray*, 163–65; and especially Schwab, "Mother's Body, Father's Tongue," 366–68.

13. In the famous sections of the *Summa theologiae* on the angels, Thomas Aquinas does not ask how many angels dance on the head of pin; rather, he poses a more general question: "Whether several angels can be at the same time in the same place?" (part 1, question 53, article 3): "I answer that, There are not two angels in the same place."

14. See Auden, *Collected Poem*, 347–400. For an analysis of Auden in relation to the question of messianicity, see Gottlieb, *"Regions of Sorrow."*

15. See Rilke, *Werke*, 1: 685 (the first of the *Duino Elegies*): "Ein jeder Engel ist schrecklich" (Every angel is terrifying).

16. "La Croyance même" was first presented at a conference "departing from the work of Jacques Derrida" and dedicated to "the ends of man," along with a brief discussion (Lacoue-Labarthe, *Les Fins de l'homme*, 391–93). For Derrida's analysis of "Toward the Critique of Violence," see "Force of Law."

17. See Freud, *Beyond the Pleasure Principle*, 8–11.

18. When I say "today," I mean the day I first began to write this chapter: November 9, 1997. Images of angels are everywhere to be found on the medium whose speed of transmission is reminiscent of angelic swiftness and whose range is almost as wide as theirs—namely, television: "Angel in the Outfield," "Touched by an Angel," and a lengthy report on "Touched by an Angel" on *Sixty Minutes* were all shown within a few hours of each other in, and beyond, the country. Images of angels appear in almost every other media as well: movies, theater, books, magazines, and the internet. Only radio, as the sphere of the purely sonorous, seems spared for now. There are, however, exceptions to the uniform pattern in which the image of the angel returns to herald the return of a belief in the return of belief: Kushner's *Angels in America* is one, and so, too, is Serres's remarkable web of dialogue, discourse, and images in which the nature of angelic orders, the multiplication of "los angeleses," the new angels—which is to say, agents—of global capital, the old world in which these angels operate come into relief. This web perhaps makes room for something other than the return of the same to the same (see *Angels: A Modern Myth*).

Bibliography

Aarsleff, Hans. *From Locke to Saussure: Essays on the Study of Language and Intellectual History.* Minneapolis: University of Minnesota Press, 1982.

Académie française, ed. *Dictionnaire de l'Académie française.* Paris: 1694. Electronic publication, Paris: Champion électronique, 1998.

Adickes, Erich. *German Kantian Bibliography.* 1893–96. New York: Burt Franklin, 1970.

———. *Kants Lehre von der doppelten Affektion unseres Ich als Schlüssel zu seiner Erkenntnistheorie.* Tübingen: Mohr, 1929.

Adorno, Theodor W. *Zur Metakritik der Erkenntnistheorie: Studien über Husserl und die phänomenologischen Antinomien.* Frankfurt am Main: Suhrkamp, 1970.

Agamben, Giorgio. *The Coming Community.* Trans. Michael Hardt. Minneapolis: University of Minnesota Press, 1993.

———. *Homo Sacer: Sovereign Power and Bare Life.* Trans. Daniel Heller-Roazen. Stanford, Calif.: Stanford University Press, 1998.

———. *Potentialities: Collected Essays in Philosophy.* Ed. and trans. Daniel Heller-Roazen. Stanford, Calif.: Stanford University Press, 1999.

———. *Le Temps qui reste.* Trans. Judith Revel. Paris: Payot and Rivages, 2000.

Aiton, E. J. *Leibniz: A Biography.* Bristol and Boston: Hilger, 1985.

Akademien der Wissenschaften at Göttingen, Leipzig, Munich and Vienna, eds. *Encyklopädie der mathematischen Wissenschaften.* Leipzig: Teubner, 1898–1904.

Altmann, Alexander. *Moses Mendelssohn.* University: University of Alabama Press, 1973.

Andersen, Jørn Erslev. *Poetik und Fragment: Hölderlin-Studien.* Trans. Joachim Schote. Würzburg: Königshausen und Neumann, 1997.

Antognazza, Maria Rosa, and Howard Hotson. *Alsted and Leibniz on God, the Magistrate, and the Millennium.* Wiesbaden: Harrassowitz, 1999.

Appelt, Hedwig, and Dirk Grathoff, eds. *Erläuterungen und Dokumente: Heinrich von Kleist, "Das Erdbeben in Chili"*. Stuttgart: Reclam, 1990.

Aquinas, Thomas. *Summa Theologiae: Latin Text and English Translation, Introductions, Notes, Appendices, and Glossaries*. New York: McGraw-Hill, 1964–81.

Arendt, Hannah. *Between Past and Future*. New York: Penguin, 1977.

———. *Men in Dark Times*. Trans. Clara and Richard Winston. New York: Harcourt Brace Javonovich, 1983.

———. *The Origins of Totalitarianism*. New York: Meridian, 1958.

Aretz. Heinrich. *Heinrich von Kleist als Journalist: Untersuchungen zum "Phöbus", zur "Germania" und den "Berliner Abendblättern."* Stuttgart: Heinz, 1983.

Aristotle. *Metaphysics*. Trans. Richard Hope. Ann Arbor: University of Michigan Press, 1952.

Arkush, Allen. *Mendelssohn and the Enlightenment*. Albany: State University of New York Press, 1994.

Assmann, Aleida. "Prädisposition und Vorgeschichte: Schriftspekulation und Spachutopien in Antike und früher Neuzeit." In *Kabbala und Romantik*, ed. Eveline Goodman-Thau, Gert Mattenklott, and Christoph Schulte, 23–41. Tübingen: Niemeyer, 1994.

Assmann, Jan. *Moses the Egyptian: The Memory of Egypt in Western Monotheism*. Cambridge, Mass.: Harvard University Press, 1997.

Auden, W. H. *Collected Poems*. Ed. Edward Mendelson. New York: Vintage, 1991.

Baeck, Leo. *The Essence of Judaism*. Trans. Irving Howe and Victor Grubenwieser. New York: Schocken, 1948.

Baeumler, Alfred. *Das Irrationalitätsproblem in der Ästhetik und Logik des 18: Jahrhunderts bis zur Kritik der Urteilskraft*. 1923. Repr., Darmstadt: Wissenschaftliche Buchgesellschaft, 1967.

Bahti, Timothy. *Ends of the Lyric*. Baltimore: Johns Hopkins University Press, 1996.

Banfi, Antonio, ed. *La crisi dell'uso dogmatico della ragione*. Rome: Fratelli Bocca, 1953.

Barilli, Renato. *Rhetoric*. Trans. Guiliana Menozzi. Minneapolis: University of Minnesota Press, 1989.

Barner, Wilfried, ed. *Der literarische Barockbegriff*. Darmstadt: Wissenschaftliche Buchgesellschaft, 1975.

Bassler, Otto Bradley. *"Labyrinthus de compositione continui": The Origins of Leibniz' Solution to the Continuum Problem (1666–1672)*. Ph.D. diss., University of Chicago, 1995.

Battistini, Andrea. "Antonomasia e universale fantastico." In *Retorica e critica letteraria*, ed. Lea Ritter Santini and Ezio Raimondi, 105–22. Bologna: Il mulino, 1978.

————. "Tradizione e innovazione nella tassonomia tropologica vichiana." *Bollettino del Centro di Studi Vichiani* 1 (1973): 73–87.

Baumgarten, Alexander Gottlieb. *Meditationes philosophicae de nonnullis ad poema pertinentibus = Philosophische Betrachtungen über einige Bedingungen des Gedichtes.* Ed. Heinz Paetzold. Hamburg: Meiner, 1983.

————. *Reflections on Poetry.* Trans. Karl Aschenbrenner and William Holther. Berkeley: University of California Press, 1954.

————. *Theoretische Ästhetik: Die grundlegende Abschnitte aus der "Aesthetica" (1750/48).* Trans. and ed. Hans Rudolf Schweizer. Hamburg: Meiner, 1983.

Bayle, Pierre. *Dictionaire historique et critique.* 3 vols. 2nd ed. Rotterdam: Reinier Leers, 1702.

Becco, Anne. "Aux sources de la monade: Paléographie et lexicographie leibniziennes." *Études philosophiques* 3 (1975): 279–94.

Beck, Lewis White. *A Commentary on Kant's "Critique of Practical Reason."* Chicago: University of Chicago Press, 1960.

Behler, Ernst, and Jochen Hörisch, eds. *Die Aktualität der Frühromantik.* Paderborn: Schoningh, 1987.

Beiser, Frederick. *The Fate of Reason.* Cambridge, Mass.: Harvard University Press, 1987.

Belaval, Yvon. *Études leibniziennes.* Paris: Gallimard, 1976.

Benjamin, Andrew, and Peter Osborne, eds. *Walter Benjamin's Philosophy: Destruction and Experience.* London and New York: Routledge, 1994.

Benjamin, Walter. *Arcades Project.* Trans. Howard Eiland and Kevin McLaughlin. Cambridge, Mass.: Harvard University Press, 1999.

————. *Correspondence of Walter Benjamin.* Trans. Manfred Jacobsen and Evelyn Jacobsen. Chicago: University of Chicago Press, 1994.

————. *Gesammelte Briefe.* 6 vols. Ed. Christoph Gödde and Henri Lonitz. Frankfurt am Main: Suhrkamp, 1995–.

————. *Gesammelte Schriften.* 7 vols. Ed. Rolf Tiedemann and Hermann Schweppenhäuser. Frankfurt am Main: Suhrkamp, 1972–91.

————. *Illuminations.* Ed. Hannah Arendt. Trans. Harry Zohn. New York: Schocken, 1969.

————. *Origin of German Tragic Drama.* Trans. John Osborne. New York: Verso, 1977.

————. *Selected Writings.* 3 vols. Ed. Michael Jennings. Cambridge, Mass.: Harvard University Press, 1996–.

Berghahn, Klaus, ed. *The German-Jewish Dialogue.* New York: Lang, 1996.

————. "On Friendship: The Beginnings of a Christian-Jewish Dialogue in the 18th Century." In *The German-Jewish Dialogue*, ed. Klaus Berghahn, 5–24. New York: Lang, 1996.

Blickle, Peter, and André Holenstein, eds. *Der Fluch und der Eid: Die meta-*

physische Begründung gesellschaftlichen Zusammenlebens und politischer Ord-nung in der ständischen Gesellschaft. Berlin: Duncker und Humblot, 1993.

Bloch, Ernst. *Literary Essays.* Trans. Andrew Joron et al. Stanford, Calif.: Stanford University Press, 1998.

Bohl, Samuel. *Disputatio prima-duodecima pro formali significationis eruendo pri-mum in explicatione Scripturae Sacrae.* Rostock: Haeredum Richelianorum, 1637.

Bolz, N. W., and W. Hübener, eds. *Spiegel und Gleichnis.* Würzburg: Königs-hausen and Neumann, 1983.

Boureau, Alain. *La Papesse Jeanne.* Paris: Flammarion, 1988.

Boyer, Carl, and Ute Merzbach. *A History of Mathematics.* New York: Wily and Sons, 1991.

Boyle, Nicholas. *Goethe: The Poet and the Age.* 3 vols. Oxford: Oxford University Press, 1991–.

Boyle, Robert. *Some Considerations Touching the Style of H. Scriptures.* London: Herringman, 1661.

Brandt, Wolfgang, ed. *Erzähler, Erzählen, Erzähltes.* Stuttgart: Steiner, 1996.

Breuer, Edward. *The Limits of Enlightenment: Jews, Germans, and the Eighteenth-Century Study of Scripture.* Cambridge, Mass.: Harvard University Press, 1996.

———. "Of Miracles and Events Past: Mendelssohn on History," *Jewish History* 9 (Fall 1995): 27–52.

Bröcker, Michael. "Sprache." In *Benjamins Begriffe*, ed. Michael Opitz and Erd-mut Wizisla, 2: 740–73. Frankfurt am Main: Suhrkamp, 2000.

Brodersen, Momme. *Spinne im eigenen Netz: Walter Benjamins Leben und Werk.* Baden-Baden: Elster, 1990.

Buber, Martin. *On Judaism.* Ed. Nahum Glazer. Trans. Eva Jospe. New York: Schocken, 1967.

Buber, Martin, and Franz Rosenzweig. *Scripture and Translation.* Trans. Lawrence Rosenwald and Everett Fox. Bloomington: Indiana University Press, 1994.

Bubner, Rüdiger. *Antike Themen und ihre moderne Verwandlung.* Frankfurt am Main: Suhrkamp, 1992.

Buci-Glucksmann, Christiane. *Walter Benjamin und die Utopie des Weiblichen.* Trans. Horst Arenz, Rolf Löper, and Renate Petzinger. Hamburg: VSA-Verlag, 1984.

Burckhardt, Jacob. *Griechische Kulturgeschichte.* Ed. Jakob Oeri. Berlin and Stutt-gart: Spemann, 1898–1902.

Burke, Carolyn, Naomi Schor, and Margaret Whitford, eds. *Engaging with Iri-garay.* New York: Columbia University Press, 1994.

Cantor, Georg, ed. *Die Rawley'sche Sammlung von zweiunddreissig Trauer-gedichten auf Francis Bacon: Ein Zeugniss zu gunsten der Bacon-Shakespeare-Theorie.* Halle: Niemeyer, 1897.

————. *Gesammelte Abhandlungen.* Ed. Ernst Zermelo. Berlin: Springer, 1932.

Caygill, Howard. *Walter Benjamin: The Colour of Experience.* London: Routledge, 1998.

Cervantes, Miguel de. *Don Quixote.* Trans. John Ormsby. Ed. Joseph Jones and Kenneth Douglas. New York: Norton, 1981.

————. *El ingenioso hidalgo Don Quijote de la Mancha.* Ed. Luis Andrés Murillo. Madrid: Clásico Castalia, 1978.

Cicero. *De republica, De legibus.* Trans. Clinton Walker Keyes. Cambridge, Mass.: Harvard University Press, 1977.

Cohen, Hermann. *Jüdische Schriften.* Ed. Bruno Strauß. Berlin: Schwetschke, 1924.

————. *Kants Theorie der Erfahrung.* Berlin: Dümmler, 1885.

————. *Logik der reinen Erkenntnis.* Berlin: Cassirer, 1902.

————. *Das Prinzip der Infintesimal-Methode und seine Geschichte: Ein Kapitel zur Grundlegung der Erkenntnisskritik.* Berlin: Dümmler, 1883.

————. *Religion of Reason from the Sources of Judaism.* Trans. Simon Kaplan. Atlanta: Scholar's Press, 1995.

Conger, George. *Theories of Macrocosms and Microcosms in the History of Philosophy.* New York: Columbia University Press, 1922.

Copi, Irving, and James Gould, eds. *Contemporary Philosophical Logic.* New York: St. Martin's, 1978.

Coudert, Allison P. *Leibniz and the Kabbalah.* Dordrecht: Kluwer, 1995.

Couturat, Louis. *La Logique de Leibniz d'après des documents inédits.* Paris: Alcan, 1901.

Craig, Hardin, ed. *Stanford Studies in Language and Literature.* Stanford, Calif.: Stanford University Press, 1941.

Curtius, Ernst Robert. *European Literature and the Latin Middle Ages.* Trans. Willard Trask. Princeton, N.J.: Princeton University Press, 1990.

Dascal, Marcel. *Leibniz, Language, Signs, and Thought.* Philadelphia: Benjamins, 1987.

————. "One Adam and Many Cultures: The Role of Political Pluralism in the Best of Possible Worlds." In *Leibniz and Adam,* ed. Marcel Dascal and Elhanan Yakira, 387–409. Tel Aviv: University Publishing Projects, 1993.

Dascal, Marcel, and Elhanan Yakira, eds. *Leibniz and Adam.* Tel Aviv: University Publishing Projects, 1993.

Dauben, Joseph Warren. *Georg Cantor: His Mathematics and Philosophy of the Infinite.* Princeton, N.J.: Princeton University Press, 1979.

Deleuze, Giles. *Logique du sens.* Paris, Minuit, 1969.

————. *Le Pli: Leibniz et le baroque.* Paris: Minuit, 1988.

de Man, Paul. *Aesthetic Ideology.* Ed. Andrzej Warminski. Minneapolis: University of Minnesota Press, 1996.

———. *Rhetoric of Romanticism.* New York: Columbia University Press, 1984.
Derrida, Jacques. *Aporias.* Trans. Thomas Dutoit. Stanford, Calif.: Stanford University Press, 1993.
———. "Force of Law: The 'Mystical Foundation' of Authority." *Cardoza Law Review* 11 (July–August 1990): 919–1045.
———. *Glas.* Trans. John Leavey and Richard Rand. Lincoln: University of Nebraska Press, 1986.
———. *Limited, Inc.* Trans. Samuel Weber. Evanston, Ill.: Northwestern University Press, 1988.
———. *Specters of Marx: The State of Debt, the Work of Mourning, and the New International.* Trans. Peggy Kamuf. New York: Routledge, 1994.
———. *Speech and Phenomenon, and Other Essays on Husserl's Theory of Signs.* Trans. David Allison. Evanston, Ill.: Northwestern University Press, 1973.
Descartes, René. *Oeuvres de Descartes.* Ed. Charles Adam and Paul Tannery. Paris: Cerf, 1897–1913.
Deuber-Mankowsky, Astrid. *Der frühe Walter Benjamin. Jüdische Werte, Kritische Philosophie, Vergängliche Erfahrung.* Berlin: Vorwerk, 2000.
Dierauer, Walter. *Hölderlin und der spekulative Pietismus Württembergs: Gemeinsame Anschauungshorizonte im Werke Oetingers und Hölderlins.* Juris: Zürich, 1986.
D'Israeli, Isaac. *A Dissertation on Anecdotes.* 1793. Repr., New York: Garland, 1972.
D'Onofrio, Cesare. *La Papessa Giovanna: Roma e papato tra storia e leggenda.* Rome: Romana società editrice, 1979.
Driehorst, Gerd. "Hebels Diebesgeschichte." In *Erzähler, Erzählen, Erzähltes,* ed. Wolfgang Brandt, 13–27. Stuttgart: Steiner, 1996.
Duchet, Michèle. *Langue et langages de Leibniz à l'Encyclopédie.* Paris: Union générale d'éditions, 1977.
Dutz, Klaus, and Stefano Gensini. *Im Spiegel des Verstandes: Studien zu Leibniz.* Münster: Nodus Publikationen, 1996.
Dyck, Joachim. *Ticht-Kunst: Deutsche Barockpoetik und rhetorische Tradition: Mit einer Bibliographie zur Forschung, 1966–1986.* Tübingen: Niemeyer, 1991.
Dyer, Denys. *The Stories of Kleist.* London: Duckworth, 1977.
Edel, Susanne. *Die individuelle Substanz bei Böhme und Leibniz.* Stuttgart: Steiner, 1995.
Eisen, Albert. "Divine Legislation as 'Ceremonial Script': Mendelssohn on the Commandments." *AJS Review* 15 (Fall 1990): 239–68.
Élie, Maurice. *Lumière, couleurs, et nature: L'Optique et la physique de Goethe et de la "Naturphilosophie."* Paris: Vrin, 1993.
Ellis, John. *Narration in the German Novelle.* Cambridge, Eng.: Cambridge University Press, 1974.

Engel, Eva. "Die Freyheit der Untersuchung: *Die Literaturbrief 72–75.*" In *Moses Mendelssohn und die Kreise seiner Wirksamkeit*, ed. Albrecht Michael, Eva Engel, and Norbert Hinske, 249–68. Tübingen: Niemeyer, 1994.

Erhart, Walter. "'In guten Zeiten giebt es selten Schwärmer': Wielands 'Agathon' and Hölderlins 'Hyperion.'" *Hölderlin Jahrbuch* 28 (1992–93): 173–91.

Ernesti, Johann Christian Gottlieb. *Lexicon technologiae Graecorum rhetoricae*. 1795. Repr., Hildesheim: Olms, 1983.

Euclid. *The Thirteen Books of Euclid's "Elements."* 2nd ed. Trans. Thomas Heath. New York: Dover, 1956.

Fauvel, John, and Jeremy Gray, eds. *The History of Mathematics: A Reader*. Basingstoke: Macmillan, 1987.

Fenves, Peter. "*Chatter*": *Language and History in Kierkegaard*. Stanford, Calif.: Stanford University Press, 1993.

———. "Continuing the Fiction: From Leibniz' 'petite fable' to Kafka's *In der Strafkolonie.*" *MLN* 116 (2001): 502–20.

———. "The Genesis of Judgment: Spatiality, Analogy, and Metaphor in Benjamin's "On Language as Such and on Human Language." In *Walter Benjamin: Theoretical Questions*, ed. David Ferris, 75–93. Stanford, Calif.: Stanford University Press, 1996.

———. "Hölderlin." In *Encyclopedia of Aesthetics*, ed. Michael Kelly, 2: 415–22. Oxford: Oxford University Press, 1998.

———. "Marx, Mourning, Messianicity." In *Identity, Violence, and Self-Determination*, ed. Sam Weber and Hent de Vries, 253–70. Stanford, Calif.: Stanford University Press, 1997.

———. *A Peculiar Fate: Metaphysics and World-History in Kant*. Ithaca, N.Y.: Cornell University Press, 1991.

———. "The Politics of Friendship—Once Again." *Eighteenth Century Studies* 32 (Winter 1998–99): 133–55.

———. Review of *Walter Benjamin*, by Howard Caygill. *Review of Metaphysics* 53 (2000): 920–23.

———. "Die Unterlassung der Übersetzung." In *Übersetzen: Walter Benjamin*, ed. Christiaan Hart-Nibbrig, 159–73. Frankfurt am Main: Suhrkamp, 2001.

———, ed. *Raising the Tone of Philosophy*. Baltimore: Johns Hopkins University Press, 1993.

Ferris, David. "Aura, Resistance, and the Event of History." Introduction to *Walter Benjamin: Theoretical Questions*, ed. David Ferris. Stanford, Calif.: Stanford University Press, 1996.

———, ed. *Walter Benjamin: Theoretical Questions*. Stanford, Calif.: Stanford University Press, 1996.

Fichte, Johann Gottlieb. *Introductions to the Wissenschaftslehre and Other Writings*. Ed. and trans. Daniel Breazeale. Indianapolis: Hackett, 1994.

————. *Sämmtliche Werke.* 11 vols. Ed. Immanuel Hermann Fichte. Repr., Berlin: De Gruyter, 1971.

————. *The Science of Knowledge.* Trans. Peter Heath and John Lachs. Cambridge, Eng.: Cambridge University Press, 1982.

Fineman, Joel. "The History of the Anecdote: Fiction and Fiction." In *The New Historicism,* ed. H. Aram Veeser, 49–76. New York: Routledge, 1989.

Fischer, Barbara. "Residues of Otherness: On Jewish Emancipation During the Age of German Enlightenment." In *Insiders and Outsiders: Jewish and Gentile Culture in Germany and Austria,* ed. Dagmar Lorenz and G. Weinberger, 30–38. Detroit: Wayne State University Press, 1994.

Fischer, Bernd. *Ironische Metaphysik.* Munich: Fink, 1988.

Fontanier, Pierre. *Commentaire raisonné à Dumarsais, "Les Tropes."* 2 vols. 1818. Repr., Geneva: Slatkine Reprints, 1967.

Fontenelle, M. de (Bernard Le Bovier). *Oeuvres complètes.* 3 vols. Ed. Georges-Bernard Depping. 1818. Repr., Geneva: Slatkine Reprints, 1968.

Foucault. Michel. *Surveiller et punir: Naissance de la prison.* Paris: Gallimard, 1975.

Frank, Manfred. "'Intellektuale Anschauung': Drei Stellungnahmen zu einem Deutungsversuch von Selbstbewußtsein: Kant, Fichte, Hölderlin, Novalis." In *Die Aktualität der Frühromantik,* ed. Ernst Behler and Jochen Hörisch, 96–126. Paderborn: Schoningh, 1987.

Frankfurt, Harry, ed. *Leibniz: A Collection of Critical Essays.* Notre Dame, Ind.: Notre Dame University Press, 1976.

Frege, Gottlieb. *Collected Papers on Mathematics, Logic, and Philosophy.* Ed. Brian McGuinness. Trans. Max Black et al. New York: Blackwell, 1984.

————. *Funktion, Begriff, Bedeutung.* Ed. Günther Patzig. Göttingen: Vandenkoeck und Ruprecht, 1986.

Freud, Sigmund. *Beyond the Pleasure Principle.* Trans. James Stachey. New York: Norton, 1961.

————. *Freud-Studienausgabe.* 11 vols. Ed. Alexander Mitscherlich, Angela Richards, James Strachey, and Ilse Grudrich-Simitis. Frankfurt am Main: Fischer, 1982.

————. *Three Case Histories.* Ed. Philip Rief. New York: Collier, 1963.

Friedman, Michael. *Kant and the Exact Sciences.* Cambridge, Mass.: Harvard University Press, 1992.

Friesenhahn, Ernst. *Der politische Eid: Mit einem Vorwort zum Neudruck sowie einem Verzeichnis neuerer Literatur zur Eidesfrage als Anhang.* 1928. Repr., Darmstadt: Wissenschaftliche Buchgesellschaft, 1979.

Gaier, Ulrich. *Hölderlin.* Tübingen and Basel: Francke, 1993.

Gasché, Rodolphe. "Saturnine Vision and the Question of Difference: Reflections on Walter Benjamin's Theory of Language." In *Benjamin's Ground,* ed. Rainer Nägele, 83–104. Detroit: Wayne State University Press, 1988.

Gallo, Ernest. *The "Poetria Nova" and Its Sources in Early Rhetorical Doctrine.* The Hague: Mouton, 1971.

García-Düttmann, Alexander. "The Violence of Destruction." In *Walter Benjamin: Theoretical Questions,* ed. David Ferris, 165–84. Stanford, Calif.: Stanford University Press, 1996.

Garin, Eugenio, ed. *Testi umanistici su la retorica.* Roma: Fratelli Bocca, 1953.

Geiger, Moritz. *Beiträge zur Phänomenologie des äesthetischen Genusses.* Tübingen: Niemeyer, 1913.

Gensini, Stefano. "The Leibnitian Concept of 'Significatio.'" In *Im Spiegel des Verstandes,* ed. Klaus Dutz and Stefano Gensini, 69–98. Münster: Nodus Publikationen, 1996.

———. "Leibniz, Linguist and Philosopher of Language: Between 'Primitive and 'Natural.'" In *Leibniz and Adam,* ed. Marcelo Dascal and Elhanan Yakira, 111–36. Tel Aviv: University Publishing Projects, 1993.

———. *Il naturale e il simbolico: Saggio su Leibniz.* Rome: Bulzoni, 1991.

Geulen, Eva. "Toward a Genealogy of Gender in Walter Benjamin's Writing." *German Quarterly* 69 (Spring 1996): 161–80.

Gibbon, Edward. *The History of the Decline and Fall of the Roman Empire.* 7 vols. Ed. John Bagnell Bury. New York: Macmillan, 1896–1901.

Gierke, Otto. *Natural Law and the Theory of Society.* Trans. Ernst Barker. Cambridge, Eng.: Cambridge University Press, 1950.

Goethe, Johann Wolfgang von. *Goethes Werke: Weimarer Ausgabe.* 50 vols. Commissioned by Großherzogin Sophie von Sachsen. Weimar: Hermann Böhlau, 1887–1917.

———. *Werke.* 14 vols. Ed. Erich Trunz. Munich: Beck, 1981.

Goodman-Thau, Eveline, Gert Mattenklott, and Christoph Schulte, eds. *Kabbala und Romantik.* Tübingen: Niemeyer, 1994.

Gössmann, Elisabeth. *Mulier papa: Der Skandal eines weiblichen Papstes: Zur Rezeptionsgeschichte der Gestalt der Päpstin Johanna.* Munich: Iudicium, 1994.

Gottlieb, Susannah Y. *"Regions of Sorrow": Anxiety and Messianism in W. H. Auden and Hannah Arendt.* Stanford: Stanford University Press, 2002.

Grimm, Jacob, and Wilhelm Grimm. *Deutsches Wörterbuch.* 16 vols. Leipzig: Hirzel, 1954.

Gritsch, Eric. "Luther und die Schwärmer: Verworfene Anfechtung?" *Luther, Zeitschrift der Luther-Gesellschaft* 47 (1976): 105–21.

Grosz, Elizabeth. *Sexual Subversions: Three French Feminists.* Sydney: Allen and Unwin, 1989.

Grothe, Heinz. *Anekdote.* 2nd ed. Stuttgart: Mezler, 1984.

Group μ. *A General Rhetoric.* Trans. Paul Burrell and Edgar Slotkin. Baltimore: Johns Hopkins University Press, 1981.

Guthke, Karl. *Schillers Dramen: Idealismus und Skepsis.* Tübingen: Francke, 1994.

Haller, Albrecht von. *Die Alpen und andere Gedichte.* Ed. Adalbert Elschen-chroich. Stuttgart: Reklam, 1965.

Hamacher, Werner. "Afformative, Strike." Trans. Dana Hollander. In *Walter Benjamin's Philosophy: Destruction and Experience,* ed. Andrew Benjamin and Peter Osborne, 110–38. London and New York: Routledge, 1994.

———. "Intensive Sprache." In *Übersetzen: Walter Benjamin,* ed. Christiaan Hart-Nibbrig, 174–235. Frankfurt am Main: Suhrkamp, 2001.

———. *pleroma.* In Hegel, *"Der Geist des Christentums": Schriften 1796–1800,* ed. Werner Hamacher, 9–333. Frankfurt am Main: Ullstein, 1978.

———. *Premises: Essays on Philosophy and Literature from Kant to Celan.* Trans. Peter Fenves. Cambridge, Mass.: Harvard University Press, 1996.

———. "The Word *Wolke*—If It Is One." Trans. Peter Fenves. In *Benjamin's Ground,* ed. Rainer Nägele, 147–76. Detroit: Wayne State University Press, 1988.

Hamann, Johann Georg. *Hamanns Hauptschriften erklärt.* 7 vols. Ed. Fritz Blanke and Lothar Schreiner. Gütersloh: Bettelsmann, 1956.

———. *Hamanns Schriften.* 9 vols. Ed. Friedrich Roth. Berlin: Reimer, 1842.

Hattenhauer, Hans. *Europäische Rechtsgeschichte.* Heidelberg: Müller Juristscher Verlag, 1992.

———. *Die geistesgeschichtlichen Grundlagen des deutschen Rechts.* 3rd ed. Heidelberg: Müller Juristscher Verlag, 1983.

———, ed. *Rechtswissenschaft im NS-Staat: Der Fall Eugen Wohlhaupter.* Heidelberg: Müller, 1987.

Hebel, Johann Peter. *Sämtliche Schriften.* 5 vols. Ed. Adrian Braunbehrens, Gustav Benrath, and Peter Pfaff. Karlsruhe: C. F. Müller, 1990–.

———. *Sämtliche Werke in acht Bänden.* 8 vols. Ed. G. F. N. Sonntag. Karlsruhe: Müller, 1832–34.

———. *The Treasure Chest.* Trans. John Hibberd. Harmondsworth: Penguin, 1994.

———. *Werke.* 2 vols. Ed. Eberhard Meckel and Robert Minder. Frankfurt: Insel, 1968.

Hegel, Georg Wilhelm Friedrich. *Faith and Knowledge.* Trans. Walter Cerf and H. S. Harris. Albany: State University of New Press, 1977.

———. *"Der Geist des Christentums": Schriften 1796–1800.* Ed. Werner Hamacher. Frankfurt am Main: Ullstein, 1978.

———. *Hegels theologische Jugendschriften nach den Handschriften der Königlichen Bibliothek in Berlin.* Ed. Herman Nohl. 1905. Repr., Frankfurt am Main: Minerva, 1966.

———. *Phenomenology of Spirit.* Trans. A. V. Miller. Oxford: Oxford University Press, 1981.

———. *Werke in zwanzig Bände.* 20 vols. Ed. Eva Moldenhauer and Karl Markus Michel. Frankfurt am Main: Suhrkamp, 1971.

Heidegger, Martin. *Erläuterungen zu Hölderlins Dichtung.* Frankfurt am Main: Klostermann, 1981.

———. *Frühe Schriften.* Frankfurt am Main: Klostermann, 1972.

———. *Hebel—der Hausfreund.* Pfullingen: Neske, 1957.

———. *Kant und das Problem der Metaphysik.* Frankfurt am Main: Klostermann, 1973.

———. *Der Satz vom Grund.* Neske: Pfullingen, 1978.

———. *Sein und Zeit.* Tübingen: Niemeyer, 1979.

———. *Wegmarken.* Frankfurt am Main: Klostermann, 1978.

Heinekamp, Albert. "Ars characteristica und natürliche Sprache bei Leibniz." *Tijdschrift voor Filosofie* 34 (1972): 446–88.

———, ed. *Leibniz et la Renaissance.* Studia Leibnitia Supplementa 23. Wiesbaden: Steiner, 1983.

Herbertz, Richard. *Die Lehre vom Unbewußten im System des Leibniz.* 1905. Repr., New York: Olms, 1980.

Hering, Jean. "Bemerkungen über das Wesen, die Wesenheit und die Idee." *Jahrbuch für Philosophie und phänomenologische Forschung* 4 (1921): 495–543.

Herse, Wilhelm. "Leibniz und die Päpstin Johanna." In *Beiträge zur Leibniz-Forschung,* ed. Georgi Schischkoff, 153–58. Reutlingen: Gryphius, 1947.

Hinske, Norbert. "Mendelssohns Beantwortung der Frage: Was ist Aufklärung? Oder Über die Aktualität Mendelssohn." In *Ich handle mit Vernunft,* ed. Norbert Hinske, 85–117. Hamburg: Meiner, 1981.

———. "Zur Verwendung der Wörter 'schwärmen' 'Schwärmer,' 'Schwärmerei,' 'schwärmerisch' im Kontext von Kants Anthropologiekolleg." In *Die Aufklärung und die Schwärmer,* ed. Norbert Hinske, 3–81. Hamburg: Meiner, 1988.

———, ed. *Die Aufklärung und die Schwärmer.* Hamburg: Meiner, 1988.

———, ed. *Ich handle mit Vernunft.* Hamburg: Meiner, 1981.

Hobbes, Thomas. *English Works.* Ed. William Molesworth. London: Bohn, 1839–45.

Hölderlin, Friedrich. *Essays and Letters on Theory.* Trans. Thomas Pfau. Albany: State University of New York Press, 1988.

———. *Sämtliche Werke.* 8 vols. Ed. Friedich Beißner and Adolf Beck. Stuttgart: Kohlhammer, 1943–85.

Holenstein, André. "Seelenheil und Untertanenpflicht: Zur gesellschaftlichen Funktion und theoretischen Begründung des Eides in der ständischen Gesellschaft." In *Der Fluch und der Eid: Die metaphysische Begründung gesellschaftlichen Zusammenlebens und politischer Ordnung in der ständischen Gesellschaft,* ed. Peter Blickle and André Holenstein, 11–63. Berlin: Duncker und Humblot, 1993.

Holz, Hans Heinz. "Idee." In *Benjamins Begriffe,* ed. Michael Opitz and Erdmut Wizisla, 1: 445–78. Frankfurt am Main: Suhrkamp, 2000.

Horn, Peter. *Heinrich von Kleists Erzählungen: Eine Einführung.* Königstein: Scriptor, 1978.

Husserl, Edmund. *Husserliana: Gesammelte Werke.* 31 vols. Ed. Husserl-Archiv in Leuven under the directorship of H. L. van Breda. The Hague: Nijhoff, 1950–.

———. *Ideas Pertaining to a Pure Phenomenology and to a Phenomenological Philosophy.* Vol. 1 of *General Introduction to a Pure Phenomenology.* Trans. F. Kersten. The Hague: Nijhoff, 1982.

———. *Phenomenology and the Crisis of Philosophy.* Trans. and ed. Quentin Lauer. New York: Harper and Row, 1965.

Idel, Moshe. *Golem: Jewish Magical and Mystical Traditions on the Artificial Anthropoid.* Albany: State University of New York Press Press, 1990.

Ingarden, Roman. *On the Motives Which Led Husserl to Transcendental Idealism.* Dordrecht: Kluwer, 1975.

Irigaray, Luce. *La Croyance même.* Paris: Galilée, 1983.

———. *An Ethics of Sexual Difference.* Trans. Carolyn Burke and Gillian C. Gill. Ithaca, N.Y.: Cornell University Press, 1993.

———. *Ethique de le différence sexuelle.* Paris: Minuit, 1984.

———. *Sex and Genealogies.* Trans. Gillian C. Gill. New York: Columbia University Press, 1993.

———. *Speculum de l'autre femme.* Paris: Minuit, 1974.

Ishiguro, Hidé. *Leibniz's Philosophy of Logic and Language.* 2nd ed. Cambridge, Eng.: Cambridge University Press, 1990.

Jacobi, Friedrich. *The Spinoza Conversations Between Lessing and Jacobi.* Trans. G. Vallée, J. B. Lawson, and C. G. Chapple. Lanham, Md.: University Press of America, 1988.

———. *Werke.* 6 vols. Ed. Friedrich Roth and Friedrich Köppen. 1812–25. Repr., Darmstadt: Wissenschaftliche Buchgesellschaft, 1968.

Jacobs, Carol. *In the Language of Walter Benjamin.* Baltimore: Johns Hopkins Univesity Press, 1999.

———. *Uncontainable Romanticism.* Baltimore: Johns Hopkins University Press, 1989.

Jäger, Lorenz. *Messianische Kritik: Studien zu Leben und Werk von Florens Christian Rang.* Köln: Böhlau, 1998.

Janik, Allan. "Haecker, Kierkegaard, and the early *Brenner.*" In *International Kierkegaard Commentary: "Two Ages,"* ed. Robert Perkins, 189–222. Macon, Ga.: Mercer University Press, 1984.

Johnson, Barbara. *The Wake of Deconstruction.* Cambridge, Mass.: Blackwell, 1994.

Jolley, Nicholas, ed. *Cambridge Campanion to Leibniz.* Cambridge, Eng.: Cambridge University Press, 1995.

Jung-Stilling, Johann. *Theobald, oder, die Schwärmer, eine wahre Geschichte.* Leipzig: Weygand, 1784.

Justinian. *The Digest of Justinian.* Ed. Theodor Mommsen and Paul Krueger. Trans. Alan Watson. Philadelphia: University of Pennsylvania Press, 1985.

Kafka, Franz, *Gesammelte Werke in zwölf Bänden.* 12 vols. Ed. Hans-Gerd Koch. Frankfurt am Main: Fischer, 1994.

Kant, Immanuel. *Critique of Judgment.* Trans. Werner Pluhar. Indianapolis: Hackett, 1987.

———. *Critique of Practical Reason.* Trans. Lewis White Beck. Indianapolis: Bobbs-Merrill, 1956.

———. *Gesammelte Schriften.* 29 vols. Ed. Königlich Preußische [later, Deutsche] Akademie der Wissenschaften. Berlin: Reimer; later, De Gruyter, 1900–.

———. *Opus postumum.* Ed. and trans. Eckart Förster and Michael Rosen. Cambridge, Eng.: Cambridge University Press, 1993.

———. "Ein Reinschriftsfragment zu Kants *Streit der Fakultäten.*" Ed. K. Weyand and G. Lehmann. *Kant-Studien* 51 (1959–60): 3–13.

Kassouf, Susan. "The Shared Pain of the Golden Vein: The Discursive Proximity of Jewish and Scholarly Diseases in the Late Eighteenth Century." *Eighteenth-Century Studies* 32 (Fall 1998): 101–10.

Kawa, Rainer. *Friedrich Schiller: "Der Verbrecher aus verlorener Ehre."* Frankfurt: Diesterweg, 1990.

Kelly, Michael, ed. *Encyclopedia of Aesthetics.* 4 vols. Oxford: Oxford University Press, 1998.

Kierkegaard, Søren. *The Concept of Anxiety.* Trans. and ed. Reider Thomte and Albert Anderson. Princeton, N.J.: Princeton University Press, 1980.

———. *Fear and Trembling—Repetition.* Trans. and ed. Howard and Edna Hong. Princeton, N.J.: Princeton University Press, 1983.

———. *Point of View of My Work as an Author: A Report to History.* Trans. Walter Lowrie. New York: Harper and Row, 1962.

———. *Two Ages.* Ed. and trans. Howard Hong and Edna Hong. Princeton, N.J.: Princeton University Press, 1978.

Kittler, Friedrich. "Ein Erdbeben in Chili und Preußen." In *Positionen der Literaturwissenschaft*, ed. David Wellbery, 24–38. Munich: Beck, 1985.

Klein, Lawrence, and Anthony La Vopa, eds. *Enthusiasm and Enlightenment in Europe, 1650–1850.* San Marino, Calif.: Huntington Library Press, 1998.

Kleist, Heinrich von. *An Abyss Deep Enough: Letters of Heinrich von Kleist.* Ed. and trans. Philip B. Miller. New York: Dutton, 1982.

———. *The Marquise of O—— and Other Stories.* Trans. David Luke and Nigel Reeves. Harmondsworth: Penguin, 1978.

———. *Sämtliche Werke und Briefe.* 2 vols. Ed. H. Sembdner. Munich: Deutscher Taschenbuch Verlag, 1987.

————, ed. *Berliner Abendblätter.* Afterword and index of sources by Helmut Sembdner. Repr., Stuttgart: Cotta, 1965.

Kommerell, Max. *Geist und Buchstabe in der Dichtung.* Frankfurt am Main: Klostermann, 1941.

Koselleck, Reinhart. *Preußen zwischen Reform und Revolution: Allgemeines Landrecht, Verwaltung, und soziale Bewegung zwischen 1791 bis 1848.* Stuttgart: Klett, 1967.

Kraft, Helga W. *Erhörtes und Unerhörtes: Die Welt des Klanges bei Heinrich von Kleist.* Munich: Fink, 1976.

Kraus, Karl. *Worte in Versen.* 2nd ed. Leipzig: Verlag der Schriften von Karl Kraus, 1919.

Krell, David Farrell, and Donald Bates. *The Good European: Nietzsche's Work Sites in Word and Image.* Chicago: University of Chicago Press, 1997.

Kugel, James, ed. *Poetry and Prophecy.* Ithaca, N. Y.: Cornell University Press, 1990.

Kully, Rolf Max. "Johann Peter Hebel als Theoretiker." In *Johann Peter Hebel: Unvergängliches aus dem Wiesental,* ed. Carl Pietzcker and Günter Schnitzler, 143–93. Freiburg: Rombach, 1996.

Kushner, Tony. *Angels in America: A Gay Fantasia on National Themes.* New York: Theatre Communications Group, 1995.

Lacan, Jacques. *Ecrits.* 2 vols. Paris: Seuil, 1971.

————. *Ecrits.* Trans. Alan Sheridan. New York: Norton, 1977.

Lacoue-Labarthe, Philippe, and Jean-Luc Nancy, eds. *Les Fins de l'homme: A partir du travail de Jacques Derrida.* Paris: Galilée, 1981.

La Vopa, Anthony. "The Philosopher and the *Schwärmer.*" In *Enthusiasm and Enlightenment in Europe, 1650–1850,* ed. Lawrence Klein and Anthony La Vopa, 85–115. San Marino, Calif.: Huntington Library Press, 1998.

Lang, Berel. *The Anatomy of Philosophical Style: Literary Philosophy and the Philosophy of Literature.* Cambridge, Mass.: Blackwell, 1990.

Lange, Victor. "Zur Gestalt des Schwärmers im deutschen Roman des 18. Jahrhunderts." In *Festschrift für Richard Alewyn,* ed. Herbert Singer and Benno von Wiese, 151–64. Cologne: Bohlau, 1967.

Lausberg, Heinrich. *Elemente der literarischen Rhetorik: Einführung für Studierende der romanischen Philologie.* Munich: Hueber, 1963.

————. *Handbuch der literarischen Rhetorik: Eine Grundlegung der Literaturwissenschaft.* 2 vols. Munich: Hueber, 1960.

Lavine, Shaughan. *Understanding the Infinite.* Cambridge, Mass.: Harvard University Press, 1994.

Leibniz, Gottfried Wilhelm. *Essais de Théodicée sur la bonté de Dieu, la liberté de l'homme et l'origine du mal.* Ed. J. Brunschwig. Paris: Garnier-Flammarion, 1969.

————. *Flores sparsi in tumulum Papissae.* In *Bibliotheca historica Goettingen-*

sis . . . , ed. Christian Ludwig Scheidt, 1: 297–368. Göttingen and Hanover: Pokwiz and Barmeier, 1758.

—. *Gesammelte Werke: Aus den Handschriften der Königlichen Bibliothek zu Hannover.* 4 vols. Ed. Georg Heinrich Pertz. 1843–47. Repr., Hildesheim: Olms, 1966.

—. *Hauptschriften zur Grundlegung der Philosophie.* Ed. Arthur Buchenau and Ernst Cassirer. Hamburg: Meiner, 1996.

—. *De l'Horizon de la doctrine humaine, Apokatastasis pantōn (la restitution universelle).* Ed. Michel Fichant. Paris: Vrin, 1991.

—. *Leibniz and Ludolf on Things Linguistic: Excerpts from Their Correspondence, 1688–1703.* Ed. and trans. John T. Waterman. Berkeley: University of California Press, 1978.

—. *Die Leibniz-Handschriften der Königlichen Öffentlichen Bibliothek zu Hannover.* Ed. Eduard Bodemann. Hannover: Hahn, 1889. Repr., Hildesheim: Olms, 1966.

—. *New Essays on Human Understanding.* Ed. and trans. Peter Remnant and Jonathan Bennett. Cambridge, Eng.: Cambridge University Press, 1981.

—. *Opera omnia.* 6 vols. Ed. Louis Dutens. Geneva: Apud Fratres de Tournes, 1768. Repr., Hildesheim: Olms, 1989.

—. *Philosophical Papers and Letters.* Ed. and trans. Leroy Loemker. Dordrecht: Reidel, 1969.

—. *Die philosophischen Schriften.* 7 vols. Ed. C. J. Gerhardt. 1875–90. Repr., Hildesheim: Olms, 1978.

—. *Political Writings.* Ed. and trans. Patrick Riley. Cambridge, Eng.: Cambridge University Press, 1988.

—. *Sämtliche Schriften und Briefe.* Multiple vols. in 7 series. Ed. Preußische [later, Deutsche] Akademie der Wissenschaften. Darmstadt and Leipzig: Akademie, 1923–.

—. *Schöpferische Vernunft: Schriften aus dem Jahren 1668–1686.* Ed. and trans. Wolf von Engelhardt. Münster: Böhlau-Verlag, 1955.

—. *Textes inédits.* 2 vols. Ed. G. Grua. Paris: Presses Universitaires de France, 1948.

—. *Theodicy: Essays on the Goodness of God, the Freedom of Man, and the Origin of Evil.* Trans. E. M. Huggard. 1951. Repr., LaSalle, Ill.: Open Court, 1985.

—. *Unvorgreifliche Gedanken, betreffend die Ausübung und Verbesserung der deutschen Sprache, Zwei Aufsätze.* Ed. Uwe Pörksen. Stuttgart: Reclam, 1983.

Lessing, Gotthold Ephraim. *Sämtliche Werke.* 23 vols. Ed. Karl Lachmann and Franz Muncker. 1886–1924. Repr., Berlin: De Gruyter, 1979.

Levinas, Emmanuel. *Théorie de l'intuition dans la phénoménologie de Husserl.* Paris: Vrin, 1963.

Liebeschutz, Hans. "Mendelssohn und Lessing in ihrer Stellung zur Geschichte."

In *Studies in Jewish Religious and Intellectual History,* ed. Siegfried Stein and Raphael Loewe, 167–82. University: University of Alabama Press, 1979.

Linke, Paul F. "Das Recht der Phänomenologie." *Kantstudien* 21 (1917): 163–221.

Longuenesse, Béatrice. *Kant and the Capacity to Judge.* Trans. Charles Wolfe. Princeton, N.J.: Princeton University Press, 1998.

Lorenz, Dagmar, and Gabriele Weinberger, eds. *Insiders and Outsiders: Jewish and Gentile Culture in Germany and Austria.* Detroit: Wayne State University Press, 1994.

Löwenbrück, Anne-Ruth. *Judenfeindschaft im Zeitalter der Aufklärung: Eine Studie zur Vorgeschichte des modernen Antisemitismus am Beispiel des Göttinger Theologen und Orientalisten Johann David Michaelis.* Frankfurt am Main: Lang, 1995.

Luther, Martin. *Von der Freiheit eines Christenmenschen.* Ed. Ludwig Schmitt. Tübingen: Niemeyer, 1954.

Maier, Anneliese. *Das Problem der intensiven Grösse in der Scholastik* (De intensione et remissione formarum). Leipzig: Keller, 1939.

Marcus, Ruth Barcan. "Modalities and Intensional Languages." In *Contemporary Philosophical Logic,* ed. Irving Copi and James Gould, 257–72. New York: St. Martin's, 1978.

Mates, Benson. *Leibniz: Philosophy and Language.* New York: Oxford University Press, 1986.

Mathieu, Vittorio. "Leibniz, Nizolius et l'histoire de la philosophie." In *Leibniz et la Renaissance,* ed. Albert Heinekamp, 143–50. Studia Leibnitia Supplementa 23. Wiesbaden: Steiner, 1983.

Mautner, Thomas. "Mendelssohn and the Right of Toleration." In *Moses Mendelssohn und die Kreise seiner Wirksamkeit,* ed. Albrecht Michael, Eva Engel, and Norbert Hinske, 191–213. Tübingen: Niemeyer, 1994.

McLaughlin, Kevin. "The Coming of Paper: Aesthetic Value from Ruskin to Benjamin." *MLN* 114 (1999): 962–90.

Mehigan, Timothy J. *Text as Contract.* Bern: Lang, 1988.

Mehlman, Jeffrey. *Walter Benjamin for Children.* Chicago: University of Chicago Press, 1993.

Mendelssohn, Moses. *Gesammelte Schriften: Jubiläumsausgabe.* 24 vols. Ed. Ismar Elbogen, Julius Guttmann, Eugen Mittwoch, Alexander Altmann. Berlin: 1929–32; Breslau, 1938. Repr., Stuttgart: Frommann-Holzboog, 1974–.

———. *Jerusalem.* Trans. Allan Arkush. Intro. and commentary Alexander Altmann. Hanover, Vt.: Brandeis University Press, 1983.

———. *Jerusalem: Oder über religiöse Macht und Judentum.* Berlin: Maurer, 1783.

———. *Moses Mendelssohn: Selections from His Writings.* Ed. and trans. Albert Jospe. New York: Viking, 1975.

———. *Philosophical Writings.* Ed. and trans. Daniel Dahlstrom. Cambridge, Eng.: Cambridge University Press, 1997.

Menninghaus, Winfried. *Walter Benjamins Theorie der Sprachmagie.* Frankfurt am Main: Suhrkamp, 1980.

Meyfart, Johannes Matthaeus. *Teutsche Rhetorica: Oder, Redekunst.* 1634. Repr., Tübingen: Niemeyer, 1977.

Michael, Albrecht, Eva Engel, and Norbert Hinske, eds. *Moses Mendelssohn und die Kreise seiner Wirksamkeit.* Tübingen: Niemeyer, 1994.

Miller, J. Hillis. "Laying Down the Law in Literature: The Example of Kleist." *Cardozo Law Review* 11 (July–August 1990): 1491–1514.

Mommsen, Theodor. *Römisches Staatsrecht.* 3 vols. Leipzig: Hirzel, 1887–88.

Monfassani, John. "Humanism and Rhetoric." In *Renaissance Humanism: Foundations, Forms, and Legacy,* ed. Albert Rabil, 171–235. Philadelphia: University of Pennsylvania Press, 1988.

Moore, A. W. *The Infinite.* London: Routledge, 1991.

Moore, Gregory H. *Zermelo's Axiom of Choice, Its Origins, Development, and Influence.* New York: Springer, 1982.

Moore, John. "The Dating of Plato's *Ion.*" *Greek, Roman, and Byzantine Studies* 15 (1974): 421–39.

Moran, Dermot. *Introduction to Phenomenology.* London: Routledge, 2000.

Morier, Henri. *Dictionnaire de poétique et de rhétorique.* 3rd ed. Paris: Presses universitaires de France, 1981.

Mosès, Stéphane. *L'Ange de l'histoire: Rosenzweig, Benjamin, Scholem.* Paris: Éditions du Seuil, 1992.

Mugnai, Massimo. *Astrazione e realtà: Saggio su Leibniz.* Milan: Feltrinelli, 1976.

———. "Der Begriff der Harmonie als metaphysische Grundlage der Logik und Kombinatorik bei Johann Heinrich Bisterfeld und Leibniz." *Studia Leibnitiana* 5 (1973): 43–73.

Nägele, Rainer, ed. *Benjamin's Ground.* Detroit: Wayne State University Press, 1988.

———. *Echoes of Translation.* Baltimore: Johns Hopkins University Press, 1997.

Nancy, Jean-Luc. *Le Partage des voix.* Paris: Galilée, 1982.

———. *Le Sens du monde.* Paris: Galilée, 1993.

Neubauer, John. "Intellektuelle, intellektuale, und ästhetische Anschauung: Zur Entstehung der romantischen Kunstauffassung." *Deutsche Vierteljahrschrift für Literaturwissenschaft und Geistesgeschichte* 46 (1972): 294–319.

Neureuther, Hans Peter. "Zur Theorie der Anekdote." *Jahrbuch des Freien Deutschen Hochstifts* (1973): 458–80.

The New Oxford Annotated Bible, with Apocryphal/Deuterocanonical Books. Ed. Bruce Metzger and Roland Murphey. New York: Oxford University Press, 1991.

Nietzsche, Friedrich. *Beyond Good and Evil.* Trans. Walter Kaufmann. New York: Vintage, 1966.

———. *Friedrich Nietzsche on Rhetoric and Language.* Ed. and trans. Sander

Gilman, Carole Blair, and David Parent. Oxford: Oxford University Press, 1989.

———. *Sämtliche Werke*. 15 vols. Ed. Giorgio Colli and Mazzino Montinari. Berlin: De Gruyter, 1967–77.

———. *Werke*. 4 vols. Ed. Karl Schlechta. Munich: Hanser, 1966.

Nizolius, Marius. *De veris principiis et vera ratione philosophandi contra pseudo-philosophos*. 2 vols. Ed. Quinirus Breen. 1553. Repr., Roma: Fratelli Bocca, 1956.

———. *Vier Bücher über die wahren Prinzipien und die wahre philosophische Methode, gegen die Pseudophilosophen*. Ed. and trans. Klaus Thieme. Munich: Fink, 1980.

Novalis (Friedrich Leopold Freiherr von Hardenberg). *Fragmente*. Dresden: Wolfgang Jess, 1929.

———. *Schriften*. 4 vols. Ed. Richard Samuel. Stuttgart: Kohlhammer, 1960.

———. *Werke*. Ed. Gerhard Schulz. 3rd ed. Munich: Beck, 1987.

Opitz, Martin. *Das Buch von der Deutschen Poeterey (1624)*. Ed. Wilhelm Braune and Richard Alewyn. Tübingen: Niemeyer, 1966.

Opitz, Michael, and Erdmut Wizisla, eds. *Benjamins Begriffe*. 2 vols. Frankfurt am Main: Suhrkamp, 2000.

Ott, Hugo. *Martin Heidegger: A Political Life*. Trans. Allan Blunden. London: HarperCollins, 1993.

Palazzi, Fernando. *Enciclopedia degli anedotti: 15.515 aneddoti storici di tutti i tempi e paesi*. Milan: Casa editrice Ceschina, 1946–50.

Parsons, Charles. "Arithmetic and the Categories." In *Kant's Philosophy of Mathematics*, ed. Carl Posy, 135–58. Dordrecht: Kluwer, 1992.

Perkins, Robert, ed. *International Kierkegaard Commentary: "The Two Ages."* Macon, Ga.: Mercer University Press, 1984.

Pietzcker, Carl, and Günter Schnitzler, eds. *Johann Peter Hebel: Unvergängliches aus dem Wiesental.* Freiburg: Rombach, 1996.

Piro, Francesco. "Are the 'Canals of Tropes' Navigable? Rhetoric Concepts in Leibniz' Philosophy of Language." In *Im Spiegel des Verstandes*, ed. Klaus Dutz and Stefano Gensini, 137–60. Münster: Nodus Publikationen, 1996.

Pitaval, François Gayot de. *Causes célèbres et interessantes, avec les jugements qui les ont decidées*. 26 vols. Amsterdam: Chatelain et fils, 1745–71.

———. *Merkwürdige Rechtsfälle als ein Beitrag zur Geschichte der Menschheit: nach dem französischen Werk des Pitaval durch mehrere Verfasser ausgearbeitet und mit einer Vorrede begleitet*. 4 vols. Ed. Friedrich Schiller. Jena: Cuno's Erben, 1792–95.

Platen, August von. *Gesammelte Werke*. 5 vols. Stuttgart-Tübingen: Cotta, 1848.

Plato. *The Collected Dialogues of Plato*. Ed. Edith Hamilton and Huntington Cairns. Princeton, N.J.: Princeton University Press, 1985.

———. *Opera*. Ed. John Burnet. Oxford: Clarendon, 1987.

———. *The Republic.* Trans. Allan Bloom. New York: Basic Books, 1991.

———. *Two Comic Dialogues: Ion and Hippias Major.* Trans. Paul Woodruff. Indianapolis: Hackett, 1983.

Posy, Carl, ed. *Kant's Philosophy of Mathematics.* Dordrecht: Kluwer, 1992.

Procopius. *Anekdota.* Ed. and trans. Otto Veh. Munich: Heimeran, 1970.

———. *The Secret History.* Trans. Geoffrey A. Williamson. Harmondsworth: Penguin, 1966.

Prodi, Paulo. *Il sacramento del potere: Il guiramento politico nella storia constitutionale dell'occidente.* Bologna: Il mulino, 1992.

Purkert, Walter, and Hans Joachim Ilgauds. *Georg Cantor, 1845–1918.* Basel: Birkhäuser, 1987.

Quanter, Rudolf. *Das deutsche Zuchthaus- und Gefängniswesen von den ältesten Zeiten bis in die Gegenwart.* Leipzig: Leipziger Verlag, 1904–5.

Quintilian. *Institutiones oratoriae.* Trans. Harold E. Butler. New York, G. P. Putnam's Sons, 1920–22.

Rabil, Albert, ed. *Renaissance Humanism: Foundations, Forms, and Legacy.* Philadelphia: University of Pennsylvania Press, 1988.

Rang, Florens Christian. *Deutsche Bauhütte: Ein Wort an uns Deutsche über Mögliche Gerechtigkeit gegen Belgien und Frankreich and zur Philosophie der Politik.* Leipzig: Eberhard Arnold, 1924.

———. *Historische Psychologie des Karnevals.* 2nd ed. Berlin: Brinckmann und Bose, 1983.

———. *Shakespeare der Christ: Eine Deutung der Sonnette.* Ed. Bernhard Rang. Heidelberg: Schneider, 1954.

Reed, T. J. *Schiller.* Oxford: Oxford University Press, 1991.

Riley, Patrick. *Leibniz' Universal Jurisprudence: Justice as the Charity of the Wise.* Cambridge, Mass.: Harvard University Press, 1996.

Rilke, Rainer Maria. *Sämtliche Werke.* 6 vols. Ed. Rilke Archive in connection with Ruth Sieber-Rilke and Ernst Zinn. Frankfurt am Main, 1955.

Robinet, André. *G. W. Leibniz: Le Meilleur des Monde par la balance de l'Europe.* Paris: Presses Universitaires de France, 1994.

———. "Leibniz: La Renaissance et l'age classique." In *Leibniz et la Renaissance,* ed. Albert Heinekamp, 12–36. Studia Leibnitia Supplementa 23, Wiesbaden: Steiner, 1983.

Rohner, Ludwig. *Kommentarband zum Faksimiledruck der Jahrgänge 1808–1815 und 1819 des "Rheinländischen Hausfreunds" von Johann Peter Hebel.* Wiesbaden: Athenaion, 1981.

Rosenfeld, Beate. *Die Golemsage und ihre Verwertung in der deutschen Literatur.* Breslau: Priebatsch, 1934.

Rosenzweig, Franz. *Der Stern der Erlösung.* 1921. Repr., Frankfurt am Main: Suhrkamp, 1988.

————. *Zweistromland.* Ed. Reinhold and Annamarie Mayer. Dordrecht: Nijhoff, 1984.

Rossi, Paolo. "Il *De principiis* de Mario Nizolio." In *Testi umanistici su la retorica,* ed. Eugenio Garin, 56–92. Rome: Fratelli Bocca, 1953.

Rotenstreich, Nathan. *Jews and German Philosophy: The Polemics of Emancipation.* New York: Schocken, 1984.

Russell, Bertrand. *A Critical Exposition of the Philosophy of Leibniz.* London, 1900. Repr., London: George Allen and Unwin, 1971.

————. *The Principles of Mathematics.* Cambridge, Eng.: Cambridge University Press, 1903.

————. "Recent Work on the Philosophy of Leibniz." In *Leibniz: A Collection of Critical Essays,* ed. Harry Frankfurt, 365–400. Notre Dame, Ind.: Notre Dame University Press, 1976.

Rüstow, Alexander. *Der Lügner: Theorie, Geschichte und Auflösung.* 1910. Repr., New York, Garland, 1987.

Rutherford, Donald. *Leibniz and the Rational Order of Nature.* Cambridge, Eng.: Cambridge University Press, 1995.

————. "Philosophy and Language in Leibniz." In *Cambridge Campanion to Leibniz,* ed. Nicholas Jolley, 224–69. Cambridge, Eng.: Cambridge University Press, 1995.

Ryan, Alan. *Property and Political Theory.* New York: Blackwell, 1984.

Ryan, Lawrence. *Hölderlins Lehre vom Wechsel der Töne.* Stuttgart: Kohlhammer, 1960.

Santini, Lea Ritter, and Ezio Raimondi, eds. *Retorica e critica letteraria.* Bologna: Il mulino, 1978.

Scheidt, Christian Ludwig, ed. *Bibliotheca historica Goettingensis worinnen allerhand bishero ungedruckte alte und neuere Schriften und urkunden, welche zur Erläuterung der Geschichte und Rechtsgelehrsamkeit dienen können, aus bewahrten Handschriften aus Licht gestellet werden.* Göttingen and Hanover: Pokwiz and Barmeier, 1758.

Schelling, Friedrich. *Historisch-kritisch Ausgabe im Auftrag der Schelling-Kommission der Bayerischen Akademie der Wissenschaften.* Multiple vols. in 4 series. Ed. H. M. Baumgartner, W. G. Jacobs, H. Krings, and H. Zeltner. Stuttgart: Frommann-Holzboog, 1976–.

————. *Philosophie der Offenbarung 1841/42.* Ed. Manfred Frank. Frankfurt am Main: Suhrkamp, 1977.

————. *Werke, nach der Originalausgabe in neuer Anordnung.* 6 vols. Ed. Manfred Schröter. Munich: Beck, 1927–54.

————. *The Unconditional in Human Knowledge.* Ed. and trans. Fritz Marti. Lewisburg, Pa.: Bucknell University, 1980.

Schestag, Thomas. "Komische Authentizität." In *Theorie der Komödie—Poetik der Komödie,* ed. Ralf Simon, 139–53. Bielefeld: Aisthesis, 2001.

————. *Para: Lucretius, Hebel, Ponge.* Munich: Boer, 1991.

Schiller, Friedrich. *On the Aesthetic Education of Man.* Ed. and trans. Elizabeth Wilkinson and L. A. Willoughby. Oxford: Clarendon, 1982.

————. *Schillers Werke: Nationalausgabe.* 43 vols. Ed. Julius Petersen and Gerhard Fricke. Weimar: Böhlaus, 1943–.

Schischkoff, Georgi, ed. *Beiträge zur Leibniz-Forschung.* Reutlingen: Gryphius, 1947.

Schlosser, Johann Georg. *Platos Briefe über die Syrakusianische Staats-Revolution aus dem griechischen übersetzt.* Königsberg: Nicolovius, 1795.

Schmalenbach, Herman. *Leibniz.* Munich: Drei Masken, 1921.

Schmitt, Carl. *Verfassungslehre.* Berlin: Duncker und Humblot, 1983.

Schneewind, Jerome. *The Invention of Autonomy: A History of Modern Moral Philosophy.* Cambridge, Eng.: Cambridge University Press, 1998.

Schneider, Helmut. "Der Zusammensturz des Allgemeinen." In *Positionen der Literaturwissenschaft,* ed. David Wellbery, 110–29. Munich: Beck, 1985.

Schoenflies, Arthur. *Die Entwicklung der Lehre von den Punktmannigfaltigkeiten.* Leipzig: Teubner, 1900. Supplemented in *Jahresbericht der Deutschen Mathematiker-Vereinigung,* Ergänzungsband 2 (1908): 1–331.

————. "Die Krisis in Cantors mathematischem Schaffen." *Acta mathematica* 50 (1927): 1–23.

————. "Mengenlehre." In *Encyklopädie der mathematischen Wissenschaften,* ed. Akademien der Wissenschaften, at Göttingen, Leipzig, Munich and Vienna, 184–207. Leipzig: Teubner, 1898–1904.

————. "Zur Erinnerung an Georg Cantor." *Jahresbericht der Deutschen Mathematiker-Vereinigung* 31 (1922): 90–106.

Scholem, Gershom. *On the Kabbalah and Its Symbolism.* Trans. R. Manheim. New York: Schocken, 1965.

————. *Tagebüche: 1913–1917.* Ed. Herbert Kopp-Oberstebrink, Karlfried Gründer, and Friedrich Niewöhner. Frankfurt am Main: Jüdischer Verlag, 1995.

————. *Walter Benjamin und sein Engel.* Ed. Rolf Tiedemann. Frankfurt am Main: Suhrkamp, 1992.

————. *Walter Benjamin: The Story of a Friendship.* Trans. Harry Zohn. New York: Schocken, 1981.

Scholz, Heinrich, ed. *Die Hauptschriften zum Pantheismusstreit zwischen Jacobi und Mendelssohn.* Berlin: Reuther und Reichard, 1916.

Schöne, Albrecht. *Goethes Farbentheologie.* Munich: Beck, 1987.

Schopenhauer, Arthur. *Werke in fünf Bänden.* 5 vols. Ed. Ludger Lütkehaus. Zürich: Haffmanns-Verlag, 1988.

————. *The World as Will and Representation.* 2 vols. Trans. E. F. J. Payne. New York: Dover, 1969.

Schulenburg, Sigrid von der. *Leibniz als Sprachforscher.* Ed. Kurt Müller. 1937. Repr., Frankfurt am Main: Klostermann, 1973.

Schulte, Christoph. "Zimzum bei Schelling." In *Kabbalah und Romantik*, ed. Eveline Goodman-Thau, Gert Mattenklott, and Christoph Schulte, 97–118. Tübingen: Niemeyer, 1994.

Schwab, Gail. "Mother's Body, Father's Tongue." In *Engaging with Irigaray*, ed. Carolyn Burke, Naomi Schor, and Margaret Whitford, 351–78. New York: Columbia University Press, 1994.

Sembdner, Helmut. *Die Berliner Abendblätter Heinrich von Kleists: Ihre Quellen und ihre Redaktion.* Amsterdam: Benjamins, 1970.

———. *In Sachen Kleist.* Munich: Hanser, 1974.

Serres, Michel. *Angels: A Modern Myth.* Trans. Francis Cowper. Paris: Flammarion, 1995.

Shell, Susan Meld. *The Embodiment of Reason: Kant on Spirit, Generation, and Community.* Chicago: University of Chicago Press, 1996.

Silz, Walter. *Heinrich von Kleist.* Philadelphia: University of Pennsylvania Press, 1961.

Singer, Herbert, and Benno von Wiese, eds. *Festschrift für Richard Alewyn.* Cologne: Bohlau, 1967.

Sommer, Benjamin. "Did Prophecy Cease? Evaluating a Reevaluation," *JBL* 115 (1996): 31–47.

Sonnino, Lee. *A Handbook to Sixteenth-Century Rhetoric.* London: Routledge and Kegan Paul, 1968.

Sorel, Georges. *Réflexions sur la violence.* Paris: Librarie de pages libres, 1908.

Sorkin, David. "The Internal Dialogue: Judaism and Enlightenment in Moses Mendelssohn's Thought." In *The German-Jewish Dialogue Reconsidered*, ed. Klaus Berghahn, 23–37. New York: Lang, 1996.

———. *Moses Mendelssohn and the Religious Enlightenment.* Berkeley: University of California Press, 1996.

———. *The Transformation of German Jewry, 1780–1840.* New York: Oxford University Press, 1987.

Spacks, Patricia Mayer. *Gossip.* New York: Knopf, 1985.

Spanheim, Friedrich. *De papa foemina inter Leonem IV. et Benedictum III., disquisitio historica: Quâ ut Onuphrii, sic praecipuè Allatii, Labbei, Blondelli, Launoji, Mabilloni, adversus papissam praesidia excutiuntur.* Lugduni Batavorum: Apud Johannem, 1691.

Spiegelberg, Herbert. *The Phenomenological Movement: A Historical Introduction.* The Hague, Nijhoff, 1965.

Spinoza, Baruch. *Opera.* 5 vols. Ed. Carl Gebhardt. Heidelberg: Winter, 1925.

———. *A Theologico-Political Treatise.* Trans. R. H. M. Elwes. Dover: New York, 1951.

Staiger, Emil. *Meisterwerke deutscher Sprache.* Zürich: Atlantis, 1948.

Steck, K. G. *Luther und die Schwärmer.* Zollikon-Zürich: Evangelischer Verlag, 1955.

Stein, Siegfried, and Raphael Loewe, eds. *Studies in Jewish Religious and Intellectual History.* University: University of Alabama Press, 1979.

Stolberg, Count Friedrich Leopold zu. *Auserlesene Gespräche des Platon.* Königsberg: Nicolivius, 1796.

———. *Über die Fülle des Herzens: Frühe Prosa.* Ed. Jürgen Behrens. Stuttgart: Reclam, 1970.

Struever, Nancy S. *Theory as Practice: Ethical Inquiry in the Renaissance.* Chicago: University of Chicago Press, 1992.

Talmud: A Hebrew-English Edition of the Babylonian Talmud. Ed. Isaac Epstein. Trans. and annotated by Maurice Simon. London: Soncino Press, 1965–89.

Tanakh: A New Translation of the Holy Bible. The New JPS Translation According to the Traditional Hebrew Text. Philadelphia: Jewish Publication Society, 1985.

Taubes, Jacob. "From Cult to Culture," *Partisan Review* 21 (1954): 387–400.

———. *Die politische Theologie des Paulus.* Munich: Fink, 1995.

Thiele-Dohrmann, Klaus. *Unter dem Siegel der Verschwiegenheit: die Psychologie der Klatsches.* Düsseldorf: Claassen, 1975.

Tillmann, Bruno. *Leibniz' Verhältnis zur Renaissance im allgemeinen und zu Nizolius im besonderen.* Bonn: Hanstein, 1912.

Tugendhat, Ernst. *Der Wahrheitsbegriff bei Husserl und Heidegger.* Berlin: De Gruyter, 1970.

Ueding, Gert, ed. *Historisches Wörterbuch der Rhetorik.* 4 vols. Tübingen: Niemeyer, 1992.

Unger, Erich. *Politik und Metaphysik.* Berlin, 1921. Repr., Würzburg: Königshausen und Neumann, 1989.

Vaihinger, Hans. *Commentar zu Kants Kritik der reinen Vernunft.* 2 vols. Stuttgart: Spemann, 1881–92.

Valla, Lorenzo. *Opera omnia.* Ed. Eugenio Garin. Turin: Bottega d'Erasmo, 1962.

Veeser, Aram H., ed. *The New Historicism.* New York: Routledge, 1989.

Velkley, Richard L. *Freedom and the End of Reason: On the Moral Foundation of Kant's Critical Philosophy.* Chicago: University of Chicago Press, 1989.

Vernant, Jean-Pierre, and Pierre Vidal-Naquet. *Myth and Tragedy in Ancient Greece.* Trans. Janet Lloyd. New York: Zone, 1990.

Vico, Giambattista. *The New Science.* Trans. Thomas Goddard Bergin and Max Harold Fisch. Ithaca, N. Y.: Cornell University Press, 1986.

Virgil. *Eclogues, Georgics, Aeneid I–VI.* Trans. H. Rushton Fairclough. Cambridge, Mass.: Harvard University Press, 1988.

Vöhler, Martin. "Hölderlins Longin-Rezeption." *Hölderlin-Jahrbuch* 28 (1992–93): 152–72.

Voigts, Manfred. *Oskar Goldberg.* Berlin: Agora, 1992.

Voit, Friedrich. *Vom "Landkalender" zum "Rheinländischen Hausfreund" Johann Peter Hebels: Das südwestdeutsche Kalenderwesen im 18. und beginnenden 19. Jahrhundert.* New York: Lang, 1994.

Volkelt, Johannes. *Ästhetik des Tragischen.* Munich: Beck, 1917.

Voss, Gerard Jan (Gerardus Johannes Vossius). *Aristarchus sive De arte grammatica.* 1662. Repr., Halis: Orphanotrophei, 1833–34.

———. *Commentariorum rhetoricum sive Oratoriarum institutionum.* Lugduni Batavorum: Joannis Maire, 1630. Repr., Ann Arbor: University of Michigan Microfilms, 1953.

———. *Elementa rhetorica.* Amsterdam: Johannem Janssonium, 1655. Repr., Ann Arbor: University of Michigan Microfilms, 1953.

———. *Etymologicon linguae latinae.* Amsterdam: Elzevirios, 1662.

———. *De vitiis sermonis, et glossematis latino-barbaris.* Amsterdam: Elzevirios, 1645.

Voss, Johann Heinrich. *Sämmtliche poetische Werke.* 5 vols. Leipzig: I. Müller, 1850.

Warburton, William. *The Divine Legation of Moses Demonstrated.* 6 vols. London: Fletcher Gyles, 1738–41.

Weber, Heinz-Dieter. "Zu Heinrich von Kleists Kunst der Anekdote." *Deutschunterricht* 30 (1978): 15–20.

Weber, Samuel. "Benjamin's Writing Style." In *Encyclopedia of Aesthetics,* ed. Michael Kelly, 1: 261–64. Oxford: Oxford University Press, 1998.

———. "Genealogy of Modernity: History, Myth, Allegory in Benjamin's *Origin of the German Mourning Play.*" *MLN* 106 (1991): 465–500.

———. "Taking Exception to Decision: Walter Benjamin and Carl Schmitt." *Diacritics* 22 (Fall–Winter, 1992): 5–18.

Weber, Samuel, and Hent de Vries, eds. *Identity, Violence, and Self-Determination.* Stanford, Calif.: Stanford University Press, 1997.

Wegenast, Margarethe. *Hölderlins Spinoza-Rezeption.* Tübingen: Niemeyer, 1990.

Weigel, Sigrid. *Body- and Image-Space: Re-reading Walter Benjamin.* Trans. Georgina Paul, Rachel McNicholl, and Jeremy Gaines. New York: Routledge, 1996.

Weinrich, Harald. *Literatur für Leser: Essays und Aufsätze zur Literaturwissenschaft.* Stuttgart: Kohlhammer, 1971.

Wellbery, David, ed. *Positionen der Literaturwissenschaft.* Munich: Beck, 1985.

Wesseler, Matthias. *Die Einheit von Wort und Sache.* Munich: Fink, 1974.

Whitford, Margaret. *Luce Irigaray: Philosophy in the Feminine.* New York: Routledge, 1991.

Wiesenthal, Liselotte. *Zur Wissenschaftstheorie Walter Benjamins.* Frankfurt am Main: Athenäum, 1973.

Wilamowitz-Moellendorff, Ulrich von. *Einleitung in die griechische Tragödie.* Berlin: Weidemann, 1907.

———, ed. and trans. *Griechische Tragoedien.* 2 vols. 4th ed. Berlin: Weidemann, 1904.

Wilson, Catherine. *Leibniz's Metaphysics: A Historical and Comparative Study.* Princeton, N.J.: Princeton University Press, 1989.

Witte, Bernd. *Walter Benjamin—Der Intellekuelle als Kritiker: Untersuchungen zu seinem Frühwerk.* Stuttgart: Metzler, 1976.

Wittgenstein, Ludwig. *Philosophical Investigations.* Trans. G. E. M. Anscombe. New York: Macmillan, 1968.

———. *Werkausgabe.* 8 vols. Frankfurt am Main: Suhrkamp, 1989.

Wittkowski, Wolfgang. "Skepsis, Noblesse, Ironie: Formen des Als-ob in Kleists 'Erdbeben.'" *Euphorion* 63 (1969): 247–83.

Wobester, Wilhelm Karol von. *Elisa, oder, das Weib, wie es seyn sollte.* Leipzig: Gräff, 1796.

Wohlhaupter, Eugen. *Dichterjuristen.* 3 vols. Tübingen: Mohr, 1953.

Wöhrmann, Klaus-Rüdiger. "Je seray ce que je seray: Nom divin et proposition identique chez Leibniz." In *Leibniz and Adam,* ed. Marcelo Dascal and El-hanan Yakira, 99–107. Tel Aviv: University Publishing Projects, 1993.

Wolf, Erik. *Richtiges Recht im nationalsozialistischen Staate.* Freiburg: Wagner, 1934.

———. *Vom Wesen des Rechts in deutscher Dichtung.* Frankfurt am Main: Klostermann, 1946.

Ziegler, Leopold. *Zur Metaphysik des Tragischen: Eine philosophische Studie.* Leipzig: Dürr, 1902.

Ziolkowski, Theodore. *German Romanticism and Its Institutions.* Princeton, N.J.: Princeton University Press, 1990.

———. *The Mirror of Justice.* Princeton, N.J.: Princeton University Press, 1997.

Zohar. 5 vols. Trans. Harry Sperling and Maurice Simon. London: Soncino Press, 1931–34.

Sources

Some of the chapters in this book have been previously published in significantly different versions.

"Autonomasia: The Fate of the Name in Leibniz" first appeared under the title "Antonomasia: Leibniz and the Baroque," *MLN* 105 (April 1990): 432–52.

"Language on a Holy Day: The Temporality of Communication in Mendelssohn" was delivered as a paper at the Franz Rosenzweig Center of the Hebrew University in Jerusalem in 1992. It first appeared in *Perspectives on Early Modern and Modern Intellectual History*, ed. Joseph Marino and Melinda Schlitt (Rochester: University of Rochester Press, 2001), 419–41.

"'The Scale of Enthusiasm': Kant, Schelling, and Hölderlin" first appeared in *Huntington Library Quarterly* 60 (1998–99): 117–52; *Enthusiasm and Enlightenment in Europe, 1650–1850*, ed. Lawrence Klein and Anthony La Vopa (San Marino, Calif.: Huntington Library Press, 1998), 117–52.

"Tragedy and Prophecy in Benjamin's *Origin of the German Mourning Play*" first appeared in *Benjamin's Ghosts: Interventions in Contemporary Theory and Cultural Studies*, ed. Gerhard Richter (Stanford, Calif.: Stanford University Press, 2001).

"'Subtracted from the Order of Number': Toward the Politics of Pure Means in Benjamin and Irigaray" was first published as "'Out of the Order of Number': Benjamin and Irigaray Toward the Politics of Pure Means," *Diacritics* 28 (Spring 1998): 43–58.

The other chapters are published here for the first time. Many thanks to Don Levine for reading the entire manuscript and Joseph Suglia for preparing the index.

Index

M E R I D I A N

Crossing Aesthetics